American Generals of the Revolutionary War

ALSO BY ROBERT P. BROADWATER
AND FROM MCFARLAND

*The Battle of Fair Oaks: Turning Point
of McClellan's Peninsula Campaign* (2011)

*Gettysburg as the Generals Remembered It:
Postwar Perspectives of Ten Commanders* (2010)

*General George H. Thomas:
A Biography of the Union's "Rock of Chickamauga"* (2009)

*Did Lincoln and the Republican Party Create the Civil War?
An Argument* (2008)

*Civil War Medal of Honor Recipients:
A Complete Illustrated Record* (2007; paperback 2012)

*The Battle of Olustee, 1864:
The Final Union Attempt to Seize Florida* (2006)

*Chickamauga, Andersonville, Fort Sumter and Guard Duty at Home:
Four Civil War Diaries by Pennsylvania Soldiers* (edited by; 2006)

*The Battle of Perryville, 1862:
Culmination of the Failed Kentucky Campaign* (2005; paperback 2011)

American Generals of the Revolutionary War

A Biographical Dictionary

ROBERT P. BROADWATER

McFarland & Company, Inc., Publishers
Jefferson, North Carolina, and London

The present work is a reprint of the illustrated case bound edition of American Generals of the Revolutionary War: A Biographical Dictionary, *first published in 2007 by McFarland.*

LIBRARY OF CONGRESS CATALOGUING-IN-PUBLICATION DATA

Broadwater, Robert P., 1958–
American generals of the Revolutionary War: a biographical dictionary / Robert P. Broadwater.
p.   cm.
Includes bibliographical references and index.

ISBN 978-0-7864-6905-5
softcover : acid free paper ∞

1. United States — History — Revolution, 1775–1783 — Biography — Dictionaries.
2. Generals — United States — Biography — Dictionaries.
3. Generals — United States — Portraits.
4. United States. Continental Army — Biography — Dictionaries.
5. United States — Biography — Dictionaries. I. Title.
E206.B76   2012   973.3'30922 — dc22   [B]   2006100331

BRITISH LIBRARY CATALOGUING DATA ARE AVAILABLE

© 2007 Robert P. Broadwater. All rights reserved

No part of this book may be reproduced or transmitted in any form or by any means, electronic or mechanical, including photocopying or recording, or by any information storage and retrieval system, without permission in writing from the publisher.

On the cover: *General George Washington Crossing the Delaware,* December 25, 1776 (Library of Congress)

Manufactured in the United States of America

McFarland & Company, Inc., Publishers
Box 611, Jefferson, North Carolina 28640
www.mcfarlandpub.com

To the memory of my Revolutionary War ancestors
who sided with the cause of liberty:
Lieutenant Charles Broadwater, 10th Virginia Infantry, and
Brevet Brigadier General Mathias Ogden

Table of Contents

Preface 1

Introduction 3

THE DICTIONARY 5

Appendix One: Reasons for Generals' Leaving the Service 165

Appendix Two: States or Countries of Origin of the Generals 167

Appendix Three: Battles of the Revolutionary War 171

Appendix Four: Numbers of Battles by State and North and South 175

Appendix Five: Colonels 177

Notes 185

Bibliography 195

Index 201

Preface

This book presents basic biographical information about the men who were the nation's first generals in the Revolutionary War. It is the intention of the author to do for these military leaders what Ezra J. Warner did for the leaders of the Civil War in his two volumes, *Generals in Gray* and *Generals in Blue*, and thereby provide researchers of the Revolutionary period a resource that brings together all of the general officers of the Continental Army, along with those holding militia commissions in the various colonies, into one easy to use reference book. Biographical sketches of all of the generals of America's first armies provide the researcher with dates and places of birth, pre-war education and occupations, wartime contributions, post war occupations, dates and places of death, and places of burial. Information on some of the generals is incomplete, with exact dates and places sometimes unavailable; but these are very few in number, and in nearly all cases sufficient information to provide at least an introduction to that general is available.

In addition, appendices have been compiled to give the Revolutionary War researcher and enthusiast easy access to statistics and other facts. Appendix One is a breakdown of reasons generals left the service (death, resignation, murder, or changing loyalties). Appendix Two lists the state or country of origin for all general officers. Appendix Three lists the battles of the Revolution in alphabetical order, and Appendix Four lists battles by state and region. Appendix Five is a listing, by state, of all the officers who held Continental and militia commissions as colonels.

Many of the names included in this volume will be very familiar to the reader, as they have become synonymous with America's revolution. Men like George Washington and Nathaniel Greene are well known to every school child in the nation. Others like Elijah Clark and Pinketam Eaton are relatively unknown to the masses, and will probably be introduced to many readers for the first time in the pages of this book.

A wide range of resources has been used in compiling this work, including death and census records, records of the Continental Congress, and contemporary writings of the period.

To be included in this book, an officer must have been commissioned to act in the capacity of general, either by the Continental Congress or by his native colony. Many other officers performed the duties of a general officer, or led bodies of men that would normally be under the command of a general officer, but did so without the commission of a general. Because they were never officially conferred the title of rank, they are not included as generals in this work. The monumental work of Francis Heitman, *Historical Register of Officers of the Continental Army During the War of the Revolution*, was invaluable in creating this listing of the generals of the war; I searched through the more than 14,000 records in Heitman's book, originally published in 1895. A few discrepancies have been found, however. There are some generals included in this work that were excluded from Heitman's book. By the same token, Heitman listed a few officers as generals that I do not, and his claims cannot be verified through other source material. John Hardin is one example of this. His Revolutionary War service record does not indicate that he rose above the rank of captain. Following the end of the war, during the campaigns against the Indians, he was commissioned as a colonel in the militia; his designation as a general most likely stems from his later service. Jedediah Preble was also classified by Heitman as a general in the war. Preble was named to that rank by the Massachusetts legislature, but refused to accept the commission. Joseph Ellis, of New Jersey, was another officer who was offered a commission as general but did not accept. He was selected to take the place of Brigadier General Philemon Dickinson when he removed from the state, but Ellis declined the promotion, serving throughout the war as a colonel. The New Jersey legislature then selected Colonel David Potter to fill the vacancy left by Dickinson, but he also declined the appointment.

Dates of birth were a particular stumbling block in compiling biographical information for many of the men included in this book. The Gregorian calendar, which is in use today, was not adopted by England until 1752. Prior to its adoption, March was considered the first month of the year, not January. For instance, General Nathaniel Greene was born on the 27th day of the fifth month of the year. In many instances, his birth date is given as July 27, because that was the fifth month of the year. But according to the Gregorian calendar, the fifth month is May, making his date of birth May 27. Whenever possible, dates of birth in this book are based on the Georgian calendar. Record keeping was not a priority to the men and women who were carving a new nation out of the wilderness, and in some cases, only the scantest of information is available for some of the individuals listed herein. For others, such as Washington, Wayne, and Marion, a wealth of material about their lives has been recorded.

Introduction

Continental militia had been involved in most of the military interventions that took place in the mid–18th century, and before, in America. Indeed, they had played a conspicuous role in the French and Indian War and contributed greatly to the success of the British in securing victory in North America. However, militia troops from the Colonies were always relegated to a subservient role, compared to Crown troops, and were always under the supervision of British officers. Colonial officers were rarely given commissions in the British Army, and had to content themselves with leading militia units. The rank of colonel was generally the highest grade that a Colonial officer could hope to attain.

With the outbreak of military hostilities at Lexington and Concord in 1775, the Colonies were faced with the problem of trying to create an American army from the various Colonial militias to defend the country from the British Army. It would be no small feat. The British Army was acknowledged as one of the finest standing armies in the world, and its leaders were touted as some of the finest military minds of the era. The Colonies could offer only a loosely tethered gathering of local militia, part-time soldiers who were more at home in their family fields than in a line of battle, men with little formal military training and less military discipline. In most cases, the leaders were just as lacking as the soldiers, and were without the training or experience to lead men in battle. True, there were such men as George Washington, who had served in the French and Indian War as a colonel of Virginia Militia, and there were also a few like Horatio Gates, a British-born patriot who had served in the British Army before adopting the American cause of freedom, but most of the generals who would lead troops in battle were just as green as their men. The Continental Army did benefit from the experience of a number of foreign-born officers who would become generals during the war. Most notable among these were men Baron DeKalb and the Marquis de Lafayette. Their experience and training would prove invaluable to the cause of liberty and would help to shape the officers and men of the Continental Army into a legitimate fighting force capable of meeting the British on equal terms on the field of battle. For most of the American generals, however, experience would be gained through on the job training, as they learned their duties through trial and error, while fighting a war against one of the greatest powers in the world. Some would fail miserably in their new vocations, while others showed a natural aptitude for command that propelled them to national prominence and won them eternal glory.

These are the stories of America's first generals. They were the men who led the first truly American Army. They came from all walks of life. Some were already of advanced age when the conflict erupted, while others were barely out of boyhood. Some had seen previous military service, while others had spent their pre-war years farming or toiling in the world of business. All were motivated by a desire to create an American nation, based on liberty and personal freedom. In the following pages, you will learn of the lives of these men, the great, the near great, and the obscure. They all share the distinction of being the first, and without their devotion, courage, and perseverance, they would also have been the last. The establishment of our nation, and all that was to follow, was a direct result of their vision and sacrifice, and the country owes a debt to their honor and memory that can only be repaid by paying tribute to their deeds.

THE DICTIONARY

ALEXANDER, WILLIAM—(New York) William Alexander was born in New York City, New York, on December 27, 1726, the son of a Scottish noble. William's father, Joseph, had been Earl of Stirling, but had been stripped of his title and lands in 1715 because of his participation in the Jacobite Rebellion. William received a fine education, fitting of nobility, and was particularly proficient in mathematics and science.

In 1748, he married Sarah Livingston, the sister of the governor of New Jersey, and the couple would have three children together. In 1756, William's father died, leaving him to make claim to what he believed to be his rightful title as Lord Stirling, and to seek reinstatement of both title and lands from the British government. The British never agreed to formally recognize his claim, but he was widely known on both sides of the Atlantic as Lord Stirling.

During the French and Indian War, he served as commissary, aide-de-camp, and secretary to General Shirley, the governor of Massachusetts. Following the conclusion of the war, Alexander accompanied Shirley to England, in an effort to pursue his Scottish claims, expending a great deal of his fortune in a failed effort before the House of Lords. Back in America, he was elected to the New Jersey legislature, and in 1765, when the British imposed the Stamp Act on the Colonies, he became one of the leading proponents of opposition, raising troops for the purpose of preventing the enforcement of the tax.

Upon the outbreak of hostilities with England, he was commissioned colonel of the 1st New Jersey Regiment on November 7, 1775. He distinguished himself when he and Elias Dayton led four boats in the capture of a British supply ship, the *Blue Mountain Valley*, on January 22–23, 1776, off the coast of Sandy Hook, New Jersey. On March 1, 1776, he was promoted by Congress to the rank of brigadier general, and six days later he was ordered to replace General Lee as commander of the New York City garrison.

Alexander commanded a brigade at the battle of Long Island, on August 27, 1776, where he fought with distinction. Noticing that the British had gotten behind him, and were threatening to cut off the escape route to Brooklyn, Alexander took Smallwood's Rifle Regiment and attacked the forces under General Cornwallis to keep the road from being closed. Alexander personally led three charges upon Cornwallis' men, detaining them long enough for the rest of his brigade to make good its escape, but in the process, Alexander was captured. The British exchanged him the following month for the governor of Florida, and Alexander was free to join the army once more.

Alexander participated in the battle of Trenton, on February 19, 1777, and was commissioned a major general in the Continental Army that same day. He was conspicuous at the battles of Brandywine, Germantown, and Monmouth, leading a division in the last battle. Alexander was instrumental in exposing the conspiracy of General Conway to have Washington replaced with General Gates as commander of the American armies. As commander of the New York City Militia, Alexander supervised the construction of several forts around the city, including Fort Stirling, on Brooklyn Heights, which he had named for himself.

In 1780, he was sent with a force of 2,500 men to attack the British force at Staten Island, but the British discovered his intentions and evacuated the position before he arrived. In 1781, he was given command of the Northern Department, and he made his headquarters at Albany, New York. While performing his duties as commander of the Northern Department, Alexander was stricken with a severe case of gout, as a result of which he died at Albany on January 15, 1783, in his fifty-seventh year.

William Alexander was buried in the Trinity Churchyard Cemetery, in Manhattan, New York.[1]

ARMAND, TUFFIN CHARLES, La Rouerie, marquis de Tuffin—(France) Charles Armand was born in France in 1750. According to the custom of French aristocrats of the day, he began his military career at the age of ten by joining an elite unit, the Garde du Corps. Armand served with this unit for ten years until he was forced to resign due to the fact that he had wounded a relative of the king in a duel. Armand retreated to a Trappist monastery for a time before deciding to come to America and join the Patriot cause. He took passage on the *Morris* which was pursued and run aground in the Chesapeake Bay by British warships in April of 1777. Thinking that Americans might be resentful of his aristocratic name, he dropped La Rouerie and adopted Charles Armand.

Armand raised a legion of volunteers, which he financed with his own money, that became the 3rd Cavalry in Pulaski's Legion, and he was commissioned a colonel by the Continental Congress on May 10, 1777. He first saw action during the defense of Philadelphia, when he was responsible for leading a rear guard action that saved the men and armament of an American outpost, winning the commendation of Washington for his actions. Armand was in command of his cavalry at the battles of Brandywine and Whitemarsh in 1777, and he wintered at Valley Forge that year. In 1778, he took part in the battle of Monmouth before being detailed to conduct partisan operations in New York and Connecticut.

In 1779, Armand succeeded Count Pulaski in command of the Pulaski Legion, following that officer's mortal wounding at Savannah. The legion was badly cut up at the battle of Camden in August of 1780, and in October of that year was redesignated Armand's Partisan Corps.

Early in 1781, Armand received leave to return to France to purchase equipment for his corps. The French government presented him with the French Order of Chevalier de Saint Louis for his accomplishments in the Continental Army. He returned to America in time to take part in the late summer operations in Virginia. His unit served under Lafayette in the action at Green Springs, on July 6, 1781. Armand remained with the Southern Department until September of 1782, when he joined Washington's main army in New York. On March 26, 1783, Armand was commissioned a brigadier general by Congress and was appointed chief of cavalry. He was discharged from service in the American army on November 25, 1783, and received the thanks and praise of Congress and General Washington. Armand stayed in America until May of 1784, when he returned to France. Once home, he returned to his birth name of La Rouerie and married a wealthy aristocrat. In 1788, he was appointed a colonel in the French army. During the French Revolution, he became a leader of the Royalist forces, taking part in the Vendee and Brittany uprisings. Tuffin Armand died from an illness at the Chateau de Guyomarais, in France, on January 29, 1793, in his forty-third year.[1]

ARMSTRONG, JOHN—(Ireland) John Armstrong was born in Brookbor, County Fermanagh, Ireland, on October 13, 1717. Little is known of his boyhood, or education. He immigrated to America and settled in Pennsylvania, prior to the French and Indian War, working as a civil engineer and surveyor. In 1747, Armstrong married Rebecca Armstrong, and the couple had two children together. Rebecca died in 1750, and Armstrong later married Mary Graham, having four children with his second wife. Armstrong took a conspicuous part in the French and Indian War, as a commander of Pennsylvania Militia. Along with Hugh Mercer, he led an expedition that destroyed the village of Indians friendly to the French, at Kittanning. His victory brought about a negotiated peace between the government of Pennsylvania and many of the Indian tribes. The city of Philadelphia awarded a silver medal to both him and Mercer for the success of the expedition. Armstrong accompanied George Washington in General Forbes' expedition against Fort Duquesne (Fort Pitt) in 1758, where Armstrong had been placed in command of 2,700 troops from the Pennsylvania Militia. When Fort Duquesne fell, it was Armstrong who was given the honor to hoist the British flag inside the works.

Following the French and Indian War, Armstrong served as a judge for the Court of Common Pleas. Washington and Armstrong had become close friends during the Fort Duquesne expedition, and when the Revolution broke out, Armstrong was commissioned a brigadier general in the Continental army on March 1, 1776, at the age of fifty-eight.

Armstrong was detailed to Charleston, South Carolina, where he helped to protect the city from a British attack later that year, defending Fort Moultrie, under General Moultrie, against the attack of Sir Peter Parker. Armstrong was assigned to hold a position at Haddrell's Point, during the defense of the city. Feeling that his contributions to the defense of Charleston were not being fully appreciated, he resigned his commission in the Continental Army on April 8, 1777, and returned home. The political leaders in Pennsylvania felt that Armstrong was the most capable man in the state to be in overall command of its militia forces. He was subsequently appointed as a major general in the Pennsylvania Militia, and served in that position for the remainder of the war, taking part in the battle of Brandywine, where he commanded the left wing of the army. He also rendered conspicuous service at the battle of Germantown. Armstrong wintered at Valley Forge, before securing permission to leave the army and return home, due to impaired health.

In 1778, he was elected as a delegate from Pennsylvania to the Continental Congress, serving till 1780. Armstrong did much to aid Washington and his army from his seat in Congress, and Washington frequently consulted with him about affairs in Pennsylvania. After the war, he was again elected to the Continental Congress, serving from 1787–1788. His two sons, John Jr. and James, also served as officers in the war, and were both elected to Congress following its conclusion. John Armstrong died at Carlisle, Pennsylvania, on March 9, 1795, at the age of seventy-seven. He was buried in the Old Carlisle Cemetery.[1]

John Armstrong (courtesy United States Military History Institute)

ARNOLD, BENEDICT—(Connecticut) Benedict Arnold was born at Norwich, Connecticut, on January 14, 1741. He was the fourth Benedict Arnold in his line, which originated with his great-grandfather. Arnold received a good primary education, including instruction in Latin. At the age of fifteen, he ran away from home to enlist in the militia during the French and Indian War. Arnold took part in the operations around Albany and Lake George before becoming disillusioned with the discipline of army life and deserting. He made his way back home, where he found employment in a drug shop in Norwich, until 1762, when he moved to New Haven to open his own druggist business, sidelining in the sale of books. Arnold's business flourished, and he was able to purchase ships with which he engaged in trade with the West Indies. He also did a brisk trade with Canada, and was a frequent visitor to Quebec. In 1767, Arnold married Margaret Mansfield, and the couple had three children together before her death in 1775, including his first son, Benedict, the fifth of the line. In the years before the Revolution, Arnold had joined the local militia, where he had risen to the rank of captain in the Governor's Guards.

When news of the fighting at Lexington and Concord reached New Haven, Arnold assembled his company and proposed to march at once to Boston. General Wooster felt that he should wait until he received orders to do so, and the supervisors of the arsenal refused to provide him with ammunition, but Arnold threatened to break into the magazine to seize the needed supplies, and the supervisors yielded. When Arnold and his command reached Cambridge, he proposed the capture of Fort Ticonderoga and Crown Point. His suggestion was adopted, and he was commissioned a colonel by the Massachusetts legislature and authorized to raise a force of 400 men for the purpose. The state of Connecticut had already undertaken an expedition to capture the strongholds and had sent state militia, along with a force of Green Mountain Boys, from Vermont, all under the command of Ethan Allen. When Arnold caught up with this force, he demanded to be in command of the combined army, but was refused that honor. Instead, he served as a volunteer, and entered Ticonderoga side by side with Allen when it fell. A few days after the capture of Ticonderoga, Arnold seized St. John's, Massachusetts, and the state of Massachusetts asked Connecticut to put him in command of the captured territory, but Ethan Allen was favored for the position by the representatives of Arnold's home state.

In July of 1775 Arnold proposed an expedition be made against Quebec, and Washington approved, placing him in command of a force of some 1,100 men that set out from Cambridge on September 11. By the time Arnold reached his objective, he had only 700 men remaining with his army. His force was insufficient to storm the works of the city, so he was forced to await the arrival of General Montgomery's army that had just taken Montreal. When the latter arrived, an assault was made upon the city on December 31, 1775, which resulted in the American forces suffering a costly repulse. Montgomery was killed in the battle, and Arnold was wounded in the leg. In recognition of his services in the campaign, the Continental Congress commissioned him a brigadier general on January 10, 1776.

During the summer of 1776 Arnold was engaged in building a fleet to try to prevent the British from advancing up Lake Champlain. On October 11, 1776, he fought a battle near Valcour Island, in which the American forces, both military and naval, were badly defeated.

Benedict Arnold

Washington crossing the Delaware in preparation for the attacks on Trenton and Princeton.

Though he lost the battle, Arnold won the campaign. His resistance had been such that it convinced the British commander, General Carleton, to call off his advance and retire to Montreal with his army. The elimination of the British threat in this quarter made it possible for 3,000 men from the northern army to be sent to General Washington in time to take part in the battles of Trenton and Princeton.

On February 17, 1777, Arnold was promoted to the rank of major general by the Continental Congress. In April of that year, the British invaded Connecticut with a 2,000-man army under the command of Governor Tryon. The British destroyed the military stores at Danbury before they were brought to battle by General Wooster, and the 600 men in his command. Wooster was killed in a skirmish with the enemy, and Arnold, who had been visiting his family, in New Haven, arrived shortly thereafter with several hundred militia reinforcements and assumed command. He gave battle to the British at Ridgefield, where after a desperate engagement, the enemy was forced to flee to their ships.

Arnold was subsequently assigned to the Northern Department again, where he took part in the Saratoga Campaign. He commanded the left wing of the army at the battle of Freeman's Farm, on September 19, 1777, and was conspicuous in the decisive battle of the campaign that took place on October 7. In the latter engagement, Arnold rushed onto the field, without orders, and conducted a series of charges that broke the British lines and assured victory to the Americans. As the fighting was ending, he received a severe wound to the same leg he had been shot in at Quebec. Arnold was taken to Albany, to recover, remaining there until the spring of 1778. In June of 1778, still being too lame to return to the rigors of the field, Washington appointed him to command at Philadelphia. It was during this time that Arnold met and fell in love with Margaret Shippen, a strong Loyalist of the city. The two were soon engaged, and Arnold began associating with numerous known Loyalists of the area. It was at this same time that he became embroiled in quarrels with Joseph Reed that led to Reed submitting a long list of charges against Arnold to Congress. That body formed a committee to investigate the charges, and the decision of the committee was that all but two of them were without substance, and the two that did seem to have merit were of such a trivial nature that the committee recommended he be acquitted of all charges. Arnold felt he had been vindicated, but Reed was not ready to let the matter rest. He indicated that there was additional evidence that had not been heard and insisted that another committee be formed to review it. This committee did not wish to overturn the verdict of its predecessor, but it also had no wish to offend an important political official from Pennsylvania, so it passed the buck by directing that the matter be handled by the military in a court-martial. The finding of the court-martial was announced on January 26, 1780. Arnold was acquitted of all but two of the charges, just as the committee had recommended. The military board differed from the committee in stating that Arnold should receive a reprimand from Washington for the two minor offenses, however. Washington issued the reprimand, but wrote it in such a manner that it praised Arnold instead of condemning him. He then offered Arnold command of the Northern Department for the coming campaign, making him second only to Washington himself in the command structure of the Continental Army.

Stung by the injustice he felt he had been forced to endure, Arnold continued his associations with Loyalists, and even opened contact with British officials. Beverly Robinson and Major John Andre were among his chief contacts. A plan was developed by which Arnold would surrender West Point and the strategic Hudson Valley to the British, thus making the American prospects of winning the war so remote that they would be favorable to peace negotiations. Arnold was assured, by Lord North, that the Colonies would be guaranteed freedom from parliamentary control, and that they would be granted the liberal terms that had been offered in 1775. In July of 1780, when Arnold received command of West Point, he intended to surrender it to the British to accomplish this mission of restoring America to British rule. When Major Andre was captured, and the plot uncovered, Arnold fled to New York and the protective care of the British. He was commissioned a brigadier general in the British army. In the spring of 1781, he commanded a raid into Virginia. In September of that same year, he led an attack on New London that was hoped to draw Washington's attention away from his march south to engage Cornwallis. In 1782, he went to London, with his new wife, Margaret Shippen, where he was well received by the king and his party. In 1787, Arnold moved to St. John's, New Brunswick, where he started a mercantile business with his sons. In 1791, he moved back to London, and settled there permanently. The Earle of Landerdale made a slander against him in 1792, and the two men fought a bloodless duel. Benedict Arnold died in London on June 14, 1801, at the age of sixty. By the time of his death, he had come to be despised by a large portion of the British population for his betrayal of his countrymen, and died virtually a man without a country.[1]

ASHE, JOHN—(North Carolina) John Ashe was born at Grovely, Brunswick County, North Carolina, in 1720. He served as a member of the North Carolina Colonial Assembly for a number of years, and was the speaker of that body from 1762 to 1765. Ashe married Mary Moore (n.d.) and the couple had eight children together. Ashe's first rebellion against the Crown took place when he opposed the Stamp Act so violently as to compel the resignation of the local stamp-master, at the head of an armed mob.

In 1771, he fought against the North Carolina Regulators, in support of Royal governor Tryon, but he soon after became a Whig and a leading proponent of the Patriot cause in North Carolina. In 1775, he led five hundred men in an attack on Fort Johnson, resulting in the capture and destruction of that place, for which he was publicly denounced as a rebel.

Ashe was a member of the first North Carolina Provincial Congress. He raised and equipped, at his own expense, a regiment of militia for state service, and on April 23, 1776, he was appointed brigadier general of the

Wilmington District. In 1778, he joined General Benjamin Lincoln's force in South Carolina, and early in 1779, he was sent to drive the British from Augusta, Georgia. In March of 1779, while en route to Augusta, his force was surprised at Briar Creek by a force of 2,300 British soldiers and Loyalists, under the command of General August Prevost. Ashe's command was outnumbered and overpowered, suffering almost four hundred casualties, while the attacking British lost only five men. The disaster at Briar Creek gave the British control of the Georgia back country for some time.

After his defeat at Briar Creek, Ashe returned home to Wilmington. When that city fell to the British in 1781, Ashe was betrayed and was captured and held under close confinement. He and his family received cruel treatment at the hands of the British. John Ashe died on October 24, 1781, as a result of smallpox contracted in the British prison.[1]

BABCOCK, JOSHUA—(Rhode Island)

Joshua Babcock was born in Westerly, Rhode Island on May 17, 1707. After graduating from Yale College in 1724, he studied medicine, establishing a practice in Westerly in 1734. On August 11, 1735, he married Hannah Stanton. After 43 years together, Hannah died in 1778. On May 28, 1780, Babcock married Ann Maxson.

In addition to his medical practice, Babcock opened a successful retail store, and entered into the political arena. Beginning in 1740, he was elected to nine terms in the Colonial Legislature, as a representative of Westerly. From 1747 to 1749, and again from 1750 to 1764, he served as Chief Justice of the Supreme Court of Rhode Island. In 1764, he was one of the original corporators of Brown University. In 1776, Benjamin Franklin appointed Babcock to be the first Postmaster of Westerly.

In 1776, Babcock was elected to the Rhode Island House of Representatives, where he cast a vote for the "Act to repeal the Maintenance of the King's authority in Rhode Island." This document effectively declared Rhode Island's independence from Great Britain, and was signed before the Declaration of Independence by the Continental Congress in Philadelphia. Babcock was commissioned a major general in the Rhode Island Militia, but it appears that his duties were administrative, or honorary, as he did not exercise field command. In fact, he resigned his commission, in December of 1776, to take his seat in the House of Representatives, where he became a member of the Board of War.

Joshua Babcock died on April 1, 1783, at Westerly, Rhode Island.[1]

BAILEY, JACOB—(Massachusetts)

Jacob Bailey (also spelled Bayley. Heitman lists Jacob Bailey and Jacob Bayley as two different generals. They are, in fact, the same person) was born in Newbury, Massachusetts, on July 19, 1726. In 1745, he moved to Hampstead. On October 16 of that same year, he married Prudence Noyes, and the couple had 13 children. He was commissioned a captain in the militia during the French and Indian War, and served with Colonel Munroe during the siege of Fort William Henry. When the fort fell on August 7, 1757, Bailey was among those who escaped the subsequent massacre. In 1759, he was present for the capture of Fort Ticonderoga and Crown Point. His service was such that he was made a colonel by General Amherst. In 1760, Bailey served with Goff's Regiment in the campaign that ended with the capture of Montreal. Following the war, Bailey moved to Vermont in 1764, where he had obtained the proprietorship for the township of Newbury. In 1776, he was commissioned a brigadier general in the New York Militia, and was later appointed commissary-general of the Northern Department. Bailey urged General Washington to construct a road from Newbury to St. John's, to help facilitate supplying the American army then in Canada, under Montgomery. Washington approved the road, without waiting for the consent of Congress, and Bailey began construction of the road with 100 men. Bailey became a chief bulwark of the Patriot cause along the northern frontier. The British offered a reward of 500 guineas for his capture, dead or alive, and he was constantly required to evade the scouts sent from Canada to accomplish this purpose. Bailey commanded a regiment in the Saratoga Campaign, and was instrumental in the capture of General Burgoyne.

After the war, he became prominent in the

Green Mountain Boys, who took such an active part in the boundary dispute between Vermont and New Hampshire. Bailey also served as a judge of the probate court, and chief judge of Orange County, Vermont. He was a leading figure in the effort to make Vermont a separate state.

Jacob Bailey died at Newbury, Vermont, on March 1, 1816, at the age of eighty-seven. He was buried in the Ox-Bow Cemetery, in Newbury, Vermont.[1]

BARNWELL, JOHN—**(South Carolina)** John Barnwell was born at Charleston, South Carolina, on July 15, 1748. He was the grandson and namesake of Colonel John "Tuscarora" Barnwell, and early inhabitant of the colony, and commander of the Tuscarora expedition and massacre in 1712.

On January 30, 1766, Barnwell married Elizabeth Fenwick, but she would die later that same year. He then married Anne Huston, on May 8, 1777, and the couple had eight children together.

Barnwell made his living as a planter, and his family enjoyed a level of prominence within the colony. On June 17, 1775, he was commissioned captain in the 1st South Carolina Regiment. He was promoted to the rank of major in 1780. He participated in the defense of Charleston when the British forces invested that place in 1780. On May 12, 1780, Barnwell was captured when the city fell. In 1781, Barnwell was commissioned a brigadier general in the South Carolina Militia, a position he would hold until the close of hostilities.

John Barnwell died at Beaufort, South Carolina, on August 27, 1800, at the age of fifty-two. The town of Barnwell, South Carolina, is named in his honor.[1]

BEALL, REAZIN—**(Maryland)** Reazin (also spelled Rezin and Reason) Beall was born at Frederick, Maryland, in 1723. In 1763, he married Amelia Beall, and the couple had seven children together.

Beall was commissioned captain of an independent company of Maryland Militia in January of 1776. In August of that same year, he was commissioned a brigadier general in the state service, and assigned to command the Maryland contingent of the Flying Camp. The Marylanders took part in the fighting at Brooklyn and White Plains, winning honor for their state at the former, and Beall distinguished himself personally at the battle of Harlem Heights. General Beall is credited with being the reason that there were no land battles fought in Maryland during the Revolution. With a small force, he successfully repelled a planned British invasion of the state at Drum Point, on the Chesapeake Bay, foiling the enemy incursion into Maryland.

Reazin Beall died at Beltsville, Maryland, on October 14, 1809, in his eighty-sixth year.[1]

BEDEL, TIMOTHY—**(New Hampshire)** Timothy Bedel (also spelled Beedle) was born at Salem, New Hampshire, about 1740. During the French and Indian War, he served as a lieutenant in the militia. At the outbreak of the Revolution, Bedel served as a captain in the New Hampshire Rangers. In June of 1775, he was commissioned colonel of the New Hampshire Rangers, serving till December of that year. He was subsequently commissioned colonel of the 1st New Hampshire Regiment. He participated in the siege of Boston, and his regiment also took part in the defense of Canada, the operations around Lake Champlain, and the battles of Trenton and Princeton. Bedel was not in command of the regiment in the last two battles, however, having been cashiered from the service on August 1, 1776. The reason for this stemmed from the battle of Cedars, near Montreal, in May of that same year. Bedel had been in command of the American force at that place when it was surrendered to Brant's Indians, without resistance. Almost 400 men had been surrendered, and a number of them were murdered by the Indians after laying down their arms. Bedel was not present with his command at the time of its surrender, however, being confined to a sickbed at Lachine. His second in command, Major Isaac Butterfield, was responsible for offering no resistance to the British force, numbering some 500. General Arnold affixed the blame for the surrender on Bedel, regardless of the fact that he was not on the scene when the action took place. He was later reinstated to command, it being felt that an injustice had been done to him. He was subsequently commissioned a colonel in the Vermont Militia in 1777, and was rapidly promoted to the rank of brigadier general in that state's service, continuing in that capacity through to the close of active campaigning in 1781. The majority of his late war service took place in the Northern District. Timothy Bedel died at Haverhill, New Hampshire, in February of 1787, in his forty-seventh year.[1]

BRICKETT, JAMES SOLDIER—(Massachusetts) James Brickett was born in Haverhill, Massachusetts, in 1737. After receiving his primary education, Brickett studied medicine, and upon completion of his studies, opened a successful practice in Haverhill. During the French and Indian War, Brickett served as a surgeon at Fort Ticonderoga in 1759 and 1760. Following the end of the war, Brickett married Edna Merrill in 1760, and seven children were born to the marriage.

At the beginning of the Revolutionary War, Brickett was commissioned a lieutenant colonel of Frye's Massachusetts Regiment, on April 20, 1775. Brickett is listed among the men who received money for losses at the battles of Lexington and Concord. He took part in the battle of Bunker Hill, on June 17, 1775, where he was wounded. He also participated in the siege of Boston. In 1776, he was commissioned a brigadier general in the Massachusetts Militia, and assigned to take part in the Canadian Expedition. John Cummings had been the original choice of the legislature, but had declined the position, leaving Brickett to receive the commission. Brickett took an active role in the Saratoga Campaign, and following the surrender of Burgoyne's army was placed in command of the escort that marched the British prisoners, some 6,000 in number, from the battlefield to Cambridge, Massachusetts.

Following the war, Brickett returned to Haverhill and resumed his practice of medicine. James Brickett died at Haverhill, Massachusetts, on December 9, 1818, in his eighty-first year.[1]

The Battle of Bunker Hill

BRODHEAD, DANIEL, III — (New York)

Daniel Brodhead III was born in Marbletown, New York, on October 17, 1736, the son of Daniel Brodhead II and Hester Wyngart Brodhead. The following year, the family moved to Danville, Pennsylvania, to settle and farm. Life was hard on what was then the Pennsylvania frontier. Indian incursions were common, and the Brodhead homestead was attacked several times. There are no records of Brodhead's education, and it can be assumed that he spent his boyhood working the family farm. His prewar occupations included: farming, running a gristmill, and working as a deputy surveyor for the state. In 1756, Daniel married Elizabeth Dupui, and the couple had two children together.

Brodhead's first appearance on the public stage was when he was selected to represent Berks County as a representative to a provincial meeting in Philadelphia in July of 1774. There, he served on a committee that called for a continental congress and acts of non-importation and non-exportation from and to Great Britain.

When the war broke out, Daniel was commissioned lieutenant colonel of the 2nd Battalion, Miles' Pennsylvania Rifle Regiment, on March 13, 1776. He transferred to the 4th Pennsylvania Regiment on October 25, 1776. On March 12, 1777, he was made colonel of the 8th Pennsylvania Regiment, with the commission being dated to rank from September 29, 1776.[1]

Brodhead was at the battle of Long Island, where he showed particular gallantry, commanding, by the end of the battle, the entire contingent of Pennsylvania troops. Washington gave him special mention in his report of the fighting. After Long Island, in 1778, Washington dispatched Brodhead to Fort Muncy, with the mission of rebuilding the fort that had previously been destroyed by Indians. Brodhead was to command the fort until Washington recommended to Congress in 1779 that he be given command of the Western Department, replacing General McIntosh. On March 5, 1779, Brodhead was ordered to Fort Pitt, Pennsylvania (present day Pittsburgh), to take command of a district that stretched from the British possessions at Detroit, to the north, to the French possessions of Louisiana. This was indeed the largest department that any officer in the Continental Army was responsible for during the war.

Brodhead established his headquarters at Fort Pitt. In addition to this stronghold, he also had within his department Fort McIntosh (Beaver, Pennsylvania), Fort Laurens (Bolivar, Ohio), Fort Tuscarora (Lisbon, Ohio), Fort Wheeling (Wheeling, West Virginia), Fort Armstrong (Kittanning, Pennsylvania), and Fort Holliday's Cove, along with dozens of lesser outposts.

In August of 1779, Brodhead mounted a campaign against the hostile Indian tribes of the frontier. With 695 soldiers and militia, he marched out of Fort Pitt, following the Allegheny River into New York, attacking the Seneca wherever he could find them. Most of the Seneca warriors were off fighting against

Daniel Brodhead (courtesy United States Military History Institute)

General Sullivan's expedition in New York. Brodhead was able to drive deep into Seneca country, killing and capturing a large number of Indians, destroying their villages, and effectually driving them out of that portion of the state. From August 11 till September 14, his forces had traveled between 300 and 400 miles in the campaign, in the roadless wilderness that was then western Pennsylvania and New York. For his action, he received the thanks of Congress, and a personal acknowledgement from General Washington.

In 1781, the Delaware tribe chose to enter the war on the side of the British, and Brodhead mounted an expedition into their lands, destroying the village of Coshocton. The result of Brodhead's action was such that the Delaware withdrew to eastern Ohio, and posed no further threat to the American frontier posts.

On September 17, 1781, Brodhead was removed from his command, and replaced by General John Gibson, over charges that he had mishandled supplies and money intended for his troops. Accusers stated that he had adopted a policy of impressment and had spent money intended to be used as bonuses for new recruits inappropriately. Washington, himself, had been aware of the impressment, and had given it his approval. So far as the misspending of the bonus money was concerned, Brodhead had used the money to buy much needed supplies for his troops. In the end, he was cleared of the charge of impressment, but not of the misappropriations. Even so, the court-martial felt that he had been justified in his actions, and he was not punished.[2]

In January of 1781, Brodhead was given command of the 1st Pennsylvania Regiment, serving with this unit for the remainder of the war. On September 30, 1783, Daniel Brodhead's services were recognized by Congress when he was promoted to brevet brigadier general.[3]

After the war, he was chosen to be one of the officers to prepare papers of the organization of the Society of the Cincinnati. In 1789, he was chosen to be surveyor-general by the Pennsylvania State Assembly, a position he would hold until 1801. His first wife having died, Brodhead married Rebecca Mifflin, the widow of General Samuel Mifflin. Daniel Brodhead died at Milford, Pike County, Pennsylvania, on November 15, 1809, at the age of seventy-three. He is buried in Milford.

BUCHANAN, ANDREW—(Maryland)

Andrew Buchanan was born at Druid Hill, Baltimore County, Maryland, on October 22, 1734. Little is known of his early life or education, but, as a result of his later vocation, he must have received a substantial primary education, and studied law. He married Susanna Lawson on July 24, 1760, and the couple had seven children together.

Buchanan adopted the Patriot cause, and in 1775 he was appointed to serve on the Baltimore Committee of Observation, in preparation for the hostilities that the Colonists were sure would be coming with Great Britain. In 1776, Buchanan was commissioned a brigadier general in the Maryland Militia. There is no date given as to his resignation, or the end of his commission, so it must be assumed that he served in this capacity until the end of the war. In 1777, Buchanan was appointed to be a judge of the Baltimore County Court. Buchanan's military commission most certainly was of an administrative nature, as he did not hold a field command. It may be assumed that his military service consisted of recruiting and readying troops for the army, possibly acquiring arms and supplies. This was a common practice during the Revolution, and a number of appointments were made to the grade of general based solely upon the individual's social status within the state, and were not based upon military experience or ability, or were not based upon the premise that that officer would command a body of men in actual combat.

Andrew Buchanan died at Druid Hill, Baltimore County, Maryland, on March 12, 1786, at the age of fifty-one.[1]

BULL, STEPHEN—(South Carolina)

Stephen Bull was born in 1734 in South Carolina. He became known as Stephen Bull of Sheldon to distinguish himself from his father's first cousin, Stephen Bull (1716–1770). As a young man, Bull inherited Sheldon Plantation from his grandfather, William Bull. (William

Bull was also the name of Stephen's uncle, who was lieutenant governor of South Carolina). On December 18, 1755, Bull married Elizabeth Woodward. The marriage produced no children, and when Elizabeth died, Bull later married Anne Barnwell on May 24, 1772. Three children were born to this union.

Bull was elected to the South Carolina House of Commons in 1757, and served until 1760. He also served as a justice of the peace of Granville County in 1756, 1765, 1767, and 1769, and in 1767 he doubled up in that capacity by also serving as justice of the peace for Colleton County. In 1763, he acquired 7,500 acres of land along the Great Satilla River, in Georgia, but never settled there. In 1775 he was elected to the first South Carolina Provincial Congress, as a representative of St. Peter Parish. He was re-elected to the second Provincial Congress that same year. In 1775, he also received a commission as colonel in the state militia. In 1776, Bull was elected to the first General Assembly, as well as to the South Carolina Legislative Council. Bull was elected to the second General Assembly in 1776, serving till 1778. In 1778, he was commissioned a brigadier general in the South Carolina Militia, a position he would hold until the end of the war. He took part in the attack on the British forces at St. Mary's in 1778. Bull continued to be active in politics, however, and served as state senator from Prince William County from 1779 to 1780. In the meantime, he served with General Moultrie in the attack on Beaufort, South Carolina, in 1779, as well as with General Lincoln in the defense of Charleston in 1780. Bull was taken prisoner when Charleston fell, and was held for some time by the British. When paroled, he and his family went into exile and lived for a time in Virginia and Maryland. Charleston was the last military service Bull performed during the war, despite the fact that he retained the rank of general until its conclusion.

Following the war, Bull was elected to the South Carolina House in 1783, but he declined to serve. In 1785, he was elected to the General Assembly, serving until 1786. He was re-elected in 1787, serving through 1788. In 1790, he was elected to the State Senate, but did not qualify for membership in that body until 1791. Following his term in the Senate, Bull retired to private life and to his plantation.

Stephen Bull died in 1800, at Sheldon Plantation, South Carolina, in his sixty-sixth year of life. He was buried in the Sheldon Churchyard Cemetery.[1]

BUTLER, JOHN—(Virginia) John Butler was born in Goochland County, Virginia, in 1727. He was married to Anne Armstrong, but the date of the marriage is unknown. The couple had no children. Prior to the Revolution, he moved to Orange County, North Carolina, where he became a planter, at his home, Mt. Pleasant Plantation. He was a member of the North Carolina Regulators before 1773, and was also sheriff of Orange County, and was elected to the North Carolina legislature. In 1775, he was a member of the Hillsboro District Committee of Safety, and became a lieutenant colonel of the state militia that same year. In 1776, he was promoted to the rank of colonel and was also elected to Congress. Butler was commissioned a brigadier general in the North Carolina Militia in 1777. During the Southern Campaign, his plantation house was burned to the ground by General Cornwallis. In 1781, Butler was elected to the North Carolina House of Commons, and he also became councilor of state, serving two terms in the latter office.

Following the war, Butler was named chairman of the Committee of Grievances, but he resigned his post later that same year. John Butler died at his home, at Mt. Pleasant, on May 20, 1785, in his fifty-eighth year. His burial site is unknown, but he was most probably interred in the family cemetery at Mt. Pleasant Plantation.[1]

BUTLER, RICHARD—(Ireland) Richard Butler was born in St. Bridget's Parish, Ireland, on April 1, 1743. In 1748, his family moved to America, settling in Pennsylvania. In the early 1770s, he was a successful trader, at Fort Pitt (present day Pittsburgh, Pennsylvania) where he became well known to the Indian tribes in that part of Pennsylvania and Ohio. Butler married Maria Smith (n.d.), and the couple had two children. He later married Catherine

Grenadier. In 1775, the Continental Congress appointed him a commissioner to negotiate with the Indians to try to gain their support against Great Britain, or at least their neutrality, in the war. He was commissioned captain of the 2nd Pennsylvania Battalion on January 5, 1776, and major of the 8th Pennsylvania Regiment on July 20, 1776. In this capacity, he took part in the battles of Saratoga and Monmouth. On March 12, 1777, he was made lieutenant colonel, with the commission being pre-dated to September 28, 1776. Near Williamsburg, Virginia, he attacked Colonel Simcoe's Rangers on June 26, 1781, and drove the enemy from the field in a small battle in which he was in command. Butler ended the war in command of the 3rd Pennsylvania Regiment. On September 30, 1783, he was granted a commission as brevet brigadier general by the Continental Congress in appreciation of his wartime services.

Following the war, Congress placed him in charge of the Indians in the Northwest Territory, and he successfully negotiated the Treaty of Fort Stanwix in 1784 that witnessed the Iroquois surrendering their lands. He also took part in the negotiations that resulted in the Treaty of Fort McIntosh in 1785. After his successful negotiations with the Indians, Butler came back to Allegheny County, Pennsylvania, where he served as judge, and from which he was elected to the state legislature. He was largely responsible for creating Allegheny County as a separate entity carved out of Westmoreland County in 1790. In all, there were eight new counties created from land that had once been part of Westmoreland County. The county immediately to the north of Allegheny County, as well as its county seat, was named Butler, in honor of Richard Butler.

In 1791, Butler was once more called to active duty in the military. He was commissioned a major general in the U.S. Army, in charge of new levies being raised to combat the Indian uprising in the Northwest. General Arthur St. Clair sent Butler and his command north from Fort Hamilton, Ohio, to bring the enemy to battle, and they were ambushed near Fort Recovery, in what is now Mercer County, Ohio, on November 4, 1791. The Indians were led by Chief Little Turtle, and Butler's force was completely surprised and thoroughly defeated. The army lost approximately 600 men killed in the battle, the worst defeat ever suffered by the U.S. Army at the hands of the Indians. Among the killed was Richard Butler. He had been conspicuous in the battle, repeatedly charging the enemy, and receiving several wounds before a tomahawk blow to the head finally killed him. He was later scalped by the Indians. Richard Butler was forty-eight years old at the time of his death.[1]

CADWALADER, JOHN—(Pennsylvania) John Cadwalader was born in Philadelphia, Pennsylvania, on January 10, 1742. He was a cousin to John Dickinson, the noted Patriot known as "the Penman of the Revolution." Cadwalader married Elizabeth Lloyd on September 25, 1768, and the couple had three children together. After Elizabeth's death, in 1776, he married Anne Dingwell, with one child resulting to the marriage. Upon Anne's death, Cadwalader married a third time, to Willamina Bond, and three children were born to this final marriage. Prior to the opening of hostilities, Cadwalader served as a member of the Philadelphia Committee of Safety, and as a captain in a local company of militia. The outbreak of hostilities found Cadwalader in command of a unit popularly known as the "Silk Stocking Company," a unit so well trained, and so versed in military tactics that nearly all of its members received commissions as officers.[1]

In 1776, he was made a colonel of a Pennsylvania militia regiment, and with that regiment, he participated in the battles of Trenton and Princeton, with George Washington's army. He was appointed a brigadier general of Pennsylvania Militia on April 5, 1777.[2] Cadwalader was offered a commission as a brigadier general in the Continental Army several times, but turned them down, preferring to remain with his own troops. As a general, Cadwalader took part in the battles of Brandywine and Germantown in 1777, and Monmouth in 1778.

On July 4, 1778, Cadwalader took part in a duel with General Thomas Conway over slanderous remarks Conway had been making about General Washington. Cadwalader was an ardent supporter of Washington, and he determined to intervene in his commanding general's behalf to answer the slanders against him. In the duel, Cadwalader shot Conway in the mouth, severely wounding him. At the conclusion of the war, Cadwalader moved to Maryland for a time, and was elected as a representative to that state's legislature.

John Cadwalader died on February 11, 1786, in Shrewsbury, Pennsylvania, at the age of forty-four.

CAMPBELL, WILLIAM—(Virginia)
William Campbell was born in Augusta County, Virginia, in 1745. After his father's death, in 1767, he moved with his mother and sisters to the Holston Valley of Fincastle County, Virginia, where they built the family plantation that came to be known as Aspenvale, near present day Abingdon, Virginia. In 1773, Campbell was appointed to the office of justice of the peace, and in 1774 he was commissioned a captain in the local militia, serving in Colonel Christian's expedition against the Shawnee that ended in the peace treaty of Camp Charlotte.

At the outset of the Revolution, he commanded a company in Patrick Henry's regiment that took part in dislodging Lord Dunmore from Gwyn's Island in July of 1776. Campbell resigned his commission on October 9, 1776, so that he could better protect his frontier home against the incursions of the Cherokee. While thus engaged, he married Elizabeth Henry, sister of Patrick Henry. He was appointed to be justice of the peace in 1777, and that same year was commissioned a lieutenant colonel in the Virginia Militia. In 1778, he served as a commissioner to establish the boundary line between Virginia and the Cherokee lands, and in 1779, he was instrumental in driving the Loyalists out of the Fincastle County region. In 1780, he was promoted to the rank of colonel, and was elected to the Virginia legislature. In October of 1780 Campbell led a regiment of riflemen at the battle of Kings Mountain, where he fought with distinction. His conduct in that battle led to his commission as a brigadier general in the state service in December of 1780. On March 15, 1781, he responded to General Greene's call for troops and led a corps of riflemen in the battle of Guilford Court House. Campbell felt that his men had not been properly supported by Colonel Lee's cavalry, and as a result of this retired from the service. He later served, under Lafayette in the battle of Jamestown on July 6, 1781. Following this battle, Campbell became ill from a sickness from which he never recovered. William Campbell died at Rocky Mills, Hanover County, Virginia, on August 22, 1781, in his thirty-sixth year. He was originally buried at Rocky Mills, but his body was removed to the family burial ground, at Aspenvale Plantation, in 1823.[1]

CASWELL, RICHARD—(Maryland)
Richard Caswell was born at Joppa, Maryland, on August 3, 1729, at the family home, called Mulberry Point. He received his primary education at the parish school, and at the age of sixteen moved to North Carolina, where he secured a position in the secretary's office of Gabriel Johnston, the royal governor of the colony.

He was made a surveyor's apprentice to James Mackilwean, and in 1747 he completed his training and was appointed deputy surveyor general, receiving a land grant on which he built his house, Newington-on-the-Hill, located near Stringer's Ferry.

On April 21, 1752, Caswell married Mary Mackilwean, the daughter of the surveyor he had been apprenticed to, and three children were born to the marriage. The family lived at Red House, a plantation near Kinston. Upon the untimely death of Mary, Caswell married Susannah Moore on June 20, 1758. This marriage produced eight children.

Caswell became an officer in the Johnston County (later Lenoir County) Militia, in a troop of cavalry prior to 1759.

At the battle of Alamance, against the North Carolina Regulators, on May 16, 1771, Caswell, a colonel of militia, commanded the right wing of Governor Tryon's army, and the victory brought the rebellion of the Regulators to a close.[1]

In 1773, Caswell was appointed to a Committee of Correspondence and Inquiry by the speaker of the Provincial General Assembly, and in 1774, he was selected to represent North Carolina in the first Continental Congress. He was re-elected to serve in the second Continental Congress, in 1775. In the meantime, the battles of Lexington and Concord had taken place, and Caswell became a strong advocate of North Carolina preparing itself for war. In a letter to his son, dated May of 1775, he stated that the residents of North Carolina must "arm and form into a Company or Companies of Independents. When their Companies are full, 68 private men each, to elect officers; viz, a captain, two lieutenants, an ensign and subalterns, and to meet as often as possible and go thro' the exercise." The fighting might have taken place in New England, but Caswell felt it was North Carolina's responsibility to "be behind their neighbors."[2]

Upon his return from the second Continental Congress, Royal governor Josiah Martin proclaimed Caswell to be a "most active tool of sedition." When the third Provincial Congress of North Carolina met in August of 1775, it made arrangements to actively support the Continental Congress by raising both money and men for the cause. In addition to the troops to be raised for the Continental army, it was determined to raise six battalions of Minutemen to serve in the state. Richard Caswell was appointed to be the commander of the Minutemen from the district of New Bern. On February 27, 1776, Caswell and his militia defeated a combined British and Loyalist force at the battle of Moore's Creek Bridge, near Wilmington. He would subsequently serve as a general in the state militia, with a commission from the North Carolina Legislature.

In November of 1776, when the fifth Provincial Congress of North Carolina met, for the purpose of drafting a new state constitution, Caswell was elected to serve as president of that body. In January of 1777, he took the oath of office as North Carolina's first elected governor, and served for three successive one-year terms, the maximum allowed by the state's new constitution.

Retiring to private life, Caswell operated his plantation, indigo works (located near Kinston), a gristmill, and a tannery. From 1784 to 1789, a number of his family members became victims of yellow fever, with two brothers and his oldest son being killed by the disease.

Richard Caswell died on November 8, 1789, at the age of sixty. He had been presiding over a session of the state senate when he was stricken by a fatal stroke of paralysis. He is believed to be buried at Caswell Memorial Park in Kinston, but the absolute certainty of that is a subject of historical debate.

CHAMBERLAIN, JAMES — (Ireland ?)

James Chamberlain was most probably born in Ireland on May 7, 1745. His family was from Ireland, coming to America and settling in Pennsylvania, and it is possible that James was born here, but is more probable that his birth occurred in Ireland and that he accompanied his family on the move to the Colonies. Chamberlain married Ann Sample on May 12, 1791, and the couple had one child together.

Chamberlain was a captain, major, and lieutenant colonel in the York County Militia, and was commissioned a brigadier general in the Maryland Militia on January 6, 1776. Owing to the fact that no battle took place in Maryland during the war, Chamberlain's duties were largely administrative, and he was instrumental in raising troops and obtaining supplies for the militia.

Following the end of the war, Chamberlain returned to private life and to his Adams County farm. James Chamberlain died on January 18, 1819, at the age of seventy-three.[1]

CLARK, GEORGE ROGERS — (Virginia)

George Rogers Clark was born in Albemarle County, Virginia, a few miles east of Charlottesville, on November 19, 1752. He received a good primary education, and by all accounts was an avid reader, reportedly buying many books during family visits to Williamsburg. He was the older brother, by eighteen years, of William Clark, who would achieve fame on his own as part of the Lewis and Clark Expedition in 1803.

In 1757, the Clarks sold their property in Albemarle County and moved to a farm in the southwest corner of Caroline County that had been willed to them by an uncle, John Clark. In 1772, Clark made a surveying trip into Kentucky, even though the British government had forbidden settlement west of the Allegheny Mountains. Over the next four years, he located prime tracts for himself and his family, and acted as a guide for families that were disregarding the edict and moving to Kentucky. Clark also participated in Lord Dunmore's War, where he gained a reputation for himself as an Indian fighter.

The coming of the Revolution brought with it increased Indian activity all along the frontier, and Kentucky was no exception. The raids became so frequent that Clark called together a meeting of representatives of all the area forts to discuss the problem in June of 1776. He and another delegate were selected to go to Williamsburg and seek the recognition and protection of the Virginia government for Kentucky, as a county of Virginia. Governor Patrick Henry granted Clark 500 pounds of gunpowder for use by the settlers, and the Virginia Assembly voted to make Kentucky a county.

In 1777, the Kentucky settlements were under almost constant attack from the Indians, and Clark decided on a bold course of action. Instead of merely defending the settlements, he proposed to take the war to the enemy by mounting a campaign against the British held settlements in the Illinois territory. Clark was granted the authority to raise a force of seven companies, of fifty men each, for the defense of Kentucky. He was given a commission as lieutenant colonel, and Patrick Henry also gave him secret permission to attack Kaskaskia and other posts in the Illinois country.

Clark had trouble raising the full complement of men he had been authorized to command. He had in his small army only 150 militia and twenty settlers and their families. With this tiny band, he struck out for Kaskaskia on June 26, 1778. The men were not informed of their intended destination until they reached the Falls of Ohio, and when it was revealed, Clark had a hard time preventing desertions. On the night of July 4, 1778, Clark's force surprised Kaskaskia, occupying the fort and town without firing a shot. Clark then negotiated with the large French population of the town, offering them American citizenship in return for their oaths of allegiance and safe conduct out of the area. The French had learned of the recent French-American alliance, and were more than willing to co-operate with Clark. A detachment was sent to the settlements of Cahokia, Prairie du Rocher, and St. Phillip, also containing large numbers of French residents, and those towns also accepted Clark's terms without resistance. Father Gibault, the priest at Kaskaskia, went to Vincennes, where he talked the French citizens there into pledging their allegiance to Clark.

During the months of August and September of 1778, Clark negotiated with the Indian tribes in the region, and succeeded in winning their neutrality in the upcoming campaign. Learning of Clark's actions, the British lieutenant governor at Detroit, Henry Hamilton, gathered his forces and proceeded down the Wabash and Maumee rivers, arriving at Vincennes on December 17, 1778. Hamilton intended to strengthen his position at Vincennes and at Sackville, but he did not plan to make a campaign against Clark until spring. Accordingly, he sent all of his Indian allies home for the winter. Clark realized that time was on the side of Hamilton. If he was permitted time to gather his superior resources, the Patriots could not hope to hold the posts they had captured in Illinois. He again decided on a bold course, and determined to attack Hamilton at Vincennes during the depth of winter. On February 6, 1779, Clark set out for Vincennes with a force of only 172 men, of which nearly half were French volunteers from the captured posts. The weather was so bad that it took seventeen days to make a trip that normally took five to six. On February 23, Clark surprised the garrison at Vincennes. He ordered his company flags to be paraded back and forth, behind a small rise, to give the British the impression that the force confronting them was 600 men, not 200. When his backwoods marksmen opened fire on the fort, their volleys were so destructive that they prevented the British from being able to open their gunports. After three days of siege and scam, Hamilton surrendered Vincennes and his army to Clark. The British never regained control of their lost posts in the Northwest, and on the basis of that, were forced to cede those lands to the United States in the Treaty of Paris in 1783. In recognition of his accomplishments, Clark was commissioned a brigadier general in the Continental Army in 1781, and he continued campaigning against hostile tribes until the end of the war.

In 1784, Clark was named the principal surveyor of the public lands that were to be used as bounty payments for Virginia veterans of the war. He subsequently served as chairman of the Board of Commissioners that supervised the allotment of land in Illinois. During the war, Clark had personally financed a great deal of the expenses for the defense of the Kentucky settlements. He was never able to obtain repayment of this money from the state of Virginia, or the Federal government, and lived most of his post-war life in debt. Hounded by creditors, he moved to Clarksburg, Indiana, in 1803, where he built a small two-room cabin. A stroke that necessitated the amputation of his right leg forced him to live with a sister at Locust Grove, Kentucky, eight miles from Louisville. On February 13, 1818, a second stroke took his life at the age of sixty-six. He was initially buried in a family plot, but in 1869, his remains were moved the Cave Hill Cemetery, in Louisville, Kentucky.[1]

CLARKE, ELIJAH—**(North Carolina)** Elijah Clarke (also spelled Clark) was born in Edgecombe County, South Carolina, in 1733. In 1774, he moved to Wilkes County, Georgia (what is now part of present day Lincoln County), because of the availability of new lands. Shortly after Clarke settled in Wilkes County, the region was threatened by Indians, and a local militia company was raised for defense, with Clarke serving as captain.

In 1776, Clark joined the Patriots and was given a commission as lieutenant colonel in the Georgia Militia, serving with Andrew Pickens. In July of 1778, he was wounded at the battle of Alligator Creek. In February of 1779, he served with Pickens at the battle of Kettle Creek, Georgia, where the Patriot force of some 300 defeated a Loyalist force of about 700 men, under the command of Colonel Boyd. This victory came as the British were trying to rally Loyalist support, following their victory at Savannah, and it forced the British to give up their recruitment efforts and retire to Augusta, freeing the Georgia back country of English control.

Clarke carried on a guerrilla war in the Georgia back country, fighting mostly against local Loyalist forces. In 1780, he defeated Major Patrick Ferguson's Loyalist force at Green Spring, South Carolina. On August 18, 1780, in another encounter with Ferguson's force, at Musgrove's Mill, South Carolina, he inflicted 150 casualties on the Loyalist force, captured another seventy, and all at the cost of only twelve casualties to his own command.

In September of 1780, Clarke took part in an attempt to retake Augusta, Georgia, from the British. The Americans were forced to retire when British re-enforcements arrived from Ninety-Six, however. The attempt to take Augusta led to violent reprisals by the Loyalists, causing some 400 women and children to flee the area, along with the Patriot forces, to North Carolina. Major Ferguson's pursuit of these forces led to the battle of Kings Mountain.

On November 20, 1780, Clarke joined Thomas Sumter in opposing Lt. Colonel Banastre Tarleton's British force at Blackstocks, South Carolina. In April of 1781, Clarke, along with General Pickens and Lt. Colonel Henry Lee, undertook a second attempt to retake Augusta from the British. They conducted a siege that resulted in the fall of that city on June 5 of that same year.

With the shifting of the war to the north of Georgia, in 1781, Clarke continued to serve in the militia, fighting Indians on the frontier. Clarke's efforts were recognized by the state of Georgia when he was commissioned a brigadier general in the militia in 1781. He was also given a plantation in Wilkes County by the people of Wilkes County and the Georgia House of Assembly.

In 1793, Clarke was commissioned a major general in the French army, at a salary of 10,000 dollars a year, and engaged in French attempts to seize control of western Florida from Spain. In 1794, he led a force across the Oconee River to build a fort and establish the Republic of Georgia, now known as the Transoconee Republic. The group set about creating a country, complete with constitution and a committee of safety. Owing to the fact that Clarke was an American, regardless of his present ties to the French, the U.S. government became alarmed over his actions, fearing they would bring on a war with Spain. On September 28, 1794, Clarke surrendered to a combined force of Georgia Militia and U.S. Regulars who were sent to put an end to his land schemes. Regardless of this incident, Clarke retained his status as a hero of the Revolution, and his reputation suffered little from his Florida expedition.[1]

Elijah Clarke died at his home in Wilkes County, Georgia, in 1799, at the age of sixty-six. He was originally buried at Graball, but his remains were moved, in 1955, to Elijah Clarke Park at Lincolnton (Lincoln County, just off US 378) in order to prevent them from being flooded by the Clark Hill Lake project.

CLINTON, GEORGE—(New York) George Clinton was born on July 26, 1739, at the family farm in Ulster County, New York, the younger brother of General James Clinton. George exhibited a disposition for the military at a young age, and in his youth he had served on a cruise aboard a privateer. In 1758, at the age of eighteen, he took part, along with his brother, in Bradstreet's expedition against Fort Frontenac, near present day Kingston, Ontario.

At the conclusion of the French and Indian War, George traveled to New York City, where he studied law in the office of William Smith. Upon completing his studies, and being accepted to the bar, George returned to Ulster County, where he established a thriving law practice. It was not long before his talents as a lawyer were recognized, and he was given a clerkship by the colonial governor, Admiral George Clinton. On February 7, 1770, Clinton married Cornelia Tappen, and the couple had four children together.

As a spokesman for the minority Whig Party in New York, he was selected to represent the state in the Continental Congress that convened in 1775. George was forced to cut short his service in the Congress by the British invasion of his native state, and returned to New York to help prepare for its defense prior to the drafting of the Declaration of Independence, thus being deprived of the opportunity that was rightfully his to have signed his name to that document.

In 1776, he was deputy of the Provincial Congress that drafted the first state constitution for New York, but his political service was once again cut short by an appeal from the Continental Congress for him to organize the militia of his state for home defense. He received a commission as a brigadier general in the Continental Army, dated March 25, 1777.

Though he and his brother, James, were unable to hold the highland Forts Montgomery and Clinton from Sir Henry Clinton's British army, the spirited defense that they displayed there caused Sir Henry to re-evaluate his campaign, and cancel his planned advance on Albany.[1]

In 1778, George was elected as the first governor of New York, a position he would hold for the next seventeen years, until 1795. At the conclusion of the war, Clinton accompanied General Washington on his tour of the

George Clinton

western forts in New York to make plans for occupying them once the British had evacuated, according to the terms of the peace treaty. On September 30, 1783, he was granted the brevet rank of major general.[2]

In 1788, Clinton presided over the state convention held to ratify the Federal Constitution. Clinton was personally opposed to ratifying the Constitution, but the Federalists were successful in garnering enough votes to offset Clinton's efforts to defeat the ratification.

Clinton continued to hold important civil posts as the 1800s were ushered in. In 1800, he was elected to Congress, and in 1801 he was once more elected to be the governor of New York. The year 1804 witnessed possibly his most important political office, when he was elected, for two terms, as vice president of the United States. George Clinton would finish out the rest of his life in Washington, D.C., and would die in the nation's capital on April 20, 1812, at the age of seventy-two.[3]

CLINTON, JAMES — (New York) James Clinton was born in Orange County, New York, on August 9, 1733. He was the older brother of Brigadier General George Clinton. James received a fine education, though he did not attend a public or private school, instead being tutored at home. At the age of twenty, James served as a captain in Lieutenant Colonel John Bradstreet's successful campaign against Fort Frontenac, at present day Kingston, Ontario, in 1758. During this expedition, Clinton and his company captured a French sloop-of-war on Lake Ontario. He was subsequently given command of four companies and charged with the mission of protecting a fifty mile line in Orange and Ulster counties from incursions by the French.[1]

James married Mary De Witt, after the close of the French and Indian War, on February 18, 1765, and retired to private life. Three children were born to the marriage. At the outbreak of the Revolution, he commanded the 3rd New York regiment of militia and accompanied General Richard Montgomery on his ill-fated expedition against Quebec in 1775. Clinton was commissioned as a brigadier general in the Continental Army on August 9, 1776.[2]

In 1777, he and his brother George, were unable to successfully defend Forts Clinton and Montgomery with his 600 men from British attacks by Sir Henry Clinton's three to four thousand man army, and the fall of the forts opened the Hudson River to navigation by the British.[3] Over 250 of his 600 man garrison fell in the battle, along with 200 British. Overwhelmed by superior numbers, Clinton was forced to abandon the forts. After securing a boat to transport his brother to safety, James attempted to make good his escape from the forts on horseback, but he received a bayonet wound in the leg during his flight. That same year, once his wounded leg had healed, along with Major General John Sullivan, Clinton defeated the Loyalists and their Indian allies at Newtown (present day Elmira). In 1781, he participated in the siege of Yorktown, Virginia, commanding a central division under General Benjamin Lincoln, where he did good service. He was later present during the British evacuation of New York. On September 30, 1783, he was granted the brevet rank of major general.[4]

James continued his public service when he was elected to serve as a delegate from New York to the Constitutional Convention, in 1787.

Clinton was described by a biographer as, "Cool, steady, and determined, he moved amid a battle with a sangfroid and firmness that astonished his soldiers. He was affectionate in his disposition, frank, generous, and kind, and when unexcited, mild. But when aroused, he was terrible as a storm. His was one of those powerful natures, which in repose exhibit only traits of gentleness, and quiet strength; yet if summoned into sudden action, put forth awful energy, and appall those, who before had never dreamed of such a slumbering volcano under so mild an exterior. He was an incorruptible patriot, a fearless and gallant soldier, and a true-hearted man."[5]

James Clinton died on December 22, 1812, in Little Britain, New York, at the age of seventy-nine.

COBB, DAVID — (Massachusetts) David Cobb was born at Attleborough, Massachusetts, on March 14, 1748. He obtained a primary education sufficient to prepare him for acceptance to Harvard, whence he graduated in 1766. He then studied medicine in Boston, and after successful completion of his studies, set up a practice in Taunton, Massachusetts. Cobb married Eleanor Bradish (n.d.), and the couple had eleven children together.

In 1774, Cobb served as secretary of the Bristol County Convention, and in 1775 he was a delegate to the Massachusetts Provincial Congress. When hostilities erupted, Cobb offered his services as a doctor, and became surgeon of Marshall's Massachusetts Regiment in May of 1775. He then took a leave of the medical practice and became lieutenant colonel of Jackson's Continental Regiment on January 12, 1777. This unit was redesignated the 16th Massachusetts Regiment in July of 1780. He transferred to the 9th Massachusetts Regiment in early June of 1781.

On June 15, 1781, Cobb became an aide-de-camp to General Washington, and in this capacity he became a close and trusted friend of the general. He would continue to serve in this position until January 7, 1783, when he was made lieutenant colonel commandant of the 5th Massachusetts Regiment. Cobb was commissioned a brevet brigadier general by Congress on September 30, 1783, in recognition of his services to the nation.[1] Washington had also showed his personal appreciation of Cobb when he designated that officer to be in charge of negotiating the British evacuation of New York with Sir Guy Carleton.

After the war, Cobb became a major general of militia, and judge of the Bristol County Court of Common Pleas. During Shay's Rebellion, he defended his courtroom from armed insurgents, refusing to give way to the mob. He was elected to Congress in 1793, serving till 1795. In 1796, Cobb became a land agent and farmer in Oldsborough, Maine, and was elected to the Massachusetts Senate from the eastern district of Maine. In 1802 he was elected president of the Massachusetts Senate, and in 1809 he became lieutenant governor of the commonwealth. He was a member of the Board of Military Defense, in 1812, and chief justice of the Hancock County Court of Common Pleas until he returned to Taunton in 1817.

David Cobb died at Taunton, on April 17, 1830, at the ripe old age of eighty-two. He was buried in the Plain Cemetery, in Taunton.

CONWAY, THOMAS—(Ireland) Thomas Coway was born in Ireland on February 27, 1733. At the age of six, his family moved to France, where the young boy was educated in the military profession. In 1749, at the age of sixteen, Conway became a lieutenant in the Regiment de Clare. By 1772, he had attained the rank of colonel, and had attained a commendable reputation in the French service. Conway sought to enlist his services in the American cause, and met with Silas Deane, in Paris, for that purpose. Deane welcomed the offer of this respected officer, and provided him with letters of introduction to General Washington, and to Congress.[1]

On December 14, 1776, Conway set sail for America. He reached Morristown, New Jersey, and Washington's encampment, on May 8, 1777. Having presented the commander in chief with his letters of introduction, he was commissioned a brigadier general and assigned to General Sullivan's Division. Conway led a brigade at Brandywine, in September of 1777, and at Germantown the following month. He distinguished himself by his conduct on those fields of battle, and had gained the support of several members of Congress. Following the battle of Germantown, Conway entered into a conspiracy with General Gates to have Washington replaced by the latter officer as commander in chief of the American armies. General Alexander, who had seen a letter written from Conway to Gates that contained several inflammatory comments about Washington, advised the commander in chief of the plot against him. Washington confronted Conway, who admitted to writing the letter Alexander had seen, but denied having part in any attempt to displace Washington from command. Conway offered his resignation to Washington, and sent a formal statement of such to Congress. When the controversy reached the Continental Congress, several members of that body decided to side with Conway. Chief among these was Thomas Mifflin and Benjamin Rush, who disliked Washington, and also wished to see him replaced with General Gates. Instead of accepting Conway's resignation, the Congress promoted him to the rank of major general and appointed him to be inspector general of the army. In doing so, Congress promoted him over the heads of twenty-three other brigadiers.

The affair soon became known as the Conway Cabal, and caused a rift in the command structure of the Continental Army. The vast majority of the officers supported Washington, leaving only the advocates of Gates and Conway to oppose him. Lafayette refused to accept Conway as second in command for his proposed (but never executed) expedition into Canada, and resolutely stood behind Washington. When Conway rejoined the army he received a cool reception from Washington, and responded by sending the commander an insulting letter. Washington forwarded the letter to Congress, with the endorsement that Conway was his "enemy." In the meantime, nine brigadier generals in the army had sent a petition to Congress complaining that Conway had been promoted above them. When Conway then sent a protest to Congress that he had not been given an independent command, but was serving under General McDougall, at Peekskill, New York, a position not to his taste or befitting his position, even those who had initially supported him decided that the time had come to wash their hands of the whole matter. Congress voted to accept his previous resignation on April 28, 1778.

General John Cadwallader, a staunch supporter of Washington, engaged in a heated argument with Conway following his official resignation from the army that led to a duel between the two men. Conway was wounded in the affair of honor, and as he lay recovering in his sickbed wrote a letter to Washington denying that he had ever conspired against him. On July 1, 1779, Conway resumed his service in the French army, where he was made the aide-major-general of the French forces in Flanders. On March 1, 1780, he was promoted to the rank of brigadier general. In 1781, Conway became colonel of the Pondicery Regiment, and in 1784 became the marechal de camp. He was appointed governor general of the French army in India in 1787, and was promoted to governor general of all French forces beyond the Cape of

Thomas Conway

Good Hope in 1789. By 1793, he was back in France, but his affiliation with the royals put him on the wrong side of the French Revolution, and he was forced to flee for his life from France. Thomas Conway is believed to have died in exile in 1800.[2]

CORNELL, EZEKIEL—(Rhode Island)
Ezekiel Cornell was born at Scituate, Rhode Island, in 1732. Cornell attended public schools before becoming a mechanic. An avid reader, Cornell established and ran a library in Scituate. He also acquired a tract of land and took up farming. Cornell married Rachael Wood on January 19, 1750, and the couple had three children together.

In 1775, he was appointed lieutenant colonel of Hitchcock's 3rd Rhode Island Regiment, and was present at the siege of Boston. He became lieutenant colonel of the 11th Continental Infantry Regiment on January 1, 1776. On October 1, 1776, he was made deputy adjutant-general of the army. Cornell and his regiment took part in the operations around New York City, and the campaigns against

Trenton and Princeton. In 1777, he was commissioned a brigadier general in the Rhode Island Militia, and appointed commander of the brigade of militia that did great service in protecting the state from 1777 to 1780, during the British occupation. When the term of enlistment of the brigade expired on March 16, 1780, Cornell was left without a command. He was subsequently elected as a delegate from Rhode Island to the Continental Congress, serving from 1780 to 1783, where he was chairman of the military committee.

On September 19, 1782, Cornell was appointed inspector of the main body of the Continental Army, under General Washington, and served in this capacity till the end of the hostilities. Following the war, Cornell retired to his farm in Scituate and devoted himself to private affairs.

Ezekiel Cornell died at Milford, Massachusetts, on April 25, 1800, in his sixty-eighth year. He was buried in the Scituate Cemetery, but the exact location of his cemetery plot has been lost.[1]

CRANE, JOHN—**(Massachusetts)** John Crane was born at Milton, Norfolk County, Massachusetts, on December 7, 1744. Crane gained his first experience at combat in the French and Indian War, the training ground for so many of the American generals in the Revolution. Following the war, he married Mehitable Wheeler, on December 16, 1766, and the couple had four children together.

In the years leading up the war, Crane joined the Sons of Liberty, becoming an active participant in the cause of liberty. Indeed, Crane was instrumental in bringing about the tension between England and the Colonies that eventually led to war. He was one of the "Indians" who took part in the Boston Tea Party, in protest of the tea tax that had been levied by Great Britain. The Sons of Liberty, dressed up as Indians, destroyed a cargo of tea that was loaded on a British ship in Boston Harbor. When the fighting erupted, at Lexington and Concord, Crane offered his services to the Patriot cause. He was considered to be an excellent

Washington at the Battle of Monmouth (courtesy United States Military History Institute)

artillerist, one of the best in the Colonies, and was accordingly commissioned a captain in Gridley's Regiment of Massachusetts Artillery on May 3, 1775. On December 10, 1775, he was commissioned a major in Knox's Continental Artillery, and on January 1, 1777, he was promoted to the rank of colonel and given command of the 3rd Continental Artillery. Crane served under Generals Knox and Gates, and fought at the battle of Brooklyn, being later wounded at Corlaer's Hook on September 14, 1776. He also served with distinction at the battles of Brandywine, Germantown, Monmouth, and Redbank. In recognition of his service and sacrifice, the Continental Congress bestowed the rank of brevet brigadier general on him on September 30, 1783.

Following the war, Crane was appointed to be one of the first judges of the Court of Common Pleas in Maine by Governor John Hancock in 1790. He moved his family to Maine to accept the position, and lived the rest of his life there.

John Crane died on August 21, 1805, at Whiting, Maine, at the age of sixty.[1]

CUSHING, JOSEPH—(**Massachusetts**) Joseph Cushing was born at Hanover, Plymouth County, Massachusetts, on March 1, 1731. After receiving a sound primary education, Cushing attended Harvard College, graduating from that institution in 1752. In 1752, Cushing also married Ruth Stockbridge, and the couple had seven children together.

Cushing studied and took up the profession of the law, and was subsequently appointed to be a judge of the Plymouth County Probate Court, and served as town clerk and representative for Hanover.

At the outset of the Revolution, Cushing sided with the Patriot cause, and was commissioned lieutenant colonel in Colonel Anthony Thomas' 2nd Plymouth County Militia Regiment. On February 1, 1776, he was commissioned a brigadier general by the Massachusetts Legislature. It would appear that Cushing's duties were largely administrative, as he never assumed a field command. He was also active in the home defense conducted by the Plymouth County Militia, responding to local alarms. On January 31, 1777, he was commissioned brigadier general for Lincoln County, Massachusetts.

Joseph Cushing died at Hanover, Massachusetts, on December 19, 1791, at the age of sixty.[1]

DANIELSON, TIMOTHY—(**Massachusetts**) Timothy Danielson was born at Brimfield, Massachusetts, in 1733. After receiving his primary education, Danielson attended Yale College, graduating in 1756. He then took up the study of theology, though he never became a minister.

In September of 1774, he served as chairman of the Hampshire County Convention, and the following month was elected a delegate to the Massachusetts Provincial Congress. Governor Gage annulled his election, however. In February and May of 1775 he was a delegate to the Provincial Congresses held in Cambridge and Watertown. On May 19, 1775, Danielson was commissioned a colonel in the Massachusetts Militia, and in 1776 he was promoted to the rank of brigadier general in that service. Danielson took part in the siege of Boston, but his contributions to the cause of liberty came from the political arena, and not from the battlefield. Though he retained his rank of general throughout the war, his wartime efforts were as a member of the Massachusetts legislature, and not in command of troops. In 1779, Danielson was elected to the Massachusetts Constitutional Convention, and he helped to draft a new constitution for the state. He subsequently served in the state senate, and as a member of the Massachusetts Executive Council. Following the war, Danielson served as chief justice of the Hampshire County Court.

Timothy Danielson died at Brimfield, Massachusetts, on September 19, 1791, in his fifty-eighth year.[1]

DAVIDSON, WILLIAM LEE—(**Pennsylvania**) William Lee Davidson was born in Lancaster, Pennsylvania, in 1746. In order to escape the Indian raids of the Pennsylvania frontier, his family moved to Rowan County, North Carolina (present day Iredell County), in 1748. In 1759, William's father died, but the boy received a good primary education at Sugaw Creek Academy, a school run by the Presbyterian Church. In 1767, at the age of twenty-one, he performed his first official duty when he escorted Governor William Tryon into Cherokee country on a boundary-setting expedition. That same year saw the announcement of his engagement to Mary Brevard. The union would produce seven children. He was appointed to be a constable of Rowan County in 1770, and in 1772 he was commissioned a captain in the Rowan County Militia. In 1774, Davidson was charged with the duty of seeing that the actions of the North Carolina Provincial Congress were being carried out in Rowan County.[1]

Davidson cast his lot with the Patriots, and on April 15, 1776, he was named major of the 4th North Carolina Regiment. He was made lieutenant colonel of the 5th North Carolina Regiment on October 4, 1777, and later transferred to the 3rd North Carolina on June 1, 1778, and to the 1st North Carolina on June 9, 1779. Davidson subsequently served as a brigadier general in the North Carolina Militia. He was instrumental in raising troops for the Patriot cause, and forwarded a body of militia to Kings Mountain in time to take part in the battle.[2]

Davidson fought at the battle of Colson's Mill, North Carolina, on July 21, 1780, where he was wounded in the stomach. His troops were victorious in the battle, driving the British from the field. His wounds had healed sufficiently by August 31 of that year to allow him to return to duty.

On February 1, 1781, Davidson led a force of Patriots who were attempting to prevent Lord Cornwallis' army from crossing the Catawba River. They met the British at Cowan's Ford, and a sharp engagement ensued, in which Davidson was shot dead by a Loyalist by the name of Frederick Hager, who accompanied Cornwallis' army. The Americans were driven from the field, but three men later went back to recover the body of Davidson. It was found, on the bank of the river, but Davidson had been stripped naked by members of the British army. His body was taken to the Hopewell Presbyterian Church cemetery, on Beattie's Ford Road, Mecklenburg County, where he was buried by torchlight in an unmarked grave, out of fears that his body might be dug up and mutilated if local Loyalists knew who was buried there. A marker was placed on the grave in later years.

In 1783, the state of North Carolina created Davidson County, in honor of the general, in the western portion of the state. When that county later became part of the state of Tennessee, North Carolina created a second Davidson County by carving out a piece of Rowan County. Davidson College, in North Carolina, which bears his name, was started with a grant from his son.[3]

DAYTON, ELIAS—(New Jersey) Elias Dayton was born at Elizabeth, New Jersey, on May 1, 1737. In his early life, he became a merchant, but in 1756 he was commissioned a lieutenant in the Jersey Blues to serve in the French and Indian War. He was subsequently promoted to the rank of captain, and with his company, fought under Wolfe at Quebec. He next took part in quelling the Pontiac Conspiracy, and was present when that chief finally surrendered, near Detroit, in 1764.

Retired from the military, Dayton returned to Elizabeth to once again make his living as a merchant and mechanic. In 1757, he had married Hannah Rolfe, and the couple had eight children. He was elected to serve as an alderman of Elizabeth, and became a member of the local committee of safety.

In 1775, along with William Alexander, he helped to capture a British transport off Elizabethtown. Dayton was commissioned as colonel of the 3rd New Jersey Regiment on January 18, 1776, and he served with this regiment for most of the war, taking part in the battles of Springfield, Germantown, Monmouth, Brandywine, and Cosswick's Bridge. His courage was such that he had three horses shot out from under him in battle. On January 1, 1781, Dayton was transferred to the 2nd New Jersey Regiment, where he helped to put down a mutiny of the New Jersey Line. With this regiment, he took part in the Yorktown Campaign. On January 7, 1783, he was commissioned a brigadier general by Congress and served in that capacity till the end of hostilities.[1]

After the war, he served several terms as a representative in the New Jersey legislature, and was commissioned a major general in the state service. In 1787, Dayton was elected to Congress, serving till 1788. He was again elected as an assemblyman from 1791–1792 and 1794–1796, and during this time served as recorder of Elizabeth. He was twice elected mayor of Elizabeth: in 1796 and 1801.

Elias Dayton died at Elizabeth, New Jersey, on October 22, 1807, at the age of seventy. He was buried at the First Presbyterian Church Cemetery, in that city.

It is a matter of historic note that Dayton's son, John, who also served in the war, as well as a variety of political positions, including being a member of the convention that framed the Constitution, was arrested in 1805 and charged with conspiracy with Aaron Burr. He was released, and never tried on the charges, however.

DE FERMOY, MATTHIAS ALEXIS ROCHE—(West Indies) Matthias Alexis Roche de Fermoy was born in the West Indies in 1737. De Fermoy was an officer in the French army, and presented himself to the Continental Congress as a colonel of engineers. He was granted a commission as a brigadier general in November 5, 1776. De Fermoy took part in the Trenton and Princeton campaigns. On January 1, 1777, he had been ordered to hold an advanced post at Mile-Run, but he deserted his post, leaving his men in a precarious position, himself returning to Trenton. Later that year, he was assigned command of Fort Independence, opposite Fort Ticonderoga, against the wishes of General Washington. When General Arthur St. Clair retreated from Fort Ticonderoga, De Fermoy, against the orders of St. Clair, set fire to his position at Fort Independence, thus drawing British attention to the evacuation, and causing St. Clair's forces to be put in danger by the British forces under General Burgoyne. In December of 1777, De Fermoy applied to Congress for a promotion to the rank of major general, but Congress declined to make the appointment. De Fermoy was permitted to resign his commission on February 16, 1777, and was given eight hundred dollars to enable him to return to the West Indies.

Matthias De Fermoy died in the West Indies in about 1778, shortly after his return to the islands.[1]

DE HAAS, JOHN P.—(Holland) John Philip De Haas was born in Holland in 1735. His family was said to have noble ties, and De Haas prided himself on his ancestry and used a seal of heraldry having "between two wings displayed a stag springing and at the bottom of the shield a stag courant." At the age of fourteen, he moved to America, with his family, and settled in Lebanon, Pennsylvania. In June of 1758, De Hass married Eleanor Bingham, and three children were born to the marriage. He entered the military service, as an ensign in the Pennsylvania Militia, during General Armstrong's Kittanning expedition, in the French and Indian War. He subsequently served under Colonels Burd and Bouquet in their expeditions, and by 1764 had attained the rank of major. De Haas received over eight hundred acres of land, in Centre County, as bounty for his services in the French and Indian War, and he purchased adjoining tracts from other officers until he owned over 3,000 acres in the county. De Hass never resided on his holdings, but his son, John De Haas, Jr. moved there in 1806.[1]

When the Revolutionary War broke out, De Haas was commissioned a major in the militia in 1775, and promoted to the rank of colonel and given command of the 1st Pennsylvania Battalion on January 22, 1776. The previous commander had been dismissed for selling furloughs to the men. With the 1st Pennsylvania Battalion he took part in the Canadian Campaign of 1776, participating in the operations around Quebec. De Hass withdrew from Quebec, with the main body, to Sorel, up the St. Lawrence River. De Hass later led a relief column to the rescue of General Arnold, at La Chine, Canada, when Arnold's force was endangered by a large detachment of British. Being apprised of the approach of De Haas' force, the British withdrew. Arnold then ordered De Haas to destroy a neighboring Indian village, but the latter officer refused to do so. The battalion had been enlisted for a period of one year, and the troops were released from the service in December of 1776. De Haas then assumed command of the 2nd Pennsylvania Regiment, and with that unit took part in the battle of Princeton on January 3, 1777. De Hass wintered that year at Morristown, New Jersey. On February 21, 1777, De Hass was commissioned a brigadier general by the Continental Congress. He had been offered the promotion previous to that date, but had been hesitant to accept it. Later that year, he took a leave of absence and returned to Philadelphia.[2]

De Hass resigned his commission on June 16, 1777, following the receipt of an order from Congress for him to immediately return to active duty. He was subsequently commissioned a major general in the Pennsylvania Militia on September 30, 1780, and held that rank until the end of the war, though he performed no further substantial service.[3]

John De Hass died in Philadelphia, Pennsylvania, on June 3, 1786, in his fifty-third year. He is believed to be buried in the Old First Reformed Church Cemetery, in Philadelphia.

DE KALB, JOHANN—**(Bavaria)** Johann De Kalb was born in Huttendorf, in the Bavarian region of present day Germany, on June 29, 1721. Little is known of De Kalb's early life, except that he adopted the life of a soldier at a young age, and became a soldier of fortune, obtaining a military education as an officer in the German Regiment of the French army. He fought for the French in the War of Austrian Succession and in the Seven Years' War. In 1768, he visited America as a secret agent of the French, seeking to gather information regarding the feelings of the Colonists for Great Britain. De Kalb, or Baron De Kalb, as he was widely known, achieved military distinction in the French army, rising to the rank of brigadier general. He was also a knight of the Order of Military Merit, winning that distinction at the battle of Wilhelmstahl in 1763, and because of this the honorary title of baron was bestowed upon him. De Kalb favored a Republican form of government, and was sympathetic to the American cause. When Lafayette decided to come to America and tender his services to the Continental Congress, De Kalb, a fellow French officer, accompanied him. In 1777, he went to see Silas Deane, the American ambassador in Paris, from whom he received the promise of a commission as a major general in the Continental Army. He then set sail for the Colonies with eleven other officers, including Lafayette. When he presented himself before Congress, that body made good Deane's promise when it granted De Kalb a major general's commission on September 15, 1777.

De Kalb was placed in command of the Maryland Division. He undertook an abortive campaign against Canada that was stopped short at Albany, but his role in the Continental Army was largely an administrative one, as he did not have a command commensurate to his rank for the first two years of his service. In 1779, he was sent south, with the Maryland and Delaware troops, some 2,000 strong, to reenforce General Lincoln in his defense of Charleston. That city fell before the arrival of De Kalb's army, however. When General Gates replaced Lincoln as commander of the Southern Department, he and De Kalb disagreed over the proper way to fight the British army that opposed them in South Carolina. De Kalb preferred to conduct a cautious campaign, and wait for the British to make a mistake that the Continentals could turn to their advantage. Gates chose to take the offensive and attack the British, playing into the hands of the enemy. Gates marched his army to Camden, where he attacked the British on August 16, 1780. De Kalb was given command of the right wing of the army, which contained the regulars in Gates' force. The left wing was composed of militia. When the British advanced across the field, with bayonets fixed, the left wing collapsed as the terrified militia fled the field. De Kalb and the right wing held firm, despite the overwhelming odds that were now arrayed against them. His regulars fought like demons, and De Kalb was at their front, extolling their courage and leading by example. He was attempting to urge the men forward in a charge when he was shot down with multiple wounds. Accounts disagree, as to the number, but he is credited with being pierced with from eight to eleven bullets. As he lay prostrate on the ground, some British soldiers prepared to finish him off with their bayonets. One of his aides, Chavalier de

Buysson, threw himself on De Kalb's body, receiving the bayonet thrusts in his stead. As he did so, Buysson cried out to his comrades, "Save the Baron De Kalb!" Upon learning of the wounded man's identity, British officers interceded and prevented any further attempts to bayonet him. De Kalb was taken prisoner, and received kind treatment at the hands of the British. When a British officer expressed sympathy for his suffering, De Kalb answered "I thank you for your sympathy — I die the death I always prayed for — the death of a soldier fighting for the rights of man." De Kalb dictated a letter to General Smallwood, who had succeeded him in the command of his division, praising the officers and men for their courage and urging them to continue the fight for freedom.

General Johann De Kalb died at Camden, South Carolina, on August 18, 1780, at the age of fifty-nine. He was buried by the British at Camden, but in 1829, his remains were moved to the New Presbyterian Church Cemetery, where a fitting monument had been erected to his memory. General Lafayette was among the honored guests who attended the ceremony to pay honor to the fallen hero.[1]

DE LAUMOY, JEAN BAPTISTE JOSEPH — (France)

Jean Baptiste Joseph de Laumoy was born in France in 1750, the son of a French infantry captain. He entered a military engineering school at the age of ten, and by 1768 was a sublieutenant in the French army. In 1770, he was promoted to the rank of full lieutenant, and by 1777 had attained the grade of major. The need for engineering officers in the American army made him a prime candidate for service in the Colonies, and De Laumoy was ordered to America in the fall of 1777.

On November 17, 1777, De Laumoy was commissioned a colonel of engineers, by the Continental Congress. He served with Lafayette, at Gloucester, New Jersey, on November 25, 1777, before going into winter quarters at Valley Forge. In 1779, De Laumoy was assigned to the Southern Department. He fought at the battle of Stono Ferry, South Carolina, where he was wounded. De Laumoy was taken prisoner at Charleston on May 12, 1780, and held by the British until his release on November 26, 1782. His services to the nation were recognized on September 30, 1783, when the Continental Congress bestowed the rank of brevet brigadier general upon him.

De Laumoy returned to France in December of 1783, having been promoted to the rank of lieutenant colonel in the French army. He was awarded the Chevalier de Saint Louis in 1784. In 1785, De Laumoy was appointed marechal general des logis at San Domingo. In 1788, he served on the army general staff. In 1789, he was second in command of the French forces employed in putting down the rebellion on Martinique, and returned to France in 1790. De Laumoy was forced to flee France, in 1792, during the French Revolution. He lived, for a time, in Holland, before coming to America and settling in Philadelphia. In 1801, he was permitted to return to France, where he retired from military service in 1810.

Jean Baptiste Joseph de Laumoy died in France on January 19, 1832, in his eighty-second year.[1]

DE WOEDTKE, FREDERICK W. — (Prussia)

Frederick William De Woedtke was born in Prussia in 1740. De Woedtke joined the military at a young age, and was an officer in the army of Frederick the Great for many years prior to the outbreak of the Revolution. De Woedtke determined to offer his services to the Patriots and fight for the cause of liberty. He visited the American ambassadors in Paris, and received letters of introduction to the Continental Congress. De Woedtke was a major in the German army when he presented himself in Philadelphia. Congress commissioned him a brigadier general, on March 16, 1776, and ordered him to join the Northern army. De Woedtke took part in a council of war at Crown Point that decided, against the advice of Colonel John Stark and others, to evacuate the position and fall back to Mount Independence.

Frederick De Woedtke did not have the opportunity to prove himself in the American army. His tour of duty with the Continental Army would last for little more than four months.

De Woedtke died near Lake George, New York, on July 31, 1776, in his thirty-sixth year.[1]

DENT, JOHN—(**Maryland**) John Dent was born in Charles County, Maryland, in 1733. Little is known of his early education, but he became a successful planter in the Durham Parish of Charles County. His plantation was called Pomonkey Hundred. On February 27, 1752, he married Sarah Marshall, and the couple had five children together. In 1775, Dent was elected to the Maryland legislature, and he was one of the signers of the Association of Freemen of Maryland. He also served on the local Council of Safety, which was preparing for hostilities with England. Though Dent was a wealthy planter, and should logically have sided with the Loyalists, he was a staunch Patriot, and sided with the cause of liberty. On January 6, 1776, he was commissioned a brigadier general in the Maryland Militia, in command of the forces of the Lower District on the Western Shore. In July of that year, he took part in resisting the fleet of Lord Dunmore that was attempting to make its way up the Potomac River and invade Maryland. When the threat from Lord Dunmore's expedition was eliminated, Dent resigned his commission in August of 1776. He then resumed his seat in the state legislature and continued to support the war from the political arena. In 1778, he was elected justice of the peace for Charles County.

Following the war, Dent retired to his plantation, and to private life. Though he was a slave owner, Dent instructed that all his slaves be trained in useful trades that would enable them to earn their way in the world, and freed them when they reached the age of twenty-one.

John Dent died in Charles County, Maryland, in 1809, in his seventy-sixth year. His burial site is unknown, but he was most probably interred in the family cemetery at Marshall Hall Plantation.[1]

DICKINSON, JOHN—(**Maryland**) John Dickinson was born at Trappe, Talbot County, Maryland, on November 8, 1732. His family moved to Delaware when Dickinson was a young boy, and he received his primary education there. He read law, in Philadelphia, before visiting London, England, for three years. Upon his return to America, Dickinson established a law practice in Philadelphia. He was elected to the Pennsylvania Assembly, and in 1765, during the Stamp Act crisis, wrote "The late Regulations respecting the British Colonies on the Continent of America considered," a protest against British encroachments on American liberty. That same year, he was a delegate to the first Congress, held in New York. In 1767, he wrote "Letters From a Farmer in Pennsylvania to the Inhabitants of the British Colonies," which had great influence in educating the colonists about their rights. On July 19, 1770, Dickinson married Mary Norris, and the couple had four children together.

In 1774, Dickinson was elected to the Continental Congress, and was prolific in his writing, penning

"Address to the Inhabitants of Quebec" (the first petition to the king), "Address to the Armies" (the second petition to the king), and "Address to the Several States." On July 6, 1775, he penned the famous "Declaration of the United Colonies of North America." He was a member of the Continental Congress when the Declaration of Independence was being debated by that body. Dickinson refused to support the action, feeling that there was still a possibility of compromise with England. He was absent from Congress when the document was signed, George Read signing in his place. His stance on the question of declaring independence made him extremely unpopular, for a time, and he withdrew from public office. In 1778, he was returned to Congress, where he actively forwarded the cause of independence. Dickinson was appointed a brigadier general in the Pennsylvania Militia, but his service to the cause of freedom came from the political arena, and not from the battlefield. He was a member of the Congressional Military Committee, however, and was influential in affairs concerning the army.

Following the war, Dickinson helped establish Dickinson College, in Carlisle, Pennsylvania, in 1783. He helped draft the Articles of Confederation, and served as president of both Pennsylvania and Delaware. He was elected to the Constitutional Convention in 1787, and was one of the signers of the Constitution. In 1788, being alarmed by the hesitation of several states to adopt the Federal Constitution, he wrote a series of nine letters, under the pen name of Fabius, intended to sway public opinion in favor of its adoption. In 1797, he was active in promoting positive American policy toward France, during the tension between the two countries that had threatened to lead to war. He then retired from public life, spending his last years in literary pursuits, at Wilmington, Delaware.

John Dickinson died at Wilmington, Delaware, on February 14, 1808, at the age of seventy-five.[1]

DICKINSON, PHILEMON—(Maryland) Philemon Dickinson was born at Crosia-dore, near Trappe, Talbot County, Maryland, on April 5, 1739. He was the brother of John Dickinson (see above). In 1740, his family moved to Dover, Delaware, where he received his education from a private tutor before attending the University of Pennsylvania, and graduating in its first class in 1759. Following college, he briefly supervised his father's estates before 1760 when he undertook the study of law, in Philadelphia, and was admitted to the bar. Philemon never set up a law practice, however. In 1767, he moved to Trenton, New Jersey. On July 14 of that same year, Dickinson married Mary Cadwalader, and the couple had two children. Mary died in 1791, and Dickinson later married Rebecca Cadwalader in 1804. On October 19, 1775, he was commissioned a brigadier general in the New Jersey Militia, and in 1776 he served as a delegate to the New Jersey Provincial Congress. On June 6, 1777, Dickinson was promoted to the rank of major general and put in command of the New Jersey Militia forces. He would serve in this capacity, which was largely administrative, through the end of the war.

In 1782, Dickinson was elected to the Continental Congress, and in 1783 he served as president of the Council of New Jersey. He was a member of the committee charged with selecting a site on which to build the national capital in 1784. In 1790, he was selected to serve the unexpired term of William Patterson, in the U.S. Senate, and served in that body until 1793. After his time in the Senate, Dickinson retired to private life, devoting himself to supervising his estates.

Philemon Dickinson died at his home, The Hermitage, near Trenton, New Jersey, on February 4, 1809, at the age of sixty-nine. He was buried at the Friends Meeting House Burying Ground, in Trenton, New Jersey.[1]

DOUGLAS, JOHN—(Connecticut) John Douglas was born at Plainfield, Windham County, Connecticut, on April 12, 1734. Little is known of his early life or education. He married Susannah Freyers (date not recorded), and the couple had seven children together. At the beginning of the war, he was commissioned lieutenant colonel of the 8th Connecticut Regiment on July 6, 1775. In 1776, he was promoted to the rank of colonel in the Connecticut Militia serving in that capacity until 1777, when he was promoted to the rank of brigadier general. Douglas served as a general in the state service until the end of the war.

John Douglas died at Windham County on September 22, 1809, at the age of seventy-five. He was buried in the Windham County Cemetery.[1]

DU BUYSSON des HAYES, CHARLES-FRANCO—(France) Charles Francois Du Buysson des Hayes (also written Dubuysson des Aix) was born in France in 1752. A French officer and contemporary of Lafayette's, Du Buysson came to America to offer his services, along with Lafayette's party of officers in 1777. Du Buysson was originally commissioned a major by the Continental Congress but rose to the rank of lieutenant colonel. He was assigned to be aide-de-camp to General De Kalb, and served in the Southern Department. At the battle of Camden, on August 16, 1780, Du Buysson was wounded and captured. In fact, it was Du Buysson who threw himself upon the prone form of De Kalb when that general was being bayoneted by the British, calling for the American troops to come and save their general. His actions alerted British officers as to the identity of De Kalb, and they immediately interceded to stop the assault upon him. Du Buysson's actions were in vain, however, as De Kalb had already been so severely wounded that he died a few days later. Du Buysson was commissioned a brigadier general in the North Carolina Militia, but following his release by the British, he left America before the end of 1780, for France.

Charles Francois Du Buysson died in France in 1786, in only his thirty-fourth year of life.[1]

DU COUDRAY, PHILIP CHARLES JEAN BAPTISTE TROUSON—(France)

Philippe Charles Jean Baptiste Tronson Du Coudray was born at Rhiems, France on September 8, 1738. As a young man, Du Coudray joined the French army, where he was trained as a mining engineer. He became a lieutenant of artillery in 1760. His services in Corsica were such that he was promoted above 180 French officers who had been senior to him to the post of adjutant general of artillery, and he had become one of the best military engineers in France.

When France began providing covert aid to America, Du Coudray was assigned to scour the French arsenals for weapons that could be sent without impairing the effectiveness of the French army. He was also detailed to supervise the selection of engineering and artillery officers who were being sent to America as advisors to the Continental Army. In 1776, Du Coudray offered his own services to Benjamin Franklin and Silas Deane. He was offered the rank of major general, and the title of general of artillery and ordnance. He set sail for America, arriving in May of 1777, and presented his credentials and letters of introduction to Congress. The rank and position offered by Deane and Franklin had not been cleared by Congress, but that body felt it necessary to honor the agreement so as not to impair the broader French assistance program. When news of the arrangement became known to the Continental Army, Generals Greene, Knox, and Sullivan threatened to resign if Du Coudray was promoted above them. Du Coudray's arrival not only produced tensions among the American officers, it also produced them among the French officers who had previously joined the army, particularly General DuPortail, who was an able and efficient officer. On August 11, 1777, Congress attempted to soothe the situation by making Du Coudray major general of the staff, a position that had no authority over the other major generals of the line. He was also made inspector general of ordnance and military manufactories. He was assigned to supervise the works on the Delaware River defenses. During the battle of Brandywine, on September 15, 1777, Du Coudray was hastening to join the main army when his horse bolted and plunged him into the Schuylkill River. Historians disagree as to exactly how the accident happened. Some state that he was crossing the river in a ferry boat when the mishap took place, while others contend that he was crossing the river on a pontoon bridge. Regardless, of which way it happened, Du Coudray ended up in the water, where he drowned, at the age of thirty-nine.[1]

DUPORTAIL, LOUIS LE BEGUE DE PRESLE—(France)

Louis Le Begue De Presle Duportail was born near Orleans, France, in 1743, the son of a French nobleman. He received a fine primary education and was enrolled in the prestigious military academy at Mezieres. Following his graduation from the academy, in 1762, he became an engineering officer in the French army. By 1777, Duportail had risen to the rank of lieutenant colonel. In 1777, during a time when the government of France was supplying covert aid to the American war effort, he was one of four engineering officers sent to the colonies at the request of Benjamin Franklin. On July 8, 1777, he received a commission as colonel of engineers from the Continental Congress. On the 22nd of that month he was elevated to the position of chief of engineers, and on November 17, 1777, Congress commissioned him a brigadier general of engineers. Duportail was assigned the duty to fortify the Delaware River defenses, as well as those in the Hud-

Louis Duportail (courtesy United States Military History Institute)

son Highlands. He also was responsible for improvements to the defenses of Philadelphia and West Point.

During the winter of 1777–78, he and General Knox were responsible for establishing the lines at the army's winter encampment at Valley Forge. While at Valley Forge, Duportail assisted Knox in the training of artillery tactics. His efforts bore fruit in the battle of Monmouth, where American artillery was largely responsible for the victory on that field. Duportail and Alexander Hamilton were sent to Sandy Hook, New York, to co-operate with French admiral D'Estang, but the campaign never materialized due to the French fleet not showing up. In 1779, Duportail was appointed commandant of the Corps of Engineers and Sappers and Miners. In 1780, he was detailed to Charleston, South Carolina, and was captured when that city fell on May, 12, 1780. Released, on parole, in November of 1780, Duportail rejoined the main body, under Washington, where he took part in the aborted plans to lay siege to New York City. Duportail later took part in the Yorktown Campaign, and following the capitulation of the British forces, on November 16, 1781, he was promoted to the rank of major general on October 26, 1781.

Duportail remained in the army until the close of hostilities, when he returned home to France. The French government recognized his service in America by making him marechal-de-camp. In 1790, he served as minister of war. During the French Revolution, he was engaged in military activities in Lorraine, when he was warned that his life was in danger from the revolutionaries. He fled to America, after two years spent in hiding, in 1794, and settled in Philadelphia for a few years until he received the permission of the French government to return home to France. Duportail started his homeward voyage in 1802, but died at sea during the passage, in his fifty-ninth year.[1]

DYER, ELIPHALET—(Connecticut) Eliphalet Dyer was born in Windham, Connecticut, on September 28, 1721. He received an adequate primary education to gain admission to Yale College, from whence he was graduated in 1740. He subsequently studied law, and was admitted to the Connecticut bar in 1746. That same year, he was appointed town clerk and justice of the peace of Windham. Dyer served several terms of office in the Connecticut legislature between 1747 and 1762. He was a promoter of the plan to form a Connecticut colony in the Susquehanna Valley of Pennsylvania, and in 1753 he was a member of a committee to purchase title to the land around Wyoming, Pennsylvania, for that purpose. The plan to colonize the Susquehanna Valley was interrupted by the French and Indian War. In August of 1755, Dyer was appointed lieutenant colonel of the Connecticut Regiment and accompanied the expedition against Crown Point. In 1758, he was promoted to the rank of colonel, and participated in General Amherst's expedition against Canada.

In 1763, as agent for the Susquehanna Land Company, he traveled to England to secure confirmation concerning the title of the land the company had acquired around Wyoming, Pennsylvania. His efforts ended in failure, however, as the Crown failed to recognize the legitimacy of the claim. When he returned to Connecticut, Dyer became comptroller of the port of New London, and in 1765, he was appointed to the Stamp Act Congress as a representative from Connecticut. He opposed the Stamp Act, and resigned from his position as comptroller rather than carry out the provisions of the act.

In 1774, Dyer was elected as a representative to the first Continental Congress. He would serve as a member of that body from 1774 to 1779, and again from 1782–1783. In 1776, he was commissioned a brigadier general in the Connecticut Militia, but he declined the appointment. He was commissioned to the same rank and grade again in 1777.[1] Dyer's position in the state military forces was largely ceremonial, however, as his service to his country came by way of the Continental Congress, and not in camp or on the battlefield. In this respect, his commission was much the same as that granted to Caesar Rodney of Delaware.

After the war, Dyer served as chief judge of Connecticut from 1789 to 1793. In 1793, he retired from public life.

Eliphalet Dyer died at Windham, Connecticut, on May 13, 1807, at the age of eighty-five. He was buried in the Windham Cemetery.

ELBERT, SAMUEL—(Georgia) Samuel Elbert was born in Savannah, Georgia, in 1740, the son of a Baptist minister. In 1754, Elbert began to establish himself as a merchant in Savannah, and over the next decade his successful business allowed him to buy several tracts of land in the Savannah area. In 1769, he married Elizabeth Rae, and the union produced six children.

In 1772, Elbert received a commission as captain in a grenadier company of Savannah's first regiment of militia. He took his military responsibilities very seriously, and later that year he sailed to England, where he studied military drill and tactics.

In 1775, he was elected to serve as a member of Savannah's Council of Safety. In August of that same year, he took his company to Augusta to protect that town from area Loyalists. On January 7, 1776, Elbert was commissioned lieutenant colonel of the 1st Georgia Regiment, and on July 5 of that same year, he became colonel of the 2nd Georgia Regiment.[1]

In 1776, Elbert was given command of an expedition against St. Augustine, Florida, that ended in failure. He was subsequently given command of the Continental line forces in Georgia, and was commissioned a brigadier general in the Georgia Militia. Elbert made another failed invasion of east Florida in 1778. In March of 1779, Elbert was captured at the battle of Brier Creek, Georgia. The American forces had been under the command of General Ashe, when they were completely surprised by a mixed force of British soldiers and Loyalists. The American center and right wing retreated at the first attack, but Elbert, who held the American left, with some two hundred men, most of them Georgia Militia, held fast. Despite the overwhelming force arrayed against him, Elbert refused to relinquish the field. His command was decimated, with nearly every officer and man in it being killed, wounded, or captured. Elbert was taken prisoner and held till after the fall of Charleston in 1781.[2]

Once he was released from British captivity, Elbert traveled to George Washington's main army, where he was given command of the "grand deposit" of arms and military stores. From June till November of 1781 he commanded a brigade at Yorktown. In 1782, he returned to Georgia, and on November 3, 1783, he was commissioned a brevet brigadier general by the Continental Congress.[3]

Elbert was elected to be a delegate to the Continental Congress, in 1784, but he declined to serve. In 1785, he was elected to a one-year term as governor, and during his term of office he oversaw the chartering of the University of Georgia. He later served as sheriff of Chatham County before his untimely death.

Samuel Elbert died on November 1, 1788, at the age of forty-eight. He was buried at Rae's Hall Plantation, but his remains were moved in 1924, due to desecration of the grave. In that year, his body was reinterred in the Colonial Park Cemetery, in Savannah.

In 1790, the state of Georgia created Elberton County, in honor of its famous son. The town of Elberton is also named for him.[4]

ENOS, ROGER—(Connecticut) Roger Enos was born at Windsor (some sources list his birth place as Simsbury), Hartford County, Connecticut, in 1729. Enos enlisted in the ranks during the French and Indian War, and by 1760 had risen to the rank of ensign in Colonel Phineas Lyman's Regiment. He took part in the Havana Campaign of 1762, and in 1764 was promoted to the rank of captain in Colonel Israel Putnam's Regiment.

On March 10, 1763, Enos married Jerusha Hayden and the couple had four children together. Following his active service in the French and Indian War, Enos was appointed to survey the lands of the Mississippi Valley. At the outbreak of the Revolution, Enos was commissioned a colonel in the Connecticut Militia, and took part in the battle of Bunker Hill, as well as the operations in and around the city of Boston during the siege of that place. He was assigned to command the rear guard of General Arnold's army during the expedition against Quebec. Enos left Arnold's army with a sizeable detachment of men, and was later charged with cowardice and brought before a court-martial. He stated the reason for his actions as stemming from the deplorable condition of the American army and the lack of food. Enos testified that he led his men away in an effort to save them from starvation. He was acquitted of the charges, and was subsequently appointed lieutenant colonel of the 16th Connecticut Regiment.

In 1781, he moved to Vermont, settling in Enosburg, the town that bears his name. That same year he was appointed brigadier general and commander of all Vermont state troops, and led the militia army resisting the British invasion from Canada. He was also appointed to the Vermont Board of War in 1781, a position he would hold until 1792. Following the war, Enos continued to serve in the Vermont Militia, and in 1787 he was promoted to the rank of major general. He resigned his commission in 1791, after thirty-two years of continuous military service. He then served several terms in the Connecticut General Assembly, was a trustee of the Vermont University, and was appointed to the committee to consider the resolutions of the U.S. Congress for the admission of Vermont as a state in the Union.

Roger Enos died at Colchester, Vermont, on October 6, 1808, in his seventy-ninth year. He was buried in the Burlington, Vermont, Cemetery in the same lot as Ethan Allen.[1]

EWING, JAMES — (Pennsylvania) James Ewing was born in Lancaster County, Pennsylvania, on August 3, 1736. Ewing's father, Thomas, served in the Pennsylvania legislature, and saw to it that the boy received a good education. As a young man, Ewing took part in General Edward Braddock's disastrous expedition against Fort Duquesne (Fort Pitt) in 1755, and he was with that officer when he was slain in battle. On May 10, 1758, he was commissioned a lieutenant in the Pennsylvania Militia and accompanied General Forbes' successful effort to capture Fort Duquesne.

In 1771, Ewing was elected to the Pennsylvania legislature, serving until 1776. He was an early advocate of the Colonies ending their association with England. His previous military experience, combined with his firm stand for independence, earned him one of two commissions as brigadier general in the Pennsylvania Militia on July 4, 1776, the other being given to Daniel Roberdeau. Ewing played a significant role in Washington's retreat across New Jersey and in his attack on Trenton on Christmas Day, 1776. He was assigned command of a brigade that was to guard the Pennsylvania side of the Delaware River during Washington's crossing of the Delaware on Christmas Eve of 1776. He was then to act in support of Washington's troops at Trenton by securing a bridge across the Assunpink River, but he could not get his troops into the assigned position because of heavy ice on the river and high winds.[1]

From November 7, 1782, till November 6, 1784, Ewing served as vice president (lieutenant governor) of Pennsylvania, under President (Governor) John Dickinson. In 1784, he was elected to the state assembly. In 1783, he became one of the trustees of Dickinson College. He chaired a committee charged with seeking improved navigation of the Susquehanna River in 1789. In 1795, Ewing was elected to the Pennsylvania Senate, and he was re-elected in 1799, finally retiring to private life in 1803.

James Ewing died at Hellam, York County, Pennsylvania, on March 1, 1806, at the age of sixty-nine.

FEBIGER, CHRISTIAN — (Denmark) Christian Febiger was born at Fiinen, Denmark, in 1746. Febiger received a military education prior to his father's death, when Christian was still just sixteen. The young man then went to Santa Cruz, where he took a position on the staff of his uncle, the governor of the island. In 1772, Febiger immigrated to America, where he took up the business of commerce in the eastern states. On April 28, 1775, Febiger joined a Massachusetts regiment at the outbreak of hostilities between the Colonies and Great Britain. He served with distinction at the battle of Bunker Hill before taking part in General Benedict Arnold's Canadian Expedition. Febiger was captured in the fighting before Quebec, on December 31, 1775. He was sent to New York, where he was confined by the British until his release on January 1, 1777. In the meantime, he had been commissioned a lieutenant colonel in the Virginia Line. Upon securing his parole, Febiger fought at the battle of Brandywine, and was promoted to the rank of colonel and assigned to command the 2nd Virginia Regiment on September 26, 1777. He commanded the right of General Nathaniel Greene's forces at Germantown, and led a force of 4,000 men and two guns at the battle of Monmouth. Febiger distinguished himself at the battle of Stony Point, personally capturing the British commander of that stronghold. In 1780, he was sent to Philadelphia with orders to forward stores collected there to the army. Febiger was present at Yorktown for the surrender of Lord Cornwallis' army. In recognition of his service, Febiger was commissioned a brevet brigadier general by the Continental Congress on September 30, 1783.

Following the end of the war, Febiger settled in Philadelphia, where he resumed his private life in business. In 1789, he was elected treasurer of the state of Pennsylvania, a position he would hold until his death. Christian Febiger died at Philadelphia on September 20, 1796, in his fiftieth year.[1]

FLOYD, WILLIAM—(New York) William Floyd was born at Long Island, New York, on December 17, 1734, the son of a wealthy landholder. His father died when William was still quite young, leaving his son heir to his vast estates. Floyd's education was in no way commensurate with the wealth and position that had been held by his father, and he received only the rudiments of schooling. Still, he was possessed of a keen mind, and connected, through position, to many of the more educated and enlightened people of the area, so he was able to improve his knowledge by association. On August 23, 1760, Floyd married Hannah Jones, and the marriage produced three children. Hannah died in 1781, and Floyd remarried, taking Joanna Strong as his second wife on May 16, 1784. William and Joanna had two children together.

Floyd was elected as a representative to the first Continental Congress in 1774, and was re-elected to serve in the second Continental Congress the following year, and continued to serve in that capacity until after the drafting of the Declaration of Independence, Floyd affixing his name to that document.

While he was in Congress, the American army evacuated Long Island, leaving it to the control of the British. Floyd's home and property were taken over by the occupying troops, and his family forced to flee to Connecticut for safety. Floyd had been appointed a major general in the New York Militia about this time, though he never took to the field, or saw any combat. For the next seven years, the family was without a home, or a means of income.[1]

In 1777, Floyd was appointed senator of the state of New York, under the new state constitution, and was a leader in organizing the new government. In 1778, he was again elected to Congress, and held a seat in that body until the ratification of the Constitution. During that time, he was continuously employed in the national Congress, or as a senator in New York.

After the war, he purchased a piece of ground on the Mohawk River, in Oneida County, New York, and spent the next several years clearing the ground until it was a well cultivated farm. In 1803, he moved his family to a house he had built there.

General Floyd died on August 4, 1821, at the age of eighty-seven. He was buried in the Presbyterian Church Cemetery, in Westernville, Oneida County, New York.

FOLSOM, NATHANIEL—(New Hampshire) Nathaniel Folsom was born at Exeter, New Hampshire, on September 28, 1726 (his birth is also listed as taking place on September 18). His father died in 1740, leaving the thirteen-year-old to help support the family. He went to work for a merchant, then invested in timber, and soon opened a sawmill. In 1747, he married Dorothy Smith, and the couple had six children together. Dorothy died in 1776, and Folsom married Mary Sprague Fisher two years later. In 1761, he went into business with two cousins, creating Folsom, Gilman & Gilman. The company opened a general store, built ships, and operated an import-export business. The partnership split up in 1768, but Folsom continued to make his living through trade, lumber and sawmilling for the rest of his life.

Folsom got his first taste of military life when he joined the New Hampshire Militia during the French and Indian War, becoming a captain in a company that accompanied Sir William Johnson's expedition against Crown Point in 1755. He was in command of ten companies that were responsible for capturing Baron Dieskau, the commander in chief of the French forces in Canada, when they captured Fort Edward, all at the loss of only six men in his command. Folsom was made a colonel in the New Hampshire militia, though his commission was revoked by the royal governor in 1774, following his raid against Fort William and Mary.

Folsom was a delegate to the New Hampshire Provincial Congress in 1774. That body then appointed him to be a representative to the first Continental Congress, later that same year.

With the outbreak of hostilities with England, the New Hampshire Provincial Congress appointed Folsom a brigadier general in the militia in May of 1775, and placed him in command of New Hampshire's military forces. Folsom went to Boston, to take part in the siege of the British forces there, but there was a great deal of confusion concerning his command status. The Provincial Assembly of Massachusetts had appointed John Stark to be the commander of the New Hampshire Militia, and he was already on the scene, in Boston. The confusion over command was straightened out in June of 1775 when the Continental Congress appointed General John Sullivan to command the New Hampshire forces then with the Continental army. With General Sullivan now in command of the New Hampshire troops, Folsom returned home. He retained command of the New Hampshire troops who were still within the state, and focused his activities on recruitment and gathering supplies. He also resumed his political career, once more taking a seat in the Provincial Congress. He would serve as a representative in that body from 1775 till 1783. In 1776, he was named judge of the Rockingham County Court of Common Pleas. In 1777 and 1779, Folsom again served as a representative in the Continental Congress.

In 1783, he became chief judge of the New Hampshire Court of Common Pleas. Folsom later served as president of the convention held

Nathaniel Folsom (courtesy United States Military History Institute)

in New Hampshire to ratify the new state constitution. One of the points in that document limited the number of offices that an individual could hold, causing Folsom to resign his seat in the Assembly, and as head of the New Hampshire Militia. He retained his place in the court, serving as chief judge in Rockingham County for the remainder of his life.

Nathaniel Folsom died at Exeter, New Hampshire, on May 26, 1790, at the age of seventy-three. He was buried at the Winter Street Cemetery in that city.[1]

FRAZER, PERSIFOR—(Pennsylvania)

Persifor Frazer was born at Newtown Square, Delaware County, Pennsylvania, on August 10, 1736. On October 2, 1766, he married Mary Worrall Taylor, and the couple had eight children together.

On January 25, 1775, Frazer was selected to a committee appointed to draft a petition to the Pennsylvania General Assembly to pray for the manumission of slaves. That same month, he was elected to the Pennsylvania Provincial Council.

On January 5, 1776, Frazer was commissioned a captain in Anthony Wayne's 4th Pennsylvania Battalion and accompanied Wayne to the Canadian frontier. At the time, he was also serving as a member of the Chester County Committee of Safety. He was promoted to the rank of major, by General Gates, at Fort Ticonderoga, on September 25, 1776. On March 12, 1777, he was commissioned a lieutenant colonel, and assigned to the 5th Pennsylvania Regiment. He fought in the battle of Brandywine, on September 11, 1777, and was captured by the British five days after the battle. Frazer was held in Philadelphia, as a prisoner of war, until he escaped on March 17, 1778. Following his escape, he was appointed clothier general of the army, but declined to accept the position. On April 1, 1780, Frazer was appointed commissioner of purchase under Quartermaster General Nathaniel Greene. He was commissioned brigadier general in the Pennsylvania Militia on May 25, 1781.

In March of 1781, Frazer was appointed treasurer of Chester County. In October of that same year, he was elected to the Pennsylvania General Assembly, and was re-elected in 1782. In June of 1786, he was appointed judge of the Chester County Court of Common Pleas. That same year, he was appointed register and recorder of wills, a position he held until his death. Frazer was a charter member of the first Masonic Lodge to be formed in Chester County.

Persifor Frazer died at Goshen, Chester County, Pennsylvania, on April 24, 1792, at the age of fifty-seven.[1]

FREEMAN, NATHANIEL—(Massachusetts) Nathaniel Freeman was born on April 8, 1741, at Dennis, Massachusetts. He studied medicine, and in 1765 settled in Sandwich, where he studied law with a relative, the noted jurist James Otis. Freeman was a respected doctor and surgeon, and was considered to be one of the best extempore speakers of his day. On May 5, 1763, Freeman married Tryphosa Colton, and the couple had four children. Tryphosa died in 1796, and Freeman married Elizabeth Handy three years later, with one child being born to this marriage. He was an ardent Patriot, and led a regiment of Massachusetts Militia in the expedition to Rhode Island. In 1781, he was made a brigadier general in the Massachusetts Militia (Heitman lists the commission as being made in 1778, but all other sources seem to agree with the 1781 date). He was also chairman of the Committee of Correspondence for the Cape Cod area.

There were a substantial number of Loyalists in the Cape Cod area, and part of the duties of the Committee of Correspondence was to monitor their activity, conduct hearings, and administer oaths of allegiance. The committee was also charged with the duty of overseeing the training and equipping of the local militia.

In 1778, the committee, with Freeman at its head, uncovered a number of Loyalists in the Cape Cod area, and also identified their contacts at Newport. In addition, they foiled the attempts of this group to distribute counterfeit money in the state.

Freeman also served as the superintendent of Barnstable County, a position he would continue to occupy after the war had ended. He would also serve as a representative in the Massachusetts House of Representatives. In the post-war years, he would resume his medical practice, as one of the most respectable doctors in the region.

Nathaniel Freeman died at Sandwich, Massachusetts, on September 20, 1827, at the age of eighty-six. He was buried in the Old Town Cemetery in that city.[1]

FRYE, JOSEPH—(Massachusetts) Joseph Frye was born in Andover, Massachusetts, on March 19, 1712, the ninth of thirteen children. Despite a certain prominence held by his family in Andover, Frye did not receive a great deal of education, though he was reported to be well read and articulate. In the 1730s he married Mehitable Poor, and the couple would have eleven children together. Frye supported himself at Andover through farming and surveying. In 1745, Frye enlisted as an ensign in Hale's 5th Massachusetts Militia to serve in King George's War. In 1746, he was promoted to lieutenant, and served at Falmouth, Maine. The end of the war in 1749 found Frye serving as captain of a company posted in Scarborough.

Following King George's War, Frye resumed private life and was elected to the Massachusetts General Court. In 1754, with the advent of the French and Indian War, Frye became a major in a regiment assigned to General John Winslow, and returned to Maine to protect the eastern frontier of Massachusetts. His regiment built Fort Halifax, at Taconic Falls, and the following year it took part in the battles at Fort Beausejour and Fort Gaspereaux. Frye was then given the assignment to burn over 250 farmsteads belonging to the French Acadians in what would become the Acadian Diaspora.

Frye and his men were present at the defeat and massacre that took place at Fort William Henry in 1757. General Montcalm led a mixed force of French and Indians, the latter numbering some 1,500. When the fort surrendered, the Indians went on a killing spree, clubbing and scalping the captured British and Provincial soldiers. Some of the prisoners were able to secure the protection of French officers, while others escaped into the woods and made their way to Fort Edward. Frye was among the latter group. In all, some 175 men were victims of the massacre, most of them being killed after they had surrendered. After serving out his parole, Frye returned to active duty, taking command of Fort Cumberland, in Nova Scotia, until after the fall of Quebec. Returning to Andover, he was again elected to the General Court.

In 1761, Frye petitioned for a tract of land along the Saco River, in Maine, as compensation for his services in the French and Indian War. In 1762, the petition was granted, and he was given six square miles of land on the Saco. The grant came with a stipulation, however. Frye was required to submit plans for the building of a town within six months of acquiring the property. Using his own abilities as a surveyor, Frye quickly laid out a town and submitted plans to have sixty families settle there, with each family to receive seven acres. He set aside one sixty-fourth part of the land for each of the following; a protestant minister, a parsonage, Harvard University, and a school. The result of his plans was the town of Fryeburg, Maine. Frye moved to Fryeburg, where he occupied all manner of civil positions during the years after the French and Indian War. During this time, he compiled a field notebook, "Tables Useful in Surveying Land," for his son. Besides being the proprietor of the town, Frye also opened a small store in his house.[1]

During the Revolution, Fryeburg occupied a place on the American frontier, and the residents were alarmed over the possibility of attacks coming from Canada. Following the battle of Bunker Hill, Frye reported to the army, at Cambridge. He was commissioned a major general in the Massachusetts Militia on June 21, 1775. In November of 1775, Frye was sent to Falmouth (present day Portsmith) to defend the town. It had already been attacked by the British, and many of the houses had been burned. Frye was able to raise five companies of militia from the surrounding area, which he posted at strategic locations around Portsmith.[2]

On January 10, 1776, the Continental Congress commissioned Frye a brigadier general of Massachusetts's forces. John Adams was one of the leading promoters of Frye receiving the commission, but it found disfavor with General Washington, who was not impressed with Frye's abilities. Nevertheless, Washington ordered Frye to report to Cambridge, where plans were underway to attack the British in Boston with the cannon that had been captured at Fort Ticonderoga. Frye took ill and spent most of the time bedridden, which earned him the further ire of Washington. On April 23, 1776, Frye resigned his commission, for health reasons, and returned to Fryeburg.[3]

For the remainder of his life, Frye served to conduct the civil and political affairs of Fryeburg. He died on July 25, 1794, at the age of eighty-two. He was buried in the town cemetery in Fryeburg, Maine.

GADSDEN, CHRISTOPHER—(South Carolina) Christopher Gadsden was born at Charleston, South Carolina, in 1724. His father was a wealthy and influential member of Charleston society, and Gadsden received a fine education, including schooling abroad, in Bristol, England. In 1741, he returned to America, and took employment in a counting house, in Philadelphia, before becoming a planter and merchant in Charleston. He married Jane Godfrey on July 28, 1746, and the couple had five children together. Following Jane's death, Gadsden married Mary Hassell, in 1759, and four more children were born to this marriage. After Mary's death, Gadsden married for a third time when he wed Ann Wragg in 1776. His last marriage produced two children. Gadsden received his first military experience in 1759 when he served as a captain in an artillery company in the expedition against the Cherokee. In 1760 he was elected to the South Carolina legislature, and served almost continuously until 1780. Gadsden was a leader in the Sons of Liberty in South Carolina in 1765. He served as South Carolina's representative in the Stamp Act Congress of 1765, and in the Continental Congress in 1774 and 1776. In 1775, while in Philadelphia, serving in Congress, Gadsden was responsible for presenting the Gadsden flag as an emblem for the ships that the Marine Committee, of which he was a member, had recently voted to outfit for war. The flag had a rattlesnake on it, and bore the motto, "Don't Tread On Me." It became one of the most famous flags and mottos of the war. It is known today as the Gadsden flag, or as the Hopkins flag, for Commodore Esek Hopkins, who first flew it. Benjamin Franklin is usually credited with helping to create the rattlesnake flag, though his name is not generally attached to it.

At the outbreak of the Revolution, Gadsden was commissioned a colonel in the state militia on June 17, 1775. In February of 1776 he was made a general in the militia and placed in command of all the military forces in South Carolina, and on September 16 of that year was commissioned a brigadier general by the Continental Congress. Gadsden retained his Continental commission for only a year. A dispute arose concerning a conflict about Federal and state authority, and he resigned on October 2, 1777. He was elected lieutenant governor of the state, and was serving in that capacity when Charleston was surrendered to the British in 1780. Gadsden was taken prisoner and was held for a period of three months before being released on parole in the city. He was active in convincing others not to exchange their paroles for the rights of British subjects, and this activity caused his arrest and confinement in a St. Augustine dungeon for almost a year. While thus confined, he refused to give his parole to his British captors, on the grounds that they had violated his previous one by virtue of his arrest.

In 1782, Gadsden was elected to the state legislature. He was also elected governor, but declined to serve because of his advanced age and poor health. In 1788, he was elected to the state convention to ratify the Federal Constitution, and in 1790 he participated in the convention that framed a new state constitution for South Carolina.

Christopher Gadsden died in Charleston on August 28, 1805, in his eighty-first year. He was buried in the St. Philip's Churchyard Cemetery, in Charleston.[1]

GANSEVORT, PETER—(New York) Peter Gansevort was born in Albany, New York, on July 16, 1749. He developed a taste for military affairs in his boyhood, and when he reached manhood, he recruited a company of grenadiers that boasted the distinction that not one of its members was less than six feet tall. Gansevort himself was six feet, three inches, considered to be a huge man in his day. At the outbreak of the Revolution, Peter received a commission as a major by the Continental Congress on July 19, 1775. The following month, he took part in General Montgomery's failed campaign. On March 19, 1776, Congress appointed him to be a lieutenant colonel, and on November 21 of that same year he was commissioned a colonel and given command of the 3rd regiment of the Continental Army. In August of 1777, Gansevort commanded the successful defense of Fort Stanwix against a combined force of British, Tories, and Indians, under the command of Colonel St. Leger. The fort was surrounded, and Gansevort was issued a demand from St. Leger that only his unconditional surrender would prevent the loss of all their lives, but Gansevort replied defiantly that he never surrendered. He was able to hold his post until a relief column arrived, prompting St. Leger to give up his siege of the fort and retire. Congress voted Gansevort its thanks on October 4, 1777.

In 1778, Gansevort was ordered to Albany, to protect that important city from British incursions, and the following year, he accompanied General Sullivan on his expedition into the Mohawk Valley to drive out the Loyalist and Indian marauders that were operating there. That same year, he married Catrina Van Schaick, and the couple had four children together.

In 1781, along with a number of other gallant officers, Gansevort was removed from the army, by an act of Congress for what can only be described as political reasons, much to the distress of General Washington.[1]

He was appointed as a brigadier general of militia by the state of New York on March 26, 1781, and served in that capacity to the close of the war.[2]

In his post-war life, Gansevort served as the sheriff of Albany County, as a commissioner to make treaties with the Indians, and as military agent for the Northern Department. In 1802, he was given a commission as a brigadier general in the United States Army, a position he would hold for the next ten years.

Peter Gansevort died on July 2, 1812, at the age of sixty-two, just when his services were most needed in the War of 1812.[3]

GATES, HORATIO — (England)

Horatio Gates was born in Malden, Essex, England, in 1728. Little is known of his early education, but he managed to obtain a commission in the British army in 1745, and served in Germany before moving to Canada prior to the doomed Braddock expedition, during the French and Indian War. At Halifax, he met Elizabeth Phillips, and the couple were married in 1754. Gates accompanied General Braddock's expedition, in command of a company of troops from Maryland, and was wounded in the fighting. When he recovered from his wound, Gates was assigned to the forts in the Mohawk Valley of New York. When the French and Indian War was over, Gates served as a staff officer, under General Robert Monkton, on an expedition to the West Indies. In 1762, Gates returned to England, where he received a commission as a major, and purchased a commission as lieutenant colonel.

Gates returned to America in 1763 in hopes of finding a vacancy for a colonel's position, but none was available. In 1763, he returned to England, where he was frustrated by an inability to secure a command. Robert Monkton had been given command of the East India Company, and had promised Gates a po-

Horatio Gates (courtesy National Archives)

sition as his deputy, but another candidate was selected for the position. Finally, in 1769, Gates and his family set sail for America once more. This time they made their way for Virginia, where Gates purchased a farm, called Traveler's Rest, near Shepherdstown, in present day West Virginia. While at Shepherdstown, Gates came in contact with many leaders of the Patriot cause, including Charles Lee.[1]

Following the fighting at Lexington and Concord, Gates offered his services to George Washington, and once the latter was made commander of the army, he recommended that Gates be given a commission because of his previous military service in the British army. On June 17, 1775, the Continental Congress commissioned Gates a brigadier general, and named him adjutant general of the army. Gates was selected to take command of the Canadian expedition, but never had the opportunity to do so, owing to General Sullivan's defeat and withdrawal prior to Gates joining that army. He was then assigned to the Northern Department, under the command of General Schuyler, where he endeavored to replace Schuyler in command. On May 16, 1776, Congress promoted Gates to the rank of major general. During British general Burgoyne's advance in New York, Gates was named to replace Schuyler on August 4, 1777. As commander of the Northern Department, Gates would win the praise of the nation for the stunning victory over Burgoyne, at Saratoga, even though Schuyler, Stark, and others had actually secured the victory. In November of 1777, Gates was named chairman of the Board of War, a position second only to the commander in chief. Congress also awarded him a gold medal, the second one that body had ever given out. The brilliant victory at Saratoga was in sharp contrast to the many defeats being suffered by Washington and the main army, and caused many people to suggest that Gates should possibly replace Washington as commander of the army. General Thomas Conway was Gates' chief ally in the efforts to effect this change. The attempt to oust Washington became known as the Conway Cabal, and threatened, for a time, to split both the army and Congress. In the end, Washington was retained, and Conway was forced to resign from the army.[2]

In 1779, Washington gave Gates a choice of commands. He could either mount an expedition against the Iroquois or assume command of the Eastern Department. Gates chose the latter. In November, he requested, and was granted, permission to winter at his home, in Virginia. While in Virginia, Gates began to lobby southern congressmen to replace General Lincoln as commander of the Southern Department. Following Lincoln's defeat at Savannah, Congress voted to replace him with Gates. With an army of some 4,000 men, almost entirely composed of militia, Gates fought Cornwallis at the battle of Camden. Though the British were outnumbered almost two to one, Cornwallis' men were all veteran troops. During the battle, Gates' undisciplined militia broke before a British bayonet charge, and fled the field. Following the disaster at Camden, Gates was replaced by General Greene as commander of the Southern Department. Gates returned to his home, at Traveler's Rest, to await reassignment. In December of 1780 Congress called for an inquiry into Gates' action at Camden, but the proceedings were later dropped.

In 1782, Gates was ordered to report to General Washington, then at Newburgh, Virginia. He was present during the Newburgh Conspiracy in March of 1783, where the soldiers threatened to revolt if they did not receive their pay. In the summer of 1783 Gates' wife died, and he retired to his home, at Traveler's Rest, where he was prominent in the creation of the Virginia chapter of the Society of the Cincinnati. In 1784, Gates proposed marriage to Janet Livingston Montgomery, the widow of General Montgomery, but she declined his offer. In 1790, Gates sold Traveler's Rest and moved to New York City. In 1800, he was elected to the New York legislature, serving one term. Horatio Gates died on April 10, 1806, in New York City, in his seventy-eighth year. He was buried at the Trinity Church Graveyard on Wall Street. The exact location of his burial was subsequently lost, and he now lies in an unknown grave.[3]

GIBSON, JOHN—**(Pennsylvania)** John Gibson was born in Lancaster, Pennsylvania, on May 23, 1740. At the age of eighteen, he accompanied General Forbes' expedition to capture Fort Duquesne at present day Pittsburgh. Gibson was taken with the area and settled there in 1763, taking up the vocation of a trader. He was taken prisoner by the Indians, and his life was spared when he was adopted by a squaw who had recently lost her son. He was detained for several years, during which time he became fluent in the languages and customs of the neighboring tribes. When he finally attained his freedom, he accompanied and served in Lord Dunmore's expedition against the Shawnee, acting as a mediator and interpreter, and in this capacity he received the surrender of Chief Logan. Gibson married Ann Shickellamy, and three children were born to the union.

Given command of a regiment in the Continental Army at the outbreak of the war, he served for a short time in New York and New Jersey before being detailed to perform a duty that he was most suited for: guarding the frontier from Indian incursions. Gibson served as commandant of Fort Laurens, near present day Bolivar, Ohio. While at Fort Laurens, Gibson and his small command, made up of 150 men of the 13th Virginia Regiment, withstood a siege from some 850 hostile Indians. He later served in the same capacity at Fort Pitt, replacing General Broadhead at that post. At the conclusion of the war, Gibson served in a variety of civil positions, and was named secretary of Indiana in 1800, a position he held until statehood was granted.

John Gibson died at the residence of George Wallace, his son-in-law, near Braddock's Field, Pennsylvania, on April 10, 1822. He was buried in the Old Allegheny Cemetery, in the Lawrenceville District of Pittsburgh, Pennsylvania.[1]

GIST, MORDECAI—(Maryland) Mordecai Gist was born in Baltimore, Maryland, on February 22, 1742. Born to a wealthy family, Gist was educated for commercial pursuits, and he entered into the family merchant and shipping business when he came of age. Being in the mercantile and shipping business, Gist's family was directly affected by British attempts at taxation such as the Navigation Acts, causing the Gists to espouse the cause of independence. Gist married Cecil Carnan in 1769, and the couple had two children before Cecil died in 1770. He later married Mary Serrett, in 1778, with whom he had one child. In 1774, he was a founder, and captain, of the Baltimore Independent Company, the first company to be raised in Maryland for the purpose of defending liberty. He was later commissioned major of the 1st Maryland Regiment, serving under General Smallwood.

In August of 1776, Gist took part in the battle of Long Island, where he commanded a force of 450 Maryland Militia. During the battle, Gist ordered six different bayonet charges against the British in his front. The first five were thrown back, only to reform to charge again. On the sixth charge, the British gave way in confusion. Washington witnessed the courage of Gist and his men, and by their valor, the unit became known as "The Bayonets of the Revolution." On December 10, 1776, Gist was promoted to colonel and given command of the 3rd Maryland Regiment, at Germantown. He served in most of the campaigns conducted by Washington's army, and on January 9, 1779, received a commission as brigadier general from the Continental Congress. In May of 1779, Gist was placed in command of the defenses of Maryland.

In 1780, Gist was transferred to the Southern Department, under the command of General Gates. He fought stubbornly at the battle of Camden, where he once more ordered a bayonet charge that drove the British from his front and netted some fifty prisoners. The British soon rallied, however, and Gist and his Marylanders were forced to retreat. Gates' role in the defeat at Camden resulted in Congress calling for an inquiry into his actions. Gist's determined stand, on the other hand, resulted in Congress tendering its thanks to that officer. After making good his escape from Camden, Gist joined Washington at Yorktown in time to be present for the surrender of Cornwallis' army.

In 1782, he was given command of the Light Corps, in General Greene's Southern Department. On August 27 of that year, he fought at the battle of Combahee Ferry, South Carolina, where the British suffered a decisive defeat. Gist served through the end of the war, when he retired from active duty, purchased a plantation near Charleston, South Carolina, and took up the life of a planter. Gist was one of the original members of the Society of the Cincinnati. Sometime in the 1780s Gist sank into a coma and was thought to be dead. The family postponed his burial until the arrival of his best friend, General Nathaniel Greene. When Greene arrived, he asked to be permitted to sit for a while with his old friend. As Greene sat beside Gist, he noticed movement in an eyelid. Gist recovered from the coma, and was spared being buried alive by Greene's intervention.

Gist was such a strong advocate of the cause of freedom that he named his two sons Independence and States. He would be the ancestor of another famous officer, General States Rights Gist, a Confederate general in the Civil War.

Mordecai Gist died on August 2, 1792, at the age of fifty. He was buried in the St. Michael's Church Cemetery, in Charleston, South Carolina.[1]

GLOVER, JOHN—**(Massachusetts)** John Glover was born at Salem, Massachusetts, on November 5, 1732, but the family moved to Marblehead following the death of John's father. Glover worked as a shoemaker before becoming a ship owner and fisherman. In the latter professions he thrived, and was able to obtain wealth and status in the Marblehead community. In 1754, he married Hannah Gale. The couple would have eight children together.

In 1759, Glover began his military career by becoming an ensign in the 3rd Military Foot Company. In 1762 he was promoted to captain lieutenant, and by 1773 he had become captain of the company. Prior to the outbreak of open hostilities, he served as a member of the Marblehead Committee of Correspondence. On May 19, 1775, Glover was commissioned colonel of the Marblehead Militia Regiment, following the death of Colonel Jeremiah Lee. He was ordered to proceed with his regiment to Boston, where he took part in the siege of the British forces there. Since the Marblehead Regiment was made up mostly of fishermen, and were used to being on boats, they were assigned to man armed ships in Massachusetts Bay. On January 1, 1776, the regiment was redesignated the 14th Continental Regiment. Glover and his regiment participated in the defense of New York City in the summer of 1776, and were largely responsible for helping the American army escape the siege of the British by ferrying them across the East River. Glover supervised this evacuation of Long Island, transporting 9,000 Continental troops, along with all of their equipment, to safety. On October 18, 1776, Glover, with 750 troops, held off a British force of some 4,000 at Pell's Point.

During the Trenton Campaign, Glover and the 14th Continental Regiment ferried Washington's army across the Delaware River prior to the attack on the town, and then took a conspicuous part in the fighting. The term of enlistment of the 14th Continental Regiment expired on December 31, 1776, and the unit was mustered out of the service. Glover returned to his home to care for his sick wife. He initially rejected an offer from Washington to become a brigadier general, but he later accepted the commission to that grade that Congress bestowed upon him dated February 21, 1777. Glover was assigned to General Schuyler and the Northern Department, where he took a significant role in the Saratoga Campaign. Following the American victory, Glover was detailed to escort General Burgoyne, and the rest of his captured British army, to Boston. In 1778, he was appointed commander of Fort Arnold, at West Point. He was subsequently detailed to serve under Lafayette, at Providence, Rhode Island, and took part in the skirmish at Quaker Hill, near Newport. In the spring of 1779 he replaced General Sullivan as commander of Providence, Rhode Island.

In 1780, he

John Glover (courtesy United States Military History Institute)

was again stationed at West Point. He served as a member of the court that tried Major John Andre for his part in the Benedict Arnold conspiracy, and was officer of the day at the execution of Andre. In 1781, he married Frances Fosdick, his first wife having died in 1778. Glover was stationed in the Hudson Highlands during 1781, and did not take part in the Yorktown Campaign. On July 22, 1782, Glover retired from the army on half pay, due to poor health. He returned to Marblehead to devote time to private business ventures. On September 30, 1783, he was brevetted a major general by Congress.

Following the war, Glover served two terms in the Massachusetts state legislature, and six terms on the Marblehead Board of Selectmen. John Glover died at Marblehead on January 30, 1797, at the age of sixty-four. He was buried in the Old Burial Hill Cemetery, in Marblehead, Massachusetts.[1]

GODFREY, GEORGE—(**Massachusetts**) George Godfrey was born at Norton (also listed as Taunton), Bristol County, Massachusetts, on March 19, 1721. Little is known of his early life or education. He married Lydia Hodges on June 30, 1739, and the couple had one child before Lydia's death in 1741. Godfrey then married her sister, Bethiah Hodges, on May 9, 1744, and this union produced another eight children. Bethiah died in 1786, where upon Godfrey subsequently entered into his third marriage, this time to the widow Abagail Shaw Dean.

Godfrey was active in the Massachusetts Militia, and was commissioned to the rank of brigadier general, from Bristol County, on January 30, 1776. His commission at this grade was renewed on several occasions. It would appear that Godfrey did not participate in any sort of active, continuous service in the militia. Instead, he seems to have been called to active duty only during times of crisis, or alarm, serving in short stints. As an example, he saw service in Rhode Island, where he served for only eight days during the alarm of August 1, 1780. His son, George Godfrey, Jr., served as a private in Colonel George William's Massachusetts Regiment. Godfrey retained his commission until the war was virtually over, in 1781.

George Godfrey died on June 19, 1793, at Norton, Massachusetts, at the age of seventy-two.[1]

GREATON, JOHN—(**Massachusetts**) John Greaton was born at Roxbury, Massachusetts, on March 10, 1741. He grew up to be a prominent member of Roxbury society, and was a member of the Old North Church, where his brother served as rector. In 1762, he married Sarah Humphrey, and the couple would have seven children together.

In 1774, Greaton was commissioned a lieutenant in the British Governor's Horse Guards. At the outbreak of the Revolution, he was commissioned lieutenant colonel of Heath's Regiment on May 19, 1775. On July 1 of that year he was promoted to colonel, serving in the operations around Boston. On January 1, 1776, he took over the command of the 24th Continental Infantry Regiment, and on November 1, 1776, assumed command of the 3rd Massachusetts Regiment. With the 24th Continental Regiment, Greaton took part in the siege of Boston, and in the Canadian expedition and the operations around Lake Champlain. He served in northern New Jersey before being assigned to the Northern Department in time to take a prominent role in the Saratoga Campaign, under General Gates. In fact, Greaton is one of the officers depicted in John Trumbull's well-known painting, "Burgoyne's Surrender at Saratoga." Following the Saratoga Campaign, Greaton and his regiment were assigned to the Highlands Department, in New York. They performed service at West Point, and the regiment was disbanded there on November 3, 1783. On January 7, 1783, the Continental Congress commissioned Greaton a brigadier general in the Continental Army, and he served in that capacity till the close of hostilities.

Greaton returned home to Roxbury, where he became an original member of the Massachusetts branch of the Society of the Cincinnati. He did not have long to re-establish himself in private pursuits, however. John Greaton died at Roxbury, Massachusetts, on December 16, 1783, at the age of forty-two. He had survived the Revolutionary War by little more than a month. He was buried at the Eustis Street Burying Ground, in Roxbury, Massachusetts.[1]

GREENE, NATHANIEL — (Rhode Island)

Nathaniel Greene was born at Warwick, Rhode Island, on May 27, 1742, the son of a Quaker minister. Greene grew up working on the family farm, and was eventually entrusted with operating a forge that his father owned. Because of Quaker religious beliefs, he was taught only reading, writing, and business math. Greene had a voracious appetite for learning, however, and studied extensively on his own, even learning Latin by self-instruction.

As relations between England and America began to deteriorate, Greene sided with the Patriot cause, and his ardor earned him election to the Rhode Island legislature. It also earned him expulsion from the Quaker society, due to his breaking the pacifistic beliefs of the order. On July 20, 1774, Greene married Catharine Littlefield, and the couple would have six children together.

In August of 1774, a militia company, called the Kentish Guards, was formed in East Greenwich, Rhode Island, with Greene being a founding member. After its formation, there was a question as to whether Greene would be allowed to serve or not. He had had a slight limp, since childhood, and the other members of the company felt that it would impede his ability to act as a soldier. The matter was finally brought to rest when James Varnum, another founding member, threatened to resign if Greene was not allowed to participate.[1]

In April of 1775 the Rhode Island legislature established an Army of Observation, and on May 3 of that year Greene was commissioned a brigadier general of state troops. On June 22, 1775, he became the youngest man to be given a commission as brigadier general in the Continental Army. (This distinction would later go to Lafayette, when Congress bestowed the rank of general upon him.) In this capacity, he took part in the siege of Boston, but missed the battle of Bunker Hill.[2]

It was during the siege of Boston that Greene first met George Washington. The army commander was much impressed with the young brigadier, and within the short span of a year had come to consider him to be the best of his generals, and the officer best suited to replace him in the event of his death or capture.

Greene took command of Long Island in 1776, where he was placed in charge of the Brooklyn defenses. On August 9, 1776, he was promoted to the rank of major general, but he missed the battle of Long Island due to being bedridden with a severe fever. Greene saw his first real combat at the battle of Harlem Heights, on September 16, 1776, where he served with distinction. Following that battle, he was placed in command of the Continental forces at Fort Lee, New Jersey. Greene also sought to hold Fort Washington, on Manhattan Island, hoping that the British would mount a frontal attack, resulting in a second Bunker Hill. The result was Greene's greatest error of the war. Vastly outmanned and outgunned, the fort fell to the British with the loss of some three thousand soldiers.

Greene played a prominent role in conducting the retreat of the army across New Jersey, and he commanded the right wing of Washington's army at the battle of Trenton on December 26, 1776. He also played a leading role at the battle of Princeton, on January 3, 1777. In March of 1778, Washington sent Greene to Congress, as his personal representative, to convince that body of the pressing needs of the army.

Greene was conspicuous with his division at the battle of Brandywine, holding a defensive position that allowed General Sullivan time to extricate his division and retreat. He held firm to his position till nightfall, allowing Washington the opportunity to disengage and retreat with the main army. At the battle of Germantown, Greene was in command of the left wing of the army.

On March 2, 1778, Greene was appointed quartermaster general of the army. The quartermaster department was in a shambles, and though Greene labored to improve its efficiency, he was less than satisfied with the assignment. He was reported as stating, "No Body ever heard of a quarter Master in History." Though he was not impressed with the position, Greene continued to perform the duties of quartermaster general until July 26, 1780, when he resigned due to a disagreement with Congress over the policy of requisitioning provisions from individual states. Greene resumed his position as a field commander at the battle of Monmouth, on June 28, 1778. On June 7, 1780, he commanded the front line at the battle of Connecticut Farms, in New Jersey, and two weeks later he commanded the force that defeated the British at the battle of Springfield, on June 23, 1780. In September of 1780, he presided over the military board that tried Major John Andre for his part in the Benedict Arnold conspiracy. In September of that year, he was assigned to be the commander at West Point.

Following General Gates' defeat at the battle of Camden, Washington assigned Greene to replace that officer as commander of the Southern Department. The army that Greene inherited was outnumbered, poorly equipped, and demoralized. He adopted a plan that would change the course of the war in the South. Greene determined not to fight the British in any stand-up battles. Instead, he would constantly harass the enemy forces, disrupt their lines of supply and communication, and wait for an opportunity to strike a telling blow. He made the best use possible of the resources he had at hand, especially the guerrilla forces under local militia commanders like Francis Marion, Thomas Sumter, and Andrew Pickens. The greatest victory of Greene's Southern Campaign came on January 17, 1781, when General Daniel Morgan defeated the British forces under the command of Tarleton at the battle of Cowpens. Greene then faced Cornwallis at the battle of Guilford Courthouse, on March 15, 1781. The Continental forces were defeated in the battle, but the British were so bloodied that a member of Parliament was led to exclaim that another such "victory" would destroy the British army. Cornwallis took his army to Wilmington, to recuperate, and from there he left the Carolinas and marched his army to Yorktown, Virginia.

When Cornwallis marched north, Greene turned his army south to attack the various isolated posts the British had left behind. The year 1781 witnessed three major battles for control of the South. On April 25, Greene fought at Hobkirk's Hill. This was followed by the siege

Nathaniel Greene

of Ninety-Six, from May 22 to June 19. On September 8, Greene fought the bloodiest engagement of the war in the battle of Eutaw Springs. While these major engagements were being fought, the partisan network set up by Greene was attacking isolated posts along the British line of forts. Greene won precious few battles, as he fought for control of the South, but his campaign and style of fighting was highly effective in forcing the British to constantly reduce their sphere of influence in the area. Greene was losing the battles, but winning the campaign. Within twenty months of being appointed commander of the Southern District, Greene had succeeded in capturing all of the British posts in the region. He had split the British army in two, effectively reducing their areas of control to Charleston and Wilmington. Greene is credited not only with winning the war in the South, but also with making possible the final victory over the British forces in America. He continued to serve in the army until its disbandment, resigning on November 3, 1783.

In recognition of his services to the country, Greene was presented an estate, Mulberry Grove, just north of Savannah, Georgia. Following his retirement from the army, he moved his family there, and began life as a Southern planter. Greene refused repeated attempts to convince him to enter into politics, preferring to attend to his estate and his personal finances. Plagued by debts incurred as a result of the war, he was forced to sell off large tracts that had been granted to him in North and South Carolina. On June 19, 1786, Greene suffered a stroke caused by overexposure to the sun. The stroke proved to be fatal, and Nathaniel Greene died at the age of forty-four. He was buried at the Nathaniel Greene Monument, in Johnson Square, Savannah, Georgia.[3]

GREGORY, ISAAC—(Virginia) Isaac Gregory was born in Virginia in 1734. Gregory married Alse Gerrard, and the couple had seven children together. In 1767, Gregory was granted 200 acres of land by Governor Tryon in the Union District region of South Carolina, and he moved his family there. Gregory became a planter, and built Fairfield Plantation on the ground he had been granted.

An ardent Patriot, Gregory was commissioned a colonel in the South Carolina Militia, following the beginning of hostilities between Great Britain and the Colonies, and was subsequently promoted to the rank of brigadier general. His efforts were primarily concentrated in defending against incursions from area Loyalists and Indians. He commanded the expeditions against the Scovillite Loyalists and the Overhill Indians. On June 20, 1779, he took part in the battle of Stono, South Carolina, where the conduct of his men won the praise of the enemy. On August 16, 1780, Gregory held a command at the battle of Camden, South Carolina, where he was wounded and captured.

Following the end of the war, Gregory returned home and resumed his private life as a planter. Isaac Gregory died at Fairfield Plantation, Camden, South Carolina, on April 3, 1797, in his sixty-third year. He was buried in the family cemetery there.[1]

GUNBY, JOHN—(Maryland) John Gunby was born in Somerset County, Maryland, on March 10, 1745. Little is known of his early life, or education. Gunby supported the Patriot cause, and raised an independent company of soldiers in Somerset County for Continental service, becoming their captain in 1776. He was subsequently promoted to the rank of lieutenant colonel in the militia in 1776, and colonel in 1777. In 1781, he assumed command of the 2nd Maryland Regiment. That regiment took part in the defense of the Carolinas and in Greene's Southern Campaign. History indicates that Gunby committed a military blunder involving a retreat while in command that was evidently confirmed by a court of inquiry. Nevertheless, he continued to exercise command, transferring to command of the 1st Maryland Regiment on January 1, 1783. Gunby received a brevet commission from the Continental Congress to the rank of brigadier general on September 30, 1783. He retired from the service on December 15 of that same year.

Following retirement, Gunby returned to Somerset County, where he purchased a small tobacco plantation. He married the widow of Dr. John Stevenson, but his bride died shortly after the marriage. He then married a Mrs. Shelby, another widow, who also died shortly after their union. Gunby's third wife was Amelia Charllier, the daughter of Colonel P. Charllier. The couple would have two children together. Gunby would have a total of four children, with one having been born to each of his first two wives.

John Gunby died on June 8, 1807, at his plantation near Stockton, Maryland, at the age of sixty-two. He was buried in the family plot, on the plantation. In 1972, his marker was moved to the Gunby Churchyard Cemetery near Stockton because of the deterioration of the burial ground on the plantation grounds. Over the years, tombstones had been knocked over and broken by farm machinery, and at the time his marker was moved, his body could not be located. Gunby's remains are still on the grounds of the plantation, and his marker at the churchyard cemetery serves only as a memorial to this patriot.[1]

HANCOCK, JOHN—(Massachusetts) John Hancock was born at Braintree, Massachusetts, on January 12, 1737. Hancock was orphaned as a small child, and raised by a wealthy uncle who was childless. After receiving his primary education, Hancock attended Harvard, graduating from that institution at the age of seventeen. He then apprenticed himself to his uncle, as a clerk, and proved himself so adept in the business world that he was sent on a business assignment to London in 1760. In 1763, Hancock's uncle died, and the young man inherited his estates and mercantile business, making him the richest man in New England. His great wealth and affluence placed him in the society of the Loyalists, but Hancock did not ascribe to their views on government. A strong populist, he believed strongly in the abilities of the common man and held unreasoned authority in contempt. Hancock was elected to the Boston Assembly in 1766, and was a member of the Stamp Act Congress. In 1768, when one of his ships was seized on a charge of carrying contraband goods, a band of citizens stormed the customs house, burned the government ship, and beat the British officers in charge. He soon after lent his support to the Boston Tea Party. In 1774, Hancock was elected to the Massachusetts Provincial Congress. When the American army was besieging Boston in the spring of 1775, some leading officers proposed to expel the British by destroying the town. Most of the proposed targets were owned by Hancock, and such a course would have surely ruined him financially, but he approved of the action, regardless of the effects it would have had on him, personally. Such was his devotion to the cause of liberty. He used his wealth to support the cause in numerous ways. It is said that hundreds of displaced families were fed daily as a result of his generosity.

In 1775, Hancock was elected to the Continental Congress, and when Peyton Randolph resigned his position as president of that body, Hancock was elected to replace him. This was, in part, due to the notoriety he had received when the British had offered a large reward for the capture of several leading Patriot leaders, Hancock included. This was also the year that he wed Dorothy Quincy, and the couple had two children together.

Hancock was the first to sign the Declaration of Independence, putting his name to the document with large letters and stating, "The British ministry can read that name without spectacles, let them double their reward." The state of Massachusetts commissioned Hancock a major general in the militia in 1776, though he never commanded an army in the field. Like many of his contemporaries, his contributions to the cause came out of the political arena, and not from the battlefield. Popular thinking, in the 18th Century, held that officers should be men of substance and society, gentlemen who were socially and intellectually superior to the men they commanded. Hancock's appointment to the grade of general followed this line of thinking, and was not due to the merits of previous military service, or a capacity for the arts of military science.

In 1777, Hancock resigned from the Continental Congress, due to ill health. He was suffering from an extreme case of gout, and retired to Massachusetts, where he was a member of the convention to frame a new state constitution. He was elected to be the first governor under this new state constitution in 1780, serving for five consecutive terms, until he declined another re-election in 1785. In 1787, however, he accepted the mantle of governor again, and served in that capacity until his death in 1793.

John Hancock died at Braintree, Massachusetts, on October 8, 1793, at the age of fifty-

John Hancock (courtesy National Archives)

five. He was buried at the Old Grainery Burying Ground in Boston, Massachusetts.[1]

HAND, EDWARD—(Ireland) Edward Hand was born in Clyduff, County Kings, Ireland, on December 31, 1744. Little is known of his early life other than an obvious education in medicine, which he received in Dublin, and an enlistment in the British army. In 1774, he was the surgeon's mate of the 18th Royal Irish Regiment when it came to America to garrison Fort Pitt. Hand resigned his commission and settled in Lancaster County, Pennsylvania, obtaining a farm just south of the city of Lancaster, which he named Rockford. In the short time between his arrival in America and the start of the Revolutionary war, Hand established himself as a doctor in Lancaster County.

Despite his short time spent in America, Hand adopted the Patriot cause, and on July 25, 1775, he became lieutenant colonel of Thompson's Pennsylvania Rifle Battalion, serving with that unit in the siege of Boston. In that same year, Hand married Catharine Ewing, on March 13, with nine children being born to the union. Hand was reported to be a superior horseman, earning the respect of his peers for his equestrian abilities. On January 1, 1776, he was transferred to the 1st Continental Infantry, and on March 7 of that year was commissioned colonel of the regiment. Hand fought at the battles of Long Island, White Plains, and Trenton, with Washington's main army, and on April 1, 1777, the Continental Congress commissioned him a brigadier general. He succeeded General Stark in command at Albany, New York, in 1778, and afterward served with General Sullivan in his expedition against the Six Nations. In August of 1780 he was assigned to command one of the two brigades of light infantry in the Continental Army. In 1781, he replaced Alexander Scammell as adjutant-general of the army. On September 30, 1783, the Continental Congress bestowed upon him the brevet rank of major general.

Hand was elected to the Continental Congress in 1784. In 1790, he was a member of the convention that drafted a new state constitution for Pennsylvania. He was elected burgess of Lancaster, and served in the Pennsylvania state legislature. In 1798, when war with France seemed apparent, Hand was commissioned a major general in the United States army, and, at the request of George Washington, was appointed adjutant-general. He was honorably discharged on July 15, 1800, when tensions between the two countries subsided.

Edward Hand died at his home at Rockford Plantation, Lancaster County, Pennsylvania, on September 3, 1802, at the age of seventy-eight. He was interred in the St. James Episcopal Church Cemetery, in Lancaster, Pennsylvania.[1]

HARRINGTON, HENRY WILLIAM— (North Carolina) Henry William Harrington was born at London, England, on May 12, 1747. (Some family histories state that he was born in North Carolina, but evidence does not support that contention.) Harrington moved from England to the West Indies, where he lived for a time in Jamaica before removing to the Carolinas and eventually settling in Anson County, North Carolina. Prior to the Revolution, Harrington served as a representative in the South Carolina Legislature. In 1775, Harrington was commissioned a captain in the local militia, a company from St. David's Parish. He was also appointed to a committee to report on the best method of manufacturing saltpeter for the colony, a commodity that would be absolutely necessary in the production of gunpowder, should the colony go to war against England. In 1776, he was promoted to colonel. That same year, Harrington married Rosanna Auld, and the couple had five children together. He was elected sheriff of the Cheraws District of South Carolina. Harrington saw service, in command of militia, at Hadrell's Point, in Charleston, South Carolina, at the beginning of the war, after he had marched the North Carolina Militia to the defense of that place. In 1778, he was commissioned a brigadier general in the militia for the Salisbury District of North Carolina. That region being along the North Carolina frontier at the time of the Revolution, Harrington's militia service was largely employed in defending against the incursions of Indians allied with the British who lived along the border of the western frontier of the state.

Henry William Harrington died in Richmond County, North Carolina, in March 31, 1809, at the age of sixty-one.[1]

HAZEN, MOSES—(Massachusetts) Moses Hazen was born at Haverhill, Massachusetts, on June 1, 1733. Little is known of his early life, except that he was apprenticed to a tanner. In 1756, he was a lieutenant in Edmond Moore's Company that took part in the campaign against Crown Point. In 1757 he was on the "alarm list" and exempt from military duty. In this year, he traveled to Halifax, Nova Scotia, where he was engaged in business, selling supplies to the British in preparation for their campaign against Louisburg. In January of 1758, Hazen was recommended as a lieutenant in Roger's Rangers, but Hazen declined. In 1759, he would accept a commission as first lieutenant, and eventually become captain of the company, leading his men on a raid against St. Anne that covered 150–180 miles in 16 days.

With his company, Hazen participated in the "Montgomery Massacre," the capture of Quebec, and the battle at Chevalier de Levis. Moses was severely wounded in the thigh in the last battle, forcing him to relinquish his command and remain in the hospital in Quebec.

At the end of the French and Indian War, Hazen became one of two hundred English landowners in Canada, and was appointed to be one of the twenty-seven justices of the peace named by the royal governor. In the years between the end of the French and Indian War and the beginning of the Revolution, Hazen acquired substantial holdings in Canada. In 1770, he married Charlotte Saussaye, the daughter of a very respectable family in Montreal. After the marriage, Hazen operated two saw mills, a forge, and an ashery for making potash. He had failed at numerous business ventures since locating himself in Canada, but his fortunes seemed to be on the rise after his marriage.

At the outbreak of the Revolution, Hazen offered his services to the British, who gave him the assignment of scouting the American movements along the New York-Canada border. In the completion of this mission, he even provided the Americans he came in contact with false information concerning the size of the British army in Canada. When the Americans learned of the inflated numbers he had been tendering, they had him arrested. He was later freed, and during General Montgomery's invasion of Canada, he gave supplies liberally to the soldiers of the American army. For doing so, he was declared to be a traitor by the British, who destroyed his property and arrested him. He was freed a second time when the British evacuated Montreal, and from that time on became a firm supporter of the American cause.

Hazen joined the Continental army, while it was still in Canada, and was given permission to recruit a Canadian corps, which he would command. He was able to secure only some 200 enlistments by the time the Americans withdrew from Canada, but they became known as the 2nd Canadian Regiment, or "Congress' Own." Hazen would serve as their colonel, and would fight with the Continental army at Brandywine and Germantown. He performed well through the entire war, and on June 29, 1781, was rewarded with a commission as brigadier general in the Continental army.

After 1783, Hazen moved to Troy, New York, and took up private life as a businessman. In recognition of his service, Hazen was given a land grant in Vermont after the conclusion of the war. He was also indemnified by Congress for the property that had been confiscated and destroyed in Canada prior to his joining the American army. Hazen moved to Vermont, along with two brothers who had also served in the Continental army and had received land grants there. Hazen would return to Troy, New York, where he died on February 3, 1803, at the age of sixty-one.[1]

HEARD, NATHANIEL—(New Jersey) Nathaniel Heard was born in Middlesex County, New Jersey, in 1730. Heard married Mary Stone, and the couple had one child together.

Nathaniel Heard was a prominent planter and horse breeder in Woodbridge, New Jersey. He also served as local tax collector and as school commissioner for Woodbridge, and managed the Pike House Tavern, which he inherited from his father.

In November of 1775, Heard was commissioned a colonel in the New Jersey Militia. On February 12, 1776, Heard was promoted to the rank of brigadier general in the state service. On June 19, 1776, Heard commanded the Middlesex County Militia in a raid on Perth Amboy, in which the royal governor, William Franklin, was captured. William was the son of Benjamin Franklin, but he had split with his father to remain loyal to the Crown. Heard offered Franklin a parole if he would agree to stay in his home and not aid the British, but Franklin refused to do so. When the British landed an army at Staten Island, in June of 1776, General Washington was there to meet them. The Americans were outnumbered, however, and were forced to retreat into New York City, and then into the Bronx and White Plains. Congress called on the state of New Jersey to send aid to Washington's forces, and the state responded by sending General Heard, with 500 New Jersey Militia. Heard was ordered to disarm the Loyalists in the New York area, and he and his men did so in Jamaica, Hempstead, Jericho, Oyster Bay, and Queens, forcing 500 Loyalists to sign oaths of allegiance and seizing a large quantity of weapons. When Washington evacuated New York City, General Heard was in command of a sixteen company brigade that covered the retreat.

Heard's home, in Woodbridge, suffered extensive damage from raids by the British army during the war. When Heard returned home after the war, he attempted to recover damages to his property from Congress. Heard petitioned Congress for the rest of his life, and his heirs continued to do so into the middle of the 1800s, but no money was forthcoming from the government.

Nathaniel Heard died at Woodbridge, New Jersey, on October 28, 1792, in his sixty-second year.[1]

HEART, SELAH—(Connecticut) Selah Heart (also spelled Hart) was born at Kensington, Connecticut, on May 23, 1732. On March 4, 1754, he married Mary Cole. The couple had a daughter, but the child did not survive infancy. They then adopted Coyprian Heart, the son of Selah's brother. Mary Cole Heart died on January 27, 1763. Heart would later marry Ruth Cole (Ruth was not the sister of Mary).

Heart was an advocate of the Patriot cause, and in May of 1775, he was appointed to a committee charged with procuring lead for the state of Connecticut, for the purpose of making musket balls. The mine from which the lead was to be obtained happened to be in Kensington, Heart's hometown. In December of 1775, he began his military service when he was commissioned a captain in Walcott's Connecticut State Regiment. Heart served in this regiment until February of 1776. He was afterward commissioned a lieutenant colonel in Gay's Connecticut State Regiment on June 20, 1776. With this unit, Heart took part in the battles and operations in and around New York City during the summer of 1776. During Washington's evacuation of New York, Heart's regiment was cut off from the main body by a force of British that had ascended the Hudson River and landed above him. Heart was taken prisoner on September 15, 1776, and was held by the British until his exchange in March of 1777. During the period of his captivity, the British released no news of his status, leaving his family and friends in doubt as to whether he was living or dead. In 1779, he was commissioned a brigadier general in the Connecticut Militia, and served as such until the end of the war.

Selah Heart died at Kensington, Connecticut, on April 10, 1806, at the age of seventy-three.[1]

HEATH, WILLIAM—(Massachusetts) William Heath was born in Roxbury, Massachusetts, on March 7, 1737. He became a farmer working the same land that had been in his family for over one hundred years. In 1759, he married Sarah Lockwood, and the couple had five children together. Heath was an early advocate of the cause of liberty, and in 1770 he wrote addresses to the public urging the coming necessity of military discipline. At the same time, he took it upon himself to organize companies of militia to prepare for the conflict that he was sure must come.[1]

When hostilities erupted, Heath was in the thick of the fighting, serving as a colonel during the combat at Lexington and Concord. His services were promptly rewarded when he was commissioned a major general of Massachusetts Militia on June 20, 1775. Two days later he was commissioned a brigadier general in the Continental Army. Heath accompanied Washington's main army to New York in 1776, where he participated in the battles of Long Island, Harlem Heights, and White Plains. His service was such that Congress promoted him to the rank of major general on August 9, 1776. He had distinguished himself on the field of battle, but the New York campaign would prove to be his last combat duty of the war. Heath was next assigned to command in the New York Highlands while Washington was making his retreat through New Jersey. From 1777 to 1778, he commanded the Eastern Department, with his headquarters at Boston. In this capacity, he was charged with superintending Burgoyne's captured army from the battle of Saratoga, quartered at Cambridge, Massachusetts.[2]

In 1779, Heath was elected commissioner of the Board of War, but he declined the honor, preferring to remain with the army in the field. He was sent to Rhode Island in 1780 to prepare for co-operation with a French fleet that was to act against the British, but the failure of the allies to co-ordinate the operation led to failure. Heath missed the Yorktown campaign, being assigned instead to once again command the army stationed in the New York Highlands.

Following the war, Heath served as a delegate to the 1788 Massachusetts Convention to ratify the Constitution. From 1791 to 1792, he was elected to a seat in the Massachusetts Senate, and at the same time, he served as judge of the Probate Court. In 1800, he was elected lieutenant governor of Massachusetts, but he declined to accept the position, opting to retire to private life on his farm.[3]

William Heath died at his home in Roxbury on January 24, 1814, at the age of seventy-six. He was buried in the Forest Hills Cemetery in Jamaica Plains, in what is now a neighborhood of Boston.

HENDERSON, WILLIAM — (Virginia)

William Henderson was born in Hanover County, Virginia, on March 5, 1748. Little is known of his early life or education. He married Letita Davis, and the couple had three children together. Henderson moved to Grindal Shoals, South Carolina, prior to the Revolution. He was a member of the second South Carolina Provincial Congress, in August of 1775.

On June 17, 1775, he was commissioned major of the 6th South Carolina Regiment, and was subsequently promoted to the rank of lieutenant colonel on September 16, 1776. The 6th participated in the defense of Charleston in 1775 and 1776, operations against the Cherokee, the failed Florida Expedition, and the siege of Savannah. On February 11, 1780, Henderson transferred to the 3rd South Carolina Regiment. Henderson commanded a flank of the American army at the battle of Stono Ferry. He took part in the siege at Charleston, was one of eleven officers to vote against surrender, and was taken prisoner when that city finally fell in May of 1780. The British held him at St. Augustine, Florida, until his exchange was effected about six months later, on November of 1780. He was then promoted to the rank of colonel in the 1st South Carolina Regiment, and put in command of Thomas Sumter's Brigade. Henderson fought with distinction at the battle of Eutaw Springs, holding his troops in an exposed position despite the fact that he had been severely wounded. In January of 1782, he was commissioned a brigadier general in the South Carolina Militia.

Following the war, Henderson was elected to the South Carolina House of Representatives. He sold his property along Grindal Shoals, and moved to the High Hills of Santee, where he lived at Prospect Hill Plantation.

William Henderson died at his plantation at High Hills, in the Sumter District of South Carolina, on January 29, 1788, at the age of thirty-nine.[1]

HERKIMER, NICHOLAS — (New York)

Nicholas Herkimer was born near present day Herkimer, New York, in 1728. Like his father, Herkimer grew up to become a farmer and an Indian trader. During the French and Indian War, the Herkimer home, at Little Falls, was fortified and became known as Fort Herkimer. Nicholas was in command of the force gathered there when the French and Indians attacked German Flats in 1758. Herkimer afterward removed his family to the Canajoharie District, where he took up residence. In 1760, he married Maria Dygert, and when she died in 1777, he later married Lany Dygert.

In 1775, he became a colonel in the state militia and was chairman of the Tryon County Committee of Safety. On September 5, 1776, he was commissioned a brigadier general of the Tryon County Militia. In 1776, Herkimer led an expedition against Sir John Johnson's force of Loyalists and Indian allies. In the fall of 1777, after the surrender of Fort Ticonderoga, a British force under the command of General Barry St. Leger lay siege to Fort Stanwix, and General Herkimer mobilized his militia forces and marched to the relief of the fort on August 6, 1777. He had arranged for the defenders of Stanwix to create a diversion when the militia got close to the fort, which was to be the firing of two cannon signifying that the garrison was making a sortie against the British. As Herkimer's men waited for the signal, a few officers in his command claimed that Herkimer was a Loyalist sympathizer and a coward. Herkimer was deeply stung by these statements, as his brother, Johan Jost Herkimer, had indeed joined the Loyalist cause and was a member of the force then besieging Fort Stanwix. His temper fired, and his honor questioned, Herkimer ordered an immediate charge, not waiting for a diversion from the fort. The result was the battle of Oriskany. As Herkimer's force crossed Oriskany Creek, they were ambushed by a large force of Indians, and fired upon from three sides. Herkimer was badly wounded in the leg, in the early part of the fighting. Tradition has it that he had his men drag him to a tree and prop him up with a saddle as he calmly filled his pipe and directed the battle. Both sides lost heavily in the severe fighting that ended up being a hand-to-hand contest. In the end, the Americans were forced to retreat from the field.

Herkimer was taken back to his home at Little Falls. The wound in his leg was festering, and the decision was made to amputate the limb. But the amputation was not a success, as the bleeding could not be arrested from his severed stump. Herkimer was supposed to have called for his pipe and Bible, and read aloud until he bled to death.

Nicholas Herkimer died on August 16, 1777, in his forty-ninth year. He was buried at his home at Little Falls.[1]

HIESTER, DANIEL—(Pennsylvania) Daniel Hiester was born in Berks County, Pennsylvania, on June 25, 1747, into the politically influential Hiester family. After receiving an adequate primary education in public schools, Hiester moved to Montgomery County, where he engaged in the mercantile business. Hiester was an early advocate of the cause of freedom, and cast his lot with the Patriots. In 1770, Hiester married Rosanna Hager, and two children were born to the marriage.

During the Revolution, Hiester and his three brothers, John, Gabriel, and William, all joined the militia. All would become officers in the Pennsylvania Militia, with Daniel serving as a colonel. John Hiester and William Hiester would also become colonels in the Pennsylvania state forces. On May 27, 1782, Daniel was promoted to the rank of brigadier general in the Pennsylvania state forces. His military career was bereft of glory however, for he saw little combat and served primarily as an administrator and district commander within the confines of the state. He would render service in this capacity through the end of the war.

Following the end of the Revolution, Hiester was elected to the supreme executive council of Pennsylvania in 1784. In 1787, he was appointed as a commissioner to negotiate the Connecticut land claims dispute. In 1789, Hiester was elected to the first U.S. Congress, under the new Constitution, as a representative from Berks County. He would serve consecutively through the fourth U.S. Congress, until he resigned his seat on July 1, 1796. Hiester then moved his family to Hagerstown, Maryland. In 1801, he was returned to the seventh Congress, as a representative of Maryland, from the district composed of Washington, Frederick, and Allegheny counties. Re-elected to the eighth Congress, Hiester was actively serving as a representative when he died, at

Washington, D.C., on March 7, 1804, at the age of fifty-six.

He was buried in the Zion Reformed Church Graveyard, in Hagerstown, Maryland.[1]

HOGUN, JAMES—(**Ireland**) James Hogun (also spelled Hogan) was born in Ireland in 1721. Little is known of his early life, but he immigrated to America, settling in Halifax, North Carolina, where he married Ruth Norfleet on October 3, 1751. The couple would have three children together.

In 1776, Hogun was a member of the North Carolina Provincial Congress. He was also commissioned colonel of the 7th North Carolina Regiment. In 1777, the regiment was released from the Southern Department and sent north to join Washington's main army. Hogun and the 7th North Carolina took part in the defense of Philadelphia and the Monmouth Campaign before the regiment was disbanded at Valley Forge in June of 1778.

In 1779, Hogun was commissioned a brigadier general in the North Carolina Militia, and was once more assigned to the Southern Department. Hogun participated in the defense of Charleston, during the British siege of March 29 to May 12, 1780, and was taken prisoner when the city was surrendered by General Lincoln. He died on January 4, 1781, at Hadrell's Point, Charleston, South Carolina, while still a prisoner of the British, his health having been broken by his extended confinement. Hogun was in his fifty-ninth year at the time of his death.[1]

HOLDEN, THOMAS—(**Rhode Island**) Thomas Holden was born at Warwick, Kent County, Rhode Island, on June 7, 1741. Holden was a farmer, in Warwick. He married a woman by the name of Freelove. Family histories state that this is Freelove Barton, but that individual, the daughter of Rowland Barton, died unmarried. Holden would have twelve children with his wife.

In April of 1775, Holden was commissioned a captain in Colonel Varnum's regiment of Rhode Island Infantry. He served for eight months, before he was recommended for promotion to the rank of major. In October of 1776, Holden was appointed quartermaster of the Rhode Island Brigade. In April of 1778, he was commissioned captain of the Warwick Alarm Company, and in May of that year was commissioned colonel of the 1st Regiment, Kent County Militia. In June of 1778, he was stationed at East Greenwich, taking part in the Newport Campaign in July and August of that year. In June of 1779, Holden was promoted to the rank of brigadier general of the Kent County Militia, a position he would hold until 1790, when he was promoted to major general. Holden was a member of the Rhode Island Council of War in 1781.

Following the end of the war, Holden was elected to the Continental Congress in 1788 and 1789, but does not appear to have taken his seat either time. In 1800, he was appointed to be a justice on the Supreme Court of Rhode Island.

Thomas Holden died at Warwick, Rhode Island, on February 22, 1823, at the age of eighty-two. He was buried in the Holden Burial Ground, in Natick, but there is no stone remaining to mark the exact spot. One of his descendants later erected a stone to his memory in the East Greenwich Cemetery, in East Greenwich, Rhode Island.[1]

HOOPER, HENRY—(**Maryland**) Henry Hooper was born in Maryland in 1720. He was actually Henry Hooper IV, being the fourth Henry in his line. His first name was not the only thing he shared in common with his ancestors. Like his father and grandfather before him, he served as a delegate in the Maryland Legislature. Hooper married Anne Ennalls (date not recorded) and the couple had four children together.

At the outbreak of hostilities, Hooper was commissioned a captain in the Maryland Militia. On January 6, 1776, he was promoted to the rank of brigadier general and given command of the Fifth District, with his headquarters at Cambridge, Maryland. Owing to the fact that there were no land battles fought in the state of Maryland, during the war, Hooper's service was largely administrative. In January of 1781, the British Navy undertook a series of raids along the Maryland coastline, and up the navigable rivers of the state. In April, three British ships of the line sailed up the Nanticoke River, and began to forage from the towns along its banks. General Hooper arrived on the scene to take command of the militia gathered there, and a small skirmish took place. Hooper determined that his force was far too small to contend with the British ships, and when the enemy offered a flag of truce, he readily accepted. The British proposed that they would pay for the provisions they were taking, and would leave as soon as they had acquired them. If the militia refused, they would mount a landing party and burn the surrounding area, including the town of Vienna. Hooper felt that he could not stop the enemy from their intentions, and thus agreed to the offer. He was roundly criticized for his decision, and was suffered the contempt of other officers in the militia, but was retained as a general of militia until the close of hostilities.

Henry Hooper died in Maryland in 1790, in his seventieth year. The exact date and location are not recorded.[1]

HOWE, ROBERT—(North Carolina)

Robert Howe was born in Brunswick County, North Carolina, in 1732. Owing to the fact that his parents died at a young age, he received little education. Howe married at a young age, when he wed Sarah Grange in 1745, and in 1764, he and his wife moved to England, as he sought to make a living in the mother country. In 1766, the Howes returned to America, and he was made captain of Fort Johnson, North Carolina, by Governor Tryon. Again settling in Brunswick County, Howe took up the life of a planter.

He served as a member of the North Carolina legislature from 1772–1773, and was elected to be a delegate to the Colonial Congress that met in New Bern in 1774. On August 21, 1775, Howe was commissioned colonel of the 2nd North Carolina Regiment, and in December of that year he was ordered to Virginia with his regiment. His forces cooperated with those of General Woodford in driving the British out of Norfolk. He received the thanks of Congress for this action, as well as a Continental commission as brigadier general, dated March 1, 1777.

Robert Howe

The British had offered royal clemency to all who would lay down their arms, but Sir Henry Clinton excepted Howe from being eligible for this offer, and sent Lord Cornwallis, with 900 men, to destroy his plantation in Brunswick County.[1]

Howe was in command of the North Carolina troops at the defense of Charleston, and shortly thereafter he replaced General Moore in command of the Southern Department. On October 20, 1777, he was commissioned a major general in the Continental Army. In January of 1778, Howe mounted an expedition against the British in Florida. He won an easy victory at Fort Barrington (Fort Howe), on the Altamaha River, but from there the campaign fell apart. An epidemic fever that ravaged his command, combined with a lack of supplies, forced Howe to retreat to Savannah with a much reduced command. In December of 1778, he attempted to defend the city from the attack of British general Prevost, but Savannah fell on December 29. Howe was widely criticized for the loss of Savannah, especially by General Christopher Gadsden, with whom he had fought a duel the previous year. His actions were tried before a court-martial, which acquitted Howe of any wrongdoing, but, at the request of the representatives of South Carolina and Georgia, he was replaced by General Benjamin Lincoln as commander of the Southern Department. He was ordered to join General Washington's main army, where he was assigned command at West Point in 1780. In 1781, he led the troops who put down the mutiny in the Pennsylvania and New Jersey lines, earning the praise of Washington for his actions. In June of 1783, he was once again employed in quelling mutiny among the troops, this time in Philadelphia.[2]

After the war, Congress appointed Howe to negotiate with the Indians on the western frontier. Upon completion of this assignment, he returned home to North Carolina, where he was elected to serve as a delegate in the state legislature. He was never able to take his seat in the assembly, however, as he was struck down with a fever. Robert Howe died on November 12, 1785, at his plantation in Brunswick County, in his fifty-seventh year.[3]

HUGER, ISAAC—(South Carolina) Isaac Huger was born at Limerick Plantation, along the Santee River, South Carolina, on March 19, 1742. His father, being one of the richest landholders in that part of South Carolina, saw to his son's future and sent him to Europe for his education. Upon young Huger's return to South Carolina, he was commissioned a lieutenant in the militia, in 1760, to serve in the war against the Cherokee. His service would bring him into contact with many of the leading Carolina Patriots of the Revolution. Henry Laurens, William Moultrie, Andrew Pickens, and Francis Marion were members of the same regiment.

On March 23, 1762, he married Elizabeth Chalmers. The marriage produced eight children.

At the outbreak of the Revolution, Huger was commissioned lieutenant colonel of the 1st South Carolina Regiment, on June 17, 1775, and on September 16, 1776, he was promoted to colonel of the 5th South Carolina Regiment. On January 9, 1779, he was commissioned a brigadier general in the Continental army, and

Isaac Huger (courtesy United States Military History Institute)

from that point on took part in every major engagement in the Southern Theater. Huger commanded the left wing of the American army at the battle of Stono Ferry, on June 9, 1779, and was severely wounded while leading his troops. He commanded the Georgia and South Carolina militia in the unsuccessful attack on Savannah. At Charleston, he was charged with harassing the enemy by cutting off the supplies of the British with a command of light troops, but his force was defeated by those under Colonel Tarleton at the battle of Monk's Corner. On March 15, 1781, he commanded the Virginia troops in General Greene's army in the battle of Guilford Courthouse, where he was again severely wounded at the head of his men. His wound had healed sufficiently by April of 1781 to allow him to command the right wing of the American army at the battle of Hobkirk's Hill, and he took part in the fighting at Camden in May of that same year. where he again commanded the Virginia brigade. Huger served till the end of the war, and at its conclusion was made vice president of the South Carolina branch of the Society of the Cincinnati, with William Moultrie serving as president.

In 1782, Huger was elected as a representative to the South Carolina Assembly. In 1789, he was appointed to be the first marshal of South Carolina, by George Washington. Huger would serve for only four years, resigning in 1793 due to poor health and a need to attend to private pursuits.[1]

Isaac Huger died on October 17, 1797, at the age of fifty-five.

HUNTINGTON, JABEZ—(Connecticut) Jabez Huntington was born at Norwich, Connecticut, on August 7, 1719. He received a substantial primary education and attended Yale University, graduating in 1741.

That same year, Jabez married Elizabeth Backus, and the couple had two children before Elizabeth died in 1745. In 1746, he married Hannah Williams, and the couple had seven children together. Huntington engaged in mercantile business in the West India trade, and was able to amass great wealth, and a large number of ships. After 1750, he was frequently elected to the Connecticut legislature, where he served as speaker for several years. In 1767, Huntington was one of the Whig leaders who proposed a boycott of British goods, and the town of Norwich adopted his stance when it forbade the purchase of tea, wines, liquors, and articles of foreign manufacture by any of the residents of the town.

When hostilities erupted between the Colonies and Great Britain, Huntington became active on the Committee of Safety. The British made him pay a particularly high price for siding with the Patriot cause as they captured a large number of his ships. In December of 1776, Huntington was commissioned a major general in the Connecticut Militia, and he undertook the duties of raising and equipping the state troops with energy and efficiency. These exertions, combined with the huge financial losses the war was causing him personally, finally affected his physical and mental health, and he resigned his commission in May of 1779 and retired to private life.

Jabez was the father of General Jedediah Huntington, as well as Ebenezer Huntington, who also served as a soldier in the Revolution, and as a representative in the Federal Congress. His grandson, Jabez Williams Huntington, served in the United States House of Representatives, as well as the United States Senate.

Jabez Huntington died at Norwich, Connecticut, on October 5, 1786, at the age of sixty-seven. He was buried in the Old Norwichtown Burying Ground, in Norwich, Connecticut.[1]

HUNTINGTON, JEDEDIAH—(Connecticut) Jedediah Huntington was born in Norwich, Connecticut, on August 4, 1743, the son of General Jabez Huntington. After receiving his primary education, he attended Harvard College, and was graduated in 1763, with distinguished honor. In 1770, he received a master's degree from Yale College. Following his academic career, he entered into commercial pursuits with his father. Prior to the war, he became a noted Son of Liberty, and a captain in the local militia. In 1767, Jedediah married Faith Trumball, and the couple had three children before Faith died in 1775. That same year, Huntington married Ann Moore, and seven children were born to this union.

In April of 1775, he was made commander of his regiment, and marched to join the army at Cambridge, arriving there just a week after the battles at Lexington and Concord. On July 8, 1775, he was commissioned colonel of the 8th Connecticut Regiment, and was charged with commanding part of the force that occupied Dorchester Heights. On January 1, 1776, Huntington was commissioned colonel of the 17th Continental Infantry. In April of that year, he helped to repulse a British force at Danbury, Connecticut. General Washington recommended Huntington for a commission as brigadier general as early as March of 1777, but there were already so many generals from Connecticut serving in the army that the appointment was postponed. On May 12, 1777, the Continental Congress finally granted Washington's request and gave Huntington the rank of general.

Huntington joined General Putnam, in New York, in July of 1777, before being ordered to Philadelphia to join the main army in September of that year. In November of 1777 he was sent, with his brigade, to intercept General Cornwallis at Red Bank, but Cornwallis anticipated the movement and withdrew. Huntington spent the winter of 1777–78 at Valley Forge, and in March of 1778 served as an officer on the panel that investigated the loss of Forts Montgomery and Clinton in New York. In May, he was ordered to the Northern Department, performing garrison duty at Camp Reading, Highlands, Nielson's Point, Springfield, Shorthills, Totowba, Peekskill, and West Point. In July of 1778 he was a member of the court-martial that tried General Lee for misconduct at the battle of Monmouth, and in September of that same year he was a member of the military board that sentenced Major John Andre to death for his part in the Benedict Arnold treason.[1]

In December of 1780, his was the only Connecticut brigade still in the Continental Army. In May of 1783, he and four other officers drafted the plan of organization that was to result in the Society of the Cincinnati. On September 30, 1783, he received the brevet commission of major general from the Continental Congress. Huntington could hardly be considered one of the fighting generals of the Revolution, but he was esteemed by all who knew him as a competent and reliable officer.[2]

Upon retiring from the army, Huntington resumed his business ventures in Norwich. He was elected sheriff of the county, and subsequently served as state treasurer. In 1789, he served as a delegate to the state convention that ratified the Federal Constitution. That same year, he received an appointment as collector of customs for the port of New London from George Washington, a post he would hold through four presidents. Jedidiah Huntington died at New London, Connecticut, on September 25, 1818, at the age of seventy-five. He was buried at New London, but his remains were later moved to the Huntington family tomb in Norwich.[3]

IRVINE, JAMES — (Pennsylvania) James Irvine was born in Philadelphia, Pennsylvania, on August 4, 1735, the son of Irish emigrants. Irvine became a hatter, in Philadelphia, prior to his entering the Pennsylvania Militia in 1760. He spent most of his time in the militia serving along the northern frontier of Pennsylvania, and by 1763 he had won a commission as captain. In 1764, he served in Colonel Henry Bouquet's expedition against the Indians in northwest Ohio.

On January 23, 1775, Irvine was selected to be a delegate to the provincial conference at Philadelphia. Upon the outbreak of hostilities, he was commissioned lieutenant colonel of the 1st Pennsylvania Battalion on November 25, 1775, and served in Montgomery's Canadian Campaign of 1776. On October 25, 1776, he was promoted to the rank of colonel and given command of the 9th Pennsylvania Regiment, and was subsequently transferred to command of the 2nd Pennsylvania Regiment. Irvine resigned his commission on June 1, 1777, owing to a dispute over rank, but he was brought back into the army when he was commissioned a brigadier general of Pennsylvania Militia in August of that same year, assuming command of the 2nd Pennsylvania Brigade.

Irvine fought with distinction at the battle of Germantown, on October 4, 1777, where his brigade fought under the command of General Armstrong, on the extreme right of the American line. At the battle of Chestnut Hill, Pennsylvania, on December 6, 1777, he was taken prisoner by the British after sustaining a wound that cost him three fingers on his left hand. Irvine would languish in British prisons for three and one-half years, until June 1, 1781, when he was finally exchanged, despite his frequent pleas to Congress to intercede in his behalf. He was subsequently appointed by Congress, after his release, to be the commander of Fort Pitt on October 11, 1781. On May 27, 1782, he was promoted to the rank of major general in the Pennsylvania Militia, a position he would hold until 1793.[1]

In 1782, he was selected as a member of the Pennsylvania Supreme Council, and was vice president of Pennsylvania from 1784 to 1785. In 1785, he was elected to the Pennsylvania State Assembly, and from 1795 to 1799, he served in the state senate. Irvine was elected as one of the original trustees of Dickinson College, serving till 1791.

James Irvine died in Philadelphia, Pennsylvania, on April 28, 1819, at the age of eighty-three. He is buried in the Christ Church Burial Ground, in Philadelphia.

IRVINE, WILLIAM—(Ireland) William Irvine (also spelled Irwine) was born at Fermanaugh, Ireland, on November 3, 1741. After receiving his primary education, he attended Trinity College, in Dublin. Following completion of his studies at Trinity, Irvine took up the study of medicine before becoming a Royal Navy surgeon during the Seven Years' War. In 1763, he resigned his commission and emigrated to America, settling in Carlisle, Pennsylvania, where he set himself up in the practice of medicine. While in Carlisle, he married Anne Callender, in 1770. Twelve children were born to this union. In July of 1774, he was a member of the Provincial Convention held in Philadelphia that recommended the formation of a general congress.[1]

When the Revolution came, Irvine was commissioned colonel of the 6th Pennsylvania Regiment on January 10, 1776, and ordered to join the army then campaigning in Canada. Irvine was taken prisoner at the battle of Three Rivers, Canada, on June 16, 1776. He was released on parole on August 3, 1776, but was not formally exchanged until May 6, 1778, and was therefore precluded from holding a command in the army. Even so, he had been commissioned colonel of the 7th Pennsylvania Regiment in January of 1777, with the commission being pre-dated to January 9, 1776. Following his exchange, Irvine served as a member of the court-martial that tried General Charles Lee.[2]

On May 12, 1779, Irvine was promoted to the rank of brigadier general in the Continental Army, and was assigned to command the 2nd Pennsylvania Brigade. He took part in the battle of Bull's Ferry, New Jersey, on July 21, 1780. Irvine then engaged in an unsuccessful attempt to recruit a corps of cavalry from Pennsylvania. On March 8, 1782, he was ordered to take command of the post at Fort Pitt (present day Pittsburgh). He continued to command at this post on the Pennsylvania frontier until October 1, 1783. During Irvine's command at Fort Pitt, the last battle of the Revolution in that region was fought on July 13, 1782, between Colonel Crawford, of his command, and the Indian Chief Guyasuta.[3]

In 1786, he was elected to the Continental Congress, and in 1793, after the adoption of the Constitution, he was a member of the third Congress, where he represented Cumberland County. In 1794, Irvine was appointed to act as a commissioner to the whiskey insurgents, and when he failed to convince them to disperse, he was appointed commander of the Pennsylvania militia that was sent to put down the rebellion. In 1801, Irvine moved to Philadelphia, where he was appointed superintendent of military stores. At the time of his death, he was president of the Pennsylvania branch of the Society of the Cincinnati. Irvine was one of the original nine trustees of Dickinson College, a position he would hold until his death.

William Irvine died at Philadelphia, Pennsylvania, on July 29, 1804, at the age of sixty-two. He is buried in the Old Swedes Church Cemetery, in Philadelphia.

JACKSON, HENRY—(Massachusetts) Henry Jackson was born at Boston, Suffolk County, Massachusetts, in October of 1747. Little is known of Jackson's early life or education.

On December 7, 1776, he was appointed lieutenant colonel of General John Hancock's Boston Independent Corps. On January 12, 1777, Jackson was commissioned colonel of the 16th Massachusetts Regiment. With this regiment, Jackson participated in the Monmouth Campaign, and fought in Rhode Island in 1778, and at Springfield, New Jersey, in June of 1780. On January 1, 1781, he transferred to the 9th Massachusetts Regiment, and served in the Northern Department. On January 1, 1783, he transferred to the 4th Massachusetts Regiment. On September 30, 1783, the Continental Congress bestowed the rank of brevet brigadier general upon Jackson, and he was retained as colonel of the Continental, or 1st American Regiment, from November of 1783 until June 20, 1784. In 1792, he was promoted to the rank of major general in the Massachusetts Militia, serving until 1796. In 1799, Jackson married Hannah Swett, and the couple had three children together.

Henry Jackson died at Boston, Massachusetts, on January 4, 1809, at the age of sixty-one.[1]

JACKSON, MICHAEL — (Massachusetts)

Michael Jackson was born at Newton, Massachusetts, on December 18, 1734. Little is known of his early education or upbringing. Jackson served as a lieutenant in the French and Indian War. In 1759, Jackson married Ruth Parker, and the couple had five children together. He later became captain of a company of Minutemen, at Newton, and took part in the initial fighting of the Revolution at Lexington and Concord on April 19, 1775. He was subsequently commissioned a major in Gardner's Massachusetts Regiment and took part in the battle of Bunker Hill, where he killed a British officer in a personal encounter, being wounded himself in the engagement. On January 1, 1776, he was commissioned a lieutenant colonel in the 8th Massachusetts, otherwise designated the 16th Continental Infantry Regiment. Jackson was wounded for a second time at the battle of Montressor's Island, on September 24, 1776. Jackson, with his regiment, took part in the battles of Trenton and Princeton, the Saratoga Campaign, the defense of Philadelphia, and the battle of Monmouth. On June 12, 1783, Jackson transferred to the 3rd Massachusetts Regiment, and commanded that unit till the end of hostilities. On September 30, 1783, the Continental Congress bestowed the rank of brevet brigadier general upon Jackson in recognition of his lengthy service to the Patriot cause. Jackson was officially discharged from the army on November 3, 1783.

The Jackson family all did their part to ensure the cause of liberty. Michael had five brothers and five sons who all served in the army during the war. Following the end of the Revolution, Jackson returned to Newton, where he resumed private life.

Michael Jackson died at Newton on April 10, 1801, in his sixty-seventh year. He was buried at the Old East Parish Burying Ground, in Newton, Massachusetts.[1]

JOHNSON, THOMAS, JR. — (Maryland)

Thomas Johnson, Jr., was born at St. Leonard's, Calvert County, Maryland, on November 4, 1732. At an early age, the family moved to Annapolis. Johnson was tutored at home, and received a fine primary education, studied law, and was admitted to the Maryland Bar in 1760. In 1762, he was elected to the Maryland legislature as a representative from Anne Arundel County, and he served consecutively until 1773. Johnson had been a leading detractor of the Stamp Act, and in 1765 had instructed the agent of the province in London to exert all opposition to any scheme to tax Maryland. In 1766, Johnson married Ann Jennings.

The rising tensions between the Colonies and Great Britain spurred Johnson to even greater efforts for the Patriot cause. In 1773, he was a member of the Annapolis Committee of Correspondence, and in 1774 and 1775 he was elected to represent Maryland in the Continental Congress. In 1774, Congress had entrusted Johnson with the task of drafting a formal address to the king, citing the grievances of the Colonies. It was Thomas Johnson who put forth on the floor of Congress the nomination for George Washington to be selected as commander in chief of the Continental Army. Johnson and Washington were close personal friends and business associates. During 1775, he also served on the Virginia Committee of Safety and as a delegate in the Virginia Provincial Congress. In 1776, he was once again elected to the Continental Congress, but delayed attending due to pressing matters in the Virginia legislature, and thus did not become a signer of the Declaration of Independence. In January of that same year, Johnson was commissioned to be the senior brigadier general of the Virginia Militia forces.

During Washington's retreat through New Jersey in 1776–77, the general sent an urgent appeal to Johnson for reinforcements, stating that he had not enough men to fight the enemy or to run away. Johnson immediately raised 1,800 militia from the western counties of Maryland and led them in person to Washington's relief. On February 14, 1777, he was elected to be the first governor of the state of Maryland, and was re-elected for two additional terms, leaving office in 1780. At the end of his term as governor, Johnson was elected deputy to the Virginia Provincial Congress, and was elected to the Maryland House of Delegates, where he introduced a bill to confiscate all British property in the state. In 1781, he used his influence to ensure that Maryland ratified the Articles of Confederation. That same year, he was re-elected to the Continental Congress, serving until 1787. In 1789, Johnson was a member of the Maryland convention to ratify the Federal Constitution. On April 20, 1790, he was appointed chief judge of the Maryland General Court, resigning from that post in 1791 when President Washington appointed him to be an associate judge on the United States Supreme Court. Upon the resignation of Chief Justice John Rutledge, Washington pressed Johnson to assume the position, but he declined. Johnson has the distinction of writing the very first decision of the U.S. Supreme Court in the case of Georgia v. Brailsford. He resigned his seat on the court in February of 1793, citing poor health as the reason. Washington offered him the position of secretary of state in 1795, but he declined, and was subsequently appointed as one of the commissioners to lay out the city of Washington. President John Adams appointed Johnson chief judge of the Territory of Washington, D.C., in 1801, and he also served as a member of the Board of Commissioners of the Federal City.

Thomas Johnson died at his home, Rosehill, in Frederick, Maryland, on October 26, 1819, at the age of eighty-six. He was buried in the All Saints Episcopal Churchyard Cemetery, but was later reinterred in the Mount Olivet Cemetery, in Frederick, Maryland.[1]

JONES, ALLEN—(**North Carolina**) Allen Jones was born in Halifax County, North Carolina, in 1739. He was the younger brother of William Jones. His father, Robin, was one of the lord proprietors of North Carolina. Allen was educated at Eaton, in England, and though his cultural ties were with Great Britain, he became an ardent Patriot upon returning to North Carolina. Allen was elected to be a delegate to the provincial conventions that met in New Berne in August of 1775 and in Halifax in April of 1776, and was subsequently commissioned a brigadier general in the state militia.

In 1779, he was elected to the Continental Congress, serving until 1780. Following the end of the war, Allen was elected to represent Northampton County in the North Carolina Senate from 1784 to 1787. In 1788, he was a delegate to the Constitutional Convention that assembled in Hillsborough. Allen favored a strong Federal government, in opposition to his brother, William, who was a strong advocate of state's rights, and actively campaigned for the adoption of the Federal Constitution in the state.

Allen Jones died in Northampton County, North Carolina, on November 10, 1798, in his fifty-ninth year.[1]

JONES, WILLIAM—(**North Carolina**) William Jones (also known as Wylie Jones) was born at Halifax County, North Carolina, in 1731. He was the older brother of Allen Jones. William was educated at Eaton, in England. Jones became a planter, and owned Grove Plantation. He married Mary Montford, the daughter of Colonel Joseph Montford. In 1775, he was appointed president of the North Carolina Committee of Safety, and as such virtually served as the governor of the state. As the leading political official in the state, William was commissioned a brigadier general in the North Carolina Militia, commensurate with his standing as commander in chief of the state forces. Like Allen, he did not command in the field, and the position was largely administrative.

In 1776, William was a delegate to the North Carolina Constitutional Convention, and served in the House of Commons from 1776 to 1778. In 1780, he succeeded his brother Allen as a delegate to the Continental Congress. Following the end of the war, William was elected to be a delegate to the Constitutional Convention in Philadelphia in 1787, but declined to attend. In 1788, he was a delegate to the Constitutional Convention that met at Hillsborough, and was largely responsible for the rejection of the Federal Constitution by that state. It is stated that the noted American naval hero, John Paul Jones, whose real name was John Paul. added the surname of Jones after staying with William Jones, and that it was Jones who recommended him when he offered his services to Congress. When the Marquis de Lafayette visited Halifax, in 1825, he spent time with Jones at Grove Plantation.

William Jones died at Raleigh, North Carolina, in 1801, in his seventieth year.[1]

KNOX, HENRY—(**Massachusetts**) Henry Knox was born in Boston, Massachusetts, the seventh of ten children, on July 25, 1750. He received a good primary education, at the Boston Latin Grammar School, and was particularly fond of reading. When his father, William, died, at the age of fifty, Henry quit school and became the sole support for his mother, taking a job as a clerk and bookbinding apprentice in a Boston bookstore. At the age of twenty-one, he opened a bookstore of his own, and earned a modest but comfortable living. He married Lucy Flucker (n.d.), and the couple had nine children. An avid reader himself, Knox showed a particular inclination for history, specifically for artillery usage in military history.[1]

In 1772, Knox joined the Boston Grenadier Corps, where he exhibited the military talent he had gained through his love of reading. During the initial phases of the Revolution, he served as a volunteer in the battle of Bunker Hill. When Washington arrived in Boston to take command of the Continental forces, he met Knox and was immediately impressed with his knowledge of artillery and artillery tactics. Washington asked for his opinion as to what the army should do in regard to the artillery arm, and Knox responded that they should move the cannon that had been taken when Fort Ticonderoga was captured to Boston, and use it against the British. Washington appointed Knox to be a colonel of artillery, and charged him with carrying out the proposition. Knox undertook his mission amid the snows and storms common to a New England winter. With great difficulty, he managed to drag the cannon from Fort Ticonderoga to Boston, using ox carts to accomplish the task, and when he had completed his assignment, 50 cannon from the fort lined the ridge of Dorchester Heights, poised to shell the British out of Boston. Despite his youth, he had won the respect of Washington, and was placed in command of all the artillery of the Continental Army. Congress appointed him brigadier general and chief of artillery on December 27, 1776. He would serve in the capacity of chief of artillery throughout the entire war.[2]

General Knox performed splendidly in all of the battles of Washington's army, including Trenton, Princeton, Brandywine, and Jamestown, but perhaps his greatest service came at Monmouth, where the British officers cited the fire of his guns as being the reason why the Patriots were able to defeat an army larger than their own. With fearful precision, his gunners mowed down the ranks of the attacking British. Washington gave him special recognition when he reported the victory to Congress, and praised his skill in handling the artillery of the army.

In 1777, Congress had come to the ill-advised decision to replace Knox with a French officer, the Count de Courdray, a move that brought forth an outcry of resentment from the army, and even threatened to evoke the resignation of other high ranking officers, General Sullivan among them. Knox was a trusted lieutenant of Washington, and one of the most beloved officers in the army, and his peers were outraged by orders for his replacement. In the end, the controversy was averted due to the fact that de Courdray died prior to the date he was to have assumed command of the artillery, and Knox was retained.

On March 22, 1782, Knox was promoted to the rank of major general in the Continental Army, with the commission to rank being dated November 15, 1781.[3]

General Knox would perform his last service to the army during the Revolution at the siege of Yorktown, where his artillery played a key role in convincing Lord Cornwallis to surrender his army. To him would fall the mantle of command, following the resignation of George Washington, and on December 23, 1783, he was named commander in chief of the American Army, and charged with making the arrangements for the disbanding of the army. In the course of the war, he had risen from a volunteer, at Bunker Hill, to the top position of the American military. This self-schooled soldier embodied the epitome of the citizen-soldier that has come to symbolize the American fighting spirit.

Following the end of hostilities, Knox became the first secretary of war under the Federal Constitution, serving from 1785 to 1794. He then retired from public service to his home in Thomastown, Maine, where he had built a

Henry Knox

Thaddeus Koscuiszko (courtesy National Archives)

magnificent home on the bank of the Georges River. On October 25, 1806, he died as a result of a chicken bone lodging in his throat. He is buried in the Elm Grove Cemetery, Thomastown, Knox County (named in his honor), Maine.[4]

KOSCIUSZKO, THADDEUS—(Poland)
Thaddeus Kosciuszko was born in Poland on February 4, 1746, to an aristocratic family of modest means. He received a good education at the local church school, and at the age of nineteen he decided to pursue a career in the military. Kosciuszko enrolled in the Royal Military School, in Warsaw, graduating in 1769, with a commission of captain. His academic performance had been such as to compel King Stanislaw August to give him a scholarship to go to Paris for advanced studies in engineering and artillery. After five years in France, he returned to Poland to find much of the country under the control of Russia, Prussia, and Austria. With his own country being occupied, he decided to travel to America and offer his services to the Patriot cause.

Kosciuszko traveled to Philadelphia, arriving there in August of 1776. When he presented himself to Congress, seeking a commission, he was the first person from Europe to offer his services to the American cause. On October 16, 1776, the Continental Congress bestowed the rank of colonel of engineers upon him, and assigned him to General Horatio Gates' Northern Department. Kosciuszko's engineering skills were largely responsible for the American victory at the battle of Saratoga the following year. His next assignment was to supervise the fortification of West Point, New York. Kosciuszko spent over two years creating a fortified camp that would deprive the British of the use of the Hudson River, and prevent the British army in New England from moving south on an overland route. Washington called West Point "the key to America," and Kosciuszko possibly performed his greatest service to the nation with the stronghold he built at that place. Under his supervision, West Point became known as the American Gibraltar. West Point would later become the site of the United States Military Academy, and the first monument erected on the grounds was to Thaddeus Kosciuszko.¹

Following the completion of the works at West Point, Kosciuszko was sent to the Army of the South, where his engineering expertise was used to help facilitate the movements of the army across rivers and through swamps. After the completion of the victorious siege of Charleston, Kosciuszko was given the honor of leading the Continental troops into that city. This was the final point of British resistance in the south. On October 13, 1783, Congress rewarded his services by promoting him to the rank of brigadier general. George Washington showed his personal gratitude by awarding him the Cincinnati Order Medal and giving him pistols and a sword as tokens of esteem for his outstanding contributions to the Revolution.²

With the war over, Kosciuszko returned to Poland in 1784 in an effort to help his own country gain its independence from Russia, Prussia, and Austria. He became a leader of the 1794 insurrection in which Warsaw and Wilno were liberated after the victory at the battle of Raclawice. The revolt was eventually put down, however, and Kosciuszko was wounded and taken prisoner by the Russians. When he was released by the Russians, it was with the condition that he leave Poland forever, so he returned to America in August of 1797. Kosciuszko settled in Philadelphia. In 1815, he was invited to the Congress of Vienna, and he journeyed to Europe hoping to effect concessions from that body that would restore Polish autonomy. Before leaving America, Kosciuszko appointed Thomas Jefferson, whom he had become great friends with, to be the executor of his will, and directed that all money coming from his estate be used to buy slaves and give them their freedom. The Vienna Congress refused to restore Poland, however, and Kosciuszko went to live with friends in Switzerland, where he died on October 15, 1817. His body was returned to Poland and buried in a crypt in Cracow's Wawel Cathedral. Upon hearing of his death, Thomas Jefferson stated: "He was a pure son of liberty as I have ever known, and of that liberty which is to go to all, not to the few and rich alone."

LACEY, JOHN—(Pennsylvania) John Lacey was born at Wrightstown, Bucks County, Pennsylvania, on December 4, 1752. A native of Buckingham Township, Bucks County, Pennsylvania, Lacey served as a captain in the Pennsylvania Associators in 1775. In 1776, he was commissioned captain in Anthony Wayne's 4th Pennsylvania Battalion, and served with Wayne along the Canadian frontier. In 1777, he served as a colonel in the Pennsylvania Militia, and fought at the battle of Germantown, on October 4, 1777, and at Gulph's Mill, in December of 1777. Lacey was commissioned a brigadier general in the Pennsylvania Militia on January 9, 1778. General Washington was so impressed with his leadership abilities and courage that he personally made him a brigadier general in the Continental service on January 28, 1778. On May 1, 1778, Lacey commanded the American forces at the battle of Crooked Billet, Pennsylvania. Lacey had been assigned to try to prevent the British from receiving supplies from the area, and the resulting battle was the only independent campaign to be assigned to the Pennsylvania State Militia during the war. Lacey had been promised a force of 1,000 men by the Pennsylvania Supreme Executive Council, but he rarely had more than a few hundred. During the battle, the British force, under the command of Lieutenant Colonel Robert Abercromby, numbered approximately 850 troops. Lacey had 300 effectives in his command. Lacey's force was surprised, and he lost one-third of his command in being routed from the field.

On January 18, 1781, Lacey married Anastasia Reynolds, and the couple had three children together. Following the end of the war, Lacey removed his family to New Jersey, where he developed Ferrago Forge, on the middle branch of Cedar Creek, in 1809. A settlement sprang up around the iron forge, called Ferrago Village. In 1810, Lacey built a road from the forge to Forked River, in order to ship the iron produced.

John Lacey died at Pemberton, Burlington County, New Jersey, on February 17, 1814, at the age of sixty-one. Lacey Park and Lacey Township, New Jersey, are both named in his honor.¹

LAFAYETTE, MARIE-JOSEPH PAUL YVES ROCH GILBERT DU MOTIER, MARQUIS DE—(France) The Marquis de Lafayette was born at Chavaniac, Auvergne, France, on September 6, 1757. His father was killed in the battle of Minden in 1759, and his mother and grandfather died in 1770, leaving him a wealthy orphan at an early age. In 1771, at the age of thirteen, Lafayette joined the French army, gaining assignment to an infantry regiment. By 1773, he had transferred to a regiment of dragoons. That same year, Lafayette married Adrienne Francoise de Nosailles, when he was still only fifteen years old. In 1774, he was promoted to the rank of captain in the French army. Lafayette became interested in the American rebellion against the British, and in December of 1776, he offered his services to Silas Deane, the American ambassador to France. Deane accepted in the name of Congress, and Lafayette left for America, arriving in April of 1777. The Continental Congress commissioned him a major general, and accepted his offer to serve without pay, or a specific command. Lafayette fought with distinction at the battle of Brandywine, in September of 1777, and his leadership at Valley Forge, during the winter encampment, brought him to Washington's attention, resulting in his being named to command a proposed expedition against Canada, to take place in 1778. The Canadian campaign was later abandoned, however. Lafayette greatly admired George Washington, who became somewhat of a father figure for the young man. Washington was equally taken with the young Frenchman, and the two became lifelong friends and supporters. Lafayette distinguished himself once more at the battle of Barren Hill, in May of 1778, and led a division at the battle of Monmouth. He then took part in the Newport, Rhode Island, campaign in July and August of 1778, before returning home to France, where he received a promotion to colonel in the French army, and was instrumental in planning for the French Expeditionary Force that was being amassed to come to America. Upon his return to America, Lafayette was given command of the Virginia Light Troops, in April of 1780. He was also a member of the military tribunal that tried Major John Andre for his part in Benedict Arnold's conspiracy, in September of 1780. In March of 1781, he was sent to Virginia, where he opposed Benedict Arnold's raid there. With the arrival of Lord Cornwallis' main body, Lafayette was forced to elude the British attempts to bring his badly outnumbered force to battle. He co-operated with General Anthony Wayne at the battle of Green Spring, on July 6, 1781. In September and October of 1781, Lafayette played a major role in the Yorktown campaign, subsequently returning to France, where he was made a major general in the French army. In 1784, he returned to America, whereupon he toured the country for six months.

When Lafayette returned to France, he was appointed to the French Assembly of Notables in 1787. He then represented Auvergne in the Estates-General of 1789. In 1789, he was appointed commander of the newly created French National Guard. During the French Revolution, Lafayette was torn by his divided loyalties and his sense of right and wrong. In October of 1789, he was responsible for saving the royal family from the mob in Paris. In 1791, he was promoted to the rank of lieutenant general and assigned to command the French Army

Marquis de Lafayette (courtesy United States Army War College)

of the Center, in 1792. Later that year he came under the suspicions of the Jacobins, and was forced to flee France, taking refuge in Belgium. While there, he was captured by the Austrians, and then by the Prussians. being held a prisoner from 1792 to 1797. Upon gaining his release, Lafayette returned to France, but distrusting Napoleon, he retired to his wife's estate at La Grange-Bleneau. He remained in retirement until 1815, when he once again entered public life in support of Napoleon's liberal constitution. He subsequently aided in securing Napoleon's second abdication of the throne. In 1818, he was elected to the Chamber, as a leader of the liberal opposition party, and served until 1824. That year, he made a trip to America, where he was warmly received as the last surviving major general of the Revolution. After a year in America, Lafayette returned to France, where he was once more elected to the Chamber, in 1827. In 1830, he was appointed to command of the National Guard, during the revolution against Charles X.[1]

Lafayette died at Paris, on May 20, 1834, at the age of seventy-six. He was buried in Le Jardin de Picpus Cemetery, in Paris. In July of 2002, the United States Congress voted to make Lafayette an honorary citizen of the United States, an honor that has been bestowed upon only six people in the history of the nation. The state of Maryland had granted Lafayette citizenship in 1785. Lafayette was still only nineteen years old when Silas Deane accepted his offer of service and promised him a commission as a brigadier general in the American army, making him the youngest officer to be promoted to that rank in the Revolution.[2]

LAWSON, ROBERT—(**Virginia**) Robert Lawson was born in Prince George County, Virginia, on January 23, 1748. He married Sarah Merriweather on November 30, 1769, and the couple had one child together.

In February of 1776, Lawson was commissioned to the rank of major in the 4th Virginia Regiment. On August 19 of that same year, he

The Battle of Guilford Court House (courtesy United States Military History Institute)

was promoted to the rank of colonel and given command of the regiment. His first service was in defending the Chesapeake Bay area from the incursions of Lord Dunmore and his British Army. Lawson and his regiment then joined Washington's main army where they participated in the campaign in northern New Jersey, and took part in the battles of Brandywine and Germantown, Trenton and Princeton. Though the regiment continued to serve with Washington's main force, Lawson was no longer with them. He resigned his commission on December 17, 1777. Lawson was subsequently commissioned a brigadier general in the Virginia Militia, and served in that capacity to the close of the war. All of his late war activities took place in the south, and he exercised a command, in General Greene's army, in the battle of Guilford Court House, North Carolina, on March 15, 1781, where he fought with distinction.

Robert Lawson died in Richmond, Virginia, in April of 1805, at the age of fifty-six.[1]

LEARNED, EBENEZER—(Massachusetts) Ebenezer Learned was born at Oxford, Massachusetts, on April 18, 1728. Learned received a good education, much of it coming from his own love of books and reading. Though a prominent and well-respected citizen, Learned was not much in the public eye in the years before the Revolution. He did serve a term in the Massachusetts provincial legislature, and was a captain in the local militia. Serving as an officer in the militia was somewhat of a tradition in his family, as his father, also named Ebenezer, had been a militia colonel. In 1749, he married Jerusha Baker, and the couple had nine children together.

Learned became an early advocate of the Patriot cause, and in 1774 he was elected to the Provincial Congress, held at Concord, that decided that Massachusetts must take a firm stance in protecting its liberties. Learned was not at the Provincial Congress when news came of the fighting at Lexington and Concord. He immediately gathered the local militia and marched them to Cambridge, where he offered his services to General Artemas Ward. During the battle of Bunker Hill, Learned was charged with holding the American position at Roxbury, and though his command came under fire, it did not participate in the general engagement.

On January 1, 1776, Learned was commissioned colonel of the 3rd Continental Infantry Regiment. With that regiment, Learned took part in the siege of the British at Boston. When the British evacuated Boston, Learned was given the honor of unbarring the gates to the city for the American army to enter. His regiment was also charged with keeping watch on the British fleet to ensure that they were indeed leaving.

Learned's regiment took part in the battles in New York, in 1776, but it did so without its commander. Poor health had forced Learned to return to his home to recuperate. He was anxious to get back to active duty, and news of the army's victories at Trenton and Princeton furthered his anxiety to return. While he was home, news came that the Continental Congress had promoted him to the rank of brigadier general. In the spring of 1777 Learned was ordered north, with his command, to try to protect the militia at Fort Edward and Fort Anne from General Burgoyne's advancing army. At Fort Stanwix, the British force, under the command of St. Leger, called off their attacks and retreated when they received word that Learned and his troops were advancing to the relief of the garrison. Learned performed well in the Saratoga Campaign, and both he and his men were publicly commended for their actions.

After the British surrender at Saratoga Learned was ordered to rejoin Washington's main army. He spent the winter of 1777 at Valley Forge, where he was in command of a division. On March 28, 1778, Learned resigned his commission due to failing health. He returned home to Oxford to recuperate. In 1779, he was a delegate to the Massachusetts state constitutional convention, and he subsequently served as a member of the state legislature, selectman of Oxford, justice of the peace, assessor, and moderator of Oxford town meetings.

Ebenezer Learned died at Oxford, on April 1, 1801, at the age of seventy-two.[1]

LEE, CHARLES—(England) Charles Lee was born in England in 1731. The exact day and month are unknown. He was the youngest son of General John Lee. Charles' early education was achieved partly in England and partly in Switzerland, where he showed a strong inclination for military tactics, and at the tender age of eleven, he received a commission in his majesty's service. At the age of twenty-four, he was commissioned a captain and placed in charge of a company of grenadiers.

In 1757, Lee's regiment was sent to America, where it took part in the expedition against Louisburg. The French position was determined to be too strong to assault, however, and Lee's regiment was sent to New York, while the army prepared for a future attempt against the stronghold. Lee was stationed at Schenectady, where he became thoroughly acquainted with the Mohawk warriors who resided in the area. Lee became a favorite of the Indians, and was eventually adopted into one of the tribes with the Indian name of Ounewaterika, or Boiling Water.

Lee next accompanied Ambercromby's failed expedition against Fort Ticonderoga, where he led his company of grenadiers in the fateful, bloody charge, receiving a serious wound in the side that required his being carried from the field. Lee was sent to Albany to recuperate, and the next winter he was stationed at Long Island. While there, he offended an army surgeon, who responded by making slanderous statements about Lee. Lee, when he heard of the falsehoods being spread by the doctor, avenged himself by giving the man a severe beating. The surgeon determined to get even with Lee, but he was not inclined to challenge that officer to a duel. Instead, he settled on a plan to ambush Lee and murder him. When he met the young captain, he seized the bridle of his horse, pointed a pistol at his chest, and fired. The flash of the pistol caused the horse to rear, and the bullet caused only a bruise to Lee, not penetrating the skin. Undeterred, the assailant then produced a second pistol and attempted to finish the job, but a companion of Lee's succeeded in knocking the weapon aside. The surgeon was subsequently forced to leave the army in disgrace.

Charles Lee

Lee's next service in the French and Indian War was in besieging the French stronghold at Fort Niagara. In 1760, he accompanied General Amherst's successful expedition against Montreal that all but ended the war in America. With the war over, Lee returned to England, where he received a commission as lieutenant colonel for his services.

Assigned to General John Burgoyne's brigade, stationed on the river Tagus, he took part in the British attempts to repel the Spanish invasion of Portugal. Lee distinguished himself in command of a detachment sent to rout a portion of the Spanish army at Villa Velha.

Upon his return from Spain, Lee entered politics, but he enjoyed little success. He violently attacked many of those in power, alienating them and making many enemies in the government. Lee spent time in Poland and Turkey, while the crisis over the Stamp Act was going on in England and America. He returned home to seek a promotion in rank, but the politicians still remembered his scathing attacks and denied promotion. He then went to Poland again, where he was made a major general in the Russian army, though he never actually served in that capacity. Instead, he caught a fever that incapacitated him for nearly a year.

When he returned to England, in 1772, he once again assailed the politicians, this time on behalf of the Americans, whose cause he had espoused. In 1773, Lee arrived in America and began a trip through the southern states. Whether he actually supported the American cause or just wanted a reason to quarrel with the politicians in England is not known, but his stand for America, combined with his past experience, soon made him one of the most prominent men in the colonies.

When the Continental Congress formed the army, Lee was the second officer it commissioned to be a major general, on June 17, 1775. Lee submitted his resignation to the British army, and forfeited his estates in England. Congress agreed to compensate him for any losses he incurred in supporting the cause, however. Lee accompanied Washington to Cambridge, where he was given command of the left wing of the army. In December of 1775, he was sent to Rhode Island, where he supervised the construction of fortifications at Newport. In January of 1776, he was ordered to New York to disarm the Tories at Long Island, and to fortify the position. Lee built four redoubts in the city, and barricaded the streets. He also captured a number of leading Tories and forced them to take an oath of allegiance.[1]

British activities in the south prompted Congress to order Lee's services there, and he hastened to Charleston, South Carolina, arriving in time for the British attack on the city. Once there, he allowed General Moultrie to retain command of the fort on Sullivan's Island, stationing himself at Haddrell's Point, too far away to be of any tactical support to Moultrie's force. The British fleet was defeated, and forced to sail away, but it was Moultrie who won fame for the victory, not Lee. After six months in Charleston, Lee was ordered to Philadelphia. General Artemas Ward had resigned his commission, making Lee second in command to Washington, himself. Lee hastened forth from Philadelphia, to join the main army, then at Harlem Heights, New York, where he took command of the right wing. He covered the retreat of the army, at White Plains, and commanded the corps that Washington left in New York when he and the rest of the army went to New Jersey to cope with General Howe. Washington's army was insufficient to deal with the British, however, and he ordered Lee to join him, as he retreated through New Jersey. Lee was slow in making the junction of forces, taking his time when speed was of the essence. While en route to join the main body, he was captured by a force of British dragoons at Baskenridge on December 13, 1776.[2]

The way in which Lee was captured gave rise to charges that it had been staged by him. He had established his headquarters three miles away from his army, in a secluded position, and with but little guard. Lee had been openly critical and contemptuous of Washington, feeling himself better qualified for the position of army commander, and it was felt that his tardiness in joining the main army was an attempt to allow Washington to be defeated while the forces were still separated. The British did not treat Lee as a prisoner of war. Instead, they considered him to be a deserter. Washington rose to Lee's defense, writing the British that if they harmed Lee in any way, he would retaliate against the Hessian officers he had captured at Trenton. In response to Washington's threat, the British allowed Lee to go to Europe, on parole, until he was eventually exchanged in May of 1778.

Once paroled, Lee rejoined the army and was reinstated to his old command. His next action was seen at the battle of Monmouth. Lee was decidedly against fighting that battle, feeling that the American army was not strong enough to face the British on an open field of battle, and should instead conduct a guerrilla campaign. During the battle, he retreated, with his wing of the army, when it did not appear necessary to do so, almost causing the Americans to suffer a terrible defeat. General Knox's artillery and General Wayne's infantry were largely responsible for saving the day from ruin. Washington retained Lee in command, willing to allow the whole matter to pass with a rebuke. Lee, on the other hand, could not get past the rebuke of Washington, or remarks made by other officers concerning his retreat. He wrote a sharp letter to Washington, and in reply, the latter finished his comments by stating that Lee was "guilty of a breach of orders and of misbehavior before the enemy, in not attacking them as he had been directed; and in making an unnecessary, disorderly, and shameful retreat." Further stung by Washington's response, Lee followed his first letter with a second that demanded to have his actions tried before a court-martial, saying, "You cannot afford me greater pleasure, sir, than in giving me an opportunity of showing to America the efficiency of her respective servants. I trust that the temporary power of office and the tinsel dignity attending it, will not be able, by all the mists they can raise, to effusate the bright rays of truth. In the mean time, your excellency can have no objection to my retiring from the army."

Lee's previous actions, combined with the insubordinate tone of his final letter, caused Washington to have him placed under arrest. He received the court-martial he had requested, and that tribunal found him guilty of disobeying orders, of making an unnecessary and disorderly retreat, and of disrespect to the commander in chief, and suspended him from the army for twelve months.

Lee could not accept the decision, and launched a series of invectives against Washington and Congress that eventually led to his being challenged to a duel by Colonel John Laurens, who took offense to the statements being made about the commander in chief. The duel was fought with pistols, and Lee was wounded. He then retired to his estate in Virginia, where he became something of a recluse. When the term of his suspension had expired, Lee heard that Congress intended to take away his commission, and he wrote that body a scathing letter of rebuke. The result was a response from Congress on January 10, 1780 that his services would no longer be needed with the army. Lee retired to his farm, but was so inefficient at its management that he was forced to sell the property to pay his debts. In the fall of 1782, he went to Baltimore to facilitate the sale of the farm when he was stricken with a fever that produced delirium. He went to Philadelphia, seeking medical attention, but the fever was beyond treatment.[3]

Charles Lee died in Philadelphia on October 2, 1782, at the age of fifty-one. He was buried in the Christ Episcopal Churchyard Cemetery, in Philadelphia. One of the leading generals in the army at the start of the war, he ended his career charged with improper actions and possible conspiracy against his commander and his adopted country.

LEWIS, ANDREW—(Ireland) Andrew Lewis was born in Ireland in 1720. In 1729, his family emigrated to America, settling in Virginia. As a young man, Lewis became well known as a frontiersman and surveyor, and in 1745 he assisted in surveying large tracts of land in the Cowpasture Valley. He married Elizabeth Govens, and the couple had seven children together. In 1751, Lewis surveyed 50,000 acres in the Greenbrier area of present day West Virginia, and discovered Lewis Spring, at which site the town of Lewisburg was established. He built a homestead, named Richfield, in Botecourt County (present day Roanoke County), near Salem.

In 1754, Lewis was commissioned a captain in George Washington's regiment of Virginia Militia. He was with Washington at Fort Necessity, Pennsylvania, the event that touched off the French and Indian War in America. He was later charged with supervising the construction of forts along the Greenbrier River, and was appointed county lieutenant of Augusta County. Lewis was captured by the French and held for thirteen months before being exchanged.

Andrew Lewis (courtesy United States Military History Institute)

In 1774, Lewis was commissioned a colonel in the Virginia Militia and given command of the men from Augusta County. With these troops, he marched 161 miles into Indian land and participated in the battle of Point Pleasant. Lewis and his 600 men were victorious in the battle, defeating the Shawnee warriors under the leadership of Chief Cornstalk. Lewis' brother, Charles, was killed in the fighting.

Lewis served as a representative of Botecourt County in the Virginia Conventions of the 1770s. On January 8, 1776, Lewis, who had been previously commissioned a brigadier general in the Virginia Militia, was placed in command of some 2,000 troops in eastern Virginia. The Continental Congress bestowed the rank of brigadier general on Lewis on March 1, 1776. On July 8–10, he engaged a combined army and navy force, under the command of Lord Dunmore, at the battle of Gwynn Island. Dunmore's military forces were entrenched on the island and were supported by a fleet of over 100 ships. Lewis used heavy artillery to win the battle. He moved his cannon into position on the night of July 7, and opened a barrage the following morning, the first round being from an 18-pounder garrison cannon, which struck Lord Dunmore's flagship. The heavy barrage caught the British completely by surprise, and Dunmore ordered the fleet to cut their anchors in order to escape it, but not before some twenty ships were lost to the fire. The expulsion of Dunmore and his army was a great victory in securing Virginia for the Patriot cause. Lewis resigned his commission in the Continental Army on April 15, 1777, though he continued to serve as a general in the Virginia Militia.

Andrew Lewis died in Bedford, Virginia, on his way home from Richmond, as the result of a fever, on September 25, 1781, in his sixty-first year. He was originally buried at his home, on the grounds of Richfield. Just prior to the end of the 19th Century, the Daughters of the American Revolution had his remains moved to the East Hill Cemetery, in Salem.[1]

LEWIS, FIELDING—(**Virginia**) Fielding Lewis was born in Warner Hall, Gloucester County, Virginia, on July 7, 1725, the son of Colonel John Lewis, a landholder and merchant in the Fredericksburg area. In 1746, he married Catharine Washington, daughter of John Washington, and the couple had three children together before Catharine died as a result of childbirth in 1749. Lewis then married Betty Washington, George Washington's only sister, in 1750, and the couple would have eleven children. In 1775, Lewis built a plantation home on 1,300 acres of what is now downtown Fredericksburg, Virginia, later named Kenmore House by a subsequent owner.

Lewis was a long-standing representative in the Virginia House of Burgesses, serving some twelve terms in the years leading up to the Revolutionary War. He was present in 1765 when Patrick Henry gave his famous speech against the Stamp Act stating, "If this be treason, make the most of it." He also served as a magistrate in Fredericksburg, as well as being a member of the local Committee of Safety.

At the beginning of the war, Lewis was a colonel in the state service and commanded the Spotsylvania County Militia. Though he was by no means a military man, and commanded in no pitched battles, Lewis was instrumental in supplying food and clothing to the troops, and for seeing to the needs of the wounded. In 1776, he was responsible for constructing and superintending a large arms manufactory, known as Gunny Green, or the Fredericksburg Gunnery, and for providing saltpeter, sulphur, powder and lead for the manufacture of ammunition. The arms factory was the first such established in America, and was reported to have produced twenty muskets, with bayonets, per week. Lewis used large sums of his own money to finance the operation of the armory. He was commissioned a brigadier general in the Virginia Militia in 1776, and assigned as the superintendent of the arsenal at Fredericksburg.

Lewis was also prominent in the building and outfitting of ships for the Virginia and Continental Navy. Among the most famous of these was the *Dragon*, built in Fredericksburg in 1777 and charged with the protection of the Rappahannock River. It was commanded by Captain Eleazor Callendar, who supervised its construction. The ship later saw duty in the Chesapeake Bay, and served throughout the Revolutionary War. Lewis' personal finances were ruined by the sums he advanced to the armory and shipbuilding efforts.

Fielding Lewis died while visiting his son, Fielding Jr., in Frederick County (now Clarke County), Virginia, on December 7, 1781, at the age of fifty-six. He was laid to rest at the St. George Church Cemetery, in Fredericksburg, where he and two of his children are buried beneath the steps of the church.[1]

LINCOLN, BENJAMIN—(Massachusetts)

Benjamin Lincoln was born on January 23, 1733, in the town of Hingham, Massachusetts. He was named for his grandfather, a prominent resident of Hingham, who had led a distinguished life and served as colonel of the local militia. Lincoln's family were farmers, and Benjamin, as the oldest son, was expected to assume his rightful spot in carrying on the family farm. The boy suffered from a slight speech impediment, and it was said that he spoke "with apparent difficulty, as though he were too full." He also suffered from narcolepsy, a condition that caused him to lapse into periods of deep sleep. It has been recorded that Lincoln would sometimes fall asleep during the dictation of dispatches, then awaken to carry on his dictation, as if nothing had happened. Though the affliction was an irritation to him, it did not impede him in any way, and though his nodding off became the source of many jests, he was always defended by those who knew him well.[1]

In 1756, Benjamin married Mary Cushing, of Pembroke, and later that year, they had a son, Benjamin Jr. At the age of twenty-five, in 1757, Benjamin was appointed to succeed his father as town clerk of Hingham, a post he would maintain for the next twenty years. He saw no action in the French and Indian War, though he served as adjutant of the 3rd Suffolk Militia. Even without the advantage of proving himself in battle, his performance of his duty was such that in 1763, upon the close of hostilities, he was appointed to the rank of major in the militia.

In 1765, Lincoln was elected as a selectman for Hingham, a position he would hold until 1771. In that same year, the passage of the Stamp Act served to polarize political activity in

Fielding Lewis (courtesy United States Military History Institute)

Benjamin Lincoln

the Colonies. The residents of Hingham tended to be more passive in their response than were those of neighboring Boston, and favored a peaceful redress of their grievances. By 1770, sentiments in Hingham had begun to change. Lincoln drafted a letter to the Boston Committee of Merchants that year indicating that the townspeople were in support of the non-importation agreement.

In 1772, Lincoln was elected as Hingham's representative to the General Court, and was also commissioned lieutenant colonel of the 2nd Suffolk Regiment. In 1774, he was elected chairman of the Hingham Committee of Correspondence. In that same year, he served as a delegate to the Provincial Congress. After the fighting at Lexington and Concord, Lincoln was appointed master of militia and assigned to the committees of supply and government organization in the Provincial Congress. During the absence of James Warren, he also served as acting president of that body.

In July of 1775 the newly elected House of Representatives declared itself to be the legal government of Massachusetts, and it elected a council of 28 members from among its ranks to perform the executive duties of government. Lincoln was appointed councilor of this body on July 28, 1775.[2]

Lincoln and his regiment took part in the siege of Boston, and in 1776 he was commissioned a brigadier general in the Massachusetts Militia, followed shortly there after by a promotion to the rank of major general. Once the British had been forced from Boston, Lincoln remained in the city, while Washington led his army south, towards New York. Lincoln had been entrusted with the duty of clearing the port completely of the British, and when this was accomplished, he joined Washington, then in New Jersey. He commanded the right wing of the American army at White Plains, on October 28, 1776.[3]

On February 19, 1777, Lincoln was commissioned a major general in the Continental army, and in July he was sent to assist in repelling General John Burgoyne's expedition into New York. Though Lincoln took no active part in the battle of Saratoga, his forces being held in reserve, he did receive a fearful wound as a result of that action. On October 8, the day after the battle, while riding forward to reconnoiter the ground, he was struck by a musket ball that shattered his leg, necessitating the removal of a portion of bone. After a long convalescence, the wound eventually healed, with one leg being shorter than the other, making him lame for the rest of his life.[4]

After his recovery, Lincoln was assigned to the Department of the South, and sent to command the defense of Charleston, South Carolina. On June 20, 1779, he fought the battle of Stono Ferry, and won a closely contested victory over the British. This was followed by a joint expedition, in conjunction with the fleet and army of D'Estaing, against the British held city of Savannah, Georgia. The works around the city were too formidable to carry by storm, so a siege was begun on September 23, 1779, that lasted until October 18 of that same year. The storm season was upon that region by that time, and D'Estaing, fearful of being able to maintain his fleet in their position, urged that an attempt be made to carry the works by storm. The ensuing attack met with dreadful carnage, and the French and American troops were repulsed by concentrated fire from British artillery and musketry, and the siege had to be abandoned.

After the repulse at Savannah, Lincoln retired to Charleston to prepare for an assault being mounted by British general Clinton against that city. Clinton had sailed, from New York, with an army of 10,000 veterans with which to seize the city. To oppose this, Lincoln had but 3,000 men in the Charleston defenses. He urgently petitioned Congress for re-enforcements, but few were available. Unable to mount a sufficient defense, Lincoln nevertheless decided that it was his duty to hold out to the last, and he determined to submit to a siege, refusing several demands from the enemy to surrender the post. From March 29 to May 12, 1780, his army withstood a constant barrage of British artillery. On May 12, as the British were preparing for a final attack on his works, Lincoln surrendered, in order to avoid a useless loss of life. He was taken, as a prisoner of war, to New York, where he was exchanged in November for British general Phillips. In 1781, he rejoined

Washington's army as it prepared to march for Yorktown.

Lincoln commanded one of the center divisions in Washington's army, during the siege of Yorktown, and performed admirably. When Lord Cornwallis determined to capitulate, Washington selected Lincoln to be the officer to receive the surrender, and Cornwallis presented his sword to the man who had so recently had to undergo the humiliation of just such a surrender, at Charleston. With the surrender of the British, at Yorktown, Lincoln's military career came to a close. He was placed in command of the War Department later that year, serving for two years, when he retired to his farm, and private life. He was called once more into his country's service in 1787, when he was appointed to command troops called out to put down Shay's Rebellion. In April of 1787, he was selected as lieutenant governor, and was subsequently chosen as a delegate to ratify the Constitution for the state of Massachusetts.[5]

Benjamin Lincoln died on May 9, 1810, at the age of seventy-seven, and was buried in the Old Ship Church Cemetery, in Hingham, Massachusetts.

LIPPITT, CHRISTOPHER—(Rhode Island) Christopher Lippitt was born in Cranston, Rhode Island, in 1744. He was descended from John Lippitt, one of the first settlers in Rhode Island, and a founder of the colonial government in 1647. Lippitt occupied a number of civil positions in his early life, and was elected to the Rhode Island General Assembly in 1765, at the age of twenty-one. He served successive terms in the state's legislature up to the outbreak of the Revolution. In 1766, he became a captain in the local militia, and that same year he was appointed as justice of the peace in Cranston.[1]

When the war broke out, Lippitt was officially commissioned lieutenant colonel of Babcock's Rhode Island State Regiment on January 15, 1776, though there is evidence that he was already performing the duties of that command in 1775.[2]

When the British threatened Prudence Island in 1775, Lippitt, with several companies of his regiment, was sent to defend it. He evacuated the inhabitants to the mainland, in the course of his duties, for their own safety.

In 1776, the commanding officer of his regiment, Colonel Babcock, was dismissed from the army for bad conduct, and Lippitt was elevated to the rank of colonel and given the command. In August of 1776, he became colonel of the 2nd Rhode Island Regiment. When General Washington ordered the 2nd Rhode Island Regiment to join the main army, Lippitt's militia commission, as colonel, was honored by a commission, at the same grade, in the Continental Army. Lippitt commanded his regiment at the battles of White Plains, Trenton, and Princeton. After wintering at Morristown, the regiment's term of enlistment expired in the spring of 1777. Most of the men in the regiment went home. In 1777, he was commissioned a brigadier general in the Rhode Island Militia, of Providence County. In this capacity, he fought under General Sullivan in the battle for Rhode Island. Following this campaign, Lippitt was again elected to the Rhode Island General Assembly, though he continued to hold his general's commission till the end of the war.

On March 23, 1777, amid the backdrop of the war, Lippitt married Waite Harris. The marriage would produce twelve children.

Lippitt was appointed judge of the Superior Court of Rhode Island at the war's end. He was a strong supporter of the Federal Constitution, and that support was responsible for costing him his political career. The Constitution faced a hard fight in Rhode Island, where opposition was so strong that the question remained in doubt for some time as to whether it would pass at all. In the end, Rhode Island did ratify the Constitution, but it was the last state in the Union to do so. Lippitt's Constitutional support was what caused him to be turned out of office by his constituents in 1787. He retired to private life.[3]

In 1807, Lippitt went into partnership with his brother, Charles, and four other men, and started the Lippitt Manufacturing Company, opening a cotton mill in the village of Centreville, Warwick, Rhode Island. This was only the third cotton mill to be opened in Rhode Island. The venture was immensely successful, with the company growing into one of the major cotton manufacturers of the 19th Century.⁴

Lippitt was a very religious man, and he spent part of his earnings building a Methodist Church, almost entirely at his own expense. During this time, he also joined the Peace Society.

Christopher Lippitt died on June 18, 1824, in Cranston, Rhode Island, at the age of eighty. He was buried in the family plot, which is now the historic Christopher Lippitt Lot, in Cranston, Warwick, Rhode Island.

LIVINGSTON, WILLIAM — (New York)

William Livingston was born at Albany, New York, on November 30, 1723. After receiving his primary education, Livingston attended Yale College, graduating from that institution in 1741. He then studied law, under James Alexander, and was admitted to the bar in 1748. He co-wrote Smith and Livingston's Laws of New York. In 1745, he married Susannah French, and the couple had five children together. In 1754, Livingston was appointed a commissioner to adjust the boundary line between New York and New Jersey. That same year, he was a member of a group that established the New York Society Library. In 1757, he wrote *A Review of Military Operations in North America*. From 1759 to 1761, Livingston served as a member of the New York Provincial Assembly. In 1774, he was elected to the Continental Congress as a delegate from New Jersey. Though he was still a member of Congress at the time the Declaration of Independence was approved, he was not able to sign that document, as he was in Elizabethtown, New Jersey, at the time, organizing forces to resist the British.

Livingston was commissioned brigadier general, and commander in chief, of the New Jersey Militia in 1776. His appointment as a general coincided with the fact that he had also been elected governor of New Jersey in 1776, a position he would hold until 1790. His rank as general and commander in chief came from the fact that he was the top executive officer in New Jersey's government.

Following the end of the war, Livingston was appointed to be a commissioner to superintend the construction of Federal buildings, in 1785. He was also offered a position as minister to The Hague that same year. He declined both positions, citing his advanced age as the reason. In 1786, he was instrumental in causing the state of New Jersey to ban the further importation of slaves. In 1787, Livingston was a delegate to the Constitutional Convention in Philadelphia, and he was a signer of the Constitution. Livingston was a member of the American Philosophical Society, and the American Academy of Arts and Sciences.

William Livingston died at Elizabethtown, New Jersey, on July 25, 1790, at the age of sixty-six. He was buried in the Trinity Churchyard Cemetery, in New York City.¹

MARION, FRANCIS — (South Carolina)

Francis Marion was born at Winyah, near Georgetown, South Carolina, in 1733. His ancestors were French Huguenots who had fled France to escape persecution. As a boy, Marion was slight of size, and was described as being of "feeble frame." By the age of twelve, however, his constitution had strengthened, and Marion began to show signs of the defiant spirit that would characterize his later life. When he was sixteen, he made a voyage to the West Indies and was shipwrecked, spending six days in a boat without food or water. Upon his return home, Marion took up farming at the home of his parents. When his father died shortly after his return from the sea, Marion remained at the family home a short time before removing to Belle Isle, near Eutaw Springs, where he established the home he would live in for the rest of his life.¹

In 1759, Marion received a commission as a lieutenant in Captain Moultrie's company of militia that was mobilized for an expedition against the Cherokee. He led an attack of thirty-one men on the Indian village of Etchoee, and was one of only ten men to escape unhurt. In 1761, he was promoted to the rank of captain and participated in a second expedition against the Cherokee. Following the war, Marion returned to his home and farm, where he took little part in public affairs. In 1775, he was elected as a delegate to the South Carolina Provincial Congress that voted to stand with the northern colonies in opposing

British aggression. At the outbreak of hostilities, Marion offered his services to the Patriot cause, and was soon commissioned a major in the militia, once again serving under Moultrie, who now held the rank of colonel. Marion served under Moultrie in the gallant defense of Charleston, South Carolina, in May of 1779.[2]

Marion is credited with firing the last shot of the battle, from Fort Moultrie, that struck the flagship of the British fleet in the cabin, killing several of the crew, and eventually causing the vessel to sink. Marion commanded Fort Moultrie for a brief time, and then took part in the fateful siege of Savannah, Georgia, in September and October of 1779. He returned to Charleston to help defend the city from the British siege from March to May of 1780, having been promoted, in the meantime, to the rank of lieutenant colonel. During the siege, Marion had one of his legs broken, which prevented him from being sent to Florida with the unwounded defenders of Charleston when the city fell to the British on May 12, 1780.

When his leg healed, Marion went to North Carolina, and was commissioned a brigadier general of South Carolina troops in August of 1780. It was during this time that Marion adopted the guerrilla tactics that would make him the scourge of the British army, and a legend in American history. Operating in the low country around the Pee Dee and Black Rivers, Marion would suddenly strike blows against unsuspecting detachments of British troops, only to then disappear again into the swampy lands that served as his base of operations. His partisan tactics were so successful that the British were forced to deploy an inordinate number of men to guard against his raids, thus reducing the number available for field operations. Marion became commonly known as the Swamp Fox, a name that would strike terror into the hearts of Redcoat garrison troops throughout the Carolinas.[3]

When General Gates was defeated at Camden, the military forces of the Southern Department all but ceased to exist, and Marion and his small band of partisans were left to face the British army virtually alone. The partisan band was undaunted by this turn of events. Instead of seeking safety from the overwhelming numbers of their enemy, they redoubled their efforts, and carried the war to the British.

At Black Mingo, Georgetown, and scores of other locations, Marion's partisans struck the British and inflicted severe losses to their ranks, keeping the invaders in a constant state of alarm. When Nathaniel Greene assumed command of the Southern Department, he at once recognized the contributions of Marion, and unlike his predecessor, General Gates, took measures to support and strengthen the operations of the Swamp Fox. Following the American victory at Guilford Courthouse, Greene was able to assume more of an offensive posture in the Carolinas, and Marion's men served to harass and confound the enemy throughout the countryside. His capture of Fort Motte, and the stores it contained, struck a serious blow at the British occupants of Charleston and Camden. At Quinby's Bridge, he assisted in routing a superior British force. Though the British won most of the battles fought during Greene's Southern Campaign, they were never able to eliminate the American forces, or subdue the

Francis Marion

countryside. The continual harassment from bands such as Marion's led to Cornwallis eventually deciding to change his base of operations to North Carolina and Virginia, leading to the Yorktown Campaign that sealed his doom.

Following the end of the war, Marion returned to his farm to once more take up the life of a quiet farmer. He was elected to the South Carolina Senate, where an incident took place that fully shows the measure of the man. The South Carolina legislature had passed a bill exonerating partisan commanders for any excesses they might have committed during the war, stating that they had been acting under extreme circumstances that were not covered by the statutes of civil law. When Marion heard of the bill, he immediately demanded that his name be removed from the list of protected officers, secure in the knowledge that his actions, during the fighting, had been of such an honorable nature that they did not require protection from prosecution. "If I have given any occasion for complaint, I am ready to answer in property and person," he said. "If I have wronged any man, I am willing to make him restitution. If in a single instance in the course of my command, I have done that which I cannot fully justify, justice requires that I should suffer for it."

Marion was offered command of Fort Johnson, at Charleston, in recognition of his services to the state, but he declined to accept the position. Instead, he married Mary Videau and retired to his plantation.

Francis Marion died at his home, at Belle Isle, on February 27, 1795, in his sixty-fifth year. He was buried in the Belle Island Plantation Cemetery, in Berkeley County, South Carolina. The city of Marion, and Marion County, South Carolina, are both named in his honor.[4]

MATHEWS, GEORGE—(Virginia) George Mathews was born in Augusta County, Virginia, on August 30, 1739. As a young man, Mathews entered into business with his brother, Sampson, that included land speculation, as well as mercantile and agricultural operations. The brothers eventually acquired vast holdings, stretching from Staunton, Virginia, to the Greenbrier district of western Virginia. In 1757, Mathews became captain of the local militia company that was raised to fight against the Indian incursions being brought about by the French and Indian War. He also led a company of militia at the battle of Point Pleasant on October 10, 1774.[1]

When the Revolution began, Mathews was commissioned colonel of the 9th Virginia Regiment on March 4, 1776. With this regiment, Mathews took part in the operations in the Chesapeake Bay area and in the defense of Philadelphia. At the battle of Germantown, on October 4, 1777, virtually his entire regiment was killed or captured by the British. Mathews was reported to have received nine bayonet wounds himself before being taken captive by the enemy. He was held in close confinement aboard a British prison ship in New York Harbor for over four years, not being released until December 5, 1781. On December 21, he joined General Nathaniel Greene's army as commander of the 3rd Virginia Regiment, and served for the remainder of the war with this unit. On September 30, 1783, the Continental Congress bestowed the rank of brevet brigadier general upon him for his service and sacrifice to the cause.[2]

In January of 1783 Mathews petitioned the legislature of Georgia for a tract of 200,000 acres on which he planned to settle 30 to 100 Virginia families, but the assembly refused to bestow such a large portion of land. Mathews then opted to purchase a tract of land in the Goose Pond region of Wilkes County, near the Broad River, and received additional adjacent land as a bounty for his Revolutionary War service. He returned to Virginia, where he was able to persuade a number of families to relocate their homes to Georgia. Mathews moved his family to his property in Georgia in 1785, and by 1787 was justice and commissioner for the new town of Washington. In that same year, he also won election to the Georgia legislature. The legislature then elected him to be governor of the state from 1787 to 1788. The year of 1787 was a busy one for Mathews, as he also served as a delegate to the Georgia Convention to ratify the Federal Constitution. Following the ratification of that document, Mathews was elected to the United States House of Representatives in 1788. In 1793, he was once again elected governor of Georgia. In 1795, he signed the Yazoo Land Bill, which opened western lands to the Mississippi River to speculators. This measure was extremely unpopular, and Mathews was accused of promoting self-interest, and was politically disgraced. He sought a new life in the Mississippi Territory, where he married Mary Carpenter, a widow of means. In 1812, his political career was revived when President James Madison commissioned him to encourage a revolt in eastern Florida against the Spanish rulers so that the United States could annex that territory. Mathews staged the revolt, and an attack on St. Augustine was about to take place when the government decided that it would be politically inexpedient to acquire Florida at that time, and called off the operation. Mathews was en route from Florida to Washington, D.C., to plead his case to be allowed to proceed with the mission when he fell ill while passing through Augusta, Georgia.

George Mathews died at Augusta, Georgia, on August 30, 1812, at the age of seventy-three. He was buried in the St. Paul Episcopal Church Cemetery in Augusta.[3]

MAXWELL, WILLIAM—(Ireland) William Maxwell was born in 1733 near Newtonstewart, County Tyrone, Ireland. His father was a small farmer, probably working the farm as a tenant. The crop failures of 1727–1739 and 1740–41 were the impetus for many Irish to leave their homes in search of a new life, and it is probable that it was a major influence in causing the Maxwells to leave Ireland. In 1747, the family landed in America, at Philadelphia, and made their way up the Delaware River, to Morris County, New Jersey (later Sussex and Warren County). The Maxwells settled in Greenwich Township, where the fertile land of New Jersey provided a good living for the family, and William doubtless spent his adolescent years helping in the fields.

According to tradition, Maxwell accompanied General Braddock's expedition in 1755, but that seems unlikely. It is more probable that the tradition came about due to Maxwell delivering provisions from New Jersey to Chambersburg, the staging area for the expedition. By Maxwell's own account, he first entered into military service in 1758, and therefore could not have taken part in the expedition.

On April 4, 1758, William Maxwell was named as one of the ensigns in the New Jersey Blues, as the militia was commonly referred to, and took part in General James Abercromby's expedition against Fort Ticonderoga. The campaign was a dismal failure, costing Abercromby's army over 2,200 casualties. After their retreat from Ticonderoga, Maxwell, and the rest of the New Jersey Blues, worked on the construction of Fort Stanwix, some 100 miles west of Albany.

In 1759, a second expedition was mounted against Fort Ticonderoga by General Lord Jeffrey Amherst. Maxwell was commissioned a lieutenant when New Jersey once more raised its quota of men. This expedition proved successful, as the French blew up the fort before retreating from the ground, and also abandoned Crown Point. Maxwell's last service in the French and Indian War was in 1760 when he accompanied Amherst on the invasion of Canada. On September 6, Amherst's army arrived before Montreal, and the French commander asked for terms, resulting in the capitulation of Montreal, Detroit, and many other western posts.

The end of the French and Indian War did not see the end of Maxwell's military career. He signed up as a British post commissary, serving in that position for twelve years. From 1761 to 1766, he superintended the provisioning of British troops stationed at Forts Schenectady, Schuyler, Stanwix, Oswego, and Niagara. In 1766, he accompanied the Royal American (60th) Regiment to Fort Michilimackinac, where he assumed the position of deputy commissary of stores and provisions for the post. In this capacity, he also assumed control for the provisioning of the local Indian tribes. Maxwell continued to perform the duties of a commissary until 1772.[1]

Maxwell's tenured service with the British army made him a natural candidate for leadership in the Revolution. On November 8, 1775, he was commissioned colonel of the 2nd New Jersey Regiment, by Congress. On October 23 of the following year, he received a promotion to brigadier general in the Continental army.² Maxwell was a steady and reliable officer, and was said to have a characteristic that is most prized by military men: luck. He was a stern disciplinarian, but always looked to the well-being of the men under his command. Possessed of superb tactical skills, his service was exemplary at Three Rivers, Brandywine, and in many small scale actions against the British in New Jersey.³

On July 25, 1780, Maxwell resigned his commission and returned to private life.⁴

William Maxwell died on November 4, 1795, at the age of sixty-three, at Union Farm, New Jersey, and was buried in the Greenwich Presbyterian Cemetery, in Greenwich Township, New Jersey.⁵

MCCLELLAN, SAMUEL—(**Massachusetts**) Samuel McClellan was born at Worcester, Massachusetts, on January 4, 1730. Little is known of his early education, but Samuel was brought up on the family farm, at Worcester, and later became a farmer himself in Woodstock, Connecticut. On November 16, 1757, he married Jimima Chandler, and the couple had four children before Jimima's death in 1764. McClellan then married Rachel Abbe, in 1766, and seven children were born to this union. Like many of his contemporaries, he gained his first military experience as a lieutenant in the French and Indian War, where he had the opportunity to observe the actions of the British officers he served under. In 1773, he was made captain of a company of militia that was raised in Woodstock, Connecticut, and in April of 1775, when news reached him of the fighting at Lexington and Concord, he immediately marched his company to Boston. He took part in the siege of Boston, and was subsequently commissioned a major, lieutenant colonel, and colonel of the 12th Massachusetts Regiment. With this regiment, he participated in the operations around Lake Champlain, the Saratoga Campaign, the defense of Philadelphia, and the battle of Monmouth.

On June 10, 1779, McClellan was commissioned a brigadier general in the Connecticut Militia by the governor. After the invasion of New London, and the massacre at Fort Groton, he was placed in command of those posts, and continued in that capacity until the end of the war.

Following the end of the war, McClellan returned to his farm at Woodstock and resumed his private life. His pursuit of personal ventures was broken by his election to the state assembly, and he served several terms before finally returning to the quiet life of a farmer.

Samuel McClellan died at Woodstock, Connecticut, on October 17, 1807, at the age of seventy-seven. He was buried for his final rest at the Old Willimantic Cemetery, in Willimantic, Connecticut.¹

MCDOUGALL, ALEXANDER—(**Scotland**) Alexander McDougall was born at Islay, Inner Hebrides, Scotland, in July of 1732. He learned the basics of reading through attending the Church of Scotland. In 1738, when McDougall was still a small boy, his family moved to New York Colony, along with some 200 Scottish Highlanders. The Scots had been led to believe that they would be landowners when they arrived in America, but the leader of the group, Lachlan Campbell, had acquired the land grant in his own name, and intended for the immigrants to become tenants on his land. McDougall's father, Robert, balked at this idea, and decided to settle in New York City, taking up residence on Manhattan Island, where he supported his family working on a dairy farm. Alexander helped his father deliver milk to the city, but he soon developed a love for the sea. At the age of fourteen, he signed on to a ship sailing out of New York and sailed out to seek his fortune.¹

For the next five years, McDougall was a member of the crews of various ships, and visited his home, at Islay, long enough to court and marry Nancy McDougall, a distant relative. He stayed in Islay a few months before returning to New York with his bride. McDougall's maritime experiences led to his becoming master of several small cargo sloops, and the eventual ownership of his own vessel, the *Schuyler*. During the French and Indian War, McDougall commanded the privateer *Tyger*, a six gun merchant vessel, and the twelve gun sloop the *Barrington*.

In 1763, Nancy McDougall died, leaving

Alexander to raise the three children they had together. McDougall gave up his privateering ventures, and invested his money in trade and land. He became a wealthy merchant and attained a level of prominence in New York society. In 1767, he married Hannah Bostwick. During this period, he also became involved in politics, protesting the hated Stamp Act. In 1769, he helped to form the Sons of Liberty in New York City. He published an anonymous broadside charging the New York Assembly with betraying the people, and was later arrested and imprisoned for sedition. McDougall became instantly famous when he refused to either plead guilty, or pay a fine, resulting in his being held by the British for 80 days. He was released because the star witness of the prosecution died, but was later arrested again, and held until 1771, when the newly elected governor released him. His sudden thrust into fame caused him to become one of the greatest activists for freedom of speech and of the press, and caused him to enter into correspondence with many of the leaders of the Revolution, including Benjamin Franklin. In 1773, he was instrumental in preventing the ship *London* from delivering its shipment of tea to New York City when he helped to organize a "tea party," where members of the Sons of Liberty dumped the tea overboard. In 1774, he drafted a non-importation resolution, which was passed at the Great Meeting in the Fields. He was appointed a deputy to the Continental Congress in 1775, and recruited the 1st New York Regiment, being commissioned colonel of the regiment on June 30, 1775. In 1776, he was a leader in creating a Continental Navy. On August 9, 1776, McDougall was commissioned a brigadier general in the Continental Army. He fought at Long Island and White Plains. When General Washington decided to evacuate New York, McDougall was entrusted with the difficult task of organizing that evacuation. His successful efforts earned him the eternal respect and admiration of Washington, and led to his promotion to the rank of major general in October 20, 1777.[2]

McDougall was conspicuous at the battle of Germantown, and during the New Jersey Campaign. In 1780, following the uncovering of Benedict Arnold's treason, he was appointed to the command at West Point, New York. The following year, he was elected to the Continental Congress. McDougall was appointed secretary of marine in 1782. He was re-elected to Congress in 1784. In 1783, he was elected to the New York State Senate, serving in that body until 1786. He was also elected the first president of the Bank of New York.[3]

Alexander McDougall died at New York City on June 9, 1786, in his sixtieth year.

McDOWELL, JOSEPH — (Virginia) Joseph McDowell was born at Winchester, Virginia, on February 15, 1756. McDowell attended common schools before being enrolled at Washington College (present day Washington and Lee). As an adult, he engaged in planting, and made his living as a member of the planter society. McDowell gained his first military experience fighting against Indian incursions along the Virginia frontier.

In July of 1776, at the age of only twenty, McDowell was named major of a frontier fort and helped defend the place, containing 120 women and children, and only nine men, from an attacking force of Cherokee. His older brother, Charles, was militia commander of the district, and McDowell served under him in the Stono Expedition, in 1779, fighting at Ramseur's Mill and all of the other battles that resulted from the British invasion of western North Carolina in 1780. He commanded the North Carolina Militia at the battle of Kings Mountain, on October 7, 1780, and was subsequently appointed a brigadier general of militia, serving at the battle of Cowpens in January of 1781.

In 1783, McDowell married Margaret Moffitt, and the couple had seven children together. By 1784, he had removed his family to Quaker Meadows, North Carolina, where he resumed private life as a planter. In 1787, McDowell was elected to the North Carolina House of Commons, serving until 1792. The year 1787 also saw his appointment as a commissioner to settle the boundary line dispute between Tennessee and North Carolina. He was a delegate to the North Carolina Constitutional Convention in 1788, where he was a leader of the faction in opposition to the Federal Constitution. In 1797, he was elected to the United States Congress, where he was an active opponent of the Federalists. In 1800, he moved to Kentucky, but returned to North Carolina in 1801.

Joseph McDowell died at Quaker Meadows Plantation, North Carolina, on February 5, 1801, at the age of forty-four. He was buried in the Quaker Meadows Cemetery, near Morganton, North Carolina. McDowell County, North Carolina, is named in his honor.[1]

McINTOSH, LACHLAN—(Scotland)
Lachlan McIntosh was born in Scotland in 1727, the son of John McIntosh, head of the McIntosh clan. In 1735, the family moved to America as part of James Oglethorpe's effort to settle Georgia. The next year, in 1736, John McIntosh established a Scottish settlement at Darien, Georgia. McIntosh's education was largely neglected during this time on the Georgia frontier, but Oglethorpe gave him the fundamentals of mathematics, and young Lachlan obtained a moderate amount of primary instruction through his own resources.

McIntosh's youth was filled with warfare, as the English in Georgia were almost constantly fighting with the Spanish in Florida. In 1740, McIntosh's father was captured by the Spanish, and his mother, unable to care for the children, sent him to an orphanage in Bethesda, near Savannah. In 1742, Oglethorpe granted him a position as cadet at Fort Frederica, thus beginning his military career at the age of fifteen. When McIntosh desired to return to Scotland to take part in the rebellion led by Bonnie Prince Charlie, it was Oglethorpe who talked him out of it, convincing the youth that his future was in Georgia.[1]

In 1748, McIntosh moved to Charleston, South Carolina, where he was employed by Henry Laurens as a clerk in his counting house. In 1756, he married Sarah Threadcraft, and returned to Georgia, where he acquired a tract of land in the Altamaha River delta and undertook the life of a rice planter. He supplemented his income by means of doing surveying work.

At the outbreak of the Revolution, McIntosh was commissioned colonel of the 1st Georgia Regiment on January 7, 1776. He helped to organize the defense of Savannah, and defeated the British at a skirmish at Rice Boats in the Savannah River. On September 16, 1776, he was commissioned a brigadier general by the Continental Congress. Button Gwinnett, the Georgia signer of the Declaration of Independence, became resentful of McIntosh's rapid advancement, and the two became embroiled in a political dispute over control of the Georgia state forces. Gwinnett attempted to restrict McIntosh's authority, and the latter responded by denouncing Gwinnett and challenging him to a duel on May 16, 1777. Both men were wounded in the exchange of fire, but Gwinnett would later die, causing his friends and supporters to level a charge of murder against McIntosh. Though he was later tried and found innocent of the charge, the incident had caused a rift between the patriot factions in the state. Accordingly, McIntosh was transferred to General Washington's headquarters, in order to ease the tensions in Georgia. After wintering at Valley Forge, McIntosh received orders on May 26, 1778, to travel to Fort Pitt (present day Pittsburgh) where he was to assume command of the fort and surrounding district. He was responsible for building Fort McIntosh at Beaverton, and Fort Laurens near Sandusky, Ohio. He was in command at Fort Pitt until May of 1779, when he was ordered south to participate in the campaign to retake Savannah, Georgia. McIntosh fought in the failed effort to take the city on October 4, 1779, and retreated with the army to Charleston following the defeat. McIntosh helped to induce enlistments into General Lincoln's depleted army as it awaited an attack on Charleston that everyone was sure the British would make. On April 9, 1780, the British fleet sailed into Charleston Harbor, and the siege of the city began. McIntosh was conspicuous in his service during the siege, but when Charleston fell on May 12 he was taken prisoner by the British. McIntosh was held by his captors for almost two years, not being exchanged until February 9, 1782. His health was much broken by his confinement. On September 30, 1783, he was given the brevet rank of major general. McIntosh retired to private life, resuming his planting and business activities.[2]

In 1784, he was elected to Congress, and was an organizer of the Georgia branch of the Society of the Cincinnati. In 1787, he served as a commissioner in the boundary dispute between Georgia and South Carolina.

Lachlan McIntosh died at Savannah on February 20, 1806, in his seventy-ninth year. He was buried in the Colonial Cemetery, in Savannah.[3]

MEAD, JOHN—(Connecticut) John Mead was born at Greenwich, Fairfield County, Connecticut, in 1725. In 1752, Mead married Mary Bush, and the couple had seven children together. Mary died in 1784, and Mead remarried in 1786, when he wed Mehitable Blackman. The couple had one child together.

In 1757, during the French and Indian War, Mead was commissioned a lieutenant in the West Company of Greenwich. He remained in the Connecticut Militia, becoming a captain in 1767, and a major in 1774, just prior to the outbreak of hostilities. In 1768, Mead was elected to the Connecticut Legislature, a position he would hold for twenty years. Mead fought at the battle of Long Island in August on 1776 and White Plains in October of that same year. He commanded the last American troops to leave the state during its evacuation by the Continental Army. Mead served as a colonel in the Connecticut Militia, from 1777 to 1781, and was subsequently appointed a brigadier general in that service, serving to the close of the war.

John Mead died at Greenwich, Connecticut, on December 3, 1790, in his sixty-fifth year.[1]

MERCER, HUGH—(Scotland) Hugh Mercer was born at Aberdeenshire, Scotland, in 1726, the son of a Presbyterian minister. After receiving his primary education, Mercer attended Marischal College (present day University of Aberdeen), where he received his diploma as a doctor. When "Bonnie Prince Charlie" landed in Scotland to start an uprising aimed at regaining the Scottish throne, Mercer joined the cause, serving as an assistant surgeon in Prince Charlie's army. The rebellion collapsed with the crushing defeat at Culloden Moor, on April 16, 1746, and Mercer became a hunted rebel, fleeing back to Aberdeenshire, where he lived in hiding for almost a year. In March of 1747 he managed to arrange passage on a ship bound for America and departed Scotland forever.

After arriving in Philadelphia, Mercer moved west into the Scots-Irish settlements of the Cumberland Valley, near the present day town of Mercersburg, where he settled and became the first doctor to practice in Franklin County, Pennsylvania. During the French and Indian War, Mercer accompanied General Edward Braddock's expedition against Fort Duquesne (Fort Pitt) in 1755. He was severely wounded in the shoulder at the battle of Monongahela, and made his way alone through the wilderness to Fort Cumberland, in Cumberland, Maryland, a distance of about 100 miles. In March of 1756, he was commissioned a captain in the militia. Along with John Armstrong, he led the Kittanning Expedition against the hostile Indians along the frontier, wiping out a number of the enemy base camps. Mercer was wounded in the right arm, and almost captured during the expedition. The city of Philadelphia awarded both him and Armstrong silver medals for their accomplishment. In 1758, Mercer was promoted to the rank of lieutenant colonel, and accompanied General Forbes' expedition that resulted in the capture of Fort Duquesne, in present day Pittsburgh, Pennsylvania. Following the capitulation of the fort, Mercer was assigned to command the post for several months. He remained in the army until his discharge in January of 1761. During that time, he was promoted to the rank of colonel, and commanded the posts of Fort Pitt, Fort Augusta, and Fort Venango. By the end of the war, Mercer had become something of a local hero. He left the army to once again practice medicine, but his time in the service had left him financially embarrassed. Mercer had met a number of prominent men during his time in the army, none more so than George Washington. The two had become fast friends, and it was largely because of that fact that Mercer decided to relocate himself and his practice to Fredericksburg, Virginia, in 1761.

Mercer's practice thrived, in Fredericksburg,

and his long patient list even included Mary Washington, George Washington's mother. By 1771, he had opened an apothecary shop in the town, near the intersection of Amelia and Caroline Streets. It was during this time that he married Isabella Gordon, the daughter of a local tavern-keeper. The couple would have five children together. In 1767, he joined the local Masonic Temple, and in 1774 he bought Ferry Farm from the Washingtons, though he never resided there. Aside from his apothecary shop and medical practice, he also dabbled in land speculation in the western frontier.

At the outbreak of the Revolutionary War, Mercer took part in the Powder Crisis in Fredericksburg in June of 1775. He was commissioned a colonel in the Virginia Militia, in December of that year, and assigned to command the 3rd Virginia Regiment. On June 5, 1776, he was commissioned a brigadier general by the Continental Congress and placed in command of the Flying Camp, the mobile militia forces of the Continental Army. He participated in the retreat through New Jersey, and in all of the engagements that took place in that state and in Pennsylvania in 1776. He has been credited with being the originator of the plan to surprise the British forces at Trenton, though that is still a subject of debate among historians. Regardless, he led the column of attack in that battle and performed with distinction. He also commanded the advance in the attack on Princeton, on January 3, 1777. During the battle, Mercer led his brigade against British reinforcements from the 17th and 55th Regiments of Foot that were coming on the field. His militia began to waver before the enemy, and Mercer was in the midst of rallying them when he was knocked to the ground by the butt of a British musket. He was quickly surrounded, and a demand was made for his surrender. Mercer refused, and from his prone position, attempted to defend himself with his sword. He was bayoneted numerous times, with some reports placing the number at more than a dozen, and was finally compelled to give up the fight. Mercer

The death of General Hugh Mercer (courtesy United States Military History Institute)

was taken to the Clarke House, on a neighboring farm, where his wounds were dressed. When Washington heard of his wounding, he sent a flag of truce to the British requesting that his aide-de-camp and nephew, Colonel George Lewis, be allowed to stay with Mercer until his death.

Hugh Mercer died, as a result of his wounds, on January 12, 1777, in his fifty-seventh year. His funeral, in Philadelphia, was attended by some 30,000 people, and he became a martyr of the Revolution. He was buried in the Christ Church Burying Ground, in Philadelphia, but in 1840, his remains were moved to the Laurel Hill Cemetery, where a monument was placed at his grave. Mercersburg and Mercer County, Pennsylvania, were named in his honor.[1]

MEREDITH, SAMUEL—(Pennsylvania)

Samuel Meredith was born in Philadelphia in 1740. His father was an emigrant from Wales, and by the time of Samuel's birth, had become one of the most influential men in the city, earning his living as a merchant. Meredith was educated at Dr. Allison's Academy, prior to taking his place in his father's business. In 1772, he married Margaret Cadwalader. Before the Revolution, Meredith served in the colonial legislature of Pennsylvania, and upon the outbreak of hostilities, he was commissioned major of the 3rd Pennsylvania Battalion in 1775. The battalion was sent to New York City, where it helped to build Fort Washington. It held the left flank of the American position covering Brooklyn following the battle of Long Island, and covered the withdrawal of the main army to Manhattan. It also took part in the battle at Fort Washington on November 16, 1776. The battalion was later redesignated the 4th Pennsylvania Regiment and took part in Washington's 1777 battles of Brandywine, Paoli, and Germantown. In the meantime, Meredith had been commissioned a brigadier general in the Pennsylvania Militia on April 5, 1777. Meredith served in this capacity until January 9, 1778.[1]

Meredith was a brother-in-law of George Clymer, a signer of the Declaration of Independence, by virtue of Clymer's marriage to Meredith's sister, Elizabeth. The two men had become partners in Meredith's merchant business, and during one of the many periods when the Continental Congress did not have the funds to continue the war, Meredith and Clymer each donated 10,000 pounds sterling to the government to facilitate the war. When Philadelphia was occupied by the British on September 26, 1777, Meredith was exiled from the city and could not return until the evacuation of the British in June of 1778.

Following the end of the war and the adoption of the Federal Constitution, Meredith served as a member of Congress from Pennsylvania from 1787 to 1788. In 1789, Meredith was appointed to be the first treasurer of the United States. The Treasury was all but bereft of funds, and Meredith advanced the country $20,000 of his own money to conduct the affairs of state. He later advanced the country another $120,000 for the same purpose. Meredith was never reimbursed for any of the money he had loaned to the country. In 1801, he resigned his position as treasurer in order to devote his attention to his estates and personal finances.

Samuel Meredith died at the family estate, Belmont, in present day Wayne County, Pennsylvania, on March 10, 1817, in his sixty-seventh year. He was buried in the family cemetery located on the grounds of the estate.

MIFFLIN, THOMAS—(Pennsylvania)

Thomas Mifflin was born in Philadelphia on January 10, 1744, the son of Quaker parents. After receiving his primary education, he attended the College of Philadelphia, graduating in 1760. Mifflin, as a man, was something of a contradiction. He became a successful businessman in the city, even though he was somewhat careless about his personal finances. His Quaker beliefs were strongly held, including pacifism, but he would serve the army in the greatest war his generation would know. He was usually dignified and reserved in his deportment, but was also prone to heated outbursts, and engaged in numerous quarrels with those with whom he came in contact. A Patriot, who believed in the cause of liberty, he felt that people were basically weak and selfish, and believed that "There can be no right to power, except what is either founded upon, or speedily obtains the hearty consent of the body of the people."

In 1765, Mifflin started an import-export business, in partnership with a younger brother. On March 4, 1767, Mifflin married Sarah Morris, and the couple had one child. In 1768, he joined the American Philosophical Society, and served as its secretary for two years. Business success, and his marriage to a wealthy, distant cousin, cemented his position among the elite of Philadelphia society. In 1771, he was appointed warden of the city, and in 1772, he was elected for the first of four terms to the Pennsylvania legislature. In 1774, Mifflin was elected to represent Pennsylvania at the Continental Congress, where he served on the committee that drafted the document boycotting the importation of British goods. He was returned to the Continental Congress the next year, following the fighting at Lexington and Concord.[1]

On July 4, 1775, Mifflin was appointed to be an aide to George Washington, with the rank of major. He was subsequently appointed to the post of quartermaster general of the Continental Army on August 14, 1775. He was promoted to the rank of colonel on December 22, 1775, and was made a brigadier general on May 16, 1776. He attained the rank of major general on February 19, 1777. Through all these advances in grade, his duties remained those of quartermaster general.[2]

Mifflin's greatest contribution to the American cause came from his recruitment efforts for the army. He had a reputation of being one of the best stump orators of his time, and it was said that no one could more effectually excite the populace with speeches than he could. His efforts resulted in large numbers of men from Pennsylvania joining the army.[3]

Shortly after his promotion to major general, Mifflin became dissatisfied with the army, and his performance as quartermaster general reflected this dissatisfaction, and contributed to the supply problems being faced by the army at Valley Forge. Mifflin resigned his position as quartermaster general on November 7, 1777, and on February 25, 1779, he resigned his commission as major general, and left the army, but not before he had become embroiled in a controversy that threatened to divide the Continental forces. Mifflin became part of the Conway Cabal, and his reputation was tainted by his support of Conway and his efforts to have Washington replaced as commander in chief. He had been appointed as a member of Congress' Board of War in 1777, and had used his influence with that body to further the designs against Washington, but when his reputation with that body began to wane, he resigned his seat at the same time he resigned his military commission.

Thomas Mifflin

Out of the army, Mifflin was somewhat shunned in national affairs for the next few years. In 1782, however, he was returned as a delegate to the Continental Congress, later serving as president of that body. In 1790, he was elected governor of Pennsylvania, and was reelected to that office through 1799. In 1794, he commanded the Pennsylvania Militia during the Whiskey Rebellion.[4]

Thomas Mifflin Died in Lancaster, Pennsylvania, on January 20, 1800, at the age of fifty-six. He was buried in the Trinity Lutheran Church Cemetery in that city. Mifflin County, Pennsylvania, was named in his honor.

MILES, SAMUEL—(Pennsylvania) Samuel Miles was born in Montgomery County, Pennsylvania, on March 11, 1740. As a boy, he received what he called a "common country education." In 1756, Miles enlisted in Captain Isaac Wayne's militia company. He later enlisted as a sergeant in Captain Thomas Lloyd's company and was promoted to the rank of captain-lieutenant. Miles participated in the expedition against Fort Duquesne, and was wounded during that campaign. In 1760, he was commissioned a captain and placed in command of the militia forces at Presque Isle (present day Erie). Miles married Catherine Wister in 1761, and the couple had ten children together.[1]

Following the war, Miles moved to Philadelphia, where he went into business as a wine merchant. In 1766, he was appointed as a manager of the House of Employ. In 1772, Miles was elected to the Pennsylvania Assembly, where he was one of the first to espouse the cause of American independence. In 1775, he was again elected to the Pennsylvania Assembly, and was appointed as a member of the Council of Safety. On March 13, 1776, he was commissioned colonel of the Pennsylvania Rifle Regiment. His command formed part of the Flying Camp, and on August 27, 1776, it took part in the battle of Long Island. Miles was captured in this battle, and held by the British until April of 1778, at which time he was exchanged. Miles was commissioned a brigadier general of Pennsylvania militia during his imprisonment, but upon his release he was unable to obtain the rank. The length of his confinement had induced the Pennsylvania assembly to confer the title on another officer who could actively command.

Miles resigned from the army as a result of his lost rank, and became auditor for settling public accounts for the state of Pennsylvania, as well as deputy quartermaster-general. He held both posts until 1782. In 1783, he was appointed to be a judge of the High Court of Errors and Appeals. In 1786, he was elected to serve as a trustee for the University of the State of Pennsylvania, and continued in that position until his resignation in 1793. He was elected to city council in 1788, and in 1789 he became an alderman. In 1790, Miles was elected mayor of Philadelphia, and he was unanimously re-elected the following year, but he declined to serve. In 1796, he was an elector for the presidential election. In 1805, he was elected to once more serve in the state assembly.[2]

Miles was a large landowner in Centre County, Pennsylvania, where he was responsible for laying out the present day town of Milesburg, which was named in his honor. In 1802, he wrote his autobiography, which was published in the *American Historical Record*.[3]

Samuel Miles died at Chesterham, Pennsylvania, on December 29, 1805, at the age of sixty-five. He was buried in the First Baptist Church Cemetery, in Philadelphia.

MILLER, NATHAN — (Rhode Island)
Nathan Miller was born at Warren, Rhode Island, on March 20, 1743. After attending private school, he became a merchant and shipbuilder. Miller married Rebecca Barton on January 8, 1764, and the couple had four children together. In 1772, he was elected to the Rhode Island legislature as deputy and served until 1774. He was subsequently re-elected to the state assembly in 1780, 1782, 1783, and 1790.

Miller had been an officer in the state service prior to the war, and had been commissioned a brigadier general in the Rhode Island Militia in 1772. He continued to hold this position during the war, serving as general for the militia from Newport and Bristol counties until 1778. His duties would appear to have been of an administrative nature, rather than as a field general.

Following the war, Miller was elected to the Continental Congress in 1786. He was re-elected, following the end of his term in office, but declined to take his seat. In 1790, he was a member of the Rhode Island convention to ratify the Federal Constitution.

Nathan Miller died at Warren, Rhode Island, on May 20, 1790, at the age of forty-seven. He was buried in the Kickamuet Cemetery, in Warren.[1]

MONTGOMERY, RICHARD — (Ireland)
Richard Montgomery was born on December 2, 1738, near Swords, County Dublin, Ireland. As a boy, Richard received a classic primary

education before attending Trinity College, in Dublin, where he acquired a particular interest in science that was to last his entire life. He was to attend Trinity for only two years, however, and did not complete the course of study, or gain his degree. With his father, grandfather, and older brother serving in the British army, Richard was groomed to follow the family tradition, and in 1756, when he was eighteen years of age, his father purchased him an ensign's commission in the 17th Regiment of Foot.

In February of 1757, the 17th Regiment of Foot received orders to proceed to Cork, where it was to prepare for shipment to America, along with five other regiments, to protect British interests in the New World from French incursion. On May 8, the regiment set sail, arriving at Nova Scotia in early July. Under the command of Colonel John Forbes, the 17th Regiment of Foot participated in the expedition against Fort Louisburg, on Cape Breton Island. The fort, supported by French naval power, proved too strong to assault, however, and the 17th was sent to New York to go into winter quarters.[1]

In May of 1758, Montgomery and the 17th participated in a second expedition against Fort Louisburg. This time, the army was to be accompanied by a large British fleet of some thirty-nine ships. On June 8, the British army, under the command of Major General Jeffrey Amherst, made an amphibious landing on the shores of Cape Breton Island, and began a siege of the fort. The defenders of the fort resisted for almost three weeks, but the works were finally surrendered on July 26, 1758. Montgomery had seen a great deal of combat during this time, and by the end of the siege he had been promoted to the rank of lieutenant. The campaign also gave the young officer experience in siege warfare that he would later use in the Revolution.

In 1759, Montgomery participated, with his regiment, in Amherst's expedition against Fort Carillon (Ticonderoga) and Crown Point. The French retreated from both places when the British army drew near, and Amherst halted the advance in order to build warships to counter the French naval presence on Lake Champlain before resuming his offensive into the interior of Canada. When the British again moved forward, Montgomery took part in the campaign that succeeded in capturing Montreal.

In 1763, Montgomery returned to England, but his time in America had made an impression on him, and he determined to settle in the Colonies and avail himself of the opportunities offered there. In 1772, he sold his commission in the British army, purchased land 100 miles above New York City, and prepared to become an American. He had more reasons than merely opportunity for relocating to New York. He had met, and been smitten with the oldest daughter of Robert L. Livingston while he had been in New York, and he would make her his bride when he returned to the colony.[2]

Being a military man for all of his adult life, Montgomery was little inclined to take part in public life, but he was quickly seen to be a leader, and his talents were sought by his new neighbors in his adopted land. In 1775, he was elected as a member of the first Provincial Convention of New York. His views over the encroachment of freedom by the mother country

Richard Montgomery

were well known, and when the Continental Congress established the army, and appointed George Washington to be its commander, Montgomery was given one of the first eight commissions as brigadier general bestowed by that body on June 22, 1775.[3]

Montgomery's previous service in the French and Indian War would be highly beneficial to the American cause, as he was to operate in the same region that he had become so familiar with in that contest. The Colonies had decided to mount an expedition against Canada, under the command of General Philip Schuyler, and Montgomery would be second in command of the American forces. Operating independently, he captured Ile aux Noix, before the forces of the two generals had made a junction. Once the two armies were joined, Schuyler became prostrated with illness, and could not continue in command. He returned to Fort Ticonderoga, leaving Montgomery to assume leadership of the expedition. Congress had promoted Montgomery to the rank of major general on December 9, 1775. He mounted his winter campaign into Canada, successfully capturing Montreal. The winter storms were such that the American army suffered terribly from exposure and cold, and Montgomery probably should have concluded his campaign at Montreal, and waited for better weather to continue, but, being a high-minded officer, he felt it his duty to complete the assignment he had been given and march against Quebec. With the greatest of difficulty, he managed to march his army to that city, and joined forces with those of General Benedict Arnold, who had marched his army from a different route. On December 31, 1775, he made a fateful assault against the city. The Americans were repulsed in a bloody conflict that in many places was fought hand to hand.

General Montgomery was killed while leading one of the charges, and though some of his men tried to recover his body, it had to be left on the field in the possession of the enemy. He was originally buried at Quebec, but in 1818, his remains were brought to New York City, where they were interred at St. Paul's Church, by a monument to his memory that Congress had previously commissioned.[4]

MOORE, ANDREW—(Virginia) Andrew Moore was born at Canniscello, Augusta County (now Rockbridge County), Virginia, in 1752. At a young age, he made a voyage to the West Indies and was shipwrecked on a desert island. Upon his return home, he took up the study of law at Augusta Academy (present day Washington and Lee University) and was admitted to the Virginia bar in 1774. Moore married Sarah Reid, and the couple had two children.

On March 19, 1776, he was commissioned a 1st lieutenant in the 9th Virginia Regiment. The unit took part in the operations around Chesapeake Bay and the defense of Philadelphia. Moore was then promoted to the rank of captain, and assigned to the Northern Department, where he took part in the Saratoga Campaign. He resigned his commission in the Continental service in 1779, and was subsequently commissioned a brigadier general in the Virginia Militia. Moore's service to the country was of a political, rather than military, nature from this time onward, and his militia duties seem to have been of an administrative nature, though he retained his commission and rank through to the end of the war. In 1780, he was elected to the Virginia state legislature, serving till 1783, and again from 1785 to 1788. In 1788, he was a member of the Virginia convention that ratified the Federal Constitution. He was elected to serve in the first Congress under that Constitution, and was re-elected until 1797. Moore served in the state legislature from 1799 to 1800, and in the state senate from 1800 to 1801. He served in the United States Senate from 1804 to 1809. In 1808, he was commissioned a major general in the Virginia State Militia. In 1810, he was appointed United States marshal

Andrew Moore (courtesy United States Military History Institute)

for the state of Virginia, and served in that capacity till the time of his death.

Andrew Moore died at Lexington, Virginia, on April 12, 1821, in his sixty-ninth year. He was buried at the Lexington Cemetery, in Lexington, Virginia.[1]

MOORE, JAMES—**(North Carolina)** James Moore was born at Rocky Point Plan, Brunswick County, North Carolina, in 1737. He was a member of a prestigious family, and his grandfather had been governor of South Carolina in 1700. Moore married Anne Ivie (n.d.) and the couple had five children together.

Moore joined the militia during the French and Indian War, and served as a captain at Fort Johnson, near Southport, in 1758. He later served as a captain of artillery, under Governor Tryon, in the defeat of the North Carolina Regulators at Alamance in 1771.

When the 1st North Carolina Regiment was raised for state defense in 1775, Moore was commissioned to be its colonel. He commanded the regiment at the battle of Moore's Creek Bridge, near Wilmington, North Carolina, in February of 1776. This was the first victory won by Patriot forces in the Revolution, over a force of some 1,500 Loyalists. Moore's conduct at Moore's Creek Bridge was praised by Congress, and he was commissioned a brigadier general in the Continental Army on March 1, 1776, and made commander in chief of the Southern Department. Ordered to join General Washington, and the main army, Moore was en route to do so when he was stricken with a fever. He stopped at the home of his brother, in Wilmington, North Carolina, where he died on January 15, 1777, as a result of the illness, in his fortieth year. James' brother, Maurice, at whose home he died, was also a patriot, serving in the North Carolina House of Burgesses in 1775 and 1776, and being instrumental in drafting the North Carolina state constitution. James and Maurice both died in the same house, on January 15, 1777, during the same hour of the day.[1]

MORGAN, DANIEL—**(New Jersey)** Daniel Morgan was born near Junction, in Hunterdon County, New Jersey, in 1736. Morgan was the first cousin of Daniel Boone. He received little or no education, and at the age of sixteen left home to escape an abusive father. He worked his way across Pennsylvania, doing odd jobs, until he reached Virginia (present day West Virginia) in 1753, where he claimed some inexpensive farmland near Charles Town, established a small sawmill, and worked as a teamster. In 1754, at the beginning of the French and Indian War, Morgan's talents as a teamster caused him to be hired to transport supplies for General Braddock's army between Winchester, Virginia; Fort Cumberland, Maryland; and southwestern Pennsylvania. After the defeat of Braddock's expedition against Fort Duquesne (Fort Pitt), Morgan used his wagon to help drive the wounded to safety. He first came into contact with George Washington during this expedition, and Washington was so impressed with his abilities as a teamster that he gave him a nickname that stuck with him the rest of his life, "The Old Wagoner."

In 1756, Morgan joined a Virginia Ranger company and was severely wounded in an Indian ambush, having a ball shot through his neck that exited through his mouth, taking the teeth on the left side of his jaw with it. Following General Forbes' capture of Fort Duquesne in 1758, Morgan returned to work as a teamster, hauling food and hardware in and out of Winchester. It was about this time that he met and fell in love with Abigail Curry. The couple would have two daughters, and would eventually marry. In the years after the French and Indian War, Morgan prospered, and his farm increased in size until it was 255 acres.[1]

In 1775, the Continental Congress voted to raise ten companies of sharpshooters from men on the frontier, and Morgan was made captain of one of the companies from Virginia. He served under General Arnold in the Canadian Expedition. Captured at Quebec, in 1776, Morgan refused to surrender his sword to his British captors, handing it to a nearby priest instead. During his captivity, he was commissioned colonel of the 11th Virginia Regiment. He was exchanged in early 1777, and rejoined Washington's main army, taking part in all the engagements of that body through 1777. Morgan served, with distinction, under Schuyler and Gates in the Saratoga Campaign, taking a prominent part in both battles. In November of 1778, Morgan rejoined Washington's army, near Philadelphia. In March of 1779, the Continental Congress commissioned Morgan colonel of the 7th Virginia Regiment. In July of that year he tendered his resignation from the army, citing poor health and dissatisfaction over Congress not advancing him further in rank as the reasons. He returned to his farm, and private life, for almost a year. Following the disastrous defeat at Camden, South Carolina, in 1780, Washington called Morgan back to active duty, with the promise that he would secure an advancement in rank for him. Morgan joined the southern army at Hillsborough, North Carolina, on October 1, 1780, and was given command of a corps. On October 13, 1780, Congress finally granted his commission as a brigadier general.[2]

Morgan performed valuable service during the southern campaigns, but his greatest claim to fame would come at the battle of Cowpens, South Carolina, on January 17, 1781. Cornwallis and Tarleton were attempting to surround his force, but Morgan engaged Tarleton, winning a stunning victory in which he killed or captured three-fourths of Tarleton's army. He then eluded Cornwallis' army, slipping into North Carolina. He is also credited with suggesting the plan of battle for Guilford Courthouse to General Greene. Congress presented Morgan with a gold medal commemorating his victory at Cowpens.

Following the surrender of Cornwallis, at Yorktown, Morgan was assigned the task of arranging housing for the British prisoners, at Winchester. While back in Winchester, he used Hessian prisoners to help build a new house for himself, which he called Saratoga. In 1782, he was elected to the Pennsylvania state legislature. Morgan continued to serve in the army until the end of the war, when he retired to his farm in Charles Town. Over time, he would increase his holding from 255 acres to over 250,000 acres.

In 1794, Washington called Morgan back into the service to help suppress the Whiskey Rebellion, and in 1795 he would command a corps of some 1,200 men. In 1797, he was elected to serve as a representative in Congress.

Daniel Morgan

Daniel Morgan died at Winchester, Virginia, on July 6, 1802, in his fifty-sixth year. He was originally buried in Winchester, but his remains were moved to Spartanburg, South Carolina, during the Civil War, for fear that Union troops would steal his body. Morgantown, West Virginia, was named in his honor, as were eight counties in various states.[3]

MORRIS, LEWIS—(New York) Lewis Morris was born at the family manor of Morrisania, near Harlem, in New York, on April 8, 1726. His family was among the wealthiest, and most aristocratic, in New York, and was well connected to the British government, with his brother, Staats, serving as an officer in the British army and an elected member of Parliament. Morris received a fine primary education before attending Yale, at the age of sixteen. He left school without graduating from that institution in 1746 and took up the business of agriculture on his family estates. At the age of twenty-three, he married Mary Walton, and the couple would have ten children together.

Despite the family ties to Britain, and the social and financial ruin that would be brought upon him, Morris sided with the cause of liberty when tensions arose between the colonies and the mother country. In 1775, he was elected to be a delegate from New York to the Continental Congress, where he was placed on a committee to procure ammunition and military supplies for the army. He was also appointed to negotiate with the various Indian tribes to seek their support, or neutrality, in the coming conflict. Morris went to Pittsburgh, Pennsylvania, for several months, where he met with Indian leaders and tried to gain their allegiance to the United States. Returning to his seat in Congress in early 1776, he was appointed to a committee charged with the purchase of muskets and bayonets and the stimulation of the production of saltpeter and gunpowder.

As the mood in Congress became increasingly one of independence, rather than rebellion, Morris faced a personal crisis. The British army was in New York, in close proximity to his home, and he would surely lose all he had if he supported the faction that advocated a split with England. Disregarding his personal ramifications, he became one of the leading advocates for the Declaration of Independence, and signed the document once Jefferson had prepared it. In retaliation, the British destroyed his home and property. Morris' three oldest sons all followed the example of their father and served as officers in the Continental army.[1]

In 1777, he was replaced in Congress by his brother, Gouverneur Morris, and he returned home to New York, where he was commissioned a brigadier general and major general in the state forces. His military duties were largely administrative, and he traveled through New England for the first few years of the war securing armaments and provisions for the army. He served as a judge in Worchester, and was elected to the upper house of the New York legislature. After the war, his brother, Gouverneur, was heavily involved in the writing of the Federal Constitution, which faced stiff opposition in New York. When it came time for the state to vote on ratification of that document, Lewis Morris used his influence and powers of persuasion to help win a narrow margin of victory for its approval.[2]

Lewis Morris (courtesy United States Army War College)

Following the war, Morris retired to his estate, at Morrisania, and attempted to rebuild both his farm and his fortunes. Though largely devoting his time to private ventures, he served on the first Board of Regents for the University of New York.

Lewis Morris died at his estate at Morrisania on January 22, 1798, at the age of seventy-one. He was buried in the Saint Anne's Episcopal Church Cemetery, in Bronx, New York.[3]

MOULTRIE, WILLIAM—**(South Carolina)** William Moultrie was born in Charleston, South Carolina, on November 23, 1730. His father was a well known physician in the area, and saw to it that the boy acquired a good education. Moultrie married Elizabeth Demaris de St. Julien in 1749, at the age of eighteen, and the couple had one child. After her death, in 1779, he would marry Hannah Motte Lynch. Moultrie would make his living as a planter in St. John's Berkeley County, but he did have the opportunity to gain military experience when he served as a militia captain in Lieutenant Colonel James Grant's expedition against the Cherokee in 1761. Francis Marion served as a lieutenant under Moultrie during this campaign. He fought in the battle of Etchoe, where the Cherokee were completely routed. An arduous campaign, conducted in the swamps and thickets of South Carolina's frontier, Moultrie gained a clear understanding of the difficulties and challenges of successful military campaigns under such conditions.

Elected to the Continental Congress, in 1774, Moultrie did not take his seat, or serve. He was, nevertheless, a political moderate, and aligned himself with the Patriot cause. On June 17, 1775, the day the battle of Bunker Hill took place, he was commissioned colonel of the 2nd South Carolina Regiment. Francis Marion was appointed a captain in one of his companies. Moultrie's first mission was an attack on Fort Johnson, on James Island, in Charleston Harbor, then in the possession of the British. The British were aware of Moultrie's intentions, however, and evacuated the fort prior to the arrival of his troops. Moultrie had three cannon placed in the fort, and this was enough to discourage a small British fleet from trying to attack the city.

In December of 1775, Moultrie placed a battery at Hadrell's Point to drive off two British men-of-war that were threatening the city. With two hundred of his men, he constructed the battery overnight, and the next morning, when the British discovered a well emplaced battery opposing them, they decided to weigh anchor and sail away.

In March of 1776, Moultrie was ordered to build a fort on Sullivan's Island to protect against an expected assault by a British fleet. Moultrie built a square pen out of Palmetto logs, with bastions at the four corners. The logs were laid horizontal, and were locked together with cross timbers. A second wall of logs was constructed sixteen feet inside of the first, and the space between them was filled with sand. It was a most unconventional structure, and when General Charles Lee, Moultrie's commanding officer, saw it he decided that it was indefensible, and ordered its evacuation. Governor Rutledge instructed Moultrie to occupy the fort, however, as that officer was under his direct command, as a militia officer, and not subject to Lee's orders when they conflicted

William Moultrie

with the governor's. A British fleet of some fifty vessels sailed into Charleston Harbor in the latter part of June 1776. On June 28, Commodore Peter Parker opened a bombardment of the fort with eight or nine of his men-of-war. The British held the same low opinion of the fort that General Lee had, and felt that they could blast it away in the space of a half hour. But both the British and General Lee were unfamiliar with the spongy nature of the green Palmetto logs, which, along with the sand, absorbed the cannon balls the British ships were firing. General Lee visited the fort, during the bombardment, and was pleasantly surprised by the lack of effect the British cannonade was having on the emplacement. The fort was struck time and time again, but the shells were causing little or no damage to it. In the meantime, the cannon in the fort were playing havoc with the British fleet, scoring many hits on the enemy vessels. Commodore Parker continued the bombardment until 9:30 that night, but was forced to concede that the fort could not be taken and sail off. Moultrie became an instant national hero, for his defense of Charleston, and he was commissioned a brigadier general in the Continental Army on September 16, 1777.[1]

Though Moultrie continued to maintain a defensive posture in Charleston, the British did not immediately return, and it was not until after the fall of Savannah, Georgia, on December 29, 1778, that he once again saw action. In February of 1779, Moultrie was in command of the defenses of Beaufort, at Port Royal Island, South Carolina, where he defeated a force of 200 British. This victory discouraged the British from making any further attempts in South Carolina until late in the year. He was later defeated at the battle of Stono Ferry, South Carolina, in June of 1779. Moultrie was once again elected to the Continental Congress in 1779, but for the second time, he declined to take his seat, preferring to remain in Charleston and attend to the defense of that important place.

A British army, under the command of General Augustine Prevost, besieged Charleston from March 29 to May 12, 1780. After a gallant defense, the American forces were forced to surrender, General Moultrie being among their number. He was held by the British for a considerable time, not being released until November of 1781, when he was exchanged for General Burgoyne. When he once again rejoined the army, Congress promoted him to the rank of major general on October 18, 1782, in which capacity he served till the end of the war.

Following the conclusion of the war, Moultrie retired to his plantation and private life, but South Carolina had need of his services, and he was elected to the state House of Representatives in 1783. In 1784, he served as lieutenant governor, and was elected governor in 1785. In 1787, he was elected to the state Senate, followed by another term as governor in 1792. In 1794, he retired from public life and began work on his *Memoirs of the American Revolution* that were published in two volumes.

William Moultrie died in Charleston on September 25, 1805, at the age of seventy-four, and was buried at Windsor Hill Plantation. Fort Moultrie, in Charleston Harbor, was named in his honor.

MUHLENBERG, JOHN PETER GABRIEL—(Pennsylvania) John Peter Gabriel Muhlenberg was born at Trappe, Pennsylvania, on October 1, 1746, the son of a Lutheran minister. He received a fine education, which included graduating from the Academy of Philadelphia (present day University of Pennsylvania). Following his completion of the course of studies at the Academy of Philadelphia, his family sent him to Germany, where he attended the University of Halle from 1763 to 1766. He was apprenticed to a grocer, in Lubeck, but was treated harshly and ran away to join a German regiment of dragoons in the British army. Muhlenberg returned to Philadelphia in 1766, and undertook the study of theology. He became an ordained minister in the Lutheran Church in 1768, and was pastor to churches in New Germantown and Bedminster, New Jersey. On November 6, 1770, Muhlenberg married Anna Barbara Meyer, and the couple had six children together. In 1771, he accepted a position as pastor of a church in Woodstock, Virginia, and traveled to England to be ordained as a minister in the Anglican Church. His work in the ministry led him into politics, and he was elected to the Virginia House of Burgesses in 1774. With the growing tensions between England and America, he was appointed chairman of the Committee of Safety for Dunmore County.[1]

In 1775, at the request of George Washington, Muhlenberg raised the 8th Virginia Regiment, composed of German-Americans from the Shenandoah Valley. He received a commission as colonel, and was given command of the regiment. With his regiment, Muhlenberg took part in the repulse of the British, at Charleston, South Carolina, in 1776. The regiment would remain in Charleston until 1778, when it was ordered to join Washington's main body. On February 21, 1777, Muhlenberg was commissioned a brigadier general by the Continental Congress. In that capacity, he took part in the defense of Philadelphia, and the battle of Monmouth, in 1778. Though Muhlenberg did not see as much combat as many other Revolutionary War generals, he was an efficient and well-respected officer in the Continental Army, and won commendation for his abilities as an administrator.

On September 30, 1783, he was given the brevet rank of major general by a grateful Congress.[2]

Following the war, Muhlenberg moved back to Pennsylvania, where he received a hero's welcome. In 1784, he was elected to the Supreme Council of the state, and served as its vice president from 1785 to 1788. In 1789, he was elected to the first United States Congress, and was re-elected to the third Congress in 1793. He was a presidential elector in 1796, and was elected to the U.S. Senate in 1801, but resigned in June of that year to accept an appointment from President Jefferson to be the supervisor of revenue for Pennsylvania and the collector of customs at Philadelphia. He served in this capacity for the remainder of his life.

John Peter Gabriel Muhlenberg died at his home, Gray's Ferry, Montgomery County, Pennsylvania, on October 1, 1807, his birthday, at the age of sixty-one. He was buried in the Augustus Lutheran Church Cemetery, in Trappe, Pennsylvania.[3]

NASH, FRANCIS—(**Virginia**) Francis Nash was born in Prince Edward County, Virginia, in 1742. His family moved to North Carolina before he reached maturity, and settled in the New Bern area. Though little is known of the particulars, Nash obviously received an adequate education to enable him to study law and gain admittance to the North Carolina bar. He established a law practice in Hillsborough, engaged in mercantile pursuits, and was appointed a justice of the peace. He served as clerk of the Superior Court of Orange County, and was elected to the North Carolina state legislature, and married Sarah Moore.

At the outbreak of hostilities with England, Nash was commissioned lieutenant colonel of the 1st North Carolina Regiment on September 1, 1775. He was promoted to the rank of colonel and given command of the regiment on April 10, 1777. In 1776, he took part in the expedition to aid Charleston, South Carolina, and was afterwards ordered to join Washington's main army with his brigade. Nash quickly became one of Washington's favorite officers, and on February 5, 1777, he received a commission, from the Continental Congress, as a brigadier general. Nash fought with distinction at the battle of Brandywine, on September 11, 1777. On October 4, 1777, at the battle of Germantown, Nash received a mortal wound, at the head of his regiment, when his thigh was shattered by a spent cannon ball. He was taken to Towamencin, to the home of Adam Gotwals, where he died on October 7, 1777, in his thirty-fifth year. Francis Nash was buried in the Mennonite Meeting House Cemetery, in Towamencin, Pennsylvania. Nash was one of the bright, rising stars of the Continental Army, and had acquired a reputation for soldierly qualities that was second to none. He had gained the attention of General Washington, and was undoubtedly on track for more responsible assignments with the army, at the time of his death. It was said that no officer's passing was more universally regretted in the army than was his. At his death, one of his friends described him as "one of the most enlightened, liberal and magnanimous gentlemen that ever sacrificed his life for his country." Nashville, Tennessee; Nashville, North Carolina; and Nashville, Georgia, were all named in his honor.[1]

NEILSON, JOHN—(**New Jersey**) John Neilson was born at New Brunswick, New Jersey, on March 11, 1745. He received an adequate primary education and attended school at Philadelphia, Pennsylvania, and afterward entered into mercantile ventures in New Brunswick from 1769 to 1775. Neilson married Catharine Voorhees on December 31, 1768, and three children were born to the union. Neilson later married Lydia Quitterfield, and eight children were born to this marriage. He adopted the cause of liberty, and at the beginning of the Revolution, Neilson raised a company of Minutemen militia and became its captain in July of 1775. On August 31, 1776, he was commissioned colonel of the 2nd Regiment of Middlesex Militia, and on February 21, 1777, he received a commission as brigadier general in the New Jersey Militia. In 1779, Neilson was assigned to command the militia in the northern portion of the state, though subsequent responsibilities in the political field impinged upon his military duties.

Neilson was elected a delegate from New

Jersey to the Continental Congress from 1778 to 1779. In 1787, he was elected to be a delegate to the Constitutional Convention, but failed to attend. He did, however, serve as a delegate in the state convention to ratify the Federal Constitution. In 1792, he was one of the founders of Alexander Hamilton's manufacturing company established at Paterson, New Jersey. Neilson was elected to the New Jersey state legislature in 1800 and served until 1801, when he retired to private life.

John Neilson died at New Brunswick, New Jersey, on March 3, 1833, at the age of eighty-seven. He was buried in the Van Liew Cemetery, in New Brunswick.[1]

NELSON, THOMAS, JR. (Virginia) Thomas Nelson, Jr. was born at Yorktown, Virginia, on December 26, 1738, the son of a wealthy merchant of the city. His received the foundation of a primary education before being sent to England, at the age of fourteen, where he was enrolled in a private school, before attending Cambridge University. In 1761, Nelson returned to Virginia, and the following year married the daughter of Philip Grymes. He had been given a sizeable fortune by his father when he married, and the couple settled in Yorktown, and enjoyed an opulent life together. Nelson added to the fortune he had been given by becoming a successful planter and merchant.

Nelson became justice of the peace for York County in 1764, and was elected to the House of Burgesses that same year, serving till 1774. In 1774, he was a member of the first general convention, held in Williamsburg. He was also a member of the second general convention, held in 1775, during which he introduced a resolution that the state organize a military force for home defense, given the rising tensions between the colonies and Great Britain. He was appointed as a delegate to the Continental Congress in 1775, at which time he resigned a commission as colonel in the Virginia militia. Nelson continued to serve in the Continental Congress until 1777, when a disease of the head that caused paralysis forced him to relinquish his seat and return home to Virginia. In 1776, while still occupying his seat, he was a signer of the Declaration of Independence.

When his health began to return, his services were again sought by the governor, who commissioned Nelson a brigadier general in the militia and made him commander in chief of the forces of the commonwealth. He would hold this position from 1777 to 1782. Nelson performed important service, in this capacity, in marshalling the militia of Virginia, and his vast personal fortune was placed at the disposal of the cause. In many instances, he used his personal wealth to forward military operations that otherwise would have to have been curtailed.

In 1779, thinking him fully recovered from his illness, he was induced to once again take a seat in Congress, but the strenuous duties produced a relapse, and he was once more forced to resign his seat and return home. For a second time, his health returned, and in 1781, he succeeded Thomas Jefferson as governor of the commonwealth, at a time when the British were threatening Virginia. Under his firm leadership, the military forces of Virginia were kept in the field until the victory at Yorktown provided the finishing stroke of the war. Following the surrender of Cornwallis, the infirmity that had plagued Nelson returned, and he was forced to resign his position as governor. Following his resignation, he was accused of abusing his powers as governor by taking actions without the approval of the council. A committee was appointed to examine the charges, and Nelson was acquitted. It was the opinion of the committee that he had acted properly, given the necessity of the situation, and had acted, in all things, in the public good. Following this acquittal, Nelson retired to private life.

Thomas Nelson died on January 4, 1789, at the young age of fifty, at his plantation, called Offley Hoo. The recurring health problems that had so hampered his career finally led to his demise. He was buried in the Grace Episcopal Church Cemetery, in Yorktown, Virginia, and his gravesite is a National Historic Site, under the care of the National Park Service.[1]

NEUVILLE, CHEVALIER DE LA— (France) Chevalier de la Neuville was born in France in 1740. He had served for some twenty years in the French army when he and his brother, Normoint, came to America in 1777 to offer their services to the Continental Army. Upon presenting himself to the Continental Congress, Neuville was made inspector of the army commanded by General Horatio Gates, in the Northern Department, on May 14, 1778. Congress had left his commission in a state of limbo, however, declaring that he would be evaluated after three months service and assigned a suitable commission at that time. Neuville served in the army for six months without receiving his evaluation from Congress or the promotion that was supposed to accompany it. He was a good officer, but was known as a strict disciplinarian among the troops, and was not popular with the men in the ranks. Dismayed by the lack of recognition he received from Congress, Neuville applied to Congress for permission to retire from the army, and that body granted his request on December 4, 1778, retiring him at the grade of brevet brigadier general. Neuville had formed a strong bond of admiration with General Gates, and kept up a lively correspondence with that officer after returning to France. His brother, Normoint, remained in America until 1779, serving in two campaigns before he too returned to France.

Chevalier de la Neuville died in France about 1800.[1]

NEVILLE, JOHN—(Virginia) John Neville was born in Prince William (present day Fauquier) County, Virginia, on July 26, 1731. In 1754, he served with George Washington in the Jumonville Campaign, that ended in the defeat of Washington's forces at Fort Necessity, Pennsylvania, and marked the beginning of the French and Indian War in America. That same year, Neville married Winifred Oldham, and the couple would have five children together. Neville established a home in Winchester, Virginia, becoming a landholder and vestryman of the Episcopal Church. He was also elected to be a justice of the peace and sheriff of Frederick County.

In 1775, Neville was ordered by the Virginia Provincial Council to take command of Fort Dunmore (the deserted Fort Pitt, in Pittsburgh, Pennsylvania, that Governor Dunmore had renamed to honor himself). On November 12, 1776, Neville was commissioned lieutenant colonel of the 12th Virginia Regiment. Neville remained at Fort Dunmore (Pitt) until 1777, when the boundary dispute between Virginia and Pennsylvania was finally settled. He then joined Washington's main army and took part in the battles of Trenton and Princeton, commanding the 8th Virginia Regiment with the rank of colonel. In October of 1777, Neville and his regiment fought in the battle of Germantown, and they performed well at Monmouth, New Jersey, in June of 1778. On September 14, 1778, Neville transferred to the 4th Virginia Regiment, and he served with this unit to the end of the war. In 1780, Neville and his command were sent to the Southern Department, where they took part in the siege at Charleston, South Carolina, from March 29 to May 12. Neville became a British prisoner following the surrender of Charleston, as did his son, Presley, who had previously served as Lafayette's aide-de-camp for two years. Father and son were held by the British for almost two years, not being released until 1782. After being granted his parole, Presley married Nancy Morgan, the daughter of General Daniel Morgan, in 1782. On September 30, 1783, the Continental Congress bestowed the rank of brevet brigadier general on John Neville, in recognition of his long and devoted service.

Following his military career, Neville, who owned property in Pennsylvania, was elected to the Superior Executive Council of that state. He also served as a delegate to the convention to ratify the U.S. Constitution. In 1794, Washington appointed Neville to be the inspector of revenue and to collect excise taxes on distilled spirits. This touched off the Whiskey Rebellion and made Neville one of the most hated men among the anti-federalist faction. On July 17, 1794, some 500 anti-federalist farmers attacked Neville's home in the Chartier's Valley, burning the house to the ground. Following this incident, Neville moved his family to Pittsburgh, Pennsylvania, and from there to Neville Island (formerly Montour's Island) in 1801.

John Neville died on July 29, 1803, at Pittsburgh, Pennsylvania, at the age of seventy-two. He was buried on property belonging to the Second Trinity Episcopal Church, but in 1900 his remains were moved to the Allegheny Cemetery when the Oliver Building was built on a portion of that burial ground.[1]

NEWCOMB, SILAS—**(Massachusetts)** Silas Newcomb was born at Edgartown, Dukes County, Massachusetts, on April 17, 1723. As a young man, Newcomb moved to New Jersey. He was married to Bathsheba Dayton, of Fairfield, New Jersey, in 1745, and the couple had four children together.

Newcomb served in the French and Indian War, taking part in General Wolfe's expedition against Quebec, where Newcomb was one of the 4,000 who scaled the heights of the Plains of Abraham, securing the victory that sealed the fate of the French defenders. Newcomb espoused the Patriot cause, and in 1774, he took part in a tea party held by citizens of Cumberland County, New Jersey. The British brig *Greyhound* had sailed into Delaware Bay and up the Cohansey Creek, laden with a shipment of tea from the East India Tea Company. The feeling of the British was that the sentiments of the people of New Jersey were less pronounced against the tea tax than was evident in Massachusetts. Newcomb and other citizens of Cumberland County proved the British wrong when they seized the ship and destroyed its cargo.

When open hostilities erupted, Newcomb offered his services to the state militia, and was commissioned a colonel on June 14, 1776, serving in the 1st Battalion of the Cumberland County Militia. On November 28, 1776, he was assigned to command of the 1st New Jersey Regiment. This regiment saw service in northern New Jersey, and in the operations in and around New York City in 1776 and 1777. On March 15, 1777, Newcomb was promoted to the rank of brigadier general in the New Jersey Militia. He resigned his commission on December 4 of that same year and returned to private life, ostensibly due to poor health.

Silas Newcomb died in 1779, at New England Cross Roads, Fairfield, New Jersey, in his fifty-seventh year.[1]

NICOLA, LEWIS—**(Ireland)** Lewis Nicola was born in Dublin, Ireland, in 1717, the son of a British army officer. Though little is known about the particulars, it is evident that Nicola received a solid educational background. There have been those who have forwarded the possibility that he was born in Germany, or in France, but the evidence would point to Ireland as being his country of nativity.[1] In 1740, at the age of twenty-three, Nicola's father purchased a commission as an ensign in the British army for him, and he started forth on his military career. In that same year, he married Christiana Doyle.

For the decade and a half from 1740 to 1755, Nicola's military service consisted mainly of garrison duty at a variety of posts, mostly in Ireland. At one time or another, he was stationed at Galway, Mannorhamilton, Londonderry, Dublin, and Cork. In 1755, he was posted to Charles Fort, near Kinsale, and promoted to the rank of fort major. For the next eleven years, Nicola would be stationed at Charles Fort. His wife, Christiana, died in 1760, and Nicola married Jane Bishop eight months later.

By the middle of the 1760s, Nicola was beginning to look about for opportunities for personal advancement. He had been "disappointed of an expected inheritance," and there was little promise of further advancement in the army. America seemed to be a land of opportunity, and accordingly, Nicola decided to move his family there, arriving in Philadelphia in August of 1766, and opening a dry goods store in the city. In 1767, he founded a circulating library, which his membership paid dues to belong to. His personal collection of two to three hundred books was considered massive by the standards of the day. Nicola's business ventures allowed him to move several times from 1766 to 1769, each time improving his circumstances until in the final year he moved to the fashionable Society Hill neighborhood. By 1771, he had expanded his library to over one thousand volumes. In 1769, Nicola gave up the dry goods business and tried his hand at publishing. He produced a magazine called the *American Magazine* or *General Repository*, but the venture was less than successful, folding after publishing only nine issues. In the early 1770s, the high cost of living in Philadelphia induced Nicola to move his family, first to Allentown, then to Easton. With the outbreak of the Revolution, he decided that the best place for him to live would again be Philadelphia, however.[2]

In 1775, Nicola was appointed to a committee to inspect the American defenses on the Delaware River. In 1776, he opened a porter house in Philadelphia, to sell beer, and shortly thereafter opened a school in the city. Nicola also got back into military service in 1776. In February of that year, he was appointed to be barrack master of the city of Philadelphia, and in December he was promoted to serve as town major. While thus employed, with all of the duties of his private ventures and public office. Nicola still found time to write a 96 page military drill handbook entitled, *Treatise of Military Exercise, Calculated for the Use of Americans*. He also translated a number of European military manuals into English.

In 1777, Nicola petitioned Congress to create an Invalid Corps, with him as its commander. It would be made up of men who were not fit for regular duty, but were still healthy enough to perform garrison duty. Congress adopted his suggestion, and on June 20, 1777, it commissioned Nicola to be the colonel of the newly created corps. The corps defended Philadelphia, until that city's capture by the British, in the fall of 1777, then relocated to Trenton. During the winter of 1777–78, the corps guarded hospitals and military stores in Easton and Bethlehem, Pennsylvania. The corps returned to Philadelphia, following its evacuation by the British in June of 1778, and for the next three years divided its time between Philadelphia and Boston. In June of 1781, Washington had the Invalid Corps ordered to West Point, New York. The corps did not arrive until July, but when it did, Nicola faced a court-martial over charges leveled at him by a subordinate officer under his command. In the end, the charges were dismissed and Nicola was cleared of any wrongdoing.[3]

In 1782, Nicola approached Washington with a proposal that has become known as the Nicola Affair. In it, he cited his personal distaste for Republican forms of government and proposed that Congress allot land, west of the frontier, to be settled by army veterans, where a new government could be established, conforming itself closely to the monarchies of Europe. Washington's response was one of surprise and repulsion. He emphatically informed Nicola that he would never be part of such a scheme, and advised his subordinate to never talk about such matters again.[4]

The Invalid Corps spent the final winter of the war doing garrison duty at West Point, Newburgh, Constitution Island, and Fishkill, New York. In May on 1783, Congress ordered the corps to be disbanded. As a reward for his services, Nicola was commissioned a brigadier general on November 27, 1783.

After the war, Nicola spent much of 1784 settling the accounts of the Invalid Corps. In the mid–1780s, he attempted to start a stage line from Philadelphia to Reading, but the state legislature refused to grant him exclusive rights to the line. In 1788, he was named commandant of the Pennsylvania Invalid Corps, and assigned to supervision of the Pennsylvania workhouse. During the Whiskey Rebellion, in 1794, Nicola was reinstated as the barrack master and town major for Philadelphia. He retired from public service in 1798, following the death of his second wife.

Lewis Nicola died in Philadelphia on August 9, 1807, in his ninetieth year. He was buried in the Old Presbyterian Meeting House Cemetery.

NIGHTINGALE, JOSEPH—(Rhode Island) Joseph Nightingale was born at Providence, Rhode Island, on September 16, 1749. After completing his primary education, Nightingale became a merchant, making an admirable living trading with overseas markets. On December 27, 1769, he married Elizabeth Waitstill Cortiss, and the couple had two children together.

In December of 1776, following the resignation of Joshua Babcock to accept the seat in the Rhode Island House of Representatives to which he had been elected, Nightingale was commissioned to replace him in the Rhode Island Militia, and given the rank of major general. It would appear that Nightingale's service was largely on alarms, and that he was called to service only during times of local crisis.

Following the war, Nightingale became a partner in a land venture that purchased the towns of Gilead and Number 31, Vermont. Present day Brighton, Vermont, was one of the towns purchased by Nightingale and his investors.

Joseph Nightingale died at Providence, Rhode Island, on November 3, 1797, at the age of forty-eight. The Nightingale-Brown House, on Benefit Street, in Providence, was built by the general in 1791.[1]

NIXON, JOHN—(Massachusetts) John Nixon was born at Framingham, Massachusetts, on March 4, 1725, the oldest of seven children. He joined the army at an early age, fighting in King George's War under the command of Sir William Pepperrill, and was present at the capture of Louisburg. After serving in the army and navy for seven years, he returned home to Framingham, where he married Thankful Berry in 1754 and settled on a 32 acre farm on Nobscot Hill, in Sudbury, Massachusetts. The couple had nine children together. The site of his home is now part of the Nobscot Boy Scout Reservation. In 1755, during the French and Indian War, Nixon was commissioned a captain and served at the battles of Fort Ticonderoga and Lake George.

In 1774, Nixon was elected captain of the Sudbury West Side Minuteman Company, and on April 19, 1775, when Paul Revere's alarm brought the countryside to arms, he marched his company to Concord, where they took part in the battle. Nixon was promoted to the rank of colonel on April 24. He fought with distinction at the battle of Bunker Hill, where he was ordered to hold an unguarded gap in the line that was exposed and offered little protection. Nixon's men held firm through two assaults by the British. By the third British attack, the men had begun to run out of ammunition, but still they held their post, fighting a desperate hand-to-hand struggle. Nixon's men left their position only after being ordered to do so by the commanding general. Nixon himself received a wound in the battle from which he never fully recovered.[1]

On January 1, 1776, Nixon was given command of the 4th Continental Infantry Regiment. With this regiment he took part in the operations around New York City during that year. His leadership was such that he received a commission as a brigadier general, from the Continental Congress, on August 9, 1776. He was entrusted with the command of Governor's Island, in New York Harbor. Nixon commanded the 1st Massachusetts Regiment, under General Gates, in the Northern Department, during the Saratoga Campaign. He was at the battle of Stillwater, in October of 1777, where a cannon ball passed so close to his head that it permanently impaired the sight in one eye and the hearing in one ear. Nixon never fully recovered from this wound, or the one received at Bunker Hill, and, as a result, he resigned his commission on September 12, 1780. Retiring to private life, he returned to his farm in Sudbury. In 1806, he moved to Middlebury, Vermont, where he died on March 24, 1815, at the age of ninety.[2]

OGDEN, MATTHIAS—(New Jersey) Matthias Ogden was born at Elizabethtown, New Jersey, on October 22, 1754, the son of Robert Ogden, a prominent lawyer and politician in the town, who was serving in the state legislature at the time of Matthias' birth. Matthias was afforded all of the opportunities of affluent society, including a fine education, and attended the College of New Jersey (modern day Princeton University).

In 1765, during the Stamp Act crisis, Ogden's father chose a stance that might possibly have alienated the family from the Patriot cause. The New Jersey Assembly had drafted a Declaration of Rights and Grievances that was to be sent to the king and to Parliament. Ogden disagreed with the way the document was to be submitted, and refused to sign it. For this, he gained the ire of the people of New Jersey and was burned in effigy. He subsequently resigned his seat in the assembly.[1]

Robert Ogden's resistance to Colonial responses in the Stamp Act crisis did not lessen his fervor, nor that of his son, for the Patriot cause. Matthias accompanied General Arnold's Canadian expedition as a volunteer, and was wounded in the assault on Quebec on December 31, 1775. In March of 1776, he was commissioned lieutenant colonel of the 1st New Jersey Regiment, being promoted to command of the regiment on January 1, 1777. With that regiment, he took part in the New York operations of 1777, the defense of Philadelphia, and the Monmouth campaign. In 1779, he participated in the expedition against the Iroquois. On October 5, 1780 he was taken prisoner at his home in Elizabethtown and held by the British until April of 1781. Ogden concluded his wartime service by taking part in the Yorktown Campaign, and by commanding the unsuccessful attempt to capture Prince William Henry (subsequently William IV), before requesting leave to travel to Europe. Congress granted the leave in 1783, and Ogden did not return to the army. Nevertheless, on September 30, 1783, Congress recognized his service to the country by bestowing the rank of brevet brigadier general upon him.[2]

After the war, Ogden served as a member of the New Jersey legislative council, in 1785. In 1789, he was chosen to be a presidential elector from New Jersey.

Matthias Ogden died on March 31, 1791, at the age of thirty-six. He was buried in the Elizabethtown Cemetery, in Elizabethtown, Essex, New Jersey.[3]

O'HARA, JAMES — (Ireland) James O'Hara was born in Ireland in 1752. He served for three years in the British army, as an ensign, before coming to America in 1772, just prior to the break between the Colonies and Great Britain. O'Hara landed in Philadelphia, but soon made his way to western Pennsylvania, where he earned a living as an Indian trader. In March of 1774, he was made the government agent among the Indians for the colony of Pennsylvania.

When the Revolutionary War broke out, O'Hara raised and equipped a company of militia, and offered his services to the Colonists. He was ordered to proceed to Fort Canhawa (now Kanawha) that had been built by the state of Virginia. O'Hara and his men remained on garrison duty in the fort until 1779. By that time, brushes with the Indians on the frontier had reduced the number of men in O'Hara's company to twenty-nine, and he was forced to abandon the fort. He attached his command to General Broadhead's northern Virginia forces. In 1780, he was appointed commissary for the General Hospital, and was stationed at Carlisle, Pennsylvania. In 1781, he was made assistant quartermaster, and that same year was commissioned a brigadier general in the Pennsylvania Militia. O'Hara was instrumental in gathering and distributing supplies for the Southern Department during the campaign of 1781, and often traveled with the army.

Following the war, O'Hara took up residence in Pittsburgh, where he built a log cabin. In 1789, he was chosen to be a presidential elector. On April 19, 1792, he was appointed to be the first quartermaster-general in the United States Army, serving in this capacity until 1796. That same year, he married Mary Carson, and plunged into a number of business ventures. O'Hara opened a sawmill in Allegheny City, and was a partner in a glass factory that was the first of its kind in western Pennsylvania. He also entered into ship building, in Pittsburgh. O'Hara ran for Congress in 1802 and 1804, but failed to win a seat in either election. In 1804, he was appointed director of the Pittsburgh branch of the Bank of Pennsylvania. In 1811, he became a partner in an iron works factory in Ligonier, Pennsylvania.

James O'Hara died at Pittsburgh, Pennsylvania, on April 8, 1834, in his seventy-third year.[1]

ORNE, AZOR — (Massachusetts) Azor Orne was born at Marblehead, Massachusetts, on July 22, 1731, the son of Deacon Joshua Orne, a wealthy merchant of Marblehead. Orne received a primary education before entering into the merchant business, like his father. On January 27, 1754, Orne married Mary Coleman, and the couple had one child. In 1773, Orne, in company with several other prominent Marblehead citizens, built a smallpox hospital on Cat Island. Though the hospital treated hundreds of cases of smallpox, there were still more than a dozen cases reported in the town, and angry residents eventually burned the hospital down in 1774.

Orne became an early advocate of the Patriot cause, joined the local militia, and became a colonel in the state service. In 1774, he was elected to be a delegate to the Essex Convention and to the Massachusetts Provincial Congress. He was also a member of the Committee of Safety and the Committee of Military Affairs. Elected as a representative to the 1st Continental Congress, Orne declined to accept the position for personal reasons. He had never attended college, and felt that his lack of education disqualified him from holding some important government offices. On April 19, 1775, when the fighting took place at Lexington and Concord, Orne was at the Black Horse Tavern with Sam Adams and John Hancock, having a meeting of the Committee of Safety and Supply. The Patriots were forced to hide in a cornfield as British soldiers searched the tavern for members of the "Rebel Congress." In 1775, Orne was appointed judge of the General Court, and in January of 1776, the Massachusetts Provincial Congress commissioned him one of three major generals in the state militia.

Orne loaned large sums of money to the government to support the war effort. In 1780, he was a representative at the Hartford Convention, where a system of finance, by means of taxes and duties, was forwarded to pay for the accumulated public debt. After the adoption of the state constitution that same year, Orne served in the state senate. He was a delegate to the Massachusetts convention to ratify the Federal Constitution, and was named as an elector for the first presidential election. Orne was offered higher stations in the new government, but refused to accept them on the basis of his lack of formal education. This probably accounts for his strong support of the public school system and his many efforts and contributions in its behalf.

Azor Orne died at Boston, Massachusetts, on June 6, 1796, at the age of sixty-four. He was buried in the Green Street Cemetery, in Marblehead, Massachusetts.[1]

PALMER, JOSEPH — (England) Joseph Palmer was born in England in 1716. Little is known of his early life in England until he emigrated to America in 1746, along with a brother-in-law. Palmer settled in the Boston area, in Roxbury, where he and his brother-in-law entered into a variety of business ventures. In 1752, they built a glassworks in Germantown (part of present day Quincy), Massachusetts, and they subsequently built a chocolate mill and salt mills. In the 1770s, Palmer became an ardent supporter of the cause of liberty. He served in the Massachusetts Provincial Congress, and as a member of the Cambridge Committee of Safety. A member of the local militia, Palmer fought at the battle of Lexington, on April 19, 1775. On February 9, 1776 he was commissioned a colonel in the state militia, and was promoted to the rank of brigadier general for Suffolk County on May 9 of that same year.

Palmer served frequently in the field in and around Boston, helping to protect the Massachusetts coastline. He undertook intelligence gathering missions in Vermont and Rhode Island, and led a failed attack on Newport, Rhode Island. Palmer served as a brigadier general of militia for the entire war. Afterward he attempted to return to private life and the operation of his factories. Poor health and ruined finances compelled him to leave Germantown, however, and try to establish himself elsewhere. In 1784, he opened a salt factory at Boston Neck.

Joseph Palmer died at his home in Dorchester, Massachusetts, on December 25, 1788, in his sixty-second year.[1]

PARSONS, SAMUEL HOLDEN — (Connecticut) Samuel Holden Parsons was born in Lyme, Connecticut, on May 14, 1737. At the age of nine, his family moved to Newburyport, Massachusetts, where his father became minister to the town's Presbyterian Church. Parsons received a substantial primary education, and attended Harvard, graduating from that institution in 1756. He then took up the study of law, under the supervision of an uncle, being admitted to the Massachusetts Bar in 1759, and establishing a practice in Lyme, Connecticut. In 1761, he married Mehitabel Mather. In 1762, he was elected to the Connecticut General Assembly.

Parsons moved to New London, where he became a member of the Committee of Correspondence, writing Sam Adams as early as 1772 to urge a congress of the colonies. He was also an early advocate of breaking ties with England. Like most political leaders of the day, Parsons was a member of the militia, being commissioned a major of Connecticut troops in 1770.

In 1775, after the battles of Lexington and Concord, Parsons, then a member of the Connecticut legislature, proposed the expedition against British-held Fort Ticonderoga, and was able to raise the funding for the project through public and private means.

On May 1, 1775, he was commissioned colonel of the 6th Connecticut Regiment, and in June of that same year he led his regiment at the battle of Bunker Hill. He remained in Boston until the British evacuation, in March of 1776. In the meantime, he had been made colonel of the 10th Continental Regiment. On August 9, 1776, Congress commissioned Parsons a brigadier general and ordered him to New York. He took part in the fighting at Battle Hill, on August 17, 1776. While in New York, Parsons was responsible for ordering the first submarine attack in American military history. David Bushnell, a Connecticut inventor, had devised a submarine that he intended to use to place torpedoes on the British ships in the harbor. Parsons readily adopted Bushnell's plan, and ordered his brother-in-law, Captain Ezra Lee, to undertake the mission. Lee was able to successfully pilot the craft to the British flagship, *Asia*, but was unable to attach the bomb to its side. The resulting explosion did little other than to excite the English sailors, doing no damage to the ship.

Parsons fought with distinction at the battle of White Plains before returning to Connecticut to recruit men to fill the army's depleted ranks. He led raids on Loyalist strongholds in Long Island, and participated in the defense of Connecticut from incursions by British forces under the command of General William Tryon.

During the winter of 1777–78, Parsons was in command at West Point, New York, where he was responsible for rebuilding many of the fortifications that had fallen into a state of disrepair. In December of 1779, Parsons was directed to take command of General Putnam's division. In September of 1780, after the uncovering of Benedict Arnold's scheme to surrender West Point, Parsons was one of the board of officers that tried Major John Andre and sentenced him to death. On October 23, 1780, he was promoted to major general in the Continental Army. During the winter of 1780–81, he helped to suppress the mutinies of the Pennsylvania and New Jersey troops, and made a raid on a Loyalist stronghold at Westchester, north of New York City. When Washington's main army departed for the Yorktown Campaign, Parsons was left behind to contain the British in New York, and prevent them from re-enforcing Cornwallis. On July 22, 1782, physically broken and financially destitute from his service in the army, Parsons tendered his resignation and retired from the army.

Parsons retired to Middletown, Connecticut, where he renewed his law practice. He was elected to the state legislature, and became involved in organizing the Connecticut branch of the Society of the Cincinnati. In March of 1787, Parsons was named director of the Ohio Land Company. Though he aspired to become governor of the Ohio Territory, he was named chief justice instead. Congress appointed him along with James Varnum and John Symmes to be the first judges of the Northwest Territory. While on a trip to survey lands for the Ohio Territory, Parsons drowned in the Beaver River on November 17, 1789, at the age of fifty-two, when his canoe overturned. His body was not recovered till the following May, and was buried with the intention of later re-interment to another site. The exact location of his grave was forgotten, however, and Samuel Holden Parsons now rests in an unmarked, unknown grave along the banks of the Beaver River.[1]

PATTERSON, JOHN — (Connecticut)
John Patterson was born at Farmington, Hartford County, Connecticut, in 1744. After receiving his primary education, he attended Yale College, graduating from that institution in 1762. Following his graduation, he taught school, and studied law, eventually establishing a legal practice and becoming a justice of the peace. On June 2, 1766, he married Elizabeth Lee, and the couple had eight children together. He represented Lenox, Massachusetts, in the General Court.

In April of 1775 he was commissioned a colonel in the 26th Regiment, Berkshire Militia, and served at the battle of Bunker Hill. He took part in the siege of Boston, and his regiment occupied a position around Roxbury. On January 1, 1776, he was assigned to the command of the 15th Continental Infantry. With this regiment, he took part in the operations around Lake Champlain. On February 21, 1777, he was commissioned a brigadier general by the Continental Congress. Patterson fought with distinction in the Saratoga Campaign, and in the battle of Monmouth. He served as a member of the military panel that tried Major John Andre for his part in Benedict Arnold's treachery, and sentenced him to be hung. On September 30, 1783, the Continental Congress bestowed the rank of brevet major general upon him in recognition of his many services to the cause.

Patterson was one of the founding members of the Society of the Cincinnati in Massachusetts, and served as its vice president. He later moved to New York, where he became chief justice of the county court. He was elected to the state legislature for four years, and in 1803 was elected to the U.S. Congress, as a representative of New York.

John Patterson died at Lisle, New York, on July 19, 1808, in his sixty-eighth year.[1]

PATTERSON, SAMUEL—(Delaware)
Samuel Patterson was born at White Clay Creek Hundred, New Castle County, Delaware. His exact date of birth is not recorded, and it is estimated that he was born in 1718, or later. Little is known of his early life or education. Patterson never married. During the French and Indian War, Patterson served as a captain in the militia. Following the end of the war, he operated a flour mill, near Christiana, Delaware.

At the outbreak of hostilities with Great Britain, Patterson was commissioned a colonel in the Delaware Militia in 1775. In 1776, he was assigned to command the Delaware contingent of the Flying Camp. That same year, he was promoted to the rank of brigadier general in the state militia, serving in that capacity through to the close of hostilities. The Delaware Regiment took part in the operations in and around New York City in 1776, and in the Trenton and Princeton Campaigns. In 1777, it participated in the defense of Philadelphia, later taking part in the Monmouth Campaign.

Following the end of the war, Patterson was elected to be the first treasurer of the state of Delaware, a position he would hold for the rest of his life.

Samuel Patterson died on May 29, 1785. The exact location of his death is not recorded, but it was most probably in New Castle County. He was buried in the Presbyterian Cemetery, in Christiana, Delaware.[1]

PICKENS, ANDREW—(Pennsylvania)
Andrew Pickens was born in Paxton, Bucks County, Pennsylvania, on September 19, 1739. His family moved to Augusta County, Virginia, when Andrew was a boy, and from there they moved to the Waxhaws region of South Carolina. Pickens participated in the Cherokee War of 1760–61, serving as an officer in Colonel James Grant's expedition against the lower Cherokee settlements. In 1764, Pickens sold his farm in the Waxhaws and bought land in the Long Cane Creek settlement, in southwestern South Carolina, along the Georgia border. Here he met Rebecca Calhoun, and the two were married in 1765, and had twelve children together. Pickens earned his living as both a farmer and an Indian trader, and enjoyed success in both.

When the war broke out, Pickens cast his lot with the Patriots, and was commissioned a captain in the South Carolina Militia in 1775. He was subsequently promoted to colonel of South Carolina state troops. On November 19, 1775, Pickens fought at the battle of Ninety-Six, South Carolina, where Major Andrew Williamson, with 600 militia, engaged a Loyalist force of some 1,800 men. During the winter of 1775, he participated in Snow's Campaign. In the fall of 1776 Pickens took part in Williamson's expedition against the Cherokee. On February 14, 1779, Pickens won a dramatic victory at the battle of Kettle Creek, which destroyed Loyalist morale in the state. In 1780, Pickens surrendered a fort in the Ninety-Six district and following his capture went home on parole, awaiting exchange. While at his home, Loyalist raiders destroyed most of his property and threatened the safety of his family. Pickens informed the British that the terms of his parole had been violated, and as a result he was soon back in the Ninety-Six district leading guerrilla operations against the enemy. On January 17, 1781, Pickens commanded the militia in General Daniel Morgan's army at the battle of Cowpens. He was promoted to the rank of brigadier general of South Carolina state troops, by a grateful governor, following the victory, and Congress voted to present him with a sword. In the spring of 1781, Pickens participated in the siege of Augusta, Georgia, which ended with the surrender of that place, by the British, on June 5, 1781. He then joined General Greene in his failed siege of Ninety-Six. He commanded the left wing of the American army at the battle of Eutaw Springs, on September 8, 1781, where he was wounded. In November of that same year, he participated in an expedition against the Cherokee that resulted in the Indians surrendering all claims to lands south of the Savannah River and east of the Chattahoochee River.[1]

In 1782, Pickens was elected to the state assembly. He was a member of the convention that framed the state constitution for South Carolina, and in 1794 he was elected to the United States Congress for one term. In 1797, he was returned to the state assembly, where he served for fourteen consecutive years. He built a new home, Hopewell, in Oconee, Georgia, and lived there a number of years before moving to the Pendleton District of South Carolina.

Andrew Pickens died on August 11, 1817, at the age of seventy-seven.

PINCKNEY, CHARLES COTESWORTH—(**South Carolina**) Charles Cotesworth Pinckney was born at Charleston, South Carolina, on February 25, 1746. His family was among the wealthiest and most influential in South Carolina, and the Pinckneys maintained close ties with England and supported the royal colonial government. His father served as the chief justice of South Carolina, as well as being a member of its Royal Council. His mother had attained fame for introducing the cultivation of indigo, which quickly became one of South Carolina's main cash crops. In 1753, the family moved to London, where the father served as the agent for South Carolina. While there, Pinckney received a good education, being enrolled at the Westminster Preparatory School. He remained in England when the family returned to America in 1758 to complete his education, first at Christ Church College, in Oxford, followed by the Middle Temple, in London, where he studied law. Pinckney concluded his time in Europe by studying botany

Charles Cotesworth Pinckney (courtesy National Archives)

and chemistry for a year at the French military academy at Caen. When he returned to South Carolina, Pinckney established himself as a lawyer, in addition to helping to run the family estates. Pinckney was truly a Southern gentleman, and was groomed to assume his proper place in the aristocracy of the planter class, but when division with England became apparent, he sided with the Patriot cause, risking everything in the cause of freedom.

In 1769, Pinckney joined the 1st South Carolina Militia Regiment, and was promptly elected lieutenant. In 1770, he was elected to the South Carolina legislature, and in 1773 he was appointed regional attorney general. Pinckney married Sarah Middleton, daughter and sister of the politically active Middletons of South Carolina who would serve in the Continental Congress and sign the Declaration of Independence. In 1775, he was elected to the Provincial Congress, and was a member of the Council of Safety, where he played an important role in organizing the military forces of the state.[1]

On June 17, 1775, he became captain of the elite Grenadiers of the 1st South Carolina Regiment, a company he had personally raised. With his company, he participated in the successful defense of Charleston in 1776. On September 16, 1776, Pinckney was commissioned colonel and given command of the 1st South Carolina Regiment. The repulse of the British at Charleston brought a period of inactivity in the South, and Pinckney took the opportunity to serve on Washington's staff in 1777, performing in that capacity at the battles of Brandywine and Germantown. In 1778, when the British were mounting a new threat against South Carolina, Pinckney returned home to resume command of his regiment in the failed campaign against the British in Florida. Pinckney led a brigade, under the command of General Benjamin Lincoln, in the failed assault on Savannah in October of 1779, and at the unsuccessful defense of Charleston in 1780. When the city fell in May of that year, Pinckney became a British prisoner of war. He was held at Haddrell's Point in Charleston Harbor, where his captors tried to induce him to abandon the Patriot cause. Pinckney's answer became a battle cry of defiance: "If I had a vein that did not beat with the love of my Country, I myself would open it. If I had a drop of blood that could flow dishonorable, I myself would let it out." He was held prisoner for an extended period, not being exchanged until 1782. By the time of his release, the fighting was largely over, but he remained with his troops until they were mustered out of the service in November of 1783. In recognition of his service, the Continental Congress gave Pinckney a commission as brevet brigadier general on November 3, 1783.[2]

Following the Revolution, Pinckney devoted himself to his plantations, and his law practice. He was a member of the South Carolina legislature until 1790. He continued to be active in the militia, rising to the rank of major general, and commander of one of South Carolina's two militia divisions. In 1784, his wife died, and in 1785 he was wounded in a duel with Daniel Huger. In 1787, he was selected to represent South Carolina at the Constitutional Convention, where he advocated for a strong national government. In 1790, he was a member of the committee that drafted a new state constitution for South Carolina. Following the creation of the state constitution, Pinckney retired from politics to devote time to personal endeavors. He repeatedly declined offers of political appointment from Washington until 1796, when he accepted a post as the ambassador to France. Here he was involved in the XYZ affair where the French refused to acknowledge his credentials and demanded a bribe from America before they would even discuss the issue of French interference with American shipping. Pinckney took affront to this slight against America's honor, broke off all negotiations and returned home. In response to the French actions, Congress voted to raise a new provisional army, and Pinckney was chosen to be one of its primary leaders, being commissioned a major general on July 19, 1798. Pinckney was given command of all forces south of Maryland, as the country prepared for a possible war with France. The differences between the two countries were successfully reconciled by negotiation in 1800, however, and Pinckney was discharged from the army on June 15, 1800.

In 1800, Pinckney made a failed bid for the vice presidency, and would run unsuccessful campaigns for the presidency against Thomas Jefferson and James Madison.

Charles Coatesworth Pinckney died at Charleston, South Carolina, on August 16, 1825, at the age of seventy-nine. He was buried at the St. Michael's Episcopal Church Cemetery in that city.[3]

POLK, THOMAS—**(Pennsylvania)** Thomas Polk was born at Carlisle, Cumberland County, Pennsylvania, in 1730. Polk moved to Mecklenburg County, North Carolina, where he married Susanna Spratt in 1755. The couple had eight children together. Polk became a farmer and planter, and was so successful in his private ventures that he was the second richest man in Mecklenburg County by the time of the Revolution. Polk also served as a justice of the peace, and was commissioner of Charlotte, North Carolina. He was a leader of the Mecklenburg Resolves, and it is said that he caused the Mecklenburg Declaration of Independence to be drawn up, and that he read it to his fellow citizens from the steps of the county court house on May 20, 1775, over a year before the united colonies adopted a stance for independence.

In 1775, Polk was commissioned a colonel in the North Carolina Militia, and on April 16, 1776, he was assigned to the command of the 4th North Carolina Regiment. Polk and his regiment joined Washington's main army, taking part in the defense of Philadelphia and the Monmouth Campaign before being ordered back to the Southern Department. Polk resigned his commission on June 28, 1778, the day the battle of Monmouth was fought. He returned to North Carolina, where he was commissioned a brigadier general in the state service in 1781, serving in that capacity until the end of the war. Polk fought at the battle of Eutaw Springs, South Carolina, on September 8, 1781, suffering a wound while leading his troops in combat.

Following the war, Polk was elected to be a representative from North Carolina to the Continental Congress in 1786. In 1791, he was host to President Washington when he visited Charlotte, North Carolina. Polk retired to private life, and resumed his farming and land interests.

Thomas Polk died at Charlotte, North Carolina, on June 26, 1794, in his sixty-fourth year. In addition to his personal accomplishments, he bears the distinction of being the great-uncle of President James Polk.[1]

POMEROY, SETH—**(Massachusetts)** Seth Pomeroy was born in Northampton, Massachusetts, on May 20, 1706. As a young man, he showed an aptitude for mechanical things, and became known as one of the best gunsmiths in the colony. In 1732 he married Mary Hunt, and the couple would have one son, Dr. Medad Pomeroy. Pomeroy served as a major in the Massachusetts Militia during King George's War, and participated in William Pepperill's expedition against Fortress Louisburg in Nova Scotia in 1745. Pomeroy used his gunsmithing skills in reconditioning the French cannon that had been spiked and put them into service during the bombardment.

During the French and Indian War, Pomeroy was made lieutenant colonel of Colonel Ephraim Williams' regiment in 1755. He took part in the expedition against Crown Point, New York. On the march to Crown Point, the regiment was ambushed by a mixed French and Indian force commanded by Baron Dieskau. Colonel Williams was killed in the engagement, and Pomeroy took command of the regiment. He retreated to the British camp at the south end of Lake George. Once there, he had a wooden wall built, supported by cannon, and prepared to make a stand. When Dieskau's force approached, they were dissuaded from making a frontal assault in the open because of the barricade Pomeroy had erected. When Dieskau was wounded in skirmishing between the forces, the French and Indians withdrew to Fort Frontenac (later Fort Ticonderoga).

Pomeroy was already a brigadier general and senior officer in the Massachusetts Militia when the fighting occurred at Lexington and Concord. When the British forces at Boston were besieged, he went to that city as a volunteer. On June 17, 1775, when the British bombardment signaled the beginning of the battle of Bunker Hill, Pomeroy borrowed a horse from General Ward and made his way to Charlestown and the front lines. When he reached the neck of the peninsula, the bombardment became so heavy that he despaired of being able to cross over to the American lines, and he accordingly turned his horse over to a soldier to return to General Ward, not wanting to be responsible for the death of the borrowed steed. He then shouldered a musket and marched across the peninsula, taking a place in the battle line and fighting as a private in the ranks, in John Stark's regiment. The week after the battle, the Continental Congress commissioned Pomeroy a brigadier general in the Continental Army. In fact, he was appointed to be the senior brigadier general in the army. When a dispute arose over this seniority, Pomeroy resigned his commission, citing his advanced age of seventy years and failing health as disqualifying him for command. He subsequently left the service and retired to his farm. In 1776, when the British overran New Jersey, General Washington issued a call for help, and Pomeroy responded, organizing the militia in his area and marching them to Washington's relief. Pomeroy never made it to New Jersey, however. He died along the line of march, at Peekskill, New York, on February 9, 1777, in his seventy-first year. Seth Pomeroy was buried in the graveyard of St. Peter's Church, in that city. The cemetery later became part of Hillside Cemetery.[1]

POOR, ENOCH — **(Massachusetts)** Enoch Poor was born in Andover, Massachusetts, on June 21, 1736. In 1755, at the age of nineteen, he enlisted in the Massachusetts Militia as a private, and took part in General Amherst's expedition against Louisburg, Nova Scotia. When that place was captured, his regiment was assigned the duty of expelling the Acadians from the area. After the French and Indian War, Poor returned home to Andover just long enough to elope with Martha Osgood. The couple settled in Exeter, New Hampshire, where Poor established himself as a merchant and ship builder.

Poor was an early opponent of British tyranny, and the passage of the Stamp Act, in 1765 caused him to take a leading role in the local politics of Exeter. In 1775, he was elected to the New Hampshire Provincial Assembly, and following the battles at Lexington and Concord, he was commissioned colonel of the 2nd New Hampshire Regiment. While the other New Hampshire regiments were sent to Boston immediately, Poor's was retained in the state to protect Portsmouth and Exeter until after the battle of Bunker Hill. It was then incorporated into the main army and accompanied General Montgomery's failed invasion of Canada. On the return from Canada, Poor's regiment was stationed at Fort Ticonderoga, where it was redesignated as the 8th Continental Regiment. In December of 1776 Poor took his regiment to Morristown, New Jersey, where it went into winter quarters. On February 21, 1777, Poor was commissioned by Congress to the rank of brigadier general, and his brigade of three New Hampshire and two New York regiments was ordered back to Fort Ticonderoga. In September and October of 1777 he performed well in the Saratoga Campaign, fighting with distinction at the battles of Freeman's Farm and Bemis Heights. In the latter engagement Poor's brigade was responsible for breaking the charge of the enemy and turning the battle in favor of the Americans. Poor wintered, with his brigade, at Valley Forge in 1777.

In June of 1778 he was responsible for leading the last maneuvers in the battle of Monmouth, and in 1779 he accompanied the Sullivan expedition against the Iroquois. Following the Sullivan expedition, Poor was assigned to General Lafayette's division, and his brigade was detailed to do garrison duty in New Jersey. On September 6, 1780, Poor was mortally wounded in a duel fought near Hackensack, New Jersey. He died as a result of the wound on September 8, 1780, at the age of forty-four. An army surgeon reported that he died of typhus, but it was the bullet wound that took his life. Enoch Poor was buried in the churchyard of the First Reformed Church, in Hackensack, New Jersey. When Washington informed Congress of his death, he stated, "He was an officer of distinguished merit, one who as a citizen and soldier had every claim to the esteem and regard of his country."[1]

POTTER, JAMES — (Ireland) James Potter was born in County Tyrone, Ireland, in 1729. In 1741, his family came to America, and eventually settled in Cumberland County, Pennsylvania, where Potter's father became the first sheriff of the county. James received little or no formal education during his childhood years. Potter took up the vocation of farming, and married Elizabeth Cathcart, of Philadelphia. In 1756, during the French and Indian War, he became a lieutenant in the militia and accompanied the Kittanning Campaign to subdue the hostile Indians along the frontier. He participated in the 1763–64 campaigns against the Indians as a captain, and was promoted to the rank of lieutenant colonel by the close of hostilities. The treaty that was signed with the Indians in 1768 opened up a large amount of land in the frontier for settlement, and Potter was selected as a commissioner to encourage settlement in the Penn's Valley region. In 1774, he bought a large tract of land for himself there and subsequently moved his family.

Potter was an early advocate of American independence, and was made a colonel in the Pennsylvania Militia in 1776. He led the Northumberland Militia in the battles of Trenton, Princeton, Brandywine, and Germantown, and was wounded at Princeton on January 3, 1777. On December 11, 1777, he received information pertaining to the location and intentions of the enemy, under Cornwallis, that prevented General Washington from marching into a trap on his way to Valley Forge. In 1778, Potter took a leave from the army to return home and look after his wife, who had become quite ill. She did not recover, and Potter would later marry Mary Patterson Chambers. Increased Indian activities along the frontier forced him to relocate his home in 1779.

In 1780, Potter was elected to the Supreme Executive Council of Pennsylvania, and the following year he became the council's vice president (lieutenant governor). In 1782, he was defeated by John Dickinson in his bid to become president of the council. On May 23 of that year, Potter was commissioned a major general in the Pennsylvania Militia, and served at that rank for the remainder of the war. In 1785, he was named deputy surveyor for Pennsylvania. He was also placed in charge of land development for Penn's Valley. In November of 1789 he died in Centre County, Pennsylvania, as the result of a construction accident, in his sixtieth year. Potter County, Pennsylvania, is named in his honor.[1]

PRESCOTT, OLIVER — (Massachusetts) Oliver Prescott was born at Groton, Middlesex County, Massachusetts, on April 27, 1731. He was the brother of Colonel William Prescott, of Bunker Hill fame, who was killed in that engagement. After receiving his primary education, Prescott attended Harvard College, graduating in 1750. He studied medicine, establishing a medical practice in Groton. On February 19, 1756, he married Lydia Baldwin, and the couple had nine children together. In 1765, he became clerk of Groton, Massachusetts, a position he would hold for twelve years, until 1777.

In 1776, Prescott was commissioned a brigadier general in the Massachusetts Militia, in place of John Cummings, whose appointment was not concurred by the Supreme Council. He was elected to the Massachusetts Supreme Council in 1777. In 1778, Prescott was promoted to the rank of major general in the Massachusetts Militia, his commission being endorsed by John Hancock. Though Prescott held the rank of general in the militia, his contributions to the cause of liberty came from the political and civil arena, as he was not a field commander of troops. In 1779, he was appointed judge of the Probate Court of Middlesex County, a position he would hold until his death.

Oliver Patterson died at Groton, Massachusetts, on November 17, 1804, at the age of seventy-three. He was buried at the Old Burial Ground, in Groton, Massachusetts.[1]

PREUDHOMME DE BORRE, PHILIPPE HUBERT — (France) Philippe Hubert Preudhomme de Borre was born in France in 1717. De Borre was a thirty-five year veteran of the French army when he offered his services to the American cause. De Borre arrived in America at Portsmouth, New Hampshire, on March 17, 1777. He went to General

Washington's headquarters at Morristown, New Jersey, where he received a commission as a brevet brigadier general on May 7, 1777. In August of that same year, De Borre held a command in General Sullivan's brigade at Staten Island. He also commanded a brigade at the battle of Brandywine, on September 28, 1777. In that battle, De Borre insisted on taking the post of honor, on the right wing of the American army. General Sullivan declined to position him there, but De Borre persisted, causing Sullivan to make a long and circuitous march to extend his line beyond De Borre's, and, in consequence, Sullivan's force was not in position and formed when the battle opened. De Borre's was the first American unit to retreat from the battlefield that day. His insubordination to General Sullivan led to a congressional investigation, and caused De Borre to resign his commission.

De Borre seems to have been one of those few French officers who felt the Continental Army to be a rabble, completely inferior to European armies. He was very unpopular with the soldiers in his command, and unsuited to leading American troops in combat. Despite the fact that he no longer exercised any official capacity in America, he remained in the country for more than a year following his resignation, not leaving for France until January of 1779. When he returned to his native country, De Borre wrote *Journal des Campagnes de 1777 et 1778 au Service des Colonies Unies de l'Amerique*, a memoir of his experiences in the Continental Army that was deposited in the French Archives of War. The exact date of Philippe Hubert Preudhomme De Borre's death is not recorded.[1]

PULASKI, COUNT CASIMIR— (Poland)

Casimir Pulaski was born at the family homestead of Winiary, in Masovia, Poland, on March 4, 1747. His father, Josef, was a successful and wealthy lawyer of the area, who became one of the largest landowners in the country by having his fees paid in land, not in money. He was also a noble and member of the ruling class, and chief magistrate of the district of Warka.[1]

Young Casimir was enrolled in the School of the Testyni, in Warsaw, where he exhibited a lack of interest in schooling. Riding was much more to his taste. Once he had completed the course of studies, he was accepted as a page to the court of Charles, Duke of Courland, at Mitau, serving as a member of the duke's personal guard. Casimir had his first taste of Russian oppression when the duke was unseated, six months after his arrival, by Catherine the Great, who installed one of her favorite courtiers in his place. Casimir was sent home to his father, having attained only the most modest of military training, but having acquired a seething hatred for the Russians. The young man may not have been adequately schooled as a soldier, but he was possessed of personal talents that compensated for his lack of training. He was reported to be an expert marksman with a pistol, and in equestrian pursuits was reputed to be the superior of even the Russian Cossacks.

In 1763, Poland's king, Augustine III, died, leaving no successor to the throne. The Polish provincial deputies met to select a new king, but Catherine the Great saw an opportunity to further expand her control of the nation. She sent a former lover, Stanislaus Poniatowaski, to sit on the throne, accompanied by 40,000 Russian soldiers, just in case the Poles had any objections to her wishes. The provincial deputies bowed to this seizure of power by the Russians, their army being too small and weak to oppose it by force of arms, and Poland effectually became a puppet state of Russia.

While most of the noble class of Poland accepted the Russian domination as a situation that was out of their control, a loud voice of opposition came from Josef Pulaski, who attempted to fan the flames of resistance as he secretly went about the business of putting together an army that could oppose the Russian rule. At first, Pulaski found few who were willing to stand up against their oppressors. The Russian control of the country seemed to be complete, and most of the citizens despaired that any attempt to cast off the Russian yoke could be successful. But Pulaski was undaunted. The sixty-four-year-old count sacrificed his personal fortune to finance the venture, and sent his two sons to all of his estates to gather men and arms. Being the largest landowner in Poland, these estates included fourteen cities and 108 villages. As fervor for the rebellion spread, some of the nobles took heart and began to offer their support to Pulaski. By December 25, 1767, the Polish patriots had gathered enough support to begin planning their insurrection, and in April of 1768 they began their war for independence. Casimir won the first victory of the rebellion when he defeated a Russian corps at Stary Konstantynow, slashing down the Russian infantry with his Polish cavalry. He repeated the act with a victory at Chmielnik. Through all the fighting, Casimir was displaying a undeniable talent for cavalry tactics.[2]

Though Casimir was able to defeat the Russian forces in his country many times, the rebellion slowly began to come apart. The Russians had hired German and Austrian mercenaries to augment their forces, and the Poles began to squabble among themselves. The death of Josef Pulaski, and the capture and murder of Casimir's brother, Francis, further weakened the cause. The Polish king, the handpicked puppet of Catherine the Great, took no part in the fighting, and when an assassination attempt was made upon him, he wrongly accused Pulaski of having a hand in the conspiracy. With all the odds against him, Pulaski refused to sacrifice the lives of the men in his army, and he thus disbanded it and fled the country, to France. Pronounced to be an assassin by the Polish king, Pulaski lived for several years in exile, in France, hoping for an opportunity to liberate his beloved Poland. It was while he was in France that he read about the American fight for liberty. He was drawn to the Patriot cause and admired the grit and determination of a people who were willing to sacrifice all for liberty. Casimir contacted a friend in the French court and asked that he arrange a meeting with the American ambassador to France, Benjamin Franklin. Franklin was impressed with the young Pulaski, and he was well acquainted with his reputation as a fighter and leader of men. He agreed to provide Casimir with letters of introduction to Congress and to General Washington, and even went so far as to grant the young Pole free passage to America. With the letters from Franklin in hand, Casimir set out to cast his lot with the freedom loving people of his newly adopted country.[3]

Casimir Pulaski (courtesy National Archives)

In America, the Patriots were facing a military dilemma. In December of 1776, a year and a half after the battle of Lexington, the Continental Army was still without an organized cavalry corps. Washington had recommended that Congress create one, and that body had appropriated funds to facilitate its creation, but there was no one to lead it once it was created. None of the colonels of Light Horse were qualified, and Washington could not spare one of his infantry generals to assume command. It was during this period when Washington was casting about searching for a qualified cavalry commander that Pulaski arrived in America, in the summer of 1777. Though he did not speak a word of English, Washington was impressed with the young Pole, whose reputation as a cavalry commander preceded him. On September 15, 1777, Pulaski was commissioned a brigadier general in the Continental Army, and appointed Chief of Dragoons.[4]

Casimir saw his first combat at Brandywine, where he led a small detachment of cavalry in a rear guard action that aided in allowing Washington to extricate his army from the field. At Chestnut Hill, Pulaski's cavalry arrived on the field as the American ranks were beginning to break, and his charge grasped victory out of defeat. At Haddonsfield, Pennsylvania, Pulaski's cavalry rode to the aide of General Wayne's surrounded men and turned what could have been a disaster into victory. Wayne later reported that without Pulaski the victory could not have been possible. Even so, Casimir was becoming outraged over the constant interference of other officers with his command, and he tendered his resignation as chief of dragoons to General Washington. Washington reluctantly accepted the resignation, but then wrote a letter of support to Congress for Pulaski's plan to raise an independent legion of cavalry and infantry to be used by Washington as a spearhead in any campaign. Congress eventually approved the plan, though it reduced the number of men Pulaski had requested to sixty-eight cavalry and two hundred infantry, the smallest unit Pulaski had ever commanded. It also approved Washington's suggestion that Pulaski retain his rank of brigadier general.[5]

The headquarters for the legion were established in Baltimore, Maryland, in part so that Pulaski and his officers could practice their Catholic faith. Men were recruited and trained until the legion became a symbol of martial pride to the residents of the city. The training paid off when the legion was responsible for defeating the British and foiling their efforts to take control of the Jersey shoreline at the battle of Egg Harbor.

The next assignment for Pulaski and the legion was to try to protect Charleston, South Carolina, from the British army that was threatening it in 1779. Pulaski had no sooner reached the city than he ordered a charge on British general Prevost's advance parties, driving them back from the city at a time when the local assembly was considering the propriety of surrendering to the superior force. Pulaski's gallant charge heartened the defenders, who determined to defend the town. General Prevost, seeing that the Americans were being reenforced, decided to withdraw to Beaufort, where he could gather together his own reenforcements. Pulaski's cavalry pursued Prevost, inflicting almost 800 casualties on the British during their withdrawal.[6]

Pulaski and his legion were present at the siege of Savannah from September 23 to October 18, 1779. The French, with a fleet and army under the command of D'Estaing, were cooperating with General Lincoln's army and had bottled up the British army in the city. But, fearing his inability to maintain his fleet at Savannah during the storm season, D'Estaing urged that the city be stormed, and Lincoln reluctantly agreed. The result was a disaster for the Americans, as the British, from behind their strong works, were able to slaughter the attackers. General Pulaski was in the thick of the fighting, and when he saw D'Estaing fall, seriously wounded, he rushed to his side, and ordered that he be carried to a place of safety. While thus employed, Pulaski was himself struck in the right groin by a piece of grapeshot from one of the British cannon. Pulaski was taken aboard the American brig *Wasp*, where he was attended by one of D'Estaing's surgeons. Pulaski's wound became infected with gangrene, and the disease took his life on October 11, 1779. His body had been so consumed by the disease that it was judged impossible to sail his remains to Charleston for burial. Instead, he was buried at sea. Nevertheless, when news of his death reached Charleston, the city held a funeral memorial for the fallen hero. Casimir Pulaski, known as the father of American cavalry, was mourned on both sides of the Atlantic. The city of Pulaski, Georgia, is named in his honor.

PUTNAM, ISRAEL—**(Massachusetts)** Israel Putnam was born in Salem, Massachusetts, on January 7, 1718. The son of a farmer, Israel received scant education at the local common school, where he learned the rudiments of reading, writing, and arithmetic. Possessed of a strong and vigorous constitution, he excelled at physical endeavors and sports. At the age of twenty, in 1739, he married Hannah Pope, of Salem, and moved to Pomfret, where he took up farming on his own ground, and raising sheep and goats. The couple would have ten children together. Hannah died in 1765, and Putnam would later marry Deborah Lothrop.

When the French and Indian War broke out, Putnam received command of a company under Sir William Johnson, who was preparing to move against Crown Point. Putnam's company was detailed to act as rangers, and were constantly in the forefront of Johnson's movements. In 1757 he was promoted to the rank of major, and took part in the disastrous campaign in which Fort William Henry was surrendered and the garrison massacred. Putnam was then stationed at Fort Edward, and he and his Rangers volunteered to march to the assistance of Fort William Henry, but were kept from doing so by orders of the fort commander. In 1758, he and his Rangers were part of General Ambercromby's failed expedition against Fort Ticonderoga, helping to cover the retreat of the British army after it had been repulsed by the French.

Once, while on a scouting mission to Fort Ticonderoga, after the failed expedition, Putnam's force was surprised and attacked by a force of French and Indians. As the battle raged, Putnam was attacked by a large brave, and when the former leveled his musket to kill his assailant, it misfired. The Indian subdued Putnam, and tied him to a tree as the battle continued. A French soldier attempted to shoot Putnam, but his musket also misfired, and the enraged Frenchman then clubbed him with the butt, leaving him stunned and senseless. Even though his men were successful in driving off their attackers, Putnam was taken away as a prisoner. When the Indians arrived at their camp, they made preparations to burn their prisoner alive, and, stripping him naked, tied him to a tree and began to pile wood in a circle around the tree. The Indians lit the pile of wood, and danced around the tree as the flames leapt higher and higher. Putnam's form was scarcely visible behind the wall of flame when a French officer entered the camp, saw what was taking place, and immediately rushed to his assistance. The officer kicked away a pile of wood and released Putnam from his bondage. Saved from death, he was eventually taken to Montreal, where he was exchanged and released.

In 1759, he was commissioned to the rank of lieutenant colonel, and participated in General Amherst's successful campaign against Fort Ticonderoga and Crown Point. Putnam continued to serve in the army until the close of hostilities, proving himself to be a brave and efficient officer. In 1762, when England declared war on Spain, Putnam was given command of a Connecticut regiment that was ordered to take part in an expedition against Havana, Cuba. The expedition was successful, though most of the American contingent failed to return home due to disease that ravaged their ranks.

In 1763, Putnam commanded a corps of Connecticut men in an expedition against the Indians, and at its successful conclusion, he retired from military endeavors and once more assumed private life. He opened a tavern, and between that and his farm, was able to earn a modest but comfortable living.

Israel Putnam was plowing in his fields when word reached him of the battles at Lexington and Concord, the preceding day. It is said that he did not even unhitch his team, or change his clothes, but immediately mounted his swiftest horse and set out for Boston, 100 miles distant, arriving there twenty-four hours later. After attending a council of war in that city, he rode to Connecticut, where he conferred with the Assembly on the best course of action to pursue. He returned to Boston with a commission of brigadier general of Connecticut troops, and he gradually assumed control

Israel Putnam

of the military forces gathering there from all parts of New England.[1]

It was Putnam who counseled that the Americans must bring about a battle with the British forces in Boston, and he was the driving force in having Breed's Hill fortified, a position from which the Americans could have shelled the enemy into submission. The British, realizing their predicament, made plans at once to storm the American position, before cannon could be placed there bring them to submission, and the battle of Bunker Hill resulted. The Americans threw back two assaults against their works, mowing down the British with destructive volley fire, but when the enemy regrouped for a third charge, it was found that the defenders were running low on ammunition. The British pressed forward the final attack with the bayonet, and the Americans, out of ammunition, and having no bayonets of their own, were forced to retreat. Putnam tried to reorganize the line on Bunker Hill, but to no avail. The Americans had punished the British in the battle, causing 1,500 English casualties, as opposed to 500 suffered by the defenders, but the British had won the day. Putnam had been defeated in the first major battle to be fought in the war. George Washington was on his way to Boston when he received news of the battle of Bunker Hill. When he reached that city, he assumed command of the forces gathered there, and Putnam became one of his major generals, commissioned by the Continental Congress on May 1, 1775.[2]

In 1776, General Putnam was sent to New York, to assume command of that district, and he erected defenses there until joined by Washington, and the main body, to resist the landing of General Clinton's British army. Putnam then took part in the battle of Long Island, where the Americans were badly defeated. Washington's army became divided in the retreat, and a portion, under Putnam, faced the prospect of being surrounded and captured. Through his personal efforts, Putnam was able to avoid the British trap, and marched his portion of the army to

The Battle of Long Island

Harlem Heights, where they joined Washington.

Putnam was assigned to the defense of Philadelphia, and held that post as Washington's army won the important victories at Trenton and Princeton. During the winter of 1776, he was detailed to garrison Princeton with a force of only fifty men.

In 1777, he was sent to New York, and placed in command of an army in the Highlands. The fall of Forts Clinton and Montgomery forced him to abandon Forts Independence and Constitution, and retreat from the Peekskill area to Fishkill. Re-enforced, he retook Peekskill, prior to the surrender of Burgoyne's army at Saratoga. Upon that victory, 5,000 men from Gates' army were added to Putnam's, and Washington, in need of re-enforcement, ordered that this number be forwarded from Putnam's army to his own, in Philadelphia. Putnam refused to obey the order, bringing a reprimand from Washington. In the spring of 1778, Washington replaced Putnam, in command of the army, with General Alexander McDougall, citing the reason for his action as being Putnam's unpopularity with the inhabitants of New York. Washington evidently felt this criticism to be undeserved, for he ordered Putnam to Connecticut to hurry forward the new recruits, before he was to join the army himself. Putnam was given command of the right wing, just after the battle of Monmouth. In 1778, he was put in command of three brigades at Danbury, where he did great service in putting down a mutiny among the troops. At West Greenwich, he faced a force of 1,500 men, under the command of Governor Tryon, even though he had but 150 men and two cannon. After a fierce little struggle, he spied the enemy dragoons making ready to charge, and he ordered his men to take refuge in a swamp. Putnam sat on his horse, in full view of the dragoons, till they were almost upon him. He then spurred his steed straight down the side of a steep precipice that none of the dragoons thought a horse and rider could survive on. Confident that Putnam had fallen to his death, they halted their horses at the crest and peered down, expecting to see the bodies of horse and rider. Instead, they saw Putnam at the bottom of the gorge, still mounted and riding away.

In 1779, Putnam was stationed with the Maryland Line, near West Point, and nothing of any real importance transpired. That winter, when the army went into winter quarters, he took the opportunity of going home to spend time with his family. In the spring of 1780, when he was returning to the army, he was stricken by a stroke that ended his military career. The stroke, and the resulting paralysis, forced Putnam into a quiet life, and kept him from public service, as well as the military.

Israel Putnam died of an inflammatory disease on May 17, 1790, at the age of seventy-two, at Brooklyn, Connecticut. He was buried in the Putnam tomb, in Brooklyn, near the junction of present day Rt. 6 and Rt. 169.[3]

PUTNAM, RUFUS—(Massachusetts) Rufus Putnam was born in Sutton, Massachusetts, on April 9, 1738. He was the cousin of General Israel Putnam. Rufus apprenticed as a millwright as a youth. In 1754, he entered the militia and served in the French and Indian War through the campaigns of 1757. He then retired to private life and the vocation of farming. Putnam married Persis Rice on April 6, 1761, and the couple had one child before Persis died in 1762. He remarried in 1765, with this union producing ten children. In 1773, Putnam traveled to east Florida, to explore lands that were supposed to have been granted to officers and men who served in the French and Indian War. When it was discovered that no land grant had been made, he was appointed to be surveyor of the province by the deputy governor. Putnam returned to Massachusetts just after the fighting at Lexington and Concord, and was commissioned lieutenant colonel of Brewer's Massachusetts Regiment.

Putnam displayed exceptional engineering talent in erecting the defenses at Roxbury, Massachusetts, and gained the attention of Generals Washington and Lee. The former wrote of Putnam's skill in engineering to Congress, which resulted in his being appointed chief engineer of the defenses in New York in the spring of 1776. He was promoted to the rank of colonel in August of 1776, and subsequently assumed command of the 5th Massachusetts Regiment. In the spring of 1777, he was assigned to the Northern Department, and served with distinction at the battle of Stillwater, New York. In 1778, he was detailed to supervise the building of fortifications at West Point, New York, and was subsequently assigned to command of a regiment in General Wayne's brigade.

In 1782, Putnam was appointed commissioner to hear the claims of New York residents who suffered losses at the hand of the Continental Army. On January 7, 1783, the Continental Congress promoted him to the rank of brigadier general, and he served as such for the remainder of the war.

Following the war, Putnam served several terms in the Massachusetts legislature. He was an aide to General Benjamin Lincoln during Shay's Rebellion, in 1787. He was appointed to be superintendent of the Ohio Company, and helped to found the town of Marietta, Ohio, the first permanent settlement in the Northwest Territory. In 1789, Putnam was appointed to be a judge of the supreme court of the territory. He was called back to active military service in 1792 when he was commissioned a brigadier general under Anthony Wayne in the latter's campaign against the Indians, and later served as Indian commissioner, negotiating the treaties with the defeated tribes. In September of 1798, he was made surveyor general of the United States, and held the office until 1808. Putnam was a member of the Ohio Constitutional Convention, held in 1803. In 1812, he formed the first Bible Society west of the Allegheny Mountains.

Rufus Putnam died at Marietta, Ohio, on May 4, 1824, at the age of eighty-six.[1]

REED, JAMES — (**Massachusetts**) James Reed was born at Woburn, Massachusetts, on January 8, 1722 or 1723. In 1745, he married Abigail Hands, and the couple had nine children together.

Reed served in the French and Indian War as a captain in Colonel Blanchard's regiment, as part of Sir William Johnson's expedition against the French and Indians around Lake George.

Reed later served as a captain in the Minutemen, and was part of the Lexington Alarm in April of 1775. On April 23, 1775, he was commissioned colonel of the 3rd New Hampshire Regiment, and took part in the battle of Bunker Hill, and the siege operations in and around Boston.[1] On January 1, 1776, he assumed command of the 2nd Continental Regiment. With this regiment, Reed took part in the defense of Canada, the operations around Lake Champlain, and the battles of Trenton and Princeton. Reed was commissioned to the rank of brigadier general on August 9, 1776, by the Continental Congress. He did not serve long in that capacity, however, as he resigned his commission, due to blindness, in September of 1776.

James Reed died at Fitzwilliam, New Hampshire, on February 13, 1803.[2]

REED, JOSEPH — (**New Jersey**) Joseph Reed was born at Trenton, New Jersey, on August 27, 1741. In 1757, at the age of sixteen, he graduated from Princeton College and moved to England to study law until the protests in the Colonies, caused by the Stamp Act, convinced him to come home. He settled in Philadelphia, where he opened a very successful law practice. In 1770, he returned to England, where he married Esther De Berdt, the daughter of the agent of Massachusetts. In November of 1774, Reed was appointed to be a member of the Committee of Correspondence for Philadelphia, and he tried to persuade the British Ministry to adopt measures of moderation. In January of 1775, he served as president of the 2nd Pennsylvania Provincial Congress. On July 4, 1775, Reed was commissioned a lieutenant colonel and appointed to be military secretary for General Washington. He served in this capacity through the siege of Boston. On June 5, 1776, he was promoted to the rank of colonel and assigned to be adjutant general of the Continental Army. Reed was very active in the New York Campaign that terminated with the battle of Long Island. Following that battle, when Admiral Howe sought to open negotiations with the Americans, it was Reed who met with the British as Washington's representative.

On May 12, 1777, Reed was promoted to the rank of brigadier general by the Continental

Congress, at the insistence of General Washington. He was assigned to command of the American cavalry. Reed preferred to remain an aide to General Washington, however, and he officially declined his promotion on June 9, 1777, earning him the distinction of being among the shortest tenured generals in the war, having held the commission for only three weeks. He continued to serve at headquarters, without pay, through the battles of Brandywine, Germantown, and Monmouth. Elected to the Continental Congress in the fall of 1777, he declined a seat on the Indian Affairs Committee, but accepted chairmanship of a committee to confer with Washington concerning the ensuing campaign and efforts to maximize the efficiency of the army. In December of 1778 he was elected president of the Supreme Council of Pennsylvania (governor), and served in that office until 1781. During his tenure, he materially aided in the founding of the University of Pennsylvania. While serving as president of the council, the British attempted to enlist him, to their side, by offering a bribe of 10,000 pounds sterling, along with the offer of any royal post in the colonies of his choosing. Reed responded, "I am not worth purchasing, but, such as I am, the king of Great Britain is not rich enough to do it."

In 1781, he was prominent in suppressing the mutiny of the Pennsylvania Line, and he was appointed by Congress as a commissioner to settle the boundary dispute between Connecticut and Pennsylvania. At the end of his term as president of the Executive Council, Reed retired from public life and resumed his law practice. Following the conclusion of the Revolutionary War, poor health caused him to make a trip to England, hoping that the sea voyage would restore him.

Joseph Reed died at Philadelphia on March 5, 1785, at the age of forty-two. He was buried at the Arch Street Presbyterian Burying Ground, but was later removed to the Laurel Hill Cemetery, when the former was built over.[1]

RICHARDSON, RICHARD—(Virginia)
Richard Richardson was born near Jamestown, Virginia, in 1704. Richardson became a surveyor in Virginia before moving to South Carolina in 1725 and settling in the Sumter District. Here he acquired a tract of land and took up farming. On October 11, 1738, Richardson married Mary Courtney, and the couple had eight children together. Mary died in 1767, and Richardson then married Dorothy Sinkler, later that year. Five children resulted from this union. Richardson entered the local militia, climbing to the rank of colonel before the Revolution. In 1775, he was elected as a member of the Charleston Council of Safety, and was commissioned a brigadier general in the South Carolina Militia. That same year, Richardson was instrumental in putting down a revolt among the Loyalists in what was known as the Back Country, along the South Carolina frontier. He was tendered the thanks of the Provincial Congress for his actions. In 1776, he served as a member of the legislative council, and assisted in framing the South Carolina state constitution. In 1780, Richardson took part in the defense of Charleston, and was taken prisoner when the city fell to the British on May 12. He was sent to St. Augustine, where he was imprisoned, and General Cornwallis made unsuccessful attempts to convince him to join the British side. Richardson's confinement severely affected his health, and given his advanced age, the British released him and sent him home. Richardson never recovered from the hardships of his prison stay, and died at his home, near Salisbury, South Carolina, in September of 1780, in his seventy sixth year. He was buried on the grounds of his home, but was later disinterred by Colonel Tarleton, when that officer burned his home, to verify that he was indeed dead.[1]

ROBERDEAU, DANIEL—(British West Indies)
Daniel Roberdeau was born on the Island of St. Christopher, in the British West Indies in 1727. Little is known of his childhood years, but his later life would indicate that he received a good education, and it is believed that he studied for a time in England. His widowed mother moved the family to Philadelphia, Pennsylvania, while Daniel was still a boy, and it is known that he finished his education there before becoming a merchant in that city. He became a respected businessman, operating a thriving importing trade. Roberdeau became

active in city politics, serving as both a warden and assemblyman. In 1756 he was selected to serve as a representative from Philadelphia County in the Pennsylvania State Assembly. On October 3, 1761, he married Mary Bostwick, of New York. During the next few years, Roberdeau devoted his energies to his new family, and his mercantile pursuits. His business thrived, making him a man of wealth and importance in the city. He took a prominent role, in 1765, in resisting the Stamp Act, and was one of the signers of the non-importation agreement drafted by the merchants of Philadelphia. Roberdeau saw clearly the coming struggle between the Colonies and the mother country. He wrote, "The merchants have engaged to sell no goods for themselves or any other person, that shall be shipped from England after the 1st of January next. The inhabitants of New York, within these few days, were within an ace of storming the King's fort in that city; and although it was guarded by regular soldiers, the Governor, on receipt of a manifesto threatening to hang him, was obliged to give up the stamps. What will be the issue I cannot foresee, but I believe from the spirit of the people, there must be a deluge of blood from one end of the continent to the other before they will submit to the Stamp Act."[1]

In June of 1775, Roberdeau was elected colonel of the second of three battalions raised in Philadelphia for local defense, known as the Associators. On June 3, 1776, Congress ordered a Flying Camp to be established in the Middle States to be composed of 10,000 men, with 6,000 of that number to be from Pennsylvania. Congress also directed that two brigadier generals be appointed to command the camp, one from Pennsylvania, and one from Maryland. On July 4, 1776, Daniel Roberdeau was elected first brigadier general of the Flying Camp. He contracted a fever while in command of the camp that incapacitated him for most of the fall and winter of 1776–1777, and was removed to Lancaster where his wife ministered to his needs. She unexpectedly died from contracting the same fever on February 15, 1777. On the fifth day of that same month and year, before he had sufficiently regained his strength to return to the army, he was elected to serve as a delegate, from Pennsylvania, to the Continental Congress. He served on committees for the Commissary Department, Foreign Affairs, and the Board of Treasury.

In 1778, Roberdeau was granted permission to superintend the operation of a lead mine at Sinking Spring, near Bellwood, Pennsylvania, lead for ammunition being then in short supply in the Colonies. He ordered a stockade fort be constructed at the site, to protect the miners from marauding Indians. The fort housed three officers and some forty enlisted men.

On December 3, 1778, Roberdeau married Jane Milligan, of Philadelphia, whereupon he retired to private life, though he continued to be active in the local politics of the city of Philadelphia. Early in 1785, Roberdeau moved his family to Alexandria, Virginia. He did not resume his import business, and it may be assumed that he and his family relied on his previously acquired wealth to subsist. In 1794, General Roberdeau moved to Winchester, Virginia. He was, at this time, prostrated by a disease that affected his nervous system, from which he never recovered.

Daniel Roberdeau died on January 9, 1795, at the age of sixty-seven. He was buried in the Presbyterian Church Cemetery, in Winchester, but his remains were later removed to Mt. Hebron Cemetery in that same city.[2]

RODNEY, CASEAR—(Delaware) Caesar Rodney was born in Dover, Delaware, on October 7, 1728, the oldest of eight children. The family was possessed of a large landed estate, which was inherited by Caesar upon his father's death. In 1756, Rodney was appointed high sheriff of Kent County, and when that term expired, he became a justice of the peace and judge of the lower court. In 1762, he was elected to the provincial legislature from Kent County. When the first general congress was organized in New York to discuss a course of action for the colonies, following the Stamp Act, Rodney was selected as one of the Delaware delegates, Once the Stamp Act was repealed, the Delaware legislature appointed Rodney to write a letter of thanks to the king. In the 1760s, Mr. Rodney became afflicted with a cancer that appeared on his nose and spread across one side of his face. He was obliged to give up his public duties, for a time, as he sought medical attention in Philadelphia. Doctors there were able to afford him considerable relief, preventing the need for him to travel to England to seek help.

In 1769, Rodney was elected speaker of the house of the Delaware legislature and was appointed chairman of the Committee of Correspondence for the colony.

He was a delegate from Delaware to the first Continental Congress, in 1774, where he was appointed to several important committees. His service earned him a second term in Congress, in 1775, as well as a commission as brigadier general in the Delaware militia in 1776, though his duties seem to have been limited to the raising, organizing and equipping of troops for the Delaware Militia.[1]

When the question of independence came before the Continental Congress, Rodney was in Delaware making a tour of the southern portion of the state. The two Delaware delegates in attendance were split on the subject of separating with England, and Rodney's vote would make the difference in whether the Declaration of Independence would receive a unanimous vote of the delegations in Congress, which was absolutely necessary. When that body prepared to vote, an urgent message was sent to Rodney that his presence was sorely needed, and he, through great personal exertions, made the journey back to Philadelphia in time to cast the swing vote in favor of liberty. He would later sign the Declaration of Independence, which he had been so instrumental in making possible.

Later in 1776, Delaware called a state convention to frame a new state constitution, and the delegates of that body replaced Rodney in the Continental Congress. He continued to serve as a member of the council of safety and the committee of inspection, and performed great service in gathering supplies for Washington's army. In 1777, he spent two months attached to the army, then near Princeton, performing this valuable service. In the fall of that year, he was once more appointed as a delegate to the Continental Congress, and was subsequently elected president of the state of Delaware, a position he would hold for four years. The cancer with which he was afflicted continued to spread, forcing him to wear a green silk screen to conceal it when he went out in public, and by 1782, it had become so severe as to force him to retire from public life and decline a re-election to the office of president of Delaware. Shortly after retiring from the presidency, he was re-elected to Congress, but was unable to take his seat.

The cancer that had plagued Rodney for most of his public career finally took his life, and he died in Dover on June 29, 1784. He was buried at the Christ Episcopal Church Cemetery in that city.

RUTHERFORD, GRIFFITH—(Ireland)
Griffith Rutherford was born in Ireland. Accounts differ regarding the year of his birth, evenly split between 1720 and 1731. Scrutiny of the events of his life would seem to establish 1731 as the proper date, however. Rutherford's parents brought him to America in 1739, and both parents died, either during the voyage, or immediately after arriving in America. Rutherford was still a young boy when this happened, and was taken in by relatives in New Jersey. The fact that he was a young orphan in 1739 would seem to credit 1731 as the correct year of his birth. Rutherford received an adequate education, and became proficient as a surveyor.

In 1753, Rutherford moved to Rowan County, North Carolina, and in 1758 he purchased two small tracts of land just outside of Salisbury. About that same time, he married Elizabeth Graham, the sister of the man who owned the property adjoining his. The couple would have twelve children. By his character and enterprise, Rutherford attained a prominent stature in Rowan County. He was elected sheriff about 1769, and was also elected to the state assembly that same year, serving for three years. In 1771, he was commissioned a captain in the local militia. In 1773, he was re-elected to the assembly, and in 1775 he was elected to the Provincial Congress, serving in all provincial congresses through the forming of the new state constitution.[1]

Rutherford led the Rowan Regiment to

South Carolina in December of 1775 to participate in the Snow Campaign. In April of 1776, he was commissioned a brigadier general in the North Carolina Militia, and in September of that year led an expedition against the Indians, fighting skirmishes at Valley Town, Ellajay, and near Franklin. From 1777 to 1778, he served in the state Senate, but returned to active military duty in 1779 when he led his brigade to Georgia to take part in General Lincoln's Savannah Campaign. In June of 1780 he fought in the battle of Ramseur's Mills, North Carolina, where he defeated a Loyalist force. In August of 1780, he took part in General Gates' campaign at Camden, South Carolina, where he was badly wounded and captured. Rutherford was held as a prisoner, in St. Augustine, Florida, until the summer of 1781, when he was finally exchanged. His captivity was a trying experience, and he almost died from being held in an unsanitary dungeon with little food. Upon his release, he immediately gathered his brigade together and marched on Wilmington, North Carolina, to engage the British force occupying that place. Before his arrival, the British commander received word of the surrender of Cornwallis, at Yorktown, and decided to evacuate the town.

Following the war, Rutherford intermittently served in the North Carolina Senate until 1786. George Washington is said to have presented him with a silver snuff box in recognition of his service in the war. Rutherford was employed to survey military land grants in Tennessee, and in 1792, he traded all his land in North Carolina for land along the Cumberland River, and moved his family to Sumner County, in that newly created territory. President Washington appointed Rutherford to be a member of the Territorial Legislative Council, and he was elected president by that body.

Griffith Rutherford died on August 10, 1805 at Sumner, Tennessee, in his seventy-fourth year. He is supposed to have been buried at Shiloh Presbyterian Church, outside Gallatin, Tennessee, but there is some controversy surrounding that. He was a member of the Lagardo Cumberland Presbyterian Church, and some accounts state that he was buried there, instead. It is unfortunate that neither records nor headstone exist to definitively pinpoint his final resting place. Rutherford County, North Carolina, and Rutherford County, Tennessee, were both named in his honor.[2]

SAFFORD, JOSEPH—(Vermont) Joseph Safford was born at Bennington, Bennington County, Vermont, on December 1, 1741. On July 30, 1766, Safford married Marcy Robinson and the couple had seven children together. Safford served in Captain John Fassett's company during the French and Indian War, in 1764, gaining his first military experience in a like manner to so many of his contemporaries, who had first seen battle in that war.

Safford bears the distinction of making the greatest rise through the ranks of any officer to become a general in the war. He served as a lieutenant in Warner's regiment of Green Mountain Boys, and when that regiment was redesignated as an official unit in the Continental Army, he was promoted to the rank of captain on September 16, 1776. Safford commanded a company in the Castleton, Vermont, Alarm. He was subsequently commissioned a colonel and brigadier general in the Vermont Militia. The vast majority of Revolutionary War generals served initially as colonels, and their rise to general was a short step.

Following the war, Safford commanded one of three companies, under the command of Ethan Allen, in driving New Yorkers out of Vermont to Massachusetts. In 1802, he moved to Malone, New York.

Joseph Safford died at Malone, New York, on January 4, 1807, at the age of sixty-five. He was buried in the Webster Street Cemetery, in Malone, New York.[1]

SAFFORD, SAMUEL—(Connecticut) Samuel Safford was born at Norwich, New London County, Connecticut, on April 14, 1737. On September 25, 1760, Safford married Mary Lawrence, and the couple had eight children together. Safford moved to Bennington, Vermont, after his marriage, and was among the earliest settlers of that town. He took an active part in the land controversy between the residents of Vermont and New York.

In 1775, at the outbreak of the Revolution, Safford joined Lieutenant Colonel Warner's regiment of Green Mountain Boys, and was chosen to be major and second in command to Warner. He served under Warner in the Canadian Expedition. When the Congress authorized Warner to raise a continental regiment in July of 1776, Safford was commissioned to be its lieutenant colonel. The regiment was assigned to the Northern Department, where it took part in the battles of Hubbarton and Bennington, Vermont, in July and August of 1777, and the Saratoga Campaign in October of 1777. Safford and the regiment also participated in the operations around New York in 1779. Safford resigned his commission on January 1, 1781, and was subsequently commissioned a brigadier general in the Vermont Militia, serving until the end of hostilities.

In 1781, he was elected chief judge of the Bennington County Court, a position he would hold for twenty-six consecutive years. In 1783, he was elected state councilor, and was continued in that office for nineteen years.

Samuel Safford died at Bennington, Vermont, on March 14, 1813, at the age of seventy-five.[1]

ST. CLAIR, ARTHUR—(Scotland) Arthur St. Clair (pronounced Sinclair) was born at Thruso, Scotland, on March 23, 1736. There is little known of his education or early years. When he was twenty-one, St. Clair enlisted in the military, receiving an ensign's commission in the army, and subsequently coming to America to fight in the French and Indian War. He was present at the capture of Montreal, in which battle he carried his regimental banner. St. Clair was promoted to the rank of lieutenant by the end of the war, but he sold his commission and endeavored to establish a trading business in the newly won territories. His business venture was a failure, and he settled in the Ligonier Valley of Pennsylvania, where fortune finally smiled upon him. In 1775, on the eve of the war, he held six different offices in the Pennsylvania government: clerk of the Court of General Quarter Sessions, prothonotary of the Court of Common Pleas, judge of the Probate Court, recorder of deeds, register of wills, and official surveyor.

When the war broke out, he accompanied the commissioners, appointed by the Continental Congress, to negotiate with the Indians in the vicinity of Fort Pitt. Granted a commission as colonel, he raised a regiment to participate in the Canadian Campaign, in December of 1775, but the regiment marched north just in time to help cover the retreat of the defeated main body. St. Clair and his regiment took part in the battle of Three Rivers, on June 8, 1776. Following that battle St. Clair was promoted by Congress to the rank of brigadier general, and in the fall of 1776 he was attached to General Sullivan's division, with whom he fought in the battle of Trenton on December 26, 1776. In January of 1777, he took a conspicuous part in the battle of Princeton, where his brigade was in the advance of Washington's army. His conduct in this battle was such that Congress promoted him to the rank of major general on February 19, 1777, and he was sent north to aide General Schuyler in opposing the advance of Burgoyne's British army. St. Clair was given command at Fort Ticonderoga, where the Americans felt sure they could stop the British from behind its heavily fortified walls. However, when Burgoyne's army arrived before that place, on July 2, 1777, St. Clair evacuated the fort and left the British in control of the area. St. Clair lost close to a thousand men, or one-third of his army, before the fort, and in making good his retreat. In 1778 he was court-martialed for his actions, but the board of officers who sat in judgment exonerated him, as Burgoyne's army had almost surrounded his position, and had managed to place artillery on top of a hill that commanded the interior of the fort.

While St. Clair was under the cloud of the court-martial, he participated in the battle of Brandywine, but he held no command, serving instead in the capacity of an aide or staff officer to Washington. Once cleared by the court, he was again entrusted with the responsibilities of his rank, and during the Yorktown Campaign, when Washington marched south to meet Cornwallis, St. Clair was placed in command of the Pennsylvania Militia that was left behind to protect Philadelphia. He arrived at Yorktown a few days before Cornwallis' capitulation, and was then sent to the assistance of General Greene's army, in South Carolina, arriving at that place too late to take part in any campaigning before the end of hostilities.

St. Clair retired from the army on November 3, 1783, and returned home to Pennsylvania. In 1786, he was elected to Congress, and in 1787 was elected president of that body. In 1788, he was appointed governor of the newly created Northwest Territory. In 1791, St. Clair mounted an expedition to subdue the Indian force under the leadership of Chief Little Turtle. An army of some 2,000 men was raised, but that force was heavily diminished through desertions by the time it reached the vicinity of the Indian camps to only about 1,400 men. St, Clair decided to assume a defensive posture, and allow the Indians to attack him, near Fort Recovery. On the morning of November 4, Chief Little Turtle attacked, and quickly put the militia in St. Clair's army in a panic. Though his regulars endeavored to hold, they were badly outnumbered and overwhelmed, and St. Clair was forced to order a retreat that soon turned into a rout. St. Clair was wounded, and lost over 900 of his men during the campaign, making it the worst defeat ever suffered by the United States Army at the hands of the Indians.

Though sustained by Washington, public opinion against St. Clair, following his defeat at Fort Recovery, was so strong that that he was never again trusted with an important military assignment. He spent the next two decades in destitute poverty trying to get Congress to settle claims for the money it owed him. During the Revolution, he had advanced large sums of his own money to cover expenses of the army, and he sought to have that money repaid. It was a black spot on the government that St. Clair died almost penniless, never receiving the money that was owed him by the nation.

Arthur St. Clair died at Philadelphia, Pennsylvania, on August 31, 1818, at the age of eighty-two. He was buried at the Old St. Clair Cemetery, in Greensburg, Pennsylvania.[1]

SALTONSTALL, GURDON—(**Connecticut**) Gurdon Saltonstall was born at New London, Connecticut, in 1708, to a very prominent Connecticut family. His father had been governor of the colony. Saltonstall received a sound primary education before attending and graduating from Yale College. On March 15, 1733, he married Rebecca Winthrop, and the couple had eleven children together. During the French and Indian War, Saltonstall served as commissary of purchase and transportation in 1756. Following the war, he was appointed collector of customs for New London.

At the outbreak of the Revolution, Saltonstall was commissioned a colonel in the Connecticut Militia. He was subsequently promoted to the rank of brigadier general and given command of the 3rd Connecticut Brigade, taking part in the operations around New York until he relinquished the command to General John Tyler. Saltonstall resigned his commission in May of 1777, and returned to private life.

Gurdon Saltonstall died at Norwich, Connecticut, on September 19, 1785, in his seventy-seventh year.[1]

SCHUYLER, PHILIP JOHN—(**New York**) Philip Schuyler was born at Albany, New York, on November 10, 1733, into one of the

Arthur St. Clair (courtesy United States Military History Institute).

most influential families of the city. His father, John, died when Philip was still a small boy, leaving his wife, Cornelia Van Cortlandt Schuyler, and his sister, Margaretta, to see after Philip's education. He was tutored at home for his initial education, then was sent briefly to school in Albany before attending Reverend Peter Steppe's Westchester County School in New Rochelle. Schuyler was a gifted student, and excelled in his studies.

In 1751, at the age of eighteen, Schuyler returned home to Albany to take part in an expedition deep into the upper reaches of the Mohawk Valley. The young man was not overly impressed with life on the frontier. The attractions of New York City were much more to his liking, and he made many extended trips there to enjoy all that the city had to offer.

In 1754, when he reached the age of majority, Schuyler showed his character when he renounced his right as first born and announced his intention of dividing the family estate equally between himself, his sister, and his two brothers.

The coming of the French and Indian War gave Schuyler the opportunity to gain his first experience as a military leader. He received a commission from the lieutenant governor, as captain, and raised a company of militia by July 14, 1755, the first company to be completed in the state. Schuyler's company was assigned to Colonel William Cockroft's regiment, at Lake George, but young Schuyler was not destined to take part in any fighting with his regiment. Prior to the fighting, he received a message from Catherine Van Rensselaer, a young lady from New York City, who he had been courting, informing him that she was pregnant with his child. Schuyler took his leave of the army to return home to marry Catherine on September 7, 1755. Their daughter, Angelica, was born in February of 1756.

His new family gave Schuyler a desire for personal advancement, and he sought an assignment to serve under Colonel John Bradstreet, the British deputy quartermaster general for New York. Schuyler's natural talent for business made it a perfect assignment for him, and he quickly won the confidence and respect of his commanding officer. It even gave him the chance to show his personal courage when

Philip Schuyler

he accompanied a supply mission to Oswego. The supply train was attacked, on its return trip, by an overwhelming force of French and Indians. Schuyler and his comrades were able to escape from the ambush, and reached relative safety by crossing the Oswego River. When Schuyler discovered that a wounded man had been left behind, on the opposite shore, he recrossed the river to rescue him, despite a heavy fire from the enemy.

Disappointed by the slow rate of advancement, Schuyler resigned from the military, but soon regretted his decision and attempted to regain his position with Colonel Bradstreet. Bradstreet was delighted to have him return. The colonel's health had been failing, and to Schuyler's competent hands he delegated a great deal of his own responsibility.

At the close of the war, Bradstreet asked Schuyler to travel to London to settle his accounts with the government. At first, Schuyler declined, but Bradstreet was able to convince him. Though he spent over a year in England, Schuyler left little record of events that transpired. He did take the opportunity to purchase a great many items for the mansion he was having built in Albany.

Upon his return from England, Schuyler engaged heavily in the business of land speculation, buying large tracts in western New York, and even acquiring parcels as far away as Detroit. Schuyler developed a part of his property at Saratoga, where he constructed saw mills, and grew, dressed and spun flax into linen. The enterprise at Saratoga thrived, and combined with the income derived from leased property, Schuyler was able to amass a large fortune. In 1768, he turned his attention to politics, gaining election to the Provincial Assembly. Schuyler was a conservative, and felt that government should be controlled by men of wealth and breeding, not by the masses. Still, he took offense to the British taxation policies, and sanctioned Colonial efforts to redress their grievances.[1]

In 1775, Schuyler was selected as a representative to the Second Continental Congress. Before he could take his seat, the clash of arms at Lexington and Concord took place. He was also commissioned as a major general in the Continental Army, on June 19, 1775.[2] When Schuyler took his seat in Congress he became so irritated with the deadlock that occurred in the passing of legislation that he left that body, never to return, opting instead to make his contributions to the cause in command of troops.

When General Burgoyne advanced his army toward Saratoga, Schuyler harassed his movements with the forces he had at hand. Bridges were destroyed, trees were felled across the roads, and the British were kept in constant alarm by irregular attacks by Schuyler's men. At the moment when the British were about to be drawn to battle, Schuyler was replaced in command by General Gates. He turned over his command with the following remarks: "I have done all that could be done, as far as the means were in my power, to injure the enemy and to inspire confidence in the soldiers of our army and I flatter myself with some success — but the palm of victory is denied me and it is left to you, General, to reap the fruits of my labor. I will not fail to second your views and my devotion to my country will cause me, with alacrity, to obey your orders."[3]

As president of the Board of Commissioner of Indian Affairs, he kept a close watch on enemy activities, and he was able to provide warning of a planned British attack against Forts Anne, Edward, and George. Enemy forays in western New York were supposed to coincide with Benedict Arnold's conspiracy at West Point, but when the latter failed to materialize, the British retreated to Canada.

On April 19, 1779, Schuyler resigned his commission and returned to private life. This did not prevent his attempted capture, by Barry St. Leger and a band of Indians, at his home in 1781. Schuyler was able to bluff his way out of the situation by pretending to issue orders to rescuers, scaring off the Indians.[4]

Following the war, and the ratification of the Constitution, Schuyler served for 12 years in the U.S. Senate.

Philip Schuyler died on November 18, 1804, at the age of seventy.

SCOTT, JOHN MORIN — (New York)

John Morin Scott was born in New York City, New York, in 1730. In his childhood, he attended common schools before being admitted to Yale College. Scott graduated from Yale in 1746, and studied law over the next few years, passing the New York Bar in 1752 and starting a practice in New York City. He served as a city alderman from 1756 to 1761. Scott was an early supporter of the Patriot cause, and was one of the founders of the Sons of Liberty in New York. In 1774, he was denied election to the Continental Congress because his views on independence were considered too extreme by his peers. He was elected as a delegate to the New York Provincial Congress in 1775, however. On June 9, 1776, he was commissioned a brigadier general in the New York Militia, and led his brigade at the battle of Long Island. He was wounded while commanding at the battle of White Plains, on October 28, 1776. Scott resigned his commission in March of 1777 to devote his time and energies to politically advancing the cause. In 1776, he was selected for the committee charged with writing a new state constitution, and in 1777 he was elected to the New York State Senate and appointed an associate justice of the New York Supreme Court. Scott declined the latter appointment. Scott was elected secretary of the state of New York in 1778, a position he would hold until 1789. He was also elected as a delegate to the Continental Congress in 1780 and 1782.

John Morin Scott died in New York City on September 14, 1784, in his fifty-fourth year. He was buried at the Trinity Church Cemetery, in New York City.[1]

SHELBY, EVAN, JR.—(**Wales**) Evan Shelby, Jr., was born on October 23, 1720, at Tregaron, Cardiganshire, Wales. In 1734, the family moved to America, settling in Maryland, where Shelby's father died in 1751. Shelby was a hunter and woodsman, and known to be a marksman with a rifle. He is variously reported as serving in Braddock's failed campaign against Fort Duquesne (Fort Pitt), but that cannot be substantiated. He did serve in General Forbes' campaign that ended in the capture of Fort Duquesne, however. Following the conclusion of the French and Indian War, Shelby entered into the fur trade, and became a trapper. In 1767, he received a commission as first lieutenant in Captain Alexander Beall's militia company.

By 1773, Shelby had moved to what was then the Virginia frontier, at Sapling Spring, and built Fort Shelby (present day Bristol, Tennessee), where he began raising cattle. In 1774, he took part in Dunmore's War, commanding the Fincastle Company, with whom he fought at the battle of Point Pleasant, against the Shawnee Indians. The year 1774 also witnessed his marriage to Letitia Cox, of Frederick County, Maryland.

Shelby continued to hold a commission in the militia when the hostilities between America and England took place, and in 1776, Virginia governor Patrick Henry promoted him to the rank of major and assigned his command to Colonel William Christian, who was mounting a campaign against the Cherokee. In December of that same year, Shelby was promoted to colonel and given command of the militia in the newly created Washington County, Virginia. In 1779, Shelby led an expedition against the villages of the Chickamauga Indians, on the lower Tennessee River. Shelby had received a commission as general in the Virginia Militia preceding his successful campaign against the Cherokee, in 1778.[1]

Shelby's most dramatic service in the war came in 1780. In October of that year, his command took part in the battle of Kings Mountain, where the American forces defeated a Loyalist army under the command of British colonel Patrick Ferguson. Most historians cite this battle as being the turning point of the war in the South.

In 1781, Shelby was elected to the Virginia state Senate, and in 1786, he was commissioned a major general of the Washington District of North Carolina. In 1787, he negotiated a truce with Colonel John Sevier, the governor of the short-lived state of Franklin, and in August of that same year was elected to succeed Sevier as governor of Franklin. Shelby declined to accept the position, however, and the state of Franklin soon ceased to exist. On October 29, 1787, Shelby resigned his commission as brigadier general in the Virginia Militia and returned to private life, retiring to Bristol, and his holdings at Fort Shelby. He also retired to a second marriage. Letitia had previously died, and in 1787, at the age of sixty-seven, Shelby married Isabella Ellicott.

Evan Shelby, Jr., died at Bristol, Tennessee, on December 4, 1794, at the age of seventy-four. He was buried at the First Presbyterian Church Cemetery, but his remains were later moved to the Bristol Cemetery. Owing to the fact that the Virginia-Tennessee state line runs through this cemetery, part of it is in Virginia, and part in Tennessee. Shelby is officially buried in the portion that is in Virginia.

SHELDON, ELISHA—(**Connecticut**) Elisha Sheldon was born in Connecticut on March 6, 1740. He was a resident of Saulsbury, Connecticut.

In June of 1776, he was commissioned a major in the battalion of Connecticut Light Horse. Sheldon offered his services to General Washington at New York, but they were refused because the Continental army did not have enough forage for the men and animals in his command. Following the American defeat at White Plains, however, Washington recognized the need for a regular mounted command with his army, and the Second Continental Dragoons was created, with Sheldon as its colonel. The 2nd Dragoons saw action at Trenton, Princeton, Woodbridge Brandywine, Germantown, Kingston, Saratoga, Schoharie, and Yorktown. In addition, Sheldon's command conducted numerous whaleboat raids against the British and Loyalists on Long Island. Elements of Sheldon's command also served as Washington's personal bodyguard, and guarded John Andre during his incarceration, trial, and execution. On September 30, 1780, Sheldon was awarded the brevet commission of brigadier general from the Continental Congress.

Following the end of the war, Sheldon purchased land in Vermont that had been granted to create the town of Hungerford. He and his three sons moved there in 1789, and were soon joined by other settlers. Elisha was elected the first selectman of the new town, and its name was changed to Sheldon. The Sheldons built a sawmill and gristmill in the town, and Samuel, General Sheldon's son, served as the town's first justice of the peace, and first representative to the Vermont Legislature.

Elisha Sheldon died in Vermont in 1805, in his sixty-fifth year.[1]

SILLIMAN, GOLD SELLECK—(Connecticut) Gold Selleck Silliman was born at Fairfield, Connecticut, on May 7, 1732. Selleck received a proper primary education before being sent to Yale, graduating from that institution in 1752. He then turned his attentions to reading law, becoming a member of the Connecticut bar and being appointed as an attorney for the Crown in Fairfield County. On January 21, 1754, Silliman married Martha Davenport. Martha died in 1774, and Silliman married Mary Fish the following year. One child was born to this marriage.

Silliman had a strong interest in the military, and in 1774, he was commissioned to be a major in the 4th Connecticut Militia Regiment. Silliman was a patriot, and when the war broke out, he was made a colonel of Connecticut cavalry, with his commission dated June 20, 1776.[1]

In March of 1776, when the British were threatening New York City, the governor directed Silliman to march his militia to the city to secure it until General Washington could arrive with his main army. Silliman took part in the battles at Long Island in August and December of 1776, and at White Plains in October of 1776, and was subsequently promoted to the rank of brigadier general in the Connecticut Militia. Washington had taken notice of him during the battle of Long Island, where Silliman was in command of a regiment. Three days following the fighting, the army commander placed him in command of a brigade of five regiments.

Following his promotion to general, Silliman was charged with the mission of defending the frontier of southwestern Connecticut from incursions by the British and their Indian allies. This assignment was a difficult one, with Silliman having to be constantly on guard for the British army that was then occupying New York City.

In 1777, Silliman defeated the British in an attempted raid on Danbury, Connecticut. On May 1, 1779, he was surprised and captured by a detail of British troops while he was at his home on Long Island. He was held as a prisoner at Flatbush and Gravesend, Long Island, for almost a year and a half, before finally being exchanged for Judge Jones of Long Island in October of 1780.

Following the war, Silliman resumed his law practice, though his health seems to have been much impaired by his long confinement as a British prisoner.

Gold Selleck Silliman died at Fairfield, Connecticut, on July 21, 1790, at the age of fifty-eight. He was buried at Old Burying Ground Cemetery in Fairfield.[2]

SMALLWOOD, WILLIAM—(Maryland) William Smallwood was born in Kent County, Maryland, in 1732. When Smallwood reached the age of majority, he became a planter in St. Mary's County, Maryland. Smallwood served as an officer in the French and Indian War, in the Maryland Militia. In 1761, he was elected to the Maryland legislature, a position he would hold for ten of the next thirteen years. In 1762, and again from 1770 to 1773, he served as judge of Charles County. In 1774, with tensions mounting between England and America, he served on the Committee of Observation for Charles County, and from 1774 to 1776, he also served the county as a delegate to the Maryland Constitutional Convention.

On January 14, 1776, he received a commission as colonel of the 1st Maryland Regiment. The 1st Maryland was part of the Flying Camp in 1776. Smallwood was promoted to brigadier general in the Continental army on October 23, 1776, and in that capacity he fought in the battle of White Plains, New York, on October 28, 1776, where he was wounded. His command suffered severe losses at the battle of Fort Washington in 1776, but in October of 1777, his troops performed well at the battle of Germantown, and were even able to capture a portion of the British camp.[1]

Smallwood was stationed at Wilmington, Delaware, during the winter of 1777–78, where he was able to capture an English brig, laden with supplies destined for the British army. In August of 1780, he distinguished himself at the battle of Camden, South Carolina, and Congress recognized his service when he was promoted to the rank of major general on September 15, 1780. Upon the reorganization of the Continental army, Smallwood commanded a division made up of the 1st and 2nd Maryland brigades. After the removal of General Gates, Smallwood threatened to resign his commission, refusing to serve under the command of Baron Steuben. Smallwood demanded, as a condition of his future service, that Congress predate his commission to major general by two years, so that he would have seniority over Steuben. Congress refused to consider such an action, and Smallwood reconsidered his threat, opting to remain in the army for the duration of the war.[2]

Following the war, Smallwood served as the first president-general of the Society of the Cincinnati, in 1783. He was elected to serve in Congress, as a delegate from Maryland, in 1785. Also, in that year, he was elected governor of the state of Maryland, for a three year term. In 1791, he was elected to the Senate, where he became Senate president.

William Smallwood died at Prince George County, Maryland, on February 14, 1792, at the age of sixty.

SPENCER, JOSEPH—(Connecticut) Joseph Spencer was born at East Haddam, Connecticut, on October 3, 1714. After completing preparatory studies, Spencer studied law, and was admitted to the Connecticut bar. He subsequently held several local offices, including judge of the probate court, in 1753, at which time he gave up his law practice. He served in King George's War, and in 1758, he served in the French and Indian War as lieutenant colonel of the Middlesex Militia.

By the time the conflict took place at Concord and Lexington, Spencer had been promoted to the rank of brigadier general of Connecticut militia. He was also colonel of the 2nd Connecticut Regiment. In this capacity, he marched the troops of the state to Boston, in April of 1775, at the age of sixty, to support the siege of the British forces. Spencer and his regiment took part in the siege, until the Continental Congress acted to form an army. When his militia units were incorporated into the Continental army, in June of 1775, Spencer was commissioned a brigadier general in the Continental service. His commission was dated June 22, 1775.

On August 6, 1776, Spencer was promoted to major general, and placed under the command of General William Heath, in the Eastern Department. He took part in the fighting in New York, at White Plains, before being transferred to New England, under Heath. In 1777, he cancelled a planned attack on the British forces in Rhode Island, and was censured by Congress for his actions. Spencer asked for, and was granted a court-martial to resolve the charges, and clear his name. The court did clear him of any wrongdoing, but following his acquittal, he promptly resigned his commission on January 13, 1778.

Upon resigning from the army, Spencer was appointed to the Continental Congress as a delegate, in 1778. He continued to serve in that body, as a delegate, the following year. When he returned to East Haddam, he was elected to the Connecticut Council, in 1780, and was regularly elected to this position for the next nine years.

Joseph Spencer died, at East Haddam, on January 13, 1789, at the age of seventy-four. He was buried in the Millington Green Cemetery, but in 1904, his remains were moved to Nathan Hale Park, east of Haddam.[1]

STANTON, JOSEPH, III — (Rhode Island)

Joseph Stanton III was born at Westerly, Rhode Island, on July 19, 1739. His parents operated a dairy business and an inn, and Stanton was familiarized with farming and business at an early age, receiving a common education proper to teach him the fundamentals needed for business. The Stanton Inn was a regular coach stop for travelers between Providence and New London.

Stanton served in the French and Indian War as a lieutenant in the Rhode Island Regiment raised for the expedition against Canada in 1759. On July 14, 1762, he married Thankful Babcock. The couple had no children. In 1768, Stanton was elected to the Rhode Island legislature, and was continued as a representative in that body until 1774. In 1776 he became a member of the local Committee of Safety, and on December 12, of that year he was commissioned a colonel in the state militia and given command of the Rhode Island State Regiment. Stanton resigned this commission on November 10, 1777, but was subsequently granted the rank of brigadier general in the state militia, a position he held until the end of the war. Stanton's duties were of an administrative nature, as he was not a combat commander by any means.

In 1790, Stanton was a delegate to the convention that adopted the United States Constitution, and that same year he became the first U.S. senator from the state of Rhode Island, serving until 1793. After his term in the Senate, Stanton was returned to a seat in the Rhode Island Legislature before being elected to Congress in 1801. He served three terms in the House of Representatives, finally leaving office in 1807. Returning to private life, Stanton attempted to salvage his finances by concentrating on the running of his inn, which he left to his nephew upon his death.

Joseph Stanton died at Charlestown, Rhode Island, on January 22, 1822, at the age of eighty-two. He was buried in the family cemetery, on the grounds of his inn, at Charlestown.[1]

The General Stanton Inn still stands today, and is among the oldest existing inns still in operation in the country today.

STARK, JOHN — (New Hampshire)

John Stark was born in Nutfield (now Londonderry), New Hampshire, on August 28, 1728. In 1736, his family moved to Manchester, and then to Derryfield, which is where Stark lived until he was twenty-seven years of age. In his late twenties, while on a hunting expedition with an older brother and two friends, Stark was captured by a band of Indians. The Indians quickly captured another member of the group, who had been walking along a river-

John Stark (courtesy National Archives)

bank, but Stark's brother and the fourth companion were in a boat, and out of reach of the Indians. The Indians ordered Stark to call out to them and beckon them in to shore, but Stark cried out instead that they were in danger of an ambush and told them to row for the opposite bank. The Indians tried several times to shoot the occupants of the boat, but Stark interceded by knocking away the barrels of their muskets just as they were about to fire. Enraged by their failure to capture the other members, and by Stark's interference, the Indians fell upon him and beat him severely. When they returned to camp they forced Stark, and his companion, to run the gauntlet. When it came Stark's turn, he grabbed a club from the nearest warrior and ran through the gauntlet of braves delivering more blows than he received. The Indians appreciated his defiant spirit, and though they kept him as a captive for several months, they were at somewhat of a loss about what to do with him. When they would order him to hoe the corn, he would cut it instead. When reprimanded for doing so, he would throw the hoe in the river. The Indians were so impressed with his spirit, that could not be broken, that they eventually adopted him into the tribe as a young chief.

When the French and Indian War broke out, a corps of Rangers was raised in New Hampshire, and placed under the command of Robert Rogers. The unit would gain everlasting fame simply as Rogers Rangers. Stark served as a lieutenant with Rogers Rangers, and was present at Fort Edward when Colonel Williams attacked that place. When his regiment was later mustered out of the service, Stark joined a second regiment of Rangers, and continued to serve under Rogers. Stark became something of a legend during a winter expedition to Fort Ticonderoga, in 1757. Major Rogers had a force of seventy men with him, including Stark, when they came across a force of the enemy numbering over two hundred. Rogers force fought it out with the French and their Indian allies from 2 p.m. till dusk, sustaining many casualties, including Rogers and Stark. Rogers was severely wounded, and Stark assumed command. Rogers' command retreated in the direction of Fort William Henry, and marched all night through snow that was reported to be four feet deep. The following morning, many of the wounded were too exhausted to go further, and Stark volunteered to press on, with two comrades, to the fort to secure help. When he arrived there, he not only informed the garrison of the plight of Rogers' men, but he marched back with them to help rescue the stranded soldiers. By the time Stark was finished, he had marched one hundred twenty miles in forty hours, through the snows of a winter blizzard, with almost nothing to eat.[1]

In 1758, Stark was with Lord Howe in his expedition against Fort Ticonderoga. The assault on the fort proved to be a disaster, but Stark's command fought with distinction. After the Ticonderoga Campaign, Stark returned home to marry Elizabeth Page, of Dumbarton. The couple would have ten children together. He spent the remainder of the winter with his new bride, then returned to the army in the spring to help build an eighty mile road through the wilderness to Crown Point.

Following the war, Stark became a staunch advocate of Colonial rights, despite the fact that his older brother had joined the British army and received a colonel's commission. He served on the local Committee of Safety, and urged the people to resist the encroachments on their freedom made by the Crown. It is said that when he received news of the fighting at Lexington and Concord he was mounted and riding toward the scene of conflict within ten minutes. He was commissioned colonel of the 1st New Hampshire Regiment on April 23, 1775, and he led that regiment at the battle of Bunker Hill. In 1776, he was ordered to proceed with his regiment to join the Canadian expedition, but he met it on its retreat from that place. He took part in the battle of Three Rivers, on June 6, 1776, and retreated to Fort Ticonderoga following the defeat there. Stark then led his regiment at the battles of Trenton and Princeton. The term of enlistment of his men was about to expire, just prior to these battles, but Stark convinced the troops to stay in the service six weeks longer so they could participate in the campaign.

Stark was commissioned a brigadier general in the New Hampshire Militia in 1777, and on August 16 of that year he fought in the battle of Bennington, Vermont, where he routed a force of 1,400 Hessians. On October 4, 1777, Congress recognized his contributions by giving him a commission as a brigadier general in the Continental Army.[2]

During the Saratoga Campaign, Stark raised a large force of militia and placed it in Burgoyne's rear, effectively cutting off his escape route and benefiting General Gates in being able to force the surrender of the British army. In 1778, Stark was given command of the northern army, and in 1780, he was one of the officers that tried Major John Andre for his part in Benedict Arnold's treason, and sentenced him to death. In the spring of 1781 he was appointed commander in chief of the Northern Department, and made his headquarters at Saratoga. On September 30, 1783, he was granted the brevet commission of major general in the Continental Army. Stark remained with the Northern Department until the disbandment of the army, then returned home to resume life a farmer.

John Stark died at his home, in Manchester, New Hampshire, on May 8, 1822, in his ninety-fourth year. He was buried at John Stark State Park, in Manchester. At the time of his death, he was the last surviving American officer to have held a general's commission in the Continental Army during the Revolution.

STEPHEN, ADAM—(Scotland) Adam Stephen was born in Phynie Parish, Aberdeenshire, Scotland, in 1721. Adam's father most likely made his living raising cattle, and he saw to it that the boy received a fine education, attending parish school, grammar school, and finally matriculating at King's College of the University of Aberdeen, where he received a master of arts degree in 1740. After graduating from

Aberdeen, Stephen attended the University of Edinburgh, where studied medicine, and probably attained his degree, though there are no records available for medical students prior to 1760. In 1745, he became a naval surgeon, serving on the *Neptune*, an army hospital ship. In 1746, he accompanied an expedition against the French city of Port l'Orient, and was offered a position by the British East India Company as a surgeon on one of its ships, but he decided instead to come to America.

Stephen arrived in Maryland in 1748, and made his way to Virginia, eventually settling in Falmouth, across the river from Fredericksburg, where he established a medical practice for the next five years. There were a number of doctors in the Fredericksburg area, however, and Stephen was able to earn only a modest living as a doctor, so he decided to try to better himself as a plantation owner. He acquired about 2,000 acres of land along the Opequon River, in Frederick County, near present day Martinsburg, West Virginia, which he named Bower Plantation. Stephen attempted to raise staple crops in the rich soil, but eventually opted to raise cattle, instead. He would be a stockman the rest of his life. Though he never married, Stephen presumably had a daughter with Phoebe Seaman, his brother's housekeeper.[1]

In 1754, Stephen received a commission as captain in George Washington's expedition to Fort Duquesne that touched off the French and Indian War. Washington promoted him to major, and he took part in the construction of Fort Necessity, at Great Meadows, (near present day Uniontown, Pennsylvania), in June. Washington tried to defend the position, but he was outnumbered by the French and Indian forces arrayed against him by more than two to one, and faced a severe shortage of supplies. When the fort was surrendered to the French on July 4, Washington retreated to Wills Creek (present day Cumberland, Maryland) where Stephen was promoted to the rank of lieutenant colonel, and aided in the construction of Fort Cumberland. In June of 1755, he would be commissioned colonel and would be given command of the fort.

In 1755, Stephen led his men in General James Braddock's failed expedition against Fort Duquesne. Braddock's army was ambushed by the French and Indians, and nearly 70 percent of his men became casualties. Stephen was very critical of the British tactics in this battle, citing their refusal to fight as the French and Indians did as being the cause of the tragedy. After the defeat, Stephen once again assumed command of Fort Cumberland, and defended it from Indian attacks in the latter part of 1755 through 1756. In 1757, he and his men were transferred to South Carolina to resist an expected attack by the French that never materialized. Transferred back to Pennsylvania, he took part in the building of Fort Ligonier, and in General Forbes' successful expedition against the French stronghold at Fort Duquesne (present day Pittsburgh).

After the conclusion of the French and Indian War, Stephen attempted to try his hand at politics, running against George Washington and George Mason for a seat in the House of Burgesses. He was defeated in the election, and a rift was caused between him and Washington.

Stephen remained in the service, and in 1763 was given command of the Virginia frontier. When tensions arose between the colonies and the mother country, he cast his lot with the Patriots, and was commissioned colonel of the 4th Virginia Regiment on February 4, 1776. On September 4, of that same year, he was commissioned a brigadier general by the Continental Congress, and he fought in that capacity at the battle of Trenton. On February 19, 1777, he was promoted to the rank of major general, and led one of the attacking columns in the battle of Brandywine. He led a division at the battle of Germantown, where he became involved in a controversy that would end his military career. On the foggy ground of that battlefield, his troops mistakenly fired on the troops of General Anthony Wayne. Stephen was held responsible for the blunder, and was later accused of intoxication during the battle. He was relieved of command and dismissed from the service on November 20, 1777.[2]

After the war, Stephen returned to farming, and to land speculation. He founded the city of Martinsburg, Virginia (present day West Virginia), and profited by the selling of lots to the inhabitants.

Adam Stephen died at Martinsburg, West Virginia, on July 16, 1791, in his seventieth year, and was buried on the southern edge of Martinsburg, off South Queen Street, next to the Martinsburg High School grounds.

STEVENS, EDWARD — (Virginia)

Edward Stevens was born in Culpepper County, Virginia, in 1745. He was married to Gilly Coleman. In 1775, he was commissioned a colonel in the Virginia Militia and commanded a battalion in the battle of Great Bridge, on December 9, 1775. On November 12, 1776, he was assigned to command the 10th Virginia Regiment, and with that regiment took part in the Northern New Jersey Campaign, the defense of Philadelphia, and the battle of Monmouth. At the battle of Brandywine, he checked the forces of General William Howe and held the road assigned him until nightfall, preventing a serious disaster to the American forces. On January 31, 1778, Stevens resigned his commission in the Continental Army. He was subsequently commissioned a brigadier and major general in the Virginia Militia, serving from 1779 to 1782. On August 12, 1780, he led 700 militia to the aide of General Horatio Gates, and took part in the battle of Camden, South Carolina. Stevens fought with distinction at the battle of Guilford Courthouse, where he was seriously wounded. He received the praise of General Greene for his conduct during the battle. Stevens also took part in the Yorktown Campaign, where he displayed the courage and leadership that had come to define him on other fields of battle.

Following the surrender at Yorktown, Stevens served in the Virginia State Senate, being re-elected to a seat in that body through 1790.

Edward Stevens died in Culpepper County, Virginia, on August 17, 1820, in his seventy-fifth year. He was buried at the Masonic Cemetery in Culpepper, Virginia.[1]

SULLIVAN, JOHN — (New Hampshire)

John Sullivan was born at Somersworth, New Hampshire, on February 18, 1740. His parents were of Irish descent, and had originally come to America as indentured servants. His father, who had taught school, saw to it that the boy received a good primary education, after which he studied law under the supervision of the Hon. Isaac Livermore, of Portsmith, Maine. Sullivan excelled at his studies, and soon attained a position on the New Hampshire bar.[1]

His law practice thrived, and at the age of twenty, in 1760, he was able to get married to

Lydia Worster, and purchase a large house in Durham, New Hampshire. The couple would have six children together. For the next decade, he devoted his talents to the law, becoming one of the most distinguished and successful jurists in the colony. He then turned his attentions to promoting manufacturing in New Hampshire, and, largely through his efforts, the New Hampshire textile industry was born. Sullivan gained large personal wealth through his affiliation with the textile industry, and if he was not rich, he was certainly well-off by the time of the Revolution. He was an ardent Patriot, who despised oppression. In the spring of 1774, he served as a representative in the New Hampshire Provincial Assembly, and in September of that same year, he was a delegate to the Continental Congress, in Philadelphia.

Though he had a taste for the military, Sullivan had had no previous experience in the army prior to the time that relations with England were reaching a crisis. That fact notwithstanding, he took part in one of the earliest acts of aggression to be committed against the Crown, when on December 12, 1774, he served as one of the leaders in an attack upon Fort William and Mary, at Newcastle, in the harbor of Portsmith. Ninety-seven kegs of powder and a quantity of small arms were captured in the fort, and were conveyed to Durham, where they were hidden for future use by the Colonials. After the battles of Lexington and Concord, Sullivan personally delivered the much needed supplies to the Patriot lines at Cambridge, Massachusetts, where he marched with a company of militia he had raised and trained.[2]

For his services, Congress commissioned Sullivan a brigadier general in the Continental Army on June 22, 1775, and he was detailed to act as an aide on General Washington's staff. During the siege of Boston, when the Connecticut Militia serving with Washington went home, due to the expiration of their term of service, Sullivan was responsible for recruiting 2,000 men from New Hampshire to replace them. His service with the army in Massachusetts was such that he was promoted to the rank of major general on August 6, 1776.[3]

Sullivan commanded a brigade at the famous crossing of the Delaware in 1776, and took part in the battle of Trenton. He did good service at Monmouth, and commanded a wing of the army at Brandywine. He was captured by the British, at Long Island, in August of 1776, being exchanged in December of that same year, before spending the cruel winter at Valley Forge.[4]

In 1777, he submitted his resignation over a controversy regarding command of the artillery in the Continental army. It had been proposed to replace General Henry Knox with the French Count de Coudray, and Sullivan rallied to Knox's support, tendering his resignation, effective the day Coudray took over as chief of artillery. In the end, the loss of Sullivan's services was averted by the fact that Coudray died before taking over his assignment, and Knox was retained in that position.

In 1778, he was given command of the Continental forces in Rhode Island, to conduct a joint campaign along with the French fleet of the Count D'Estang against Newport Island.

John Sullivan

The French fleet was intercepted by the British fleet, and in the ensuing battle the ships of both navies were widely dispersed by a violent storm. When Sullivan assailed the British position, he did so without the support of the big French naval guns, and the attack proved to be a failure.

General Washington appealed to Sullivan, in the spring of 1779, to mount an expedition against the Six Nations of the Iroquois, to stop the incursions the Indians had been making in New York and Pennsylvania, and to acquire the store of grain that the Indians were then providing to the British army. Sullivan led a force of some 5,000 troops deep into Iroquois country, and fought his first engagement at the Iroquois village of Newtown, southeast of present day Elmira. The enemy was a mixed force of British regulars, Tories, and Indians, and numbered some 1,250 men, under the command of Colonel John Butler. Butler planned to ambush Sullivan's column, but the trap was discovered, and Sullivan attacked, dispersing the enemy with volleys of musketry and artillery fire. This was the only real battle of the campaign, though there were numerous forays and delaying actions undertaken by the British and their allies. Sullivan's campaign was a huge success, and many Indians were taken prisoner, their towns and cities destroyed. The influence of the Iroquois had been largely negated, and the attacks made by them on the frontier of New York and Pennsylvania came almost to a halt. After the campaign, Sullivan's forces hurried to New Jersey, to once more join Washington's army, but their commander did not accompany them. Five years of fighting had broken Sullivan's constitution, and he resigned his commission in November of 1779, due to poor health.

Retiring from the military did not bring with it an end to Sullivan's public service. He served in the Continental Congress in 1780 to 1781, before a four year term as attorney general of his state. This was followed by a term as speaker of the New Hampshire House of Representatives, and his serving as president of the convention that ratified the Constitution in New Hampshire. In 1789, Sullivan was a presidential elector, casting his vote for Washington. Later that same year, he was appointed a federal judge for the New Hampshire district, a position he would hold until 1795.[5]

John Sullivan died on January 23, 1795, at Durham, New Hampshire.

SUMNER, JETHRO—(Virginia) Jethro Sumner was born at Nasemond, Virginia, in 1730. He moved to North Carolina prior to 1760, when he was to be found as the paymaster of the provincial troops in that state, and the commander of Fort Cumberland. He was married to Mary Hurst, and the couple had three children together. Sumner was a Mason and was active in the Blandford Bute Lodge. He served as a justice of the peace in Bute County, as well as high sheriff. As tensions increased between the Colonies and England, he was a member of the Bute County Committee of Safety.

On April 15, 1776, he was commissioned a colonel in the North Carolina Militia and given command of the 3rd North Carolina Regiment. Sumner was ordered north, to join Washington's main army, where he took part in the defense of Philadelphia and the battle of Monmouth. On January 9, 1779, he was commissioned a brigadier general by the Continental Congress, and was subsequently ordered to join General Horatio Gates' army in the Southern Department. Sumner took part in the battle of Camden, under Gates, on August 16, 1780. Sumner fought at Lower Cape Fear and Stone Ferry, as part of the army of the Southern Department. On September 8, 1781, he was part of Nathaniel Greene's army that fought at the battle of Eutaw Springs. Sumner was credited with ordering a bayonet charge in that battle that helped to keep the enemy in check. Following Eutaw Springs, Sumner was occupied in campaigning against the Loyalist forces in North Carolina, and served in this capacity until the end of the war, performing the duties of commander of all state forces.

Jethro Sumner died at Warren, North Carolina, in 1790, in his sixtieth year. He was buried at the Guilford Battle Ground in Guilford County, North Carolina.[1]

SUMTER, THOMAS—(Virginia) Thomas Sumter was born in Hanover County, Virginia, on August 14, 1734. He received a common education before taking up the profession of surveying. When his father died at an early age, Sumter took care of his mother and tended the family sheep herd. During the French and Indian War, Sumter became a sergeant in the Virginia Militia and campaigned against the Cherokees. When the Indians sued for peace, Sumter accompanied the Cherokee representatives to the court of King George III, where he acted as a translator for them. When he returned to America, in 1762, he landed at Charleston, South Carolina, and spent that winter with the Cherokees. While he was with the Indians, he was responsible for capturing Baron Des Onnes, a French emissary that had been sent to stir up hostilities between the Cherokee and the British. Sumter returned briefly to Virginia, but was arrested for an old debt, and thrown in jail. He escaped from the Stanton Prison and made his way to Eutaw Springs, South Carolina, where he purchased a tract of land and became a planter. He also opened a small country store, and by 1766 had won the respect of his neighbors to the extent that they made him justice of the peace. Sumter married Mrs. Catey Gemstone, a wealthy widow seven years his senior. The couple moved to St. Mark's Parish, where they opened another store, a sawmill and a grist mill, and in 1768, they had their only child, a son, Thomas Jr.

In 1775, Sumter was elected to the First Provincial Congress, and he was re-elected to that body in 1776, when he was made a member of the Council of Safety. Following the outbreak of hostilities, he was commissioned a captain of Rangers and soon after promoted to lieutenant colonel of the 2nd South Carolina Rifle Regiment. With this regiment, he participated in the battle of Sullivan's Island on June 28, 1778, and Williamson's campaign against the Cherokee in the fall of that same year. He also participated in the Georgia Campaign defending against the British raid from St. Augustine, Florida.

He helped to adopt the constitution for the state of South Carolina, the second of the colonies to declare itself an independent sovereignty, and was elected to serve in the first General Assembly under that constitution in 1778.

After the fall of Charleston, in 1780, Governor Rutledge evacuated the government to North Carolina, leaving South Carolina completely in the hands of the British. During this critical time, Sumter formed the militia to oppose British movements in the state, and he stood as the only organized vestige of government authority in South Carolina. On July 30, 1780, he was defeated in the battle of Rocky Mount. On August 6, 1780, he defeated the British at the battle of Hanging Rock, destroying the Prince of Wales Regiment in the process. He was defeated by Tarleton at the battle of Fishing Creek, on August 18, 1780. On October 6, 1780 he was commissioned a brigadier general in the South Carolina Militia by Governor Rutledge. Sumter won a victory at the battle of Fish Dam Ford on November 9, 1780, capturing the British commander. On November 20, 1780, he defeated Tarleton at the battle of Blackstock's. British efforts were then shifted to other theaters, and South Carolina was spared from further scenes of conflict.

Sumter was elected to the state senate in

Thomas Sumter

1782. In 1785, he was elected to the state assembly, winning re-elections through 1789. In 1789, he was elected to the first U.S. Congress, and was re-elected in 1791. In 1796, he was returned to Congress, and in 1801 he was selected to fill Charles Pinckney's unexpired term as U.S. senator when the latter became minister to Spain. Sumter was continued in the Senate until 1810, when he retired to private life. In later life, Sumter became a great proponent of states' rights and a Calhoun supporter.

Thomas Sumter died at Stateburg, South Carolina, on June 1, 1832, in his ninety-eighth year. He was buried at his home at South Mount, at Stateburg. Thomas Sumter was the last surviving general officer commissioned in the militia to have served in the Revolution.[1]

SWARTWOUT, JACOBUS—(New York) Jacobus Swartwout was born at Fishkill, Dutchess County, New York, on November 5, 1734. Little is known of his early life or education. On March 7, 1760, he married Aaltje Brinckerhoff, and the couple had seven children together. Swartwout was an advocate of the Patriot cause, and the beginning of the war found him a colonel in command of a New York Minuteman Regiment. He was commissioned a colonel in the New York Militia in 1776, and served as such until 1780. Swartwout took part in the operations in and around New York City during the campaign of 1776. On March 3, 1780, he was commissioned a brigadier general in the state service, and continued in that capacity until the close of the war.

Following the war, he founded the town of Swartwoutville, in Duchess County, New York. Jacobus Swartwout died at Swartwoutville on January 23, 1827, at the age of ninety-two.[1]

SWIFT, HEMAN—(Massachusetts) Heman Swift was born at Sandwich, Barnstable County, Massachusetts, on October 14, 1733. Little is known of his early education. Swift acquired his first taste of military leadership and combat during the French and Indian War, serving as a lieutenant in Colonel David Wooster's regiment from 1758 till 1760. On February 29, 1760, he married Mary Skiff, and the couple had eleven children together. Mary died in 1788, and Swift later married Eleanor Johnson.

Swift was a personal friend of George Washington, and a staunch supporter of the cause of liberty, and offered his services to his state at the outbreak of hostilities. He was commissioned a colonel in 1776, and on January 1, 1777, was assigned to command the 7th Connecticut Regiment. The regiment was assigned to the Highlands Department, but did take part in the defense of Philadelphia and the Monmouth Campaign. On January 1, 1781, Swift transferred to the 2nd Connecticut Regiment, and was once again assigned to the Highlands Department. On September 30, 1783, the Continental Congress bestowed the rank of brevet brigadier general on Heman Swift in recognition of his distinguished service during the war. Swift continued to serve in the army until December of that same year.

Following the war, Swift served for many years in the Connecticut House of Representatives before retiring to private life.[1]

Heman Swift died at Cornwall, Connecticut, on November 12, 1814, at the age of eighty-one.

TEN BROECK, ABRAHAM—(New York) Abraham Ten Broeck (also spelled Tenbroeck) was born at Albany, New York, on May 13, 1734, into a prominent family of the colony. On November 1, 1763, Ten Broeck married Elizabeth Van Rensselaer, and the couple had five children together.

Ten Broeck was elected to be a delegate to the second Continental Congress in 1775. He was commissioned a colonel of New York Militia in 1775, and a brigadier general of Albany and Tryon County Militia on June 25, 1778. Ten Broeck held a command at the battle of Bemis Heights, New York, in September of 1777, and commanded the New York Militia at the battle of Saratoga, in October of that same year.

In 1779, he was elected mayor of Albany, serving until 1783. During these same years, he was also elected to the New York State Senate. In 1781, Governor Clinton appointed Ten

Broeck to be the first judge of the Court of Common Pleas. Ten Broeck resigned his commission in the New York Militia on March 26, 1781, due to poor health.

Following the war, Ten Broeck became the first president of both the Bank of Albany and the Albany Public Library, and a trustee of Union College. In 1797, his house in Albany was destroyed by fire, and Ten Broeck built the manor house, named Prospect, in Watervliet Township. The mansion sparked development in what was to become Arbor Hill, New York.

Abraham Ten Broeck died on January 19, 1801, at the age of sixty-six.[1]

TEN BROECK, PETRUS—(New York) Petrus Ten Broeck (also spelled Tenbroeck) was born at Kingston, Ulster County, New York, on October 4, 1720. Little is known of his early life or education. On June 24, 1749, he married Catharina Rutsen. Ten Broeck was a citizen of Rhinebeck, and at the outbreak of the war was commissioned a colonel in the Rhinebeck Militia. In November of 1775, he was chosen to be deputy of the New York Provincial Congress. He later served as secretary of the Committee of War. Ten Broeck was subsequently commissioned a brigadier general in the state militia. His commission as general seems to have been motivated by his position with the Committee of War, as he did not serve in the field or command troops in camp or in battle.

Petrus Ten Broeck died on March 5, 1777, at the age of fifty-six.[1]

THOMAS, JOHN—(Massachusetts) John Thomas was born at Marshfield, Plymouth County, Massachusetts, on November 9, 1724. After completing his primary education, Thomas studied medicine and established himself in the medical practice. Thomas rose to become a prominent member of Plymouth County society, and was highly regarded as a leader of the community. In 1746, he was appointed surgeon to a regiment that was sent to Annapolis Royal, Nova Scotia, and in 1747, he served on the medical staff of General William Shirley. In 1759, he became a colonel in the militia, and in 1760 he commanded a regiment under General Jeffrey Amherst, at Crown Point. On September 12, 1761, he married Hannah Thomas, and the couple had four children together.

Thomas was quite active in the Massachusetts Militia prior to the Revolution, holding the rank of colonel, and when that state mobilized for war, following the battles at Lexington and Concord, he was appointed major general of the Massachusetts state forces in June of 1775. Thomas was promoted to the rank of lieutenant general of state forces in January of 1776. On March 4, 1776, Thomas was responsible for the fortification of Dorchester Heights, a movement that caused the British to evacuate the town. He was also commissioned to the rank of general by the Continental Congress, being given the rank of brigadier general in the Continental service on June 22, 1775, and being promoted to major general on March 6, 1776.

Thomas took part in the siege of Boston, and in the operations in and around that city during 1775. He then led his forces in support of General Montgomery's Canadian Expedition, and took part in operations against Quebec. After the death of General Montgomery, Thomas was entrusted with the command in Canada. The severe Canadian winter, combined with an epidemic of smallpox, took an extreme toll on the American army during their retreat from Quebec in May of 1776. Thomas was stricken with smallpox and died of the disease during the retreat at Fort Chambly, Quebec, Canada. Sources differ as to the exact date, ranging from May 30 to June 3. Thomas was fifty-one years old at the time of his death. He was buried at Fort Chambly, along with a number of soldiers who had succumbed to the disease, mostly in unmarked graves.[1]

THOMPSON, WILLIAM—(Ireland) William Thompson was born in Ireland in 1736. As a young man, he migrated to the Cumberland Valley of Pennsylvania, and settled in the Carlisle area, where he became a well known surveyor and justice of the peace. During the French and Indian War, Thompson was assigned to raise a troop of cavalry, of which he was commissioned the captain. He accompanied Armstrong's expedition against Kittanning, which resulted in the destruction of the Indian stronghold. After the end of the war, Thompson served on the committee that was charged with establishing the western boundaries of Pennsylvania. On March 29, 1762, he married Catherine Ross, and the couple had seven children together.

In 1774, Thompson was a member of a convention held in Cumberland County, Pennsylvania, to denounce the closing of the port of Boston by the British, and he was subsequently appointed to be a member of the Committee of Correspondence.

On June 14, 1775, the Continental Congress approved the raising of six companies of expert riflemen from Pennsylvania, and Thompson was instrumental in spurring enlistments and enrolling the quota of men. The Pennsylvania riflemen became part of the 1st Continental Infantry, and marched to Cambridge, joining the main army there on August 14, with Thompson commanding as colonel. In November of 1775, when the British landed a force at Lechmore's Point, Thompson was ordered to drive the enemy back, which he successfully accomplished. On March 1, 1776, Thompson was promoted to the rank of brigadier general by the Continental Congress. It was intended to send him to Virginia, to command the military forces there, but, after conference with Washington, Thompson decided against the assignment for reasons that an officer from that state would receive better support than he could hope to obtain. General Lee was selected for the position instead, and Thompson was sent to New York, to replace that officer when he went south. Thompson took part in the Canadian Expedition of 1776, and was in command of the New York contingent that was co-operating with General Sullivan. Thompson commanded at the battle of Three Rivers, Canada, on June 8, 1776, where he suffered a defeat. Thompson was captured during the battle, and his exchange became a point of concern with General Washington. Initially, Thompson was supposed to be exchanged for William Franklin, the son of Benjamin Franklin and royal governor of New Jersey who had remained loyal to the crown instead of following the example of his Patriot father. Washington initiated the exchange, only to be informed by Congress that they were no longer willing to trade Franklin. Thompson was forced to remain a British prisoner for over four years. He was not exchanged until the fall of 1780. Thompson desired to resume active service with the army, but his health had been so completely broken by his confinement that he was forced to return to his home at Carlisle.

William Thompson died at Carlisle in 1781, as a result of his imprisonment, in his forty-fifth year. He was buried in the Old Graveyard in Carlisle.[1]

TUPPER, BENJAMIN—(Massachusetts)
Benjamin Tupper was born in Stoughton, Massachusetts, on March 11, 1738. The death of his father at an early age caused Tupper to be apprenticed to a tanner till the age of sixteen. He then became a farmhand, and in 1756 enlisted in the Massachusetts Militia to serve in the French and Indian War. Following the war, Tupper became a school teacher in 1762. He was married that same year to Huldah White, and the couple would have one child together. In April of 1775, Tupper was commissioned a major in the militia, serving in Fellow's Massachusetts regiment. He was promoted to lieutenant colonel in November, and on January 1, 1776, became lieutenant colonel of the 21st Continental Regiment. Tupper took part in the siege of Boston and the battles around New York with this regiment. On November 1, 1776, Tupper was made colonel of the 2nd Massachusetts Regiment. Tupper took part in the engagements at Trenton and Princeton with the 2nd Massachusetts. He was transferred to the 11th Massachusetts Regiment on July 7, 1777, and fought in the Saratoga Campaign, the defense of Philadelphia, and the battle of Monmouth with that regiment. On January 1, 1781, Tupper assumed command of the 10th Massachusetts Regiment, leading it till January of 1783, when he took command of the 6th Massachusetts Regiment.

On September 30, 1783, the Continental Congress bestowed the rank of brevet brigadier general on Benjamin Tupper, in recognition of his extensive service. Before retiring from the army, Tupper became one of 238 officers to sign the Newburgh Petition, asking the federal government to pay off the soldiers of the army with land grants in Ohio. Following the war, Tupper served in the Massachusetts legislature. In 1786, he was called back into active service to assist in putting down Shay's Rebellion. That same year, he also helped to survey land in the Seven Ranges, and used the knowledge he gained in doing so to persuade Congress into allowing him to establish settlements in the Ohio Territory. He was one of the original founders of Marietta, Ohio. In 1788, along with General Putnam, he became one of the first judges to be appointed to the Court of Common Pleas for the territory. He lived in the Northwest Territory for the remainder of his life.

Benjamin Tupper died on June 7, 1792, at the age of fifty-four. He was buried in the Mound Cemetery, in Washington County, Ohio.[1]

TWIGGS, JOHN—(Georgia) John Twiggs was born in Maryland (some sources state Virginia) on December 12, 1750. He moved to Georgia, where he owned a plantation, Good Hope, near Augusta. The property was a grant from King George III. In 1775, Twiggs married Ruth Emanuel, and the couple had six children together.

At the outbreak of the Revolution, Twiggs became a militia leader, under Colonel Samuel Jack, and saw service mostly against the Cherokee Indians, who were allied with the British. He was called the Savior of Georgia for his efforts in keeping the Patriot cause alive in that state after it had been occupied by British forces in 1779. Twiggs fought at the battle of Camden on August 16, 1780, where he was wounded. In 1781, he was commissioned a brigadier general in the Georgia Militia, serving in that capacity until the end of hostilities.

Following the end of the war, Twiggs prospered in the running of his plantation, and in business ventures. He purchased the tobacco crop of neighboring plantations, cured it in his warehouses, and shipped it to Savannah to be sold. In 1785, he signed a peace treaty with the Creeks, at Galphinton, and secured another treaty with other Creek tribes at Shoulderbone in 1786. Twiggs founded the settlement of New Savannah, Georgia. He was a trustee of the Academy of Richmond County, and a member of the committee charged with selecting a location to build the University of Georgia. Twiggs served as a justice of the peace, and was a member of the committee that welcomed President Washington to Augusta when he visited there in 1791.

John Twiggs died at Richmond, Georgia, on March 29, 1816, at the age of sixty-five. He was buried in the Twiggs Family Cemetery, at Good Hope Plantation, in Richmond County, Georgia. Twiggs County, Georgia, is named in his honor.[1]

TYLER, JOHN—(Connecticut) John Tyler was born at Preston, New London County, Connecticut, on December 29, 1721. On December 14, 1742, he married Mary Colt, and the couple had seven children together.

Tyler joined the local militia in 1752, being appointed lieutenant of the third company of the town of Preston. From 1756 till 1760, he served in various companies that were raised to defend against the French and Indians, rising to the rank of captain. In 1756, he was elected to the Connecticut General Assembly, and served nine terms in that body before hostilities with Great Britain erupted.

When the Revolutionary War broke out, Tyler was commissioned lieutenant colonel of the 6th Connecticut Regiment, performing garrison duty at New London until June of 1775, when the regiment was ordered to Boston. He was present at the siege of Boston, and on January 1, 1776, was promoted to the rank of colonel and assigned to the 10th Continental Regiment. With this regiment, he took part in the campaigns in and around New York in the summer of 1776, seeing action in the battles of Long Island and White Plains. On June 3, 1777, he succeeded Gurdon Saltonstall as brigadier general of the 3rd Connecticut Militia Brigade. In 1778, he attempted to dislodge the British from Newport, Rhode Island, fighting at Quaker Hill. He commanded the militia during the New Haven alarm of 1779, and defended the coast at New London, New Haven, and Groton. When the army was disbanded, his troops had not been paid for some time.

Tradition has it that Tyler paid off his men with his own money.

Following the war, Tyler returned to Preston, where he was elected to his first of two terms in the Connecticut Assembly in 1783.

John Tyler died at Preston, Connecticut, on July 29, 1804, at the age of eighty-two. He was buried at the Old Griswold Cemetery in New London County.[1]

VAN CORTLANDT, PHILIP — (New York)
Philip Van Cortlandt was born in New York City on September 1, 1749. He received his primary education in a schoolhouse his father had built upon the grounds of the family farm, before being sent to Coldenham Academy. Van Cortlandt only spent nine months at the academy, dropping out when he received news that his uncle had died at sea. He was then apprenticed to Nathaniel Merritt, to learn the art of surveying, and upon completion, set himself up as a surveyor. At the same time, he had started a milling business and a small retail store.

In 1774, Van Cortlandt received a commission as major in the provincial militia. His appointment came directly from the governor, who was trying to convince Van Cortlandt to remain loyal to England. Cortlandt's father had served in the New York legislature, and was a local leader, and Governor Tryon sought to cultivate his influence by offering various inducements, such as land grants, if the family would give their full support to the crown. The Van Cortlandts were Patriots, however, and could not be swayed from the cause of freedom. Philip accepted the commission as major, and trained with his troops, but, on June 30, 1775, after the fighting at Lexington and Concord, he accepted a commission as lieutenant colonel in the 4th New York Regiment. The regiment was ordered to support Montgomery's expedition to Canada. Van Cortlandt did little campaigning that winter. He had been stricken with a fever that nearly killed him, and spent most of the winter months recuperating. His regiment was engaged at the battle of White Plains, but Van Cortlandt was not with it during the fighting. Following that battle, on November 21, 1776, he was commissioned to be colonel of the 2nd New York Regiment.[1]

Philip Van Cortlandt (courtesy United States Military History Institute)

Following the battle, Van Cortlandt was ordered to the White Plains area, where his command was charged with monitoring the actions of the British from Morrisania to the North River. In August of 1777, Van Cortlandt was ordered, with his command, to the support of Fort Stanwix. He served under General Arnold during the Saratoga Campaign, where he was responsible for discovering the enemy position, prior to the battle. Following the battle, Van Cortlandt's command joined the main army, at Valley Forge to go into winter quarters.

In June of 1778, Van Cortlandt was appointed, by Washington, to command the encampment at Valley Forge, and thereby missed the battle of Monmouth. Following this assignment, Governor Clinton requested that Washington release him from the main army to serve in protecting the New York frontier from Indian incursions, and Van Cortlandt spent the winter of 1778–79 in the performance of this duty. On August 29, 1779, he took part in the battle of Newton, New York, in which his regiment was instrumental in routing the Indian force. The winter of 1779–80 was spent in winter quarters at Morristown, New Jersey, before being once again detailed to guard the New York frontier.

Van Cortlandt served with distinction in the Yorktown Campaign, seeing a great deal of combat during the siege under the command of Lafayette. In recognition of his contributions to the cause, during the war, Congress awarded him a commission as brevet brigadier general in the Continental service on September 30, 1783.

Following the war, Van Cortlandt was made an officer in the Society of the Cincinnati. In 1788, he was a delegate to the New York convention to ratify the Constitution. He served in the state assembly from 1788 to 1790 and in the state senate from 1791 to 1793. From 1793 to 1809 he served as a representative from New York in the United States Congress. He then retired from public service to attend to agricultural pursuits.

Philip Van Cortlandt died at Croton, New York, on November 21, 1831, at the age of eighty-two. He was buried in the Hillside Cemetery, in Peekskill, New York.

VAN RENSSELAER, ROBERT—**(New York)** Robert Van Rensselaer was born at Crailo, New York, on December 5, 1740. He was the grandson of Ninian Van Rensselaer, one of the Dutch men responsible for the colonization of New Amsterdam, and his descendants became leading citizens in the Albany area. On April 23, 1765, Van Rensselaer married Cornelia Rutsen, and the couple had four children together.

In 1775, Van Rensselaer was commissioned a colonel in the New York Militia. In 1777, he was elected to the New York State Assembly, as a delegate from Albany County, serving until 1779. He was re-elected in 1780, and served until 1781. On June 16, 1780, Van Rensselaer was commissioned a brigadier general in the New York Militia. His most significant service came during Sir John Johnson's raid in the Mohawk Valley. Johnson's force of some 1,000 Loyalists, Germans, and Indians had burned a swath of destruction down the valley, and had defeated an American force in the battle of Stone Arabia on October 19, 1780. Van Rensselaer arrived on the scene just as the battle of Stone Arabia was concluding, and received news of the disaster from survivors. Van Rensselaer's army consisted of some 1,500 militia and Oneida Indians, and he prepared to engage the inferior forces of the enemy in a fight that was to become known as the battle of Klock's Field. For unknown reasons, Van Rensselaer delayed his attack until just before dusk, however, and even though the American forces drove the enemy from the field, the victory was not complete due to the attack being halted at nightfall. The following morning, Van Rensselaer called off the American pursuit and allowed Sir John, and the beaten remnant of his command, to escape back to Canada. Van Rensselaer then established his headquarters at Fort Plain, renaming the works Fort Rensselaer, after himself. The name change did not stick, however.

Following the battle of Klock's Field, Van Rensselaer came under severe criticism for his actions upon that field. Strong sentiment against him charged that he had intentionally allowed Sir John to escape, and it was even suggested that he was, at heart, a Loyalist himself. (Sir John and Van Rensselaer had been contemporaries, before the war.) Van Rensselaer was brought before a court-martial, in which he was exonerated of the charges, but his reputation with the troops and the people of the Mohawk Valley was forever stained.

Robert Van Rensselaer died at Claverack, New York, on September 11, 1802, at the age of sixty-one. He was buried in the Claverack Dutch Reformed Cemetery.[1]

VAN SCHAICK, GOSEN "GOOSE"— **(New York)** Gosen Van Schaick was born in Albany, New York, in 1736, the oldest son of the mayor of Albany. Named for a family patriarch, he soon acquired the nickname of Goose, by which he became commonly known.

In 1756, at the age of twenty-one, he was appointed a lieutenant in the New York Militia, in Captain Philip Schuyler's company, and served in the expedition against Crown Point in his first military experience in the French and Indian War. In 1758, he was promoted to captain and took part in the operations against Forts Frontenac and Niagara. During an expedition against Fort Carillon, he was severely wounded in the face in a skirmish near Lake George. The wound permanently disfigured him, and would eventually cost him his life, but he quickly returned to the command of his company. In 1759, he was promoted to major, and in 1762 Van Schaick was commissioned lieutenant colonel of the 1st New York Regiment. At the close of the French and Indian War he was among the most experienced and respected military men in New York.

After the war, Van Schaick returned to Albany, where he entered into business as an exporter of farm and forest products from New York's rich Hudson Valley. In 1766, he became a member of the Sons of Liberty and of Albany's Committee of Correspondence, joining his neighbors in signing a protest against the Stamp Act. In 1770, he married Maria Ten Broeck, and the couple had six children together.

Following the battles at Lexington and Concord, Van Schaick was commissioned colonel of the 2nd New York Regiment on June 28, 1775. His face wound, from the French and Indian War, had by this time become malignant, and would be a constant affliction during his service. General Schuyler placed him in command at Albany, with orders to forward men and supplies to the northern front. On March 8, 1776, Van Schaick was given command of the 1st New York Regiment, and with this unit fought and was wounded at Fort Ticonderoga on July 6, 1777. In 1778, Van Schaick was ordered to report to Valley Forge, and he subsequently took part in the battle of Monmouth, before being deployed in the lower Hudson Valley and upper Mohawk Valley to guard against incursions by the Iroquois. In 1779, General James Clinton placed him in charge of an expedition against the Onondaga Indians, in the Mohawk Valley, in conjunction with the Sullivan-Clinton expedition. In 1780, Van Schaick returned to Albany, where he served as an administrator for the Northern Department, focusing on recruiting and gathering supplies, and commanded at Fort Orange. During the last years of the war, he made numerous trips to Philadelphia to seek medical attention for the ever growing cancer on his face, and endured a number of surgeries to have it cut away. Though he had been regularly passed over for promotion, the Continental Congress recognized his service to the country when it bestowed the rank of brevet brigadier general upon him on October 10, 1783. Van Schaick continued to serve until November of 1783, when he was discharged from the army, and retired to private life.

After the war, Van Schaick gave his attentions to personal matters, including applications for bounty land for his military services. His health continued to decline, as a result of the cancer, and Goose Van Schaick died at Albany on July 4, 1789, in his sixty-third year. He was buried in the Albany Rural Cemetery, in Menands, Albany County, New York.[1]

VARNUM, JAMES M.—(Massachusetts)
James Mitchell Varnum was born at Dracut, Massachusetts, on December 17, 1748. He received a substantial primary education and attended Harvard, being expelled for unknown reasons. He later attended Rhode Island College (present day Brown), where he graduated in the first class from that institution in 1769. His graduation thesis was an argument as to why America should not rebel against Great Britain. Following his graduation from college, Varnum taught school for a brief period before deciding to study law. After completing the course of study, he was admitted to the Massachusetts bar in 1771. Varnum served in the Rhode Island Militia, prior to the Revolution, and once hostilities erupted, offered his services to the Continental Army. On May 3, 1775, he was commissioned colonel of the Rhode Island Regiment, and on January 1, 1776, he was given command of the 9th Continental Regiment. With this regiment, he participated in the siege of Boston, and the battles of Long Island, White Plains, Red Bank, Trenton and Princeton. On January 1, 1778, he was given command of the 1st Rhode Island Regiment, but

he had little time to lead that unit. On February 27, 1777, he was commissioned a brigadier general by Congress. Varnum took part in the failed Rhode Island Campaign, where planned co-operation with the French fleet, and D'Estang, failed to materialize. On March 5, 1779, Varnum resigned his commission in the Continental Army and returned home to resume his law practice.

Though no longer in the army, Varnum continued to aide the cause of freedom, serving in the Continental Congress from 1780 to 1782, and again in 1786.

In 1788, he was one of the original founders of the Ohio Company of the Northwest Territory. Territorial government in the Northwest Territory was a pet project of George Washington, and he embraced the company, appointing Varnum to act as its first federal judge. In the spring of 1788, Varnum traveled to Adelphia, Ohio (present day Marietta). He opened the first court in the territory, and began to bring the constitutional law of the United States to the territory, and assisted Governor St. Clair in forming a government. In December of 1788 Varnum became severely ill. James Varnum died on January 10, 1789, from consumption, at the age of fifty. He was buried at Campus Martius, in Marietta, Ohio.[1]

VON STEUBEN, FRIEDRICH WILHELM AUGUSTUS—(Prussia) Friedrich Wilhelm Augustus Von Steuben was born at Fortress Magdeburg, Germany, in 1730, where his father, an engineering officer in the German army, was stationed. Most of Von Steuben's early years were spent in Russia, but his family returned to Germany when he was ten years old, where he received schooling in Breslau by the Jesuits. At the age of seventeen, Von Steuben entered military service as an officer in the Prussian army. Von Steuben served in the Seven Years' War, being promoted to the rank of captain. Following the war, he was assigned to the General Staff, and his performance was such that it eventually earned him a position on the staff at Frederick the Great's headquarters. In 1763, Von Steuben was discharged from the army for unknown reasons. In 1764, he obtained the title of baron when he became chamberlain at the Petty Court of Hohenzollern-Hechingen. He also was named grand-marshal to the court, and was aide-de-camp to the king of Prussia. Prince Margrave, of Baden, appointed him knight of the order of Fidelity and made him commander in chief of all his military.

In 1771, Von Steuben accompanied the prince to France, in an effort to secure a loan. Failing to find a willing lender, they returned home in 1775, deeply in debt. Searching for a means to reverse his fortunes, Von Steuben looked to America. He had heard that Benjamin Franklin was in Paris, and speculated that he might find work with the Continental Army. In 1777, Von Steuben traveled to Paris to meet with Franklin. He had the endorsement of the French minister of war, Count de St. Germain, and soon won Franklin's approval and a letter of introduction to General Washington. On September 26, 1777, he landed in New Hampshire, and on February 5, 1778, he appeared before Congress. Von Steuben offered to volunteer,

James Varnum (courtesy United States Military History Institute)

Baron Friedrich von Steuben drilling the troops (courtesy United States Army War College)

without pay, to prove himself worthy of remuneration. If, after Congress saw the measure of his abilities they wished to retain his services, then he would request compensation equivalent to what he had been paid in Europe. Congress accepted his offer, and on March 28, 1778, appointed him volunteer inspector general of the army.

Von Steuben was responsible for molding the American forces into a real army, capable of giving battle to the British on equal terms. His system of training and discipline remain as the basis of military training in the American army to this day. On May 5, 1778, Congress recognized his accomplishments with the army by commissioning him a major general. It was Von Steuben who was the first to report the approach of the British army at Monmouth. During the winter of 1778–79, Von Steuben wrote *Regulations for the Order and Discipline of the Troops of the United States*. He participated in the Southern Campaign in the spring of 1781, leading a corps of Virginia troops south to join Lafayette. Following this, he was forced to take a leave from the army due to sickness, but rejoined it in time to take part in the final operations around Yorktown.

Von Steuben served till the end of the war, being discharged on March 24, 1784. In recognition of his service to the American cause, Congress voted to present him with a gold-hilted sword. Following the war, he located himself in New York, where he attempted to go into business. Von Steuben was not well versed in mercantile ventures, however, and his business efforts proved to be a failure. In 1790, he received a pension from the United States government, amounting to $2,500 a year. He was also given approximately 16,000 acres of ground in New York.

Baron Von Steuben died on his farm, near New York City, on November 28, 1794, in his sixty-fourth year. In his will, Von Steuben requested to be buried in an unmarked grave. In 1804, however, his remains were moved to Steuben Memorial Historic Park, in Oneida County, New York.[1]

VOSE, JOSEPH—**(Massachusetts)** Joseph Vose was born at Milton, Norfolk County, Massachusetts, on December 7, 1738. On December 27, 1761, he married Sarah Howe, and the couple would have three children together.

Vose joined the Patriot cause shortly after the fighting at Lexington and Concord, and was appointed major of Heath's Massachusetts Regiment on May 19, 1775. He was promoted to the rank of lieutenant colonel in July of that same year. On January 1, 1776, he was assigned to the 24th Continental Infantry Regiment. With these two units, Vose took part in the operations in and around Boston during the early stages of the war, and in the defense of Canada and operations around Lake Champlain. On January 1, 1777, Vose was promoted to the rank of colonel and given command of the 1st Massachusetts Regiment. This regiment took part in the battle of Princeton, the Saratoga Campaign, the defense of Philadelphia, the Monmouth Campaign, and the Rhode Island expedition.

Vose served with the 1st Massachusetts through to the close of the hostilities. On September 30, 1783, he was granted a commission as brevet brigadier general, in recognition of his many services in the war. He retired from the service on November 3 of that same year, returning to private life.

Joseph Vose died on May 22, 1816, at his home at Milton, Massachusetts, at the age of fifty-four.[1]

WADSWORTH, JAMES—**(Connecticut)** James Wadsworth was born at Durham, Middlesex County, Connecticut, on July 8, 1730. He received a thorough primary education and attended Yale College, graduating from that institution in 1748. He subsequently studied law and was admitted to the Connecticut bar. In 1756, he was made town clerk of Durham, a position he would hold for thirty years. On January 13, 1757, Wadsworth married Katherine Guernsey, and the couple had two children together.

In 1762, he was appointed justice of the peace, and in 1773 he was appointed to be a judge of the New Haven County Court. Wadsworth was a member of the local Committee of Safety, and was commissioned a colonel in the state militia in 1775. On June 20, 1776, he was promoted to the rank of brigadier general, and in May of 1777 was advanced to the grade of major general in the state service. In the latter capacity, he was charged with the defense of the Connecticut coastal towns, with his headquarters being in New Haven. Wadsworth resigned his commission in 1779, but he did not retire from public life. In 1783, he was elected to the Continental Congress, serving until 1786. From 1785 to 1790, he served as a member of the Connecticut Executive Council. From 1786 to 1787 he served as the state comptroller. Wadsworth was a delegate to the state convention to ratify the Federal Constitution in 1788, but he was an opponent of that document, and argued against its adoption.

James Wadsworth died at Durham, Connecticut, on September 22, 1817, at the age of eighty-seven. He was buried in the Old Cemetery, at Durham.[1]

WADSWORTH, PELEG—**(Massachusetts)** Peleg Wadsworth was born in Duxbury, Massachusetts, on May 6, 1748. After completing his primary education in public and common school, Wadsworth attended Harvard College, where he graduated with a B.A. in 1769 and a M.A. in 1772. Following college, he taught school in Plymouth for several years before entering into commercial pursuits in Kingston, Massachusetts. In 1772, he married Elizabeth Bartlett, and the couple had ten children together.

Early in 1775, Wadsworth recruited a company of militia, and was elected captain by the men. On April 19 of that year, upon receiving news of the fighting at Lexington and Concord, Wadsworth assembled his men and marched to the scene of conflict. He did not arrive in time to take part in the fighting at either of those two battles, but did participate in the siege of Boston. On January 1, 1776, he was commissioned captain of the 23rd Continental Regiment, and on February 23 of that year was assigned as aide-de-camp to General Artemas Ward. Later that year he served as an engineer under General Thomas, helping to lay out the defenses of Roxbury, Massachusetts. Wadsworth was present at the battle of Long Island, New York, on August 1, 1776. In 1777, he was commissioned a brigadier general in the Massachusetts Militia, and in 1778 was appointed to the post of adjutant general for the state. In 1779 he participated in an expedition against the British force at Castine, Maine, known as the Penobscot Expedition. Wadsworth was second in command to Paul Revere even though Revere was only a lieutenant colonel. The expedition was to be a three-prong mission with two ground columns and a naval detachment. The naval detachment, under Commodore Dudley Saltonstall, and Revere's ground column were both badly defeated, leading to the court-martial of both of those officers for their part in the disaster. For his part, Wadsworth led his column well, and kept them well in hand during the retreat.

In March of 1780, Wadsworth was given command for all the defense forces in the province of Maine, and he made his headquarters at Thomaston. On February 17, 1781, he was wounded and captured by a British raiding party at his headquarters and was imprisoned at Fort George, in Castine, Maine. The British planned to send Wadsworth to England, to stand trial for treason, but before they could do so, he escaped, along with another prisoner, by cutting a hole in the ceiling of his cell. Wadsworth returned to his family in Plymouth, where he remained until the end of the war.

In 1784, he moved his family to Portland, Maine, where he engaged in surveying and opened a store. In 1792, Wadsworth was chosen to be a presidential elector, and was elected to the Massachusetts Senate. In 1793 he was elected to the United States Congress, and served consecutively until 1807. Wadsworth then moved his family to Hiram, Maine, in 1807, to a tract of land that he had been given from the state for his war services. He served as selectman, treasurer, and magistrate for the town, before retiring from public life to devote himself to farming and private concerns.

Peleg Wadsworth died at Hiram, Maine, on July 18, 1829, at the age of eighty-one. He was buried in the family cemetery at Wadsworth Hall, in Hiram, Maine. He was the grandfather of Henry Wadsworth Longfellow, the celebrated American poet.[1]

WARD, ANDREW—(Connecticut) Andrew Ward was born at Guilford, Connecticut, on November 19, 1727. Little is known of his early life, or education. On September 7, 1750, he married Diana Hubbard. The marriage would bear five children to the couple.

Like so many generals in the Revolution, Ward served as an officer during the French and Indian War. In 1758, he was a captain in Colonel Phineas Lyman's regiment, and in 1759 he served in the same capacity in Colonel Nathan Whiting's regiment.

In May of 1775, Ward was commissioned colonel of the 1st Connecticut Regiment, serving in that capacity until December 20, 1775. This regiment participated in General Montgomery's invasion of Canada. He was then assigned to command the Connecticut State Regiment on May 10, 1776, and held that position until May of 1777. In June of 1777, Ward was commissioned a brigadier general in the Connecticut Militia, and continued in that capacity through the end of the war.

Andrew Ward died on January 10, 1799, at Guilford, Connecticut, at the age of seventy-one.[1]

WARD, ARTEMAS—(Massachusetts) Artemas Ward was born at Shrewsbury, Massachusetts, on November 26, 1727, the son of a sea captain and merchant. He was enrolled at Harvard, after receiving a primary education in common schools and by tutors, and graduated from that institution in 1748. After graduation, he taught briefly at Harvard. In 1750, Ward married Sarah Trowbridge. The couple would have seven children together. Ward opened a general store in Shrewsbury in 1750, and in 1751, he was named township assessor for Worcester County. In 1752, Ward was elected a justice of the peace as well as a member of the Massachusetts Assembly.

In 1755, during the French and Indian War, Ward was commissioned a major in the 3rd Massachusetts Regiment. From 1755 till 1757, the regiment performed mainly garrison duty on the Massachusetts frontier, but in 1758 it took part in Abercrombie's expedition against Fort Ticonderoga. Ward had been promoted to colonel by this time but was not able to accompany the regiment during the battle for the fort as he was incapacitated by illness. In 1762 Ward returned to Shrewsbury and was appointed to be a judge on the Court of Common Pleas, being placed on the taxation committee with John Hancock and Samuel Adams. Because of Ward's numerous attacks against the crown, on the floor of the assembly, the royal governor revoked his military commission in 1767, and banned him from the assembly in 1768. On October 3, 1774, the 3rd Massachusetts Regiment resigned from the British service, en masse, and marched to Shrewsbury to inform Ward that they had unanimously elected him to be their colonel. Ward was officially commissioned to the rank of colonel by the Provincial Congress of Massachusetts, of which he was a delegate, on October 27, 1774. On May 19, 1775, following the fighting at Lexington and Concord, Ward was appointed commander in chief of the Massachusetts Militia. New Hampshire and Connecticut soon followed suit, naming Ward to command their militia forces, as well. He was in command of the army during the battle of Bunker Hill, though he remained at his headquarters, in Cambridge, and took no active part in the battle. In fact, it was alleged that he was largely responsible for the American loss from a failure, on his part, to supply enough ammunition to the troops to be able to hold the ground. On June 17, 1775, he was named as the first major general in the Continental Army, by Congress, and as such was commander of the army that was besieging Boston until the arrival of George Washington. When Washington took charge of the army, Ward was named second in command, and was assigned to the right wing of the army, on Roxbury Heights. Following the British evacuation of Boston, when Washington marched the army to New York, Ward was given command of the Eastern Department. He held that post until he was forced to resign, for reasons of poor health.

Ward became president of the Massachusetts Executive Council in 1777, and was a delegate in the Massachusetts House of Representatives from 1779 to 1785. He was also elected to the Continental Congress in 1780 and 1781. In 1785, he became Speaker of the House, in Massachusetts. From 1791 to 1795, he served in the United States Congress, under the new Federal Constitution, before retiring to private life.

Artemas Ward died at Shrewsbury, Massachusetts, on October 28, 1800, at the age of seventy-two. He was buried in the Mountain View Cemetery, in Shrewsbury.[1]

Artemas Ward (courtesy United States Military History Institute)

WARNER, JONATHAN — (Massachusetts)
Jonathan Warner was born at Hardwick, Worcester County, Massachusetts, on July 14, 1744. On February 5, 1766, he married Hannah Mandell, and the couple had twelve children together.

Warner joined the Massachusetts Militia

prior to the open hostilities with Great Britain, becoming an officer in a regiment of Minutemen from Worcester County, and served as a colonel during the Lexington Alarm. He was subsequently appointed to be colonel of the 4th Worcester County Regiment of militia, with his commission dated February 7, 1776. On February 12, 1776, the Massachusetts House of Representatives commissioned Warner a brigadier general in the state militia. The first choice of the House for brigadier general of Worcester County troops had been John Witcomb, but when that officer declined the appointment it was then bestowed upon Warner. Warner served in and around Boston during the siege of the British forces in that city. In 1777, Warner was chosen to lead an expedition to the St. John's River, but he was later instructed to disband the soldiers he had collected for that mission and to return the weapons and provisions that had been provided by the Continental Army for that purpose. Warner continued to serve as a brigadier general within the state of Massachusetts until 1780, when he returned to private life. Following the war, Warner moved his family to Vermont.

Jonathan Warner died at Craftsbury, Orleans County, Vermont, on January 7, 1803, at the age of fifty-eight.[1]

WARREN, JOSEPH—(Massachusetts) Joseph Warren was born in Roxbury, Massachusetts, on June 11, 1741. Warren was born into an influential family, his father earning his living through farming and running an orchard. Warren was well educated, graduating from Harvard in 1759. In 1760, he found employment as the master of the Roxbury Grammar School. He studied medicine, and opened a medical practice in 1764. That same year, Warren married Elizabeth Hooton. In 1765, the passage of the Stamp Act caused Warren to adopt an alias of "A True Patriot" and write articles condemning the acts in the *Boston Gazette*. Warren's written protests were so inflammatory that the royal governor threatened to prosecute the owners of the newspaper for printing them, charging the paper with distributing seditious material. Warren was at every town meeting, held in Boston, from the arrival of British troops in 1768, till their removal, following the Boston Massacre, in March of 1770. Following the massacre, he was appointed to the Committee of Safety.

In March of 1772, Warren delivered the anniversary oration for the massacre, and in November of that year joined James Otis and Samuel Adams as a member of the Committee of Correspondence. In September of 1774, Warren penned the Suffolk Resolves, which stated that a king who violated the rights of his people had no right to their allegiance. They also declared the Regulating Acts null and void, advised local towns to choose their own militia officers, and advised tax collectors to refuse to turn the money collected over to the royal treasury. The Continental Congress approved the Suffolk Resolutions, placing it in a position of open rebellion against the crown.

When news of the fighting at Lexington reached Warren, he left his office and rode to the scene of the conflict. He joined General Heath during the hottest part of the fighting, where he had a pin struck from his head by a musket ball. In May of 1775, Warren was unanimously elected to be chairman of the Provincial Congress, and was named chief executive officer of the Massachusetts military. On June 14, 1775, he was commissioned a major general, with his commission being the second issued, right behind Artemas Ward.

On June 17, 1775, Warren learned of the pending assault on the American position at Bunker (Breed's) Hill, and hastened to take part in the battle. Arriving at the Patriot position, he was offered command of the defenses, but declined to do so, preferring to take his place in the line as a volunteer, under the command of Putnam and Prescott. When the American army was finally forced to retreat, due to a shortage of ammunition, Warren was conspicuous in rallying the men to keep the withdrawal from becoming a rout. A British officer recognized Warren, and taking a musket from one of the enlisted men, fired a shot that struck Warren in the head, killing him instantly. Joseph Warren was thirty-four years old at the time of his death. He was buried, by the British, upon the battlefield, but was later removed to the Granary Burying Ground. In 1825, his remains were moved to the Warren Tomb, at St. Paul's Church, and in 1855 they were moved again, this time to the Forest Hills Cemetery, in Boston, where they now repose.[1]

WASHINGTON, GEORGE—(Virginia)

George Washington was born in Westmoreland County, Virginia, on February 22, 1732. Washington received little formal education in his youth, but his early notebooks indicate that he was self-schooled, and that he studied geography, military history, agriculture, and composition. He showed an early aptitude for surveying and mathematics. Washington's father, Augustine, died in 1743, when George was still a young boy, and the lad was sent to live with his older brother, Lawrence, at Mount Vernon Plantation. Washington had exhibited an early disposition to go to sea, but was talked out of that vocation by his mother. Instead, Washington took up the vocation of surveying, becoming assistant surveyor of Culpepper County in 1748, and chief surveyor in 1749. When Lawrence died, in 1752, George inherited Mount Vernon and took up the life of a planter. In 1752, Washington also began his military career, being appointed adjutant for southern Virginia, with the rank of major. In 1753, he was assigned to be adjutant of the Northern Neck and Eastern Shore. In the fall and winter of 1753–54, Washington was charged, by Governor Dinwiddie, with ascertaining the intentions of the French military in the Ohio Valley. He was subsequently placed in command of an expedition toward Fort Duquesne (Fort Pitt), and promoted to the rank of colonel. The French presence forced him to build Fort Necessity, which he was compelled to surrender to a superior army of French and Indians on July 3, 1754, sparking the beginning of the French and Indian War in America. In 1755, he became aide-de-camp to General Edward Braddock, and accompanied his army on its expedition against Fort Duquesne. When Braddock's army was ambushed at the battle of Monongahela, on July 9, 1755, it was Washington's

The surrender of Cornwallis' army at Yorktown

bravery and command of the situation that enabled the survivors of the ambush to escape. He was then placed in command of all Virginia Provincial forces, and assigned the task of protecting the Virginia frontier. He accompanied General John Forbes' successful expedition against Fort Duquesne in 1758, a campaign that helped to end the war and eliminate incursions on the frontier.

In 1758, Washington was elected to the Virginia House of Burgesses, a position he would hold until 1774. That same year, he was promoted to the brevet rank of brigadier general, resigning his commission in December of 1758. On January 6, 1759, Washington married Martha Custis. He was appointed justice of the peace, for Fairfax County, in 1760. In 1774, he was elected to the Virginia Provincial Congress, and in September of that year, he was elected as a representative of Virginia to the First Continental Congress. He was returned to the Continental Congress in 1775. On June 15, 1775, Washington was appointed to command the Patriot army besieging the British forces at Boston. Washington's use of cannon, captured at Fort Ticonderoga, forced the British to evacuate the city in March of 1776.

From August to November of 1776, Washington campaigned to defend New York from the British. The battles of Long Island, Harlem Heights, and White Plains were all defeats for the Continental Army, but Washington proved to be masterful in delaying the British and keeping his little army together. He withdrew across New Jersey, into Pennsylvania. On December 25, 1776, he launched the successful surprise attack on the Hessian forces at Trenton, followed by the defeat of the British at Princeton, on January 3, 1777. In the spring of 1777, Washington sent most of his best officers and men to oppose General Burgoyne's expedition up the Hudson Valley, in New York. While the campaign against Burgoyne was in progress, Washington faced the forces of General Howe at the battles of Brandywine and Germantown. With the surrender of Burgoyne's army, at Saratoga, Washington went into winter quarters, at Valley Forge. In November and December of 1777, Washington was forced to defend himself against the plot of General Thomas Con-

George Washington (courtesy United States Military History Institute)

way to replace him with General Gates, the hero of Saratoga. Washington was successful in uncovering and blunting this plan to disgrace and supplant him, and Conway resigned from the army under a cloud of suspicion. Following the British evacuation of Philadelphia, Washington fought in the battle of Monmouth, on June 28, 1778. After General Gates' failed Southern Campaign, Washington assigned General Nathaniel Greene to the command of the Southern Department, while he planned the Yorktown Campaign with French general Rochambeau. From August to September of 1781, Washington led the movement of the combined French-American army to Yorktown, where he laid siege to the British forces under the command of Lord Cornwallis. The British were forced to surrender on October 19, 1781, freeing Washington's army to return his attention to General Clinton's British army in New York. Clinton was forced to evacuate the city, and Washington took possession on November 25, 1783. With the hostilities now at an end, Washington resigned his commission on December 23, 1783. Washington rebuffed suggestions that he become the king of America, following the end of the war, putting his full support in a democratic form of government. He was a leader in the Maryland-Virginia Conference, in 1785. In 1787, he presided over the Constitutional Convention, in Philadelphia. In February of 1789, Washington was unanimously elected to be the first president of the United States of America, inaugurated in New York City on April 30, 1789. He was re-elected to the Presidency in 1792, but refused to accept a third term of office, retiring to his estate at Mount Vernon in 1797. During his second term as president, Washington had to quell the Whiskey Rebellion on the western frontier of Pennsylvania. In 1798, he was appointed commander in chief of the American army during the tensions that had arisen with the leaders of the French Revolution.

George Washington died at his home, at Mount Vernon, on December 14, 1799, from complications arising from a severe case of laryngitis. He was sixty-seven years old at the time of his death. Washington was buried in the family cemetery, at Mount Vernon. George Washington was not only the first commanding general of the American army and the first president of the United States, he was also the first, and the greatest hero of the new nation he struggled so hard to create. The nation's capital was named in his honor, as well as countless streets, towns, schools and landmarks throughout the country to honor the memory of the man who was "first in war, first in peace, and first in the hearts of his countrymen."[1]

WATERBURY, DAVID — (Connecticut)

David Waterbury was born at Stamford, Connecticut, on February 12, 1722. In 1734, he married Mary Holly, and the couple had three children together. He later married Mary Maltby, and two children were born to this union. During the French and Indian War, he served under Sir William Johnson at the battle of Lake George in 1755. Waterbury later served in General James Abercrombie's attack on Fort Ticonderoga in 1758.

On May 1, 1775, Waterbury was commissioned colonel of the 5th Connecticut Regiment. He was assigned to General Montgomery's army for the Canadian Expedition, and was present at the siege of St. John's and the surrender of Montreal.

On June 3, 1776, he was commissioned a brigadier general in the Connecticut Militia and assigned to the Northern Department. Waterbury assumed command of the post at Skeensborough (present day Whitehall), New York, to supervise the building of a fleet that was to operate on Lake Champlain. Waterbury has been described as being an uncompromising Patriot who used harsh measures in dealing with those who did not support the cause of the Colonies. Numerous defectors to the Loyalist cause cited "the excessive rigor" of Waterbury as being the reason why they chose to remain loyal to the British. He remained at Skeensborough through the summer of 1776, expediting the completion of the ships, and on October 11, 1776, took part in the battle of Valcour Bay between the British and American fleets.

General Waterbury struck his colors and surrendered his vessel, the *Washington*, becoming a prisoner of the British. General Wilkinson alleged that he did so without firing a shot, and accused him of cowardice. Wilkinson was not present during the fight, but his allegations cast a stain on the reputation of General Waterbury. Waterbury's reputation was redeemed by the official report of General Arnold, the overall commander in the battle. Arnold stated that Waterbury had fought the *Washington* with distinguished gallantry, and had surrendered the ship only after it had been hit in the hull several times by the enemy. The British were elated over their capture of the general and the ship, and General Carleton reported the capture to Lord Germaine with great pride. Waterbury was held by the British for four years, being exchanged in October of 1780. Following his release, Waterbury commanded a brigade in General Washington's main army in the summer of 1781, and took part in the Yorktown Campaign. He served till the end of the war, when he returned to his home and a private life of farming. He was elected as a delegate to the Connecticut General Assembly in 1783, 1794, and 1795.

David Waterbury died at Stamford, Connecticut, on June 29, 1801, at the age of seventy-nine. He was buried in the Woodland Cemetery, in Stamford, Connecticut.[1]

WAYNE, ANTHONY—(Pennsylvania) Anthony Wayne was born in Chester County, Pennsylvania, on January 1, 1745. He received his primary education from an uncle, before being sent to the Philadelphia Academy, where he studied until the age of seventeen. Wayne was particularly interested in mathematics, and having completed his education, he returned home to open a surveyor's office. In 1765, he was commissioned by some Pennsylvania gentlemen to survey a tract of land they had obtained in Nova Scotia from the Crown. Wayne performed his duties so efficiently that he was asked to supervise the settlement of the land, and he retained this post until 1767. In that same year, he married Polly Primrose, the daughter of Benjamin Primrose, of Philadelphia, and returned to Chester County, resumed his surveying business.

Wayne took no hand in the political events of his day, preferring action to the stuffy business of politics. As tensions heated between the colonies and the mother country, Wayne left politics to the politicians, opting instead to raise a regiment of militia for home defense, should it be needed. When the break with England came, he was ready to offer the services of himself and his regiment. Congress assigned him to the Northern Department, then preparing for the invasion of Canada, and appointed him colonel of the 4th Pennsylvania Battalion on January 3, 1776.[1]

Wayne took part in the failed attack on Trois Rivieres (Three Rivers), in which the commanding officer, General William Thompson, was taken prisoner, and the second in command, Colonel Arthur St. Clair, was wounded. Command of the column devolved upon Wayne, though he was more seriously wounded than was St. Clair. Wayne conducted a skilled retreat from Trois Rivieres, falling back to Fort Ticonderoga, where he joined forces with General Arnold. In recognition of his service Congress promoted him to the rank of brigadier general in the Continental Army on February 21, 1777.[2]

In 1777, Wayne was given command of a

Anthony Wayne

brigade in Sullivan's Division of Washington's army. Prior to the battle of Brandywine, he kept his brigade constantly in the rear of the British army, harassing and attacking it, when the opportunity presented itself, with such skill and daring that he won the praise and admiration of his commander. So forceful and daring were his attacks, that the nickname of "Mad" Anthony soon became how he was known throughout the army. The nickname was originally given him by a soldier in his camp who always made it a point to walk a wide circle around the general, mumbling to himself, "Mad Anthony! Mad Anthony!" Wayne's other soldiers were amused by his antics, but the fearless actions of their commander caused the nickname to stick.[3]

At the battle of Brandywine, on September 11, 1777, Wayne valiantly defended his position, at Chadd's Ford, throwing back the repeated attacks of the British. He maintained his position till nightfall, and only then withdrew to catch up with the rest of the defeated American army. Wayne's conduct was conspicuous at the battle of Germantown, on October

4, 1777, and though the day ended in a defeat for the Continental Army, Wayne had swept everything before him, despite being wounded twice, and having his horse shot out from under him. Wayne was given command of the rear guard, during the retreat, and punished the pursuing British regiments with such a destructive fire from artillery and musketry that they were forced to abandon the pursuit.

At the battle of Monmouth, Wayne once more displayed a talent for tactical command that was rapidly winning him a reputation as one of the best young generals in the army. He won the praise of his direct commander, Lafayette, and the recognition of Washington, for his valiant defense of his position on the field, launching furious charges against the British, and disputing every inch of ground.

The most brilliant example of Wayne as a commander came at Stony Point, New York. The British fortress was considered to be impregnable, situated on a hill, with two sides protected by the Hudson River and a third guarded by a swamp. It was heavily fortified, bristled with cannon, and contained 600 veteran troops. Any attack through the narrow defile that constituted the land approach was considered to be suicide. Wayne sent two detachments, of twenty men each, forward to clear the abatis that circled the fort. Behind them were two columns of 150 men each, that were to attack the fort, from the right and left. Wayne knew that everything depended upon speed and surprise, and he determined that the fort must be taken with the bayonet in a headlong charge. Accordingly, he ordered every man to remove the load from his musket, and issued orders that any man who uttered a word would be immediately put to death by the officer nearest him. Wayne began his attack at midnight, hoping to catch the majority of the garrison in slumber. As the columns charged in toward the fort, they noticed that the tide was up, causing all of the surrounding ground to be flooded. Without hesitation, they surged forward. The British sentinels had spied their movements, and the fort was being roused to action as Wayne's soldiers pushed forward. Casualties began to mount, as the Americans were being shot down, unable to reply with their empty muskets. Wayne was shot down, with a wound to the head, but he managed to get to his knees and cried, "March on! Carry me into the fort, for I will die at the head of my column." His men obeyed, and the column he was leading entered the fort, and fought its way through the British defenders, till it was met in the middle of the structure by Wayne's other column. Wayne had done the impossible, he had captured what had been considered an impregnable position with a force that was inferior to that of the garrison. Wayne's wound proved not to be serious, the ball only grazing his head.[4]

In 1781, he was put in command of the American forces in Georgia. In a number of small but sanguinary engagements, he was able to drive the British from the state. The people of Georgia were so grateful that they presented him with a plantation, as a token of their esteem. Wayne continued to serve in the army until the end of hostilities, and was recognized for his accomplishments when Congress promoted him to the rank of major general on September 30, 1783.[5]

In 1789, Wayne was a member of the Pennsylvania convention to ratify the Constitution, and in 1792, he was given command of the army operating against the Indians on the frontier. Wayne defeated the Indians in a battle near Miami Rapids, and eliminated the incursions that they had previously been making. The result of his victory was the negotiation of a peace treaty with many of the warring tribes, that was ratified in 1795. General Wayne was then charged with supervising the construction of a chain of forts, along the frontier, which he himself had proposed. He was actively engaged in this work when he was stricken with disease in December of 1796.[6]

General Wayne died on December 15, 1796, at Presque Isle, Pennsylvania, while overseeing the construction of the forts on the frontier. His body was buried there, but, in 1809, his son removed his remains, and they were buried in the St. David's Church Cemetery, in Waynesboro, Pennsylvania.[7]

WEBB, SAMUEL BLACHLEY—(Connecticut) Samuel Blachley Webb was born at Wethersfield, Connecticut, on December 15,

1753. His father died when he was quite young, and his mother then married Silas Deane. Webb would become his stepfather's private secretary upon reaching the age of maturity.

At the outbreak of hostilities, Webb was commissioned a lieutenant in the 2nd Connecticut Regiment on May 1, 1775. He commanded a company of light infantry at the battle of Bunker Hill, on June 17, 1775, where he was wounded and commended for his gallantry. He was subsequently appointed aide-de-camp to General Putnam, and on June 21, 1776, he was promoted to the rank of lieutenant colonel and assigned to General Washington as his private secretary. He was responsible for writing the order that made public the Declaration of Independence in New York City on July 9, 1776. Webb took part in the battles of Long Island, White Plains, and Trenton, in 1776, and was at Princeton in January of 1777. He received a second wound at White Plains. In 1777, he raised the 3rd Connecticut Regiment, almost entirely at his own expense, and was commissioned to be its colonel. In December of that year, he participated in General Samuel Parson's expedition against Long Island, where he was captured by the enemy on December 10, 1777. Webb was held for three years, not being exchanged by the British until December of 1780. Upon his release, he replaced General Steuben as commander of the light infantry. On September 30, 1783, the Continental Congress bestowed the rank of brevet brigadier general on him in appreciation of his wartime services and sacrifices.[1]

He was a founder of the Society of the Cincinnati in 1783. When George Washington was inaugurated as the first president of the United States, in New York City, Webb served as the grand marshal, and held the Bible as Washington took the oath of office.

In 1789, Webb moved to Claverack, New York, where he married Catherine Hageboom. The marriage would result in the birth of a son in 1802.

Samuel Blachley Webb died at Claverack on December 3, 1807, at the age of fifty-three. He was buried in the Dutch Reformed Church Cemetery, in Claverack.[2]

WEEDON, GEORGE—(Virginia) George Weedon was born in Fredericksburg, Virginia, in 1734. Like most of the young men of the era, he received his introduction to the military during the French and Indian War. Weedon served in George Washington's regiment during the conflict, though he spent most of his time doing garrison duty. He did manage to rise to the rank of captain-lieutenant by the end of the war, however.

Following the end of the French and Indian War, Weedon became an inn-keeper and tavern owner, in Fredericksburg, and married Catharine Gordon, sister of Isabella Gordon, the wife of General Hugh Mercer. He was a member in good standing of the local Masonic lodge.

Weedon was a staunch Patriot, and was commissioned lieutenant colonel in the 3rd Virginia Regiment on February 13, 1776, and was promoted to colonel and given command of the regiment on August 13 of that year. With this regiment, Weedon participated in the battles around New York. He also took part in Washington's crossing of the Delaware and in the battle of Trenton. On February 20, 1777, he was appointed acting adjutant general to General Washington, and a week later was commissioned a brigadier general by the Continental Congress. Weedon led his brigade at Brandywine, where he rendered invaluable service in arresting the British pursuit and rallying the routed army. He also served with distinction at the battle of Germantown, on October 4, 1777. Shortly after the battle of Germantown, Weedon retired from the service over a controversy concerning superiority in rank between himself and General Woodford. When Congress reordered the seniority of Virginia generals, Woodford, who was outranked by Weedon, was placed in front of that officer. Weedon considered this to be a slight to his honor, and thus left the service. Congress accepted his resignation only on the condition that he could be called back to active duty should it ever become necessary. He resumed the command of a brigade in 1780, in time to take part in the Yorktown Campaign, where he was in command of the Virginia Militia that seized and controlled Gloucester Point, opposite

Yorktown on the York River, thus cutting off Cornwallis' route of escape. Weedon resigned his commission in June of 1783, after the signing of the Treaty of Paris.

In 1785, Weedon was elected mayor of Fredericksburg. He lived out the rest of his life operating his inn and tavern and giving his attentions to private pursuits.

George Weedon died at Fredericksburg in 1793, in his fifty-ninth year. He was buried in the Fredericksburg Masonic Lodge Cemetery, in Fredericksburg, Virginia.[1]

WEST, WILLIAM—(Rhode Island) William West was born at North Kingston, Rhode Island, in 1732. Little is known of his early education. In 1750, he married Ellen Brown, and the couple had eight children together. Following his marriage, West moved to Scituate, Rhode Island, where he was a very successful farmer, and kept a large herd of dairy cattle. It is recorded that he often set out to market with a load of cheese valued at $1,500, a huge sum for those days. In 1775, West built one of the largest and most showy houses ever to be built in Scituate. That same year, he was chosen to be second in command of the troops being raised to defend the coastline around Narragansett. He was subsequently commissioned a brigadier general in the Rhode Island Militia. In May of 1777, West was appointed chairman of a committee to ascertain the number of men still needed to complete the Continental battalion then being raised by the state. He was also a member of the Rhode Island Council of War, serving as chairman of that body. In 1781, West was elected lieutenant governor of the state.

Following the war, West served as a justice on the Rhode Island Superior Court, and was elected to the state Senate. Like many of his Patriot comrades, West was financially ruined by the devaluation of the Continental money, and lived out the last years of his life in modest means.

William West died at Providence, Rhode Island, in 1816. He was buried in the cemetery on the West Farm, in North Scituate, Rhode Island.[1]

WHIPPLE, WILLIAM—(Maine) William Whipple was born at Kittery, Maine, on January 14, 1730. His father was a maltster, but had been earning a living putting to sea by the time William was born. Whipple received a primary education in his home town, where he acquired the basics of learning. On leaving school, he signed on to a merchant vessel and for the next several years conducted business in the West Indies, where he made a sizeable fortune.

In 1759, he left the sea and went into a trading business with his brother, at Portsmith, Maine, a livelihood that he would continue right up to the time of the Revolution. In 1770, he married Katherine Moffat, and one child was born to the marriage. Whipple represented Portsmith in the Provincial Congress held in Maine in 1775, for the purpose of electing delegates to the Continental Congress, and he served on the local Committee of Safety.

In 1776, he was appointed to be a delegate to the Continental Congress, and in that capacity signed the Declaration of Independence, continuing to hold his seat until September of 1777.

When he left Congress, in 1777, the assembly of New Hampshire commissioned him, along with John Stark, to be a brigadier general in the state militia. New Hampshire was in a state of alarm due to the American evacuation of Fort Ticonderoga and Burgoyne's advance toward the state. The New Hampshire Militia was organized into two brigades, commanded by Whipple and Stark. Whipple commanded his New Hampshire brigade at the battle of Saratoga. His conduct on that field was so conspicuous that he, along with Colonel Wilkinson, was selected to meet with two British officers to settle the articles of capitulation. Whipple was also chosen to be one of the American officers to conduct the surrendered British army to their encampment at Winter Hill, near Boston. On the way to Winter Hill, Whipple had with him a black servant by the name of Prince. Along the line of march, Whipple commented to Prince that the column might be called to combat, and stated that he hoped Prince would do his duty and fight for his country. Prince replied that he had no wish to fight. Furthermore, he had no reason to do so, as he did not possess his personal freedom, and did not feel he had a country to fight for. Whipple, seeing the inconsistency of an army fighting for its freedom, while men were in bondage, immediately granted Prince his freedom. Prince had stated, "Had I my liberty, I would fight in defense of the country to the last drop of my blood."

In 1778, General Whipple commanded a detachment of New Hampshire Militia, under the command of General Sullivan, that was co-operating with the Count D'Estaing for the purpose of driving the British out of Rhode Island. Through a misunderstanding, the French fleet never made a rendezvous with the Americans, who were forced to give up the campaign and retreat. Whipple's commission as a general in the New Hampshire Militia was ended in 1778.

In 1780, he was elected as a representative to the New Hampshire General Assembly and was re-elected to that post several times. In 1782, he was appointed receiver of public monies for the state of New Hampshire. He resigned from this post in 1784, partly due to failing health. Subsequent to his resignation as receiver of monies, he was appointed to be a judge of the superior court. It was during this time that he began to be troubled by strictures of the breast that greatly curtailed his physical activities. He nonetheless rode his court circuits until the fall of 1785, when the disease became so advanced that he was forced to return home. From this time, to the end of his life, Whipple was confined to his bedroom by the disease.

William Whipple died at his home, in Portsmith, Maine, on November 28, 1785, at the age of fifty-five. He was buried in the North Cemetery in that city.[1]

WHITCOMB, JOHN — (Massachusetts)

John Whitcomb was born at Lancaster, Massachusetts, in 1720 (also listed to be 1713 in some family histories). On June 12, 1735, he married Mary Carter, and one child was born to the couple. Mary died in 1744, and later that year John married Becke Whitcomb. One child was also born to this union. During the French and Indian War, he served as a colonel of militia in the campaign against Crown Point in 1755.

At the beginning of the Revolution, he was not called into service, due to his advanced age. The soldiers in his regiment were so attached to him, however, that they refused to serve under any other officer, and Whitcomb, failing to convince them otherwise, agreed to remain in the army and to join them in the ranks. During the siege of Boston, Whitcomb assumed command of the regiment. He was commissioned a brigadier general in the Massachusetts Militia, and was advanced to the rank of major general in that service in 1775. On June 5, 1776, he was commissioned a brigadier general in the Continental Army, but he declined to accept the position, citing his age as being too advanced for field duty. He was subsequently allowed to retire from the army.

John Whitcomb died at Bolton, Worcester County, Massachusetts, on November 17, 1785, in his sixty-fifth year.[1]

WILKINSON, JAMES — (Maryland)

James Wilkinson was born in Benedict, Maryland, in 1757. After receiving a substantial primary education, Wilkinson attended the University of Pennsylvania, where he studied medicine, and after graduation became a doctor in Maryland.

At the beginning of the war, Wilkinson enlisted as a volunteer in Thompson's Pennsylvania Rifle Battalion on September 9, 1775. In March of 1776 he became captain of the 2nd Continental Infantry Regiment. With this commission, Wilkinson began a meteoric rise in rank that included serving on the staff of General Greene, aide-de-camp to General Arnold, and brigade major on the staff of General Gates.

By January of 1777, he had risen to the rank of lieutenant colonel in Hartley's Continental Regiment. Wilkinson was appointed deputy adjutant general of the Northern Department in May of 1777, and served under Gates in the Saratoga Campaign. His association with General Gates would pay immediate dividends, but would embroil him in lifelong controversy. On November 6 of that year he was commissioned a brigadier general by a thankful Congress, in recognition of his services at Saratoga. Following that campaign, Wilkinson became a harsh critic of General Washington and his policies, and endeavored to secure his replacement, as commander in chief, with General Gates. He was part of the Conway Cabal, that for some time caught the attention of certain members of Congress and caused a division between the new nation's leadership. In the end, the supporters of Washington prevailed, and those who had conspired against him were held in contempt. Wilkinson had been appointed to the Board of War on January 6, 1778, and had been in a position to fully vent his opposition to General Washington. When the Conway Cabal came unraveled, Wilkinson resigned his commission in the Continental Army on March 6, 1778, and his position on the Board of War on March 31. While embroiled in this controversy, Wilkinson married Ann Owen Biddle, on November 12, 1778, and the couple would have one child together. Wilkinson was appointed clothier-general of the Continental Army on July 24, 1779, but resigned the post on March 27, 1781, and was subsequently commissioned a brigadier general in the Pennsylvania Militia, serving till the end of the war.

Following the Revolution, Wilkinson retired to private life, his medical practice, and a land scheme in Kentucky, until he was called to military duty in 1791. He was commissioned a lieutenant colonel during the Ohio River Territory Indian Campaigns on October 22, 1791. On March 5, 1792, he was promoted to the rank of brigadier general and replaced General Anthony Wayne. In 1803, he participated in the transfer of the Louisiana Purchase from France, and briefly served as governor of the vast new territory. He was publicly criticized for heavy-handed tactics during his governorship, and was reassigned to frontier military duty. His reputation was further impaired when he was implicated in Aaron Burr's scheme to establish an independent western nation, and narrowly escaped being indicted by Congress during the Burr trial. He was twice investigated by Congress, and was brought up on court-martial charges for his activities, but, following his successful defense in the court-martial, he assumed a military command in New Orleans.

Wilkinson was commissioned a major general on March 2, 1813, during the War of 1812, and was posted to Canada, where he failed in an expedition against Montreal. As in the Revolution, Wilkinson was a vocal critic of those in charge, this time aiming his criticism at President Madison and his policies. He was relieved of his command and ordered to Washington, where he was discharged from the service on June 15, 1815.

In 1825, Wilkinson traveled to Mexico seeking a Spanish land grant in Texas. James Wilkinson died in Mexico on December 28, 1825, in his sixty-fifth year. Biographer Temple Bodley said of him, "He had considerable military talent, but used it only for his own gain."[1]

WILLIAMS, OTHO HOLLAND—(Maryland)

Otho Holland Williams was born in Prince George County, Maryland, on March 1, 1749. His ancestors were among the first settlers in Maryland, arriving from England shortly after Lord Baltimore became proprietor of the province. At the age of one, his family moved to western Maryland to Frederick County (present day Washington County). Williams lost both parents in 1762, when he was thirteen years old, and he took a job in the office of the Frederick County Clerk to help support himself and his siblings. He would later take over the position of clerk. In 1767, he moved to Baltimore to assume the post of clerk there, returning to Frederick (Washington) County in 1774 to go into business for himself.

In 1775, Williams was commissioned lieutenant in a rifle company of militia that was raised in Frederick County, known as Cresap's Company Maryland Riflemen. Following the fighting at Lexington and Concord, his company was marched to Boston to join the army assembling there. Williams assumed command of the company, and was promoted to captain when his immediate commander received promotion to a higher grade. With his company, he participated in the siege of the British army in Boston. In June of 1776 Williams' company was combined with another Maryland rifle company, as well as one from Virginia, to form the Maryland and Virginia Rifle Regiment. Williams was commissioned major of the regiment on June 27, 1776. The regiment took part in the battle of Fort Washington, New York, on November 16, 1776, in which a large portion was captured by the British. Williams was among the number who were captured, and he was taken to New York City, where he was released, on parole. Fearing that Williams might try to contact Washington and provide him with useful military information, the British revoked his parole and placed him in close confinement. He was held in British prisons for fifteen months before being exchanged on January 16, 1778. Williams' health was greatly impaired by his imprisonment, where he suffered from acts of cruelty committed by his British captors.[1]

While Williams was confined to a British prison, Congress commissioned him colonel of the 6th Maryland Regiment on December 10, 1776. Upon his being exchanged, Williams commanded this regiment in the battle of Monmouth on June 28, 1778. He and his regiment were then transferred to the Southern Department, where Williams became deputy adjutant-general under General Gates and adjutant-general when General Greene assumed command. Williams took part in the battles of Guilford Courthouse and Hobkirk Hill, and at the battle of Eutaw Springs he led a charge that saved the day for the Americans. In the spring of 1782, General Greene dispatched Williams to Congress with reports from the department, and that body recognized his services by promoting him to the rank of brigadier general on May 9, 1782.[2]

Following the end of the war, Williams moved to Baltimore, where he was appointed collector of the port by the governor. He held that position until the adoption of the Federal Constitution, at which time he received a second appointment for the same position by President Washington. Williams served as collector of the port of Baltimore until his death. In 1785, Williams married Mary Smith, and in 1788 he founded and laid out the present day city of Williamsport, Maryland. When the federal government was searching for a site to establish the national capitol, Williams suggested Williamsport, and in 1791, Washington came to see for himself if the town would be suitable. Washington was forced to reject the site due to the fact that the Potomac River contained rapids that were at that time unable to be navigated located below the town.

Williams' health was much impaired as a result of his imprisonment, and it deteriorated with each passing year. Doctors could do little to ease his suffering, and Williams turned to alternative treatments like those offered at the hot springs of Bath, Virginia (present day Berkeley Springs, West Virginia). He was on his way to Bath, to seek a treatment at the springs, when he died at Millar's Town, Virginia, on July 15, 1794, at the age of forty-five. Otho Holland Williams was buried in the Riverview Cemetery, in Williamsport, Pennsylvania.

WILLIAMSON, ANDREW—(Scotland)
Andrew Williamson was born in Scotland in 1730, and is said to have come to America at a young age, settling in South Carolina. Williamson probably had little or no schooling, and was said to be illiterate but highly intelligent. He was an excellent woodsman, and, as a young man, earned his living as a cow driver. He served as a lieutenant in the militia in James Grant's expedition against the Cherokee, and by 1765 had acquired several small tracts of land and begun to assume the life of a planter. Williamson married Eliza Tyler (n.d.), of Virginia, and the couple had four children together. By 1770, he had established his plantation, Whitehall, just west of Ninety Six.

When hostilities broke out with England, Williamson was commissioned a major in the militia, and was elected to the first Provincial Congress, where he was awarded a contract to supply the troops. He participated in the capture of Loyalist leader Robert Cunningham in 1775. On November 21 of that same year, he was overcome by Loyalists in the Ninety Six area, and signed a treaty with them. In December of 1775, he renewed hostilities when he participated in the Snowshoe Campaign.

Williamson's next service came against the Cherokee. In 1776, he led an expedition that ended in the defeat of the Patriot forces at the battle of Essenecca, where he had a horse shot out from under him. He was promoted to colonel and given command of 2,000 militia that mounted an all-out campaign against the

Cherokee, resulting in a peace treaty, signed on May 20, 1777, that ceded large sections of the Cherokee land. In 1778, he was promoted to the rank of brigadier general in the South Carolina Militia, and took part in General Howe's failed Florida expedition. In 1779, he served under General Lincoln at Savannah and Charleston. He was accused of treason, after the fall of Charleston. Williamson had 300 men, camped near Augusta, where he supposedly kept the news of the fall of Charleston from them, and kept them out of any action. It was reported that he received a commission in the British army for advising his officers to go home. Charged with treason, Williamson was captured by American troops, at his home at Whitehall, but escaped and fled to the protection of British lines, at Charleston. Sentiment against Williamson was so strong that it was taken for granted that he would be hung if he fell into American hands. He later redeemed himself, however, by providing the Patriots valuable information, sent to the army by way of John Lauren. Because of this, General Greene intervened, in 1783, to prevent the confiscation of his property. After the war, Williamson retired to his plantation, and to private concerns.[1]

Andrew Williamson died at his home on March 21, 1786, in his fifty-sixth year.

WILLIAMSON, MATTHIAS — (New Jersey) Matthias Williamson, Sr., was born at Elizabethtown, New Jersey, in 1716. Little is known of his early life or education, but Williamson served as a lieutenant in the New Jersey Militia during King George's War. In 1750, he married Susannah Halstead, and the couple had seven children together. Williamson operated a successful saddlery business in Elizabethtown, and in 1757 he was elected high sheriff of Essex County.

At the outbreak of the war, Williamson was commissioned colonel of a New Jersey light horse regiment, on October 27, 1775. In September of 1776, he served as aide-de-camp for General Elias Dayton. On September 26, 1776, Williamson was commissioned a brigadier general in the New Jersey Militia, and on November 27, 1776, he was commissioned brigadier general of the New Jersey Brigade. Williamson resigned his commission on February 5, 1777, when he became assistant deputy quartermaster general for the Continental Army. He was subsequently advanced to the positions of assistant quartermaster general and quartermaster general. Williamson was taken prisoner by the British at Connecticut Farms in June of 1780, and was later released.

Following the end of the war, Williamson returned to Elizabethtown and private life. Matthias Williamson, Sr., died at Elizabethtown on October 31, 1807, in his ninety-first year.[1]

WILSON, JAMES — (Scotland) James Wilson was born at Carskerdo, Scotland, on September 14, 1742. He attended numerous colleges in Scotland, including St. Andrews, Glasgow, and Edinburgh, but did not attain a degree from any of them. In 1765, he immigrated to America, residing in New York until 1766, when he moved to Philadelphia and began studying law at the College of Philadelphia (present day University of Pennsylvania). In 1767, Wilson was admitted to the bar and set up his law practice in Reading and Carlisle. Wilson's law practice was substantial enough for him to purchase a farm, near Carlisle, and to amass a small fortune. He also taught classes in English literature at Philadelphia College. On November 5, 1771, he married Rachel Bird, and the couple had six children together. Rachel died in 1786, and Wilson later married Hannah Gray, in 1793. In 1774, Wilson was a delegate to the Pennsylvania Provincial Convention, and was a member of the local Committee of Correspondence. In 1774, he also wrote a pamphlet entitled, "Considerations on the Nature and Extent of the Legislative Authority of the British Parliament" that asserted that England had no authority to pass laws for the colonies. In 1775, Wilson was elected to the Continental Congress, where he became one of the then minority members who advocated a break with the mother country. His convictions were realized when he later became a signer of the Declaration of Independence. He was returned to the Congress in 1777, 1783, and 1785–86.

His military career in the Revolution began with his being commissioned colonel of the 4th Pennsylvania Battalion in 1775. He was also a member of the Board of War, and instrumental in negotiating the legal relations between the United States and France. On May 24, 1782, he was commissioned a brigadier general in the Pennsylvania Militia, and served in that capacity till the close of the war, though his efforts were administrative in nature. In 1781, Wilson was appointed to be the original director of the Bank of North America.

Following the war, Wilson sought an appointment in the new federal government, and secured a position as an associate justice on the Supreme Court in 1789. He was, by this time, financially ruined, however, and spent some time in debtor's prison while he was serving on the Supreme Court. In 1790, he served as a law professor at the College of Philadelphia. By 1798, Wilson complained of great mental fatigue and the inability to work, and made a trip to North Carolina to visit a friend.

James Wilson died at the Hayes Plantation, near Edenton, North Carolina, on August 21, 1798, at the age of fifty-five. He was buried there, with reinterment to the Christ Churchyard Cemetery in Philadelphia in 1906.[1]

WINDS, WILLIAM — (New York) William Winds was born at Southhold, Long Island, New York, in 1727. As a young man, he moved to Morris County, New Jersey, where he attained wealth and prominence, becoming a leader of the region. In 1758, he was commissioned a captain in the New Jersey Militia, and took part in the expedition against Canada that ended with the capture of Montreal. Following the war, he was appointed as a justice of the peace in Morris County, and in this capacity, he boldly resisted the enforcement of the Stamp Act. Winds even went so far as to substitute the white bark of birch trees for the stamped paper the British were trying to tax. In 1772, he was elected to the New Jersey General Assembly, and he was re-elected to that body in 1775. In 1776, he was elected to be a delegate in the New Jersey Provincial Congress. On November 7, 1775, Winds was commissioned a lieutenant colonel in the 1st New Jersey Battalion. He was assigned to protect Perth Amboy, New Jersey, and while there was also responsible for guarding William Franklin, the last of the royal governors of New Jersey, who was being held as a prisoner. On March 7, 1776, he was promoted to colonel and given command of the battalion, and on March 4, 1777, he was promoted to the rank of brigadier general and ordered north to take part in the expedition against Canada. Winds was among the lucky few to survive that disastrous campaign and he returned to New Jersey, where he served for the remainder of the war.

William Winds died at Rockway, Morris County, New Jersey, on October 12, 1789, in his sixty-second year. He was buried at the Rockaway Presbyterian Church Cemetery, in Rockaway.[1]

WOLCOTT, ERASTUS — (Connecticut) Erastus Wolcott was born at Windsor, Connecticut, on September 21, 1722. On February 10, 1746, he married Jerusha Wolcott, and the couple had six children together. Jerusha was his second cousin, once removed.

Wolcott was quite active in the politics of the colony, serving as a delegate to the Connecticut General Assembly, where he was speaker of the Lower House. He was also a justice of the peace, judge of the Probate Court, and chief justice of the Hartford County Court. His accomplishments were such as to earn him an honorary degree from Yale College. In 1775, he was commissioned a colonel in the Connecticut Militia, and was sent to conduct an interview with General Gage, then in command of the British forces in Boston, with a view to determining the state of affairs and the possible need to prepare for defensive measures. In 1776, he was assigned to the command of a regiment, and ordered to join General Washington's army that was then investing the British at that place, where he took an active part in the siege. Following the evacuation of Boston by the British, Wolcott went to New London, where he supervised the construction of fortifications at that place. He then performed garrison duty at Forts Trumbull and Griswald during the summer of 1776. He was subsequently commissioned a brigadier general in the Connecticut Militia.

serving in the area around Peekskill, New York, and being active on alarms. Wolcott resigned his commission in January of 1781. Following the end of the war, Wolcott was elected to the United States Congress, and was appointed judge of the Connecticut Superior Court.

Erastus Wolcott died at East Windsor, Connecticut, on September 14, 1793, at the age of forty-seven. He was buried in the Old Church Yard Cemetery of South Windsor, Connecticut.[1]

WOLCOTT, OLIVER—(Connecticut) Oliver Wolcott was born in Litchfield, Connecticut, on December 1, 1726, into one of the most prominent families of the state. His father was a man of means, having been a judge in the state and also served a term as colonial governor of Connecticut. His father saw to it that Oliver received a good education, and was suited to assume the mantle of the Wolcott family as a leader in local affairs. Oliver was a scholarly student, and graduated from Yale in 1747. In this same year, he received a commission to serve as a captain in King George's War, and he led his company in defense of the frontier until the ratification of the peace at Aix-la-Chapelle, when he returned to Connecticut and commenced the study of medicine. He never practiced medicine, however.

In 1751, he was appointed to be the sheriff of the newly created Litchfield County. His political career began in 1774, when he received an appointment to the state council. He was re-elected to this post every year until 1786. In 1776, he was selected to be a delegate to the Continental Congress, where he became a signer of the Declaration of Independence. Wolcott returned to Connecticut, immediately after signing the Declaration of Independence, where he was given the command of fourteen regiments of state militia that had been raised for the defense of New York. In November of 1776, he returned to his seat in Congress, and remained there through the winter of 1777–78.

General Wolcott took part in several military movements during the summer of 1778, but his most memorable contribution was joining the army under General Gates to take part in the battle of Saratoga. Here, he commanded a corps of several hundred volunteers, and his actions were conspicuous in the battle that forced General Burgoyne to surrender his army. From 1778 to the end of the war, Wolcott spent his time between sitting in Congress and service in the Connecticut Militia, where he was subsequently commissioned a major general. He had also been appointed commissioner of Indian affairs for the Northern Department, and, at the war's conclusion, was responsible for creating the peace terms for the Six Nations of the Iroquois People.

In 1786, he was elected lieutenant governor of Connecticut, and was re-elected to the position for the next ten years, when he was elected to serve as governor. Wolcott had little time to serve out his election as governor, however, as he died during the first year of his term.

Oliver Wolcott died at Litchfield, Connecticut, on his birthday, December 1, 1797, at the age of seventy-one. He was buried in the East Cemetery, in Litchfield, Connecticut.[1]

WOODFORD, WILLIAM—(Virginia) William Woodford was born in Caroline County, Virginia, in 1735. Woodford fought for six years in the French and Indian War, before settling in Fredericksburg, Virginia, and becoming a farmer and businessman. In 1763, he married Mary Thornton, and the union would produce four children.

When the war broke out, Woodford was commissioned colonel of the 2nd Virginia Regiment in the fall of 1775, and that was converted to a Continental commission, of the same rank, on February 21, 1776. In the meantime, Woodford had fought the first battle of the Revolution to take place in Virginia. The fighting took place at Hampton, on October 26, 1775, when Woodford and his men successfully prevented Lord Dunmore from destroying the town, and in the process sank five of his ships. On December 9, 1775, he again engaged the Royal forces of Lord Dunmore at Great Bridge, on the Elizabeth River, forcing the enemy to retire with a loss of fifty-five casualties, while not one man of the Virginia Militia was killed or wounded. Less than a week later, on December 14, 1775, Woodford and his militia occupied Norfolk, fulfilling Washington's belief that holding Virginia depended on Lord Dunmore being forced to evacuate that city.

On February 21, 1777, Woodford was commissioned a brigadier general in the Continental Army, and assumed command of the Virginia Brigade, serving with Washington's main body. He distinguished himself at the battle of Brandywine, where he was wounded in the hand. The wound did not necessitate his leaving his brigade, and he took an active part in the battles of Germantown and Monmouth. In the spring of 1780, he was ordered to march his troops to the relief of Charleston, and his column covered the 500 miles in only twenty-eight days, arriving at Charleston in April. On May 12, he was taken prisoner in the fighting around the city. The British sent him to New York, where he was confined as a prisoner of war.

William Woodford died in a British prison, in New York City, on November 13, 1780. He was buried in the Trinity Churchyard Cemetery, in Manhattan, New York.[1]

WOODHULL, NATHANIEL—(New York) Nathaniel Woodhull was born at Mastic, the family home at Brookhaven, Suffolk, New York, on December 30, 1722, to a well-to-do landholding family. His family's holdings ensured that he would be well educated and a member of New York's elite society. He married Ruth Floyd, sister of General William Floyd, a signer of the Declaration of Independence, and the marriage produced two children. In 1758, he joined the provincial forces from New York to fight in the French and Indian War.

In 1775, he was elected as president of the New York Provincial Congress, and that body commissioned him a brigadier general of militia, in command of the units from Suffolk and Queens Counties.

In August of 1776, on the eve of the battle of White Plains, Woodhull was assigned to the task of moving a large herd of cattle, that were on Long Island, east, to keep them out of the hands of the British. For the performance of this task, he had but 190 militia under his command. Fearful of being in such close proximity to the enemy, his men deserted at an alarming rate. By August 27, there were but ninety left with Woodhull and the herd. Despite the desertions, Woodhull had been able to move 1,400 cattle to the Hempstead Plains, and had 300 more to move when a thunderstorm forced him to take refuge in a tavern owned by Increase Carpenter, about two miles east of Jamaica, near present day Hollis. A patrol of British cavalry learned of Woodhull's presence in the tavern and captured him there. What happened next is a matter of conjecture. The popular version states that Woodhull's captors demanded that he say "God save the King," to which he defiantly responded, "God save us all." His answer supposedly enraged his captors, who slashed him on the head and arm with their sabers. A second, less popular version is that he sustained his wounds while trying to escape capture, and in the process of climbing over a wooden fence. Neither version can be substantiated, and the former did not appear in print for the first time until 1821. What is certain is that Woodhull was severely wounded in the head and arm by his captors, who took him to Jamaica, where the wounds were dressed by a British surgeon. He was then taken to Gravesend, where he was loaded onto a prison ship at anchor in the harbor. The wound to his arm developed gangrene, and he was moved to an improvised hospital at New Utrecht, where the limb was amputated.

The amputation failed to save the general's life, however. Nathaniel Woodhull died on September 20, 1776, at the age of fifty-four. He was buried at his home at Mastic, Suffolk, New York.[1]

WOOSTER, DAVID—(Connecticut) David Wooster was born in Stratford, Fairfield County, Connecticut, on March 2, 1710, making him one of the oldest men to become a general during the Revolution. In his early life, he attended Yale College, graduating from that institution in 1738. The following year, during the war with Spain, he was commissioned a first lieutenant, then captain of a ship armed to guard the Connecticut coast from Spanish raiders.

In 1745, he served as a captain in the Connecticut Militia in the expedition against Louisburg, where he distinguished himself by his gallantry. Chosen to take charge of a cartel ship bound for France and England, he was warmly received in the latter country, being presented to the king, and making a good impression in the court. The king admitted him in the regular service, and he was presented a captaincy in Sir William Pepperell's regiment with half pay for life. On March 6, 1746, Wooster married Mary Clapp, and the couple would have three children together.

Wooster was commissioned a colonel during the French and Indian War in 1756, and was afterward appointed a brigadier general in the British service. At the conclusion of the French and Indian War, Wooster became involved in the mercantile business, and served as royal customs collector in New Haven, while retaining his commission in the British army. Wooster founded the Masons in Connecticut, receiving a charter from the grand provincial lodge in Massachusetts to set up the first Connecticut lodge in New Haven.

Though he had reached the age that he should have been considering retiring when the Revolution broke out, he at once offered his services to the Patriot cause, and they were immediately accepted. Wooster was made a major general in the Connecticut Militia in April of 1775. He was also commissioned colonel of the 1st Connecticut Regiment on May 1, 1775, and received a commission as a brigadier general in the Continental Army on June 22, 1775. Wooster was one of the first eight brigadier generals commissioned by Congress, and was the third in rank. He declined the latter commission, however, preferring to retain his position with the Connecticut Militia.[1]

He is reported to have been a driving force in the expeditions against Fort Ticonderoga and the forts on Lake Champlain, and of helping to finance those expeditions with his own money. He accompanied the expedition into Canada, and when it ended in failure, returned to his native Connecticut to direct militia forces there.

David Wooster

In April of 1777, the British landed a force at Campo Beach, at Westport, Connecticut, and marched to Danbury, where they burned many houses and buildings. On their return, they marched through Ridgefield, where American forces under the command of Generals Benedict Arnold and David Wooster awaited them. The Americans attacked, on April 27, and in the heavy fighting that followed Arnold had a horse shot out from under him and Wooster was seriously wounded by a musket ball, which broke his backbone, while at the head of his troops, trying to rally them. Wooster was taken to Danbury for medical attention, but his wound proved to be mortal.

David Wooster died on May 2, 1777, in his sixty-seventh year. Wooster's last words were reported to be his hope that his country would gain its independence. He was buried at the Wooster Cemetery, in Danbury, Connecticut.[2]

Appendix One: Reasons for Generals' Leaving the Service

Resigned

Armstrong, John
Babcock, Joshua
Conway, Thomas
De Fermoy, Matthias Alexis Roche
Dent, John
Frye, Joseph
Glover, John
Maxwell, William
Mifflin, Thomas
Miles, Samuel
Miller, Nathan
de la Neuville, Chevalier
Newcomb, Silas
Parsons, Samuel Holden
Preudhomme de Borre, Philippe Hubert
Roberdeau, Daniel
Saltonstall, Gurdon
Schuyler, Philip
Scott, John Morin
Spencer, Joseph
Sullivan, John
Varnum, James
Wadsworth, James
Williamson, Mathias, Sr.

Killed in Battle (including mortal wounds)

Davidson, William Lee
De Kalb, Johann
Herkimer, Nicholas
Hogun, James
Mercer, Hugh
Montgomery, Richard
Nash, Francis
Pulaski, Casimir
Warren, Joseph
Woodhull, Nathaniel
Wooster, David

Drowned

Du Coudray, Philippe Charles Jean Baptiste Tronson

Killed in Duel

Poor, Enoch

Died in the Service (sickness or disease)

Alexander, William
Ashe, John
Campbell, William
Hogun, James
Lewis, Andrew
Moore, James
Pomeroy, Seth
Richardson, Richard
Thomas, John
Woodford, William

Dismissed or Court-Martialed

Gunby, John
Lee, Charles
Stephen, Adam

Traitor

Arnold, Benedict
Williamson, Andrew

Sickness or Disease (nonfatal)

Huntington, Jabez
Learned, Ebenezer
Nixon, John
Putnam, Israel
Reed, James
Ten Broeck, Abraham
Ward, Artemas

Appendix Two: States or Countries of Origin of the Generals

Bavaria (1)
De Kalb, Johann

British West Indies (1)
Roberdeau, Daniel

Connecticut (24)
Arnold, Benedict
Babcock, Joshua
Douglas, John
Dyer, Eliphalet
Enos, Roger
Heart, Selah
Huntington, Jabez
Huntington, Jedediah
Mead, John
Parsons, Samuel Holden
Patterson, John
Safford, Samuel
Saltonstall, Gurdon
Sheldon, Elisha
Spencer, Joseph
Swift, Heman
Tyler, John
Wadsworth, James
Ward, Andrew
Waterbury, David
Webb, Samuel Blachley
Wolcott, Erastus
Wolcott, Oliver
Wooster, David

Delaware (2)
Patterson, Samuel
Rodney, Caesar

Denmark (1)
Febiger, Christian

England (4)
Gates, Horatio
Harrington, Henry William
Lee, Charles
Palmer, Joseph

France (7)
Armand, Tuffin Charles
Du Buysson des Hayes, Charles Francois
Du Coudray, Philippe Charles Jean Baptiste Trouson
Duportail, Louis Le Begue De Presle
Lafayette, Marie-Joseph Paul Yves Roch Gilbert du Motier, Marquis de
Neuville, Chevalier de la
Preudhomme de Borre, Philippe Hubert

French West Indies (1)
De Fermoy, Matthias Alexis Roche

Georgia (1)
Elbert, Samuel

Ireland (15)
Armstrong, John
Butler, Richard
Chamberlain, James
Conway, Thomas
Hand, Edward
Hogun, James
Irvine, William
Lewis, Andrew
Maxwell, William
Montgomery, Richard
Nicola, Lewis
O'Hara, James
Potter, James
Rutherford, Griffith
Thompson, William

Maine (1)
Whipple, William

Maryland (14)
Beall, Reazin
Buchanan, Andrew
Casswell, Richard
Dent, John
Dickinson, John
Dickinson, Philemon
Gist, Mordecai
Gunby, John
Hooper, Henry
Johnson, Thomas, Jr.
Smallwood, William
Twiggs, John
Wilkinson, James
Williams, Otho Holland

Massachusetts (38)
Bailey, Jacob
Brickett, James Soldier
Cobb, David
Crane, John
Cushing, Joseph
Danielson, Timothy
Freeman, Nathaniel
Frye, Joseph
Glover, John
Godfrey, George
Greaton, John
Hancock, John
Hazen, Moses
Heath, William
Jackson, Henry
Jackson, Michael
Knox, Henry
Learned, Ebenezer
Lincoln, Benjamin
McClellan, Samuel
Newcomb, Silas
Nixon, John
Orne, Azor
Pomeroy, Seth
Poor, Enoch
Prescott, Oliver
Putnam, Israel
Reed, James
Swift, Heman
Thomas, John
Tupper, Benjamin
Varnum, James
Vose, Joseph
Wadsworth, Peleg
Ward, Artemas
Warner, Jonathan
Warren, Joseph
Whitcomb, John

Netherlands (1)
De Haas, John P.

New Hampshire (4)
Bedel, Timothy
Folsom, Nathaniel
Stark, John
Sullivan, John

New Jersey (7)
Dayton, Elias
Heard, Nathaniel
Morgan, Daniel
Neilson, John
Ogden, Mathias
Reed, Joseph
Williamson, Matthias, Sr.

New York (19)
Alexander, William
Brodhead, Daniel
Clinton, George
Clinton, James
Floyd, William
Gansevort, Peter
Herkimer, Nicholas
Livingston, William
Morris, Lewis
Schuyler, Philip
Scott, John Morin
Swartwout, Jacobus
Ten Broeck, Abraham
Ten Broeck, Petrus
Van Cortlandt, Philip
Van Rensselaer, Robert
Van Schaick, Goose
Winds, William
Woodhull, Nathaniel

North Carolina (5)
Ashe, John
Howe, Robert
Jones, Allen
Jones, William
Moore, James

Pennsylvania (14)
Cadwalader, John
Davidson, William Lee
Ewing, James
Frazer, Persifor
Gibson, John
Hiester, Daniel
Lacey, John
Meredith, Samuel
Mifflin, Thomas
Miles, Samuel
Muhlenberg, John Peter Gabriel
Pickens, Andrew
Polk, Thomas
Wayne, Anthony

Poland (2)
Kosciuszko, Thaddeus
Pulaski, Casimir

Prussia (2)
De Woedtke, Frederick William
Von Steuben, Friedrich Wilhelm Augustus

Rhode Island (8)
Cornell, Ezekiel
Greene, Nathaniel
Holden, Thomas
Lippitt, Christopher
Miller, Nathan
Nightingale, Joseph
Stanton, Joseph, III
West, William

Scotland (7)
McDougall, Alexander
McIntosh, Lachlan
Mercer, Hugh
St. Clair, Arthur
Stephen, Adam
Williamson, Andrew
Wilson, James

South Carolina (8)
Barnwell, John
Bull, Stephen
Clarke, Elijah
Gadsden, Christopher
Huger, Isaac
Marion, Francis
Moultrie, William
Pinckney, Charles Cotesworth

Vermont (1)
Safford, Joseph

Virginia (20)
Butler, John
Campbell, William
Clark, George Rogers
Gregory, Isaac
Henderson, William
Lawson, Robert
Lewis, Fielding
Mathews, George
McDowell, Joseph
Moore, Andrew

Nash, Francis
Nelson, Thomas, Jr.
Neville, John
Richardson, Richard
Stevens, Edward
Sumner, Jethro
Sumter, Thomas
Washington, George
Weedon, George
Woodford, William

Wales (1)

Shelby, Evan, Jr.

Appendix Three: Battles of the Revolutionary War

Amboy, New Jersey, March 8, 1777
Amelia Island, Florida, May 18, 1777
Anderson, Fort, Georgia, July 23, 1780
Anne, Fort, New York, July 8, 1777
Assumpsick Bridge, New Jersey, January 2, 1777
Augusta, Georgia, January 29, 1777; September 14 to 18, 1789; and April 16 to June 5, 1781
Balfour, Fort, South Carolina, April 12, 1781
Barren Hill, Pennsylvania, May 20, 1778
Beaufort, South Carolina, August 10, 1776, and February 3, 1779
Beattie's Mill, South Carolina, March 21, 1781
Bedford, New York, July 2, 1779
Bemis Heights, New York, September 19, 1777
Bennington, Vermont, August 16, 1777
Bergen, New Jersey, July 19, 1780
Biggin's Bridge, South Carolina, April 14, 1780
Black Mingo, South Carolina, April 14, 1780
Blackstocks, South Carolina, November 20, 1780
Block House, New Jersey, July 21, 1780
Blue Licks, Kentucky, August 19, 1782
Bordertown, New Jersey, May 8, 1778
Boston, Massachusetts, June 1775 to March 1776
Bound Brook, New Jersey, April 13, 1777
Brandon's Camp, South Carolina, July 12, 1780
Brandywine, Pennsylvania, September 11, 1777
Brattonville, South Carolina, July 12, 1780
Breed's Hill (Bunker Hill), Massachusetts, June 17, 1775
Brewerton, Georgia, December 29, 1778
Brier Creek, Georgia, March 3, 1779
Bristol, Pennsylvania, April 17, 1778
Bristol, Rhode Island, October 7, 1775
Broad River, South Carolina, November 12, 1780
Brookland, Long Island, New York, August 28, 1776
Brooklyn, New York, August 27, 1776
Bruce's Cross Roads, North Carolina, February 12, 1781
Brunswick, New Jersey, December 1, 1776, and October 26, 1779
Buford Massacre, South Carolina, May 29, 1780
Bulltown Swamp, Georgia, November 19, 1778
Bull's Ferry, New Jersey, July 21, 1780
Bushwick, New York, August 27, 1776
Butts Hill, Rhode Island, August 29, 1776
Camden, South Carolina, August 16, 1780, April 25 and May 10, 1781
Cane Break, South Carolina, December 22, 1775
Cane Creek, South Carolina, September 12, 1780, and September 13, 1781
Cars, Fort, Georgia, February 10, 1779
Catawba Ford, South Carolina, August 18, 1780
Caughnawaga, New York, May 22, 1780
Cedars, The, Canada, May 19, 1776
Cedar Springs, South Carolina, July 13 and August 8, 1780
Chad's Ford, Pennsylvania, September 11, 1777
Chambly, Canada, October 19, 1775, and June 16, 1776
Charles City Courthouse, Virginia, January 8, 1781
Charleston, South Carolina, May 11 to 13, 1779, and March 29 to May 12, 1780
Charleston Neck, South Carolina, May 11, 1779
Charlestown, Massachusetts, January 8, 1776
Charlotte, North Carolina, September 26, 1780
Chatterton's Hill, New York, October 28, 1776
Chemung, New York, August 29, 1779
Cherokee Ford, South Carolina, February 14, 1779
Cherokee Indian Town, South Carolina, July 13, 1780
Cherry Valley, New York, November 10, 1778
Chesapeake Bay, July 8 to 10, 1776
Chestnut Creek, New Jersey, October 6, 1778
Chestnut Hill, Pennsylvania, December 6, 1777

Appendix Three

Clapp's Mill, North Carolina, March 2, 1781
Clinton, Fort, New York, October 6, 1777
Clouds Creek, South Carolina, November 7, 1781
Cobleskill, New York, June 1, 1778
Cock Hill, Fort, New York, November 16, 1776
Combahee Ferry, South Carolina, August 27, 1782
Concord, Massachusetts, April 17, 1775
Connecticut Farms, New Jersey, June 7 to 23, 1780
Coosawathcie, South Carolina, May 11 to 13, 1779
Coran, New York, November 21, 1780
Cornwallis, Fort, Georgia, September 14, 1780, and June 5, 1781
Cowan's Ford, North Carolina, February 1, 1781
Cowpens, South Carolina, January 17, 1781
Crompo Hill, Connecticut, April 28, 1777
Crooked Billet, Pennsylvania, May 1, 1778
Croton River, New York, May 14, 1781
Crown Point, New York, May 12, 1775; October 14, 1776; and June 16, 1777
Cumberland, Fort, Nova Scotia, November 20, 1776
Currytown, New York, July 9, 1781
Danbury Raid, Connecticut, April 25 to 27, 1777
Diamond Island, New York, September 23, 1777
Dorchester, South Carolina, December 1 and 29, 1781, and April 24, 1782
Dorchester Neck, Massachusetts, February 14, 1776
Dreadnaught, Fort, Georgia, May 21, 1781
Dutch Island, Rhode Island, August 2, 1777
Earle's Ford, North Carolina, July 15, 1780
East Chester, New York, January 18, 1780
Ebenezer, Georgia, June 23, 1782
Edge Hill, Pennsylvania, December 7, 1777
Egg Harbor, New Jersey, October 15, 1778
Elizabethtown, New Jersey, January 26 and June 6, 1780
Elmira, New York, August 29, 1779
Esopus, New York, October 13, 1777
Essenecca Town, South Carolina, August 1, 1776
Eutaw Springs, South Carolina, September 8, 1781
Fairfield, Connecticut, July 8, 1779
Falmouth, Maine, October 18, 1775
Fayette, Fort, New York, June, 1, 1779
Fish Dam Ford, South Carolina, November 9, 1780
Fishing Creek, South Carolina, August 18, 1780
Flatbush, New York, August 22 to 23, 1780
Flat Rock, South Carolina, July 20, 1780
Fogland Ferry, Rhode Island, January 10, 1777
Fort Plain, New York, August 2, 1780, and September 7, 1781
Four Corners, New York, February 3, 1780
Four Holes, South Carolina, April 7 and 15, 1781
Freehold Courthouse, New Jersey, June 28, 1778
Freeman's Farm, New York, September 19, 1777
Galphin Ford, Georgia, May 21, 1781

Geneseo, New York, September 14, 1779
George, Fort, New York, November 16, 1776, and October 11, 1780
George, Fort, Long Island, November 21, 1781
Georgetown, South Carolina, January 24, 1781
German Flats, New York, October 29, 1780
Germantown, Pennsylvania, October 4, 1777
Glouster, Massachusetts, August 13, 1775
Granby, Fort, South Carolina, May 15, 1781
Grape Island, Massachusetts, May 21, 1775
Great Bridge, Virginia, December 9, 1775
Great Savannah, South Carolina, August 20, 1780
Great Spring, South Carolina, August 1, 1780
Green Springs, Virginia, July 6, 1781
Greenwich, Connecticut, June 19, 1779
Grierson, Fort, Georgia, September 14, 1780, and May 24, 1781
Griswold, Fort, Connecticut, September 6, 1781
Groton Hill, Connecticut, September 6, 1781
Guilford, North Carolina, March 15, 1781
Gulph's Mill, Pennsylvania, December 11, 1777
Gum Swamp, South Carolina, August 16, 1780
Gwyn's Island, Chesapeake bay, July 8 to 10, 1776
Hampton, Virginia, October 26, 1775
Hancock's Bridge, New Jersey, March 21, 1778
Hanging Rock, South Carolina, August 1 to 6, 1780
Harlem Cove, New York, November 16, 1776
Harlem Heights, New York, October 16, 1776
Harlem Plains, New York, September 16, 1776
Haw River, North Carolina, February 25, 1781
Hayes' Station, South Carolina, November 9, 1781
Henry, Fort, Virginia, September 1, 1777, and February 26 to 28, 1778
Hickory Hill, Georgia, June 28, 1779
Highlands, New York, March 24, 1777
Hillsborough, North Carolina, April 25, 1781
Hobkirk Hill, South Carolina, April 25, 1781
Hogg Island, Massachusetts, May 28, 1775
Horseneck, Connecticut, February 26, 1779, and December 9, 1780
Hubbarton, Vermont, July 7, 1777
Hunt's Bluff, South Carolina, August 1, 1780
Hutchinson's Island, Georgia, March 7, 1776
Indian Field and Bridge, New York, August 31, 1778
Iron Hill, Delaware, September 3, 1777
Isle Aux Noix, Canada, June 24, 1776
Jamaca, New York, August 28, 1776
James Island, South Carolina, July 1782
Jamestown Ford, Virginia, July 6, 1781
Jefferd's Neck, New York, November 7, 1779
Jersey City, New Jersey, July 18, 1779
Jerseyfield, New York, October 30, 1781
John's Island, South Carolina, November 4, 1782
Johnson, Fort, South Carolina, September 14, 1775
Johnson Hall, New York, October 24, 1781

Johnstown, New York, May 22, 1780, and October 24, 1781
Kanassoraga, New York, October 23, 1780
Kemp's Landing, Virginia, November 14, 1775
Kettle Creek, Georgia, February 14, 1779
Keyser, Fort, New York, October 19, 1780
King's Bridge, New York, January 17, 1777, and July 3, 1781
Kings Mountain, North Carolina, October 7, 1780
Kingston, New York, October 13, 1777
Kingstree, South Carolina, August 27, 1780
Klock's Field, New York, October 21, 1780
Lake Champlain, October 11 to 13, 1776
Lake George, New York, September 18, 1777
Lanneau's Ferry, South Carolina, May 6, 1780
Lee, Fort, New Jersey, November 18, 1776
Le Nud's Ferry, South Carolina, May 18, 1780
Lexington, Massachusetts, April 19, 1775
Lindley's Mill, North Carolina, September 13, 1781
Lloyd's Neck, New York, September 5, 1779
Long Cane, South Carolina, December 11, 1780
Long Island, New York, August 27 to 30, 1776, and December 10, 1777
Mamaroneck, New York, October 21, 1776
Manhattanville, New York, November 6, 1776
Martha's Vineyard, Massachusetts, May 5, 1775
McDonnell's Camp, South Carolina, July 15 to 16, 1780
McIntosh, Fort, Georgia, February 2 to 4, 1777
Medway Church, Georgia, November 24, 1778
Mercer, Fort, New Jersey, October 22, 1777
Middleburg, New York, October 15, 1780
Middletown, New Jersey, April 17, 1779, and June 12, 1780
Mifflin, Fort, Pennsylvania, October 23 and November 10 to 15, 1777
Millstone, New Jersey, January 22 and June 17, 1777
Mincock Island, New Jersey, October 15, 1778
Minisink, New York, July 22, 1779
Mohawk Valley, New York, August 2, 1780
Monk's Corner, South Carolina, April 14, 1780, and October 1781
Monmouth, New Jersey, June 28, 1778
Montgomery, Fort, New York, October 6, 1777
Montreal, Canada, September 25 and November 12, 1775
Montressor's Island, New York, September 24, 1776
Moore's Creek Bridge, North Carolina, February 27, 1776
Morris, Fort, Georgia, January 9, 1779
Morrisania, New York, August 5, 1779, and March 4, 1782
Moses Kill, New York, August 2, 1777
Motte, Fort, South Carolina, May 12, 1781
Moultrie, Fort, South Carolina, June 28, 1776, and May 7, 1780
Mount Washington, New York, November 8, 1776
Musgrove's Mills, South Carolina, August 19, 1780
Nelson, Fort, Virginia, May 9, 1779
Nelson's Ferry, South Carolina, August 29, 1780, and May 14, 1781
Newark, New Jersey, April 15, 1780
New Bridge, New Jersey, April 15, 1780
New Haven, Connecticut, July 5, 1780
New London, Connecticut, September 6, 1781
New Rochelle, New York, October 18, 1776
Newton, New York, August 29, 1779
New York City, New York, August 29, 1775
Ninety Six, South Carolina, November 19 to 21, 1775, and May 22 to June 19, 1781
Noodles Island, Massachusetts, May 27, 1775
Nook's Hill, Massachusetts, March 8, 1776
Norfolk, Virginia, January 1, 1776, and May 9, 1779
Norwalk, Connecticut, July 12, 1779
Oconote, South Carolina, August 1, 1776
Ogeechee Road, Georgia, May 21, 1782
Old Iron Works, South Carolina, August 8, 1780
Onondagas, New York, April 21, 1779
Orangeburg, South Carolina, May 11, 1781
Oriskany, New York, August 6, 1777
Osborne's, Virginia, April 27, 1781
Pacolet River, North Carolina, July 14, 1780
Paoli, Pennsylvania, September 20, 1777
Paramus, New Jersey, March 22 and April 16, 1780
Paulus Hook, New Jersey, August 19, 1779
Peekskill, New York, March 22, 1777
Pelham Manor, New York, October 18, 1776
Petersburg, Virginia, April 25, 1781
Philadelphia, Pennsylvania, occupied September 26, 1777, to June 18, 1778
Philips Heights, New York, September 16, 1778
Phipp's Farm, Massachusetts, November 9, 1775
Piscataway, New Jersey, May 8, 1777
Plain, Fort, New York, August 2, 1780
Plains of Abraham, Canada, May 6, 1776
Pon Pon, South Carolina, March 23, 1780
Port Royal Island, South Carolina, February 3, 1779
Poundridge, New York, July 2, 1779
Princeton, New Jersey, January 3, 1777
Punk Hill, New Jersey, March 8, 1777
Pyles' Defeat, North Carolina, February 25, 1781
Quaker Hill, Rhode Island, August 29, 1778
Quebec, Canada, December 8 to 31, 1775
Quinby's Bridge, South Carolina, July 17, 1781
Quinton's Bridge, New Jersey, March 18, 1778
Rahway Meadow, New Jersey, June 26, 1781
Ramseur's Mill, North Carolina, June 20, 1780
Rayborn Creek, South Carolina, July 15, 1776
Red Bank, New Jersey, October 23, 1777

Appendix Three

Rentowie, South Carolina, March 27, 1780
Richmond, Virginia, January 5, 1781
Ridgefield, Connecticut, April 27, 1777
Rocky Mount, South Carolina, July 30, 1780
Roxbury, Massachusetts, July 8, 1775
Rugh's Mills, South Carolina, December 4, 1780
Sag Harbor, New York, May 23, 1777
St. George, Fort, New York, November 23, 1780
St. John, Fort, Canada, May 14, 1775
Salkahatchie, South Carolina, March 8, 1780
Sandusky Ohio, June 4, 1782
Saratoga, New York, October 7 to 17, 1777
Savannah, Georgia, occupied by British December 29, 1778, to July 11, 1782. Siege September 23 to October 18, 1779
Schoharie, New York, October 17, 1780
Schuyler, Fort, New York, August 4 to 22, 1777
Shallow Ford, North Carolina, February 6, 1781
Sharon, Georgia, May 24, 1782
Short Hills, New Jersey, June 26, 1777
Silver Bluff, South Carolina, May 21, 1781
Skanesborough, New York, July 7, 1777
Smith's Point, New York, November 23, 1780
Somerset Courthouse, New Jersey, January 20, 1777
Spencer's Hill, Georgia, November 19, 1778
Spencer's Tavern, Virginia, June 16, 1781
Springfield, New Jersey, December 17, 1776, and June 23, 1780
Sorrel River, Canada, July 24, 1776
Stallions, South Carolina, July 12, 1780
Stanwix, Fort, New York, August 4 to 22, 1777
Staten Island, New York, August 21 to 22, 1777
Stillwater, New York, September 19 and October 7, 1777
Stone Arabia, New York, October 19, 1780
Stonington, Connecticut, September 30, 1775
Stono Ferry, South Carolina, June 20, 1779
Stony Point, New York, June 1 and July 16, 1778
Sullivan, Fort, South Carolina, June 28 to 29, 1776
Sullivan's Island, South Carolina, June 28 to 29, 1776, and May 8, 1780
Sunbery, Georgia, January 6 to 9, 1779
Tappan, New York, September 28, 1778
Tarcote, South Carolina, September 4, 1780
Tarcote Swamp, South Carolina, October 25, 1780
Tarrytown, New York, August 30, 1779, and July 15, 1781
Thickety, Fort, South Carolina, July 30, 1780
Thomassy, South Carolina, August 11, 1776
Threadwell's Neck, New York, October 10, 1781
Three Rivers, Canada, June 8, 1776
Throg's Neck, New York, October 12, 1776
Ticonderoga, New York, May 10, 1775, and July 6, 1777
Tiger River, South Carolina, November 20, 1780
Tiverton, Rhode Island, May 31, 1778
Tom's River, New Jersey, July 18, 1780
Torrence's Tavern, North Carolina, February 1, 1781
Trenton, New Jersey, December 26, 1776, and January 2, 1777
Tyron, Fort, New York, November 16, 1776
Valcour Island, New York, October 11, 1776
Valley Grove, New York, August 26, 1776
Vandreuil, Canada, May 26, 1776
Verplank's Point, New York, June 1, 1779
Vincennes, Indiana, July 5 and December 17, 1778, and February 23, 1779
Wahab's Plantation, South Carolina, September 21, 1780
Wanbaw Creek, South Carolina, February 14, 1782
Ward's House, New York, March 16, 1777
Warwarsing, New York, August 22, 1781
Washington, Fort, New York, November 16, 1776
Wateree, Ford of the, South Carolina, August 15, 1780
Watson, Fort, South Carolina, April 15 to 23, 1781
Waxhaws, South Carolina, may 29, 1780
Weehawken, New Jersey, August 19, 1779
West Canada Creek, New York, October 30, 1781
West Chester, New York, September 16, 1778
West Chester County, New York, March 15, 1777
West Farms, New York, January 25, 1777
West Greenwich, Connecticut, March 26, 1779
West Haven, Connecticut, September 1, 1781
Wetzell's Mills, North Carolina, March 6, 1781
Wheeling, (West) Virginia, September 1, 1777, and September 26 to 28, 1778
White House, Georgia, September 15, 1780
Whitemarsh, Pennsylvania, December 5 to 8, 1777
White Plains, New York, October 28, 1776
Wiboo Swamp, South Carolina, March 6, 1781
Wiggin's Hill, Georgia, April 1781
Williamson's Plantation, South Carolina, July 12 and December 31, 1780
Wilmington, North Carolina, February 1, 1781
Wolford's Iron Works, South Carolina, August 8, 1780
Woodbridge, New Jersey, April 19, 1777
Wright's Bluff, South Carolina, February 27, 1781
Wyoming, Pennsylvania, July 1 to 4, 1778
Yamacrow Bluff, Georgia, March 4, 1776
Yorktown, Virginia, September 28 to October 19, 1781
Young's House, New York, December 25, 1778, and February 3, 1780

Appendix Four: Numbers of Battles by State and North and South

Canada — 10
Connecticut — 14
Delaware — 1
Florida — 1
Georgia — 24
Indiana — 1
Kentucky — 1
Maine — 1

Massachusetts — 14
New Jersey — 38
New York — 97
North Carolina — 18
Nova Scotia — 1
Ohio — 1
Pennsylvania — 14
Rhode Island — 6

South Carolina — 83
Vermont — 2
Virginia — 13
West Virginia — 1

Battles in the North — 199
Battles in the South — 142

Appendix Five: Colonels

Colonels and Lieutenant Colonels, holding commissions from the Continental Congress or their state militia. Listed alphabetically, by state or country.

Canada

De Roussi, Pierre Regnier
Prentiss, Samuel
Torrey, Joseph

Connecticut

Arnold, James
Baldwin, Jonathan
Beebe, Bezaleel
Belden, Thomas
Benjamin, Aaron
Blagden, Samuel
Bradley, Philip Burr
Brown, John
Brown, Thomas
Buell, Nathaniel
Bulkley, Elippalat
Burrall, Charles
Canfield, Samuel
Chandler, John
Chapman, Samuel
Clark, Joel
Cochran, Robert
Coit, Samuel
Cook, Isaac, Jr.
Cooke, Joseph Platte
Danielson, William
Denison, Nathan
Dimon, David
Dorrance, George
Durkee, John
Dyer, Thomas
Elderkin, Jedediah
Elmore, Samuel
Ely, John
Enos, Roger
Gallup, Nathan
Gay, Fisher
Gould, Abraham
Gray, Ebenezer
Grosvenor, Thomas
Hait, Joseph
Hall, Street
Harris, Joseph
Hayden, Thomas
Hinman, Benjamin
Hobby, Thomas
Holdridge, Hezekiah
Hooker, Noadiah
Horsefield, Obadiah
Hull, William
Humphreys, David
Huntington, Ebenezer
Hutchins, Benjamin
Johnson, Jonathan
Johnson, Obadiah
Knowlton, Thomas
Lattimer, Jonathan
Ledyard, William
Lee, Isaac
Lewis, Ichabod
Lyman, Moses
Mason, Jeremiah
McClellan, Samuel
Meigs, Return Jonathan
Moseley, Increase
Mott, Samuel
Moulton, Stephen
Neill, Henry
Newberry, Roger
Orcutt, William
Parsons, Marshfield
Penfield, John
Pettibone, Jonathan
Pettibone, Ozias
Phelps, Noah
Pitkin, George
Porter, Joshua
Porter, Phineas
Rodney, Thomas
Root, Jasse
Russell, Giles
Sage, Comfort
St. John, Stephen
Sedgwick, John
Selden, Samuel
Smith, Oliver
Staley, Gad
Starr, Josiah
Storrs, Experience
Talcott, Elizur
Talcott, Matthew
Tallmadge, Benjamin
Thompson, Joseph
Trumbull, Jonathan
Trumbull, Jonathan, Jr.
Webb, Charles
Wells, Levi
Wells, Stephen
Whiting, Samuel
Williams, Ebenezer
Williams, William
Wills, Soloman
Worthington, Elias
Wyllys, Hezekiah
Wyllys, Samuel

Delaware

Couch, Thomas
Foster, Henry
Gooch, Thomas

Hall, David
Haslet, John
Hodgson, Robert
Hudson, Robert
Latimer, George
Latimer, James
McDonough, Thomas
McKean, Thomas
McKinley, James
Pope, Charles
Vaughan, Joseph
Wade, Francis

France

Balme, Mottin de la
Bedaulx, Charles Frederick de
Brahm, Ferdinand de
Briffault, Augustin
Britigney, Marquis de
Cambray, du Monsieur
De Corney, Louis Ethis
De Crenis, Chevalier
De Fayals, _____
De Franchessin, Jacques Antoine
De Frauval, _____
De Monfort, Julius, Count
De Vienna, Marquis
Du Buysson, Chevalier
Failly, Chevalier de
Faneuil, Monsieur
Fleury, François Louis de
Gimat, de
Gouvion, Jean Baptiste Obrey de
Holtzendorf, Louis Casimer de
Laumoy, _____ de Mons
Mullens, Thomas
Murnan, John Barnard de
Pelliser, Christopher
Plessis, de Maduit du
Radiere, Lewis Mons. de la
Rogers, Nicholas
St. Martin, _____
Ternant, Jean Baptiste
Tousard, Louis de
Villefranche, _____

Georgia

Branham, Samuel
Clarke, Elijah
Dooley, John
Few, Benjamin
Few, William
Habershem, Joseph
Harden, William
Hovenden, Thomas
Howe, Caleb
Jack, Samuel
Jackson, James
Jones, John
Little, James
Marbury, Leonard
McIntosh, John
Mosby, Littlebury
Neal, Thomas
Pannill, Joseph
Rae, Robert
Stirk, John
Taylor, Thomas
Walton, George

Maryland

Adams, Peter
Addison, John
Beall, William
Beatty, William
Boyd, Abraham
Buchanan, William
Chaille, Peter
Cockey, Edward
Earle, Joseph
Earle, Richard Tilghman
Eccleston, John
Ewing, Thomas
Ford, Benjamin
Forrest, Uriah
Griffin, Charles Greenberry
Hall, Elihu
Hall, Josias Carvil
Hindman, James
Hollingsworth, Henry
Howard, John Eager
Hughes, Thomas
Hyde, William
Johnson, James
Marbury, Luke
Ramsey, Nathaniel
Rawlings, Moses
Richardson, William
Rumsey, Charles
Shryock, Henry
Sim, Patrick
Smith, Samuel
Stewart, John
Stone, John Hawkins
Stricker, George
Thompson, John D
Tillard, Edward
Ware, Francis
Weltner, Ludowick
Whiteley, William
Winder, Levin
Woolford, Thomas

Massachusetts

Alden, Ichabod
Allen, John
Bacon William
Badlam, Ezra
Baldwin, Jedutham
Baldwin, Loammi
Bancroft, Ebenezer
Barnes, Edward
Barrett, Nathan
Bassett, Barachiah
Bigelow, Timothy
Bond, William
Brewer, David
Brewer, Samuel
Bridge, Ebenezer
Bridge, Ebenezer (shared name, different men)
Brooke, Eleaser
Brooks, John
Brown, Abijah
Buck, Jonathan
Buckmaster, William
Burbeck, William
Butterick, John
Carey, Simeon
Carpenter, Thomas
Carter, Josiah
Chapin, Israel
Clarkson, Matthew
Cogswell, Jonathan
Cogswell, Thomas
Collins, James
Converse, James
Cotton, Theopjilus
Crafts, Edward
Cushing, David
Dean, Isaac
Doggett, John
Doolittle, Ephraim
Eager, Nahum
Farrington, Thomas
Fellows, John
Fernald, Tobias
Foster, Benjamin
French, Jacob
Frost, John
Frye, James
Fuller, Nathan
Gardner, Thomas
Gerrish, Jacob
Gerrish, Samuel
Gibbs, Caleb

Green, David
Gridley, Richard
Hammond, Edward
Haskell, Henry
Hatch, Jabez
Hathoway, John
Hawes, Benjamin
Henly, David
Henshaw, William
Herrick, Rufus
Holden, Benjamin
Holman, John
Holman, Jonathan
Howe, Ezekiel
Hutchinson, Israel
Hyde, Caleb
Jackson, Ephraim
Jackson, Giles
Jacobs, John
Johnson, Samuel
Jobonot, Gabriel
Jordan, Nathaniel
Kempton, Thomas
Keyes, Danforth
Learned, David
Lee, William Raymond
Leonard, Nathaniel
Leonard, Zaphaniah
Little, Moses
Littlefield, Noah Moulton
Longley, Robert
Loring, Jotham
Lothrop, Thomas
Lovell, Soloman
Mansfield, John
March, Samuel
Marshell, Thomas
Mason, David
Maxwell, Hugh
McIntosh, William
Mellan, James
Metcalf, James
Mitchell, Abiel
Mitchell, Jonathan
Mitchell, Thomas
Morrell, Henry
Moseley, John
Moulton, Johnson
Murray, Seth
Newhall, Ezra
Oliver, Robert
Page, Jeremiah
Palfrey, William
Patten, Jonathan
Perry, Abner
Peters, Andrew
Phinney, Edmund

Pickering, Timothy
Pierce, Samuel
Poor, Thomas
Pope, Edward
Pope, Frederick
Popkin, John
Porter, Elisha
Prescott, William
Putnam, Enoch
Rand, John
Read, Joseph
Reed, Seth
Roberts, James
Robinson, john
Robinson, Lemuel
Robinson, Timothy
Root, Aaron
Rosseter, David
Sargena, Paul Dudley
Sawyer, Ephraim
Scammon, James
Sheppard, William
Simonds, Benjamin
Smith, Calvin
Smith, Jonathan
Sperhawk, Nathaniel
Sprout, Ebenezer
Stacey, William
Stearns, Abijah
Trawbridge, John
Tudor, William
Turner, William
Vose, Elijah
Wade, Nathaniel
Waggoner, John Peter
Walker, Timothy
Ward, Jonathan
Ward, Joseph
Wells, David
Wesson, James
Wheelock, Ephraim
Wheelock, Moses
Whitcomb, Asa
Whiting, Daniel
Whitney, Josiah
Wigglesworth, Edward
Willard, Aaron
Williams, George
Williams, Samuel

Netherlands
Derick, Jacob Gerhard

New Hampshire
Adams, Winborn

Allen, Ebenezer
Ashley, Samuel
Badger, Joseph
Baldwin, Nahum
Bartlett, Thomas
Bell, John
Bellows, Benjamin
Chase, Jonathan
Cilley, Joseph
Colburn, Andrew
Dane, Theophilus
Dearborn, Henry
Evans, Stephen
Gale, Jacob
Gilman, David
Gilman, Israel
Gilman, Jeremiah
Gilman, Nicholas
Gregg, William
Hale, Nathan
Hammond, Joseph
Heald, Thomas
Hobart, David
Hunt, Samuel
Hutchins, Gordon
Johnson, Charles
Kelley, Moses
Langdon, John
Long, Pierce
Lovewell, Noah
McClary, John
Mooney, Hercules
Morey, Israel
Moulton, Jonathan
Nash Thomas
Nichols, Moses
Peabody, Stephen
Reed, Jonathan
Reid, George
Reynolds, Daniel
Smith, Eleazer
Stickney, Thomas
Tash, Thomas
Thornton, Matthew
Titcomb, Benjamin
Walbridge, Ebenezer
Waldron, John
Walker, Abel
Warner, Seth
Warren, Gideon
Webster, John
Welch, Joseph
Williams, William
Wingate, Joshua
Wyman, Isaac

Appendix Five

New Jersey

Barber, Francis
Beavers, Joseph
Bond, William
Borden, Joseph
Bott, William
Boudinot, Elias
Brearley, David
Breese, Samuel
Burr, Aaron
Chamberlain, William
Clark, Elijah
Conway, John
Cook, Ellis
Covenhoven, John
Crane, Jacob
Cripps, Whitton
Cumming, John Noble
De Hart, William
Dey, Theunis
Dick, Samuel
Drake, Jacob
Dunham, Azariah
Dunn, Micajah
Ely, George
Fell, Peter
Fleming, Stephen
Ford, Jacob, Jr.
Forman, David
Forman, Jonathan
Hadden, Thomas
Haight, Joseph
Hand, Elijah
Hand, Henry
Hankinson, Aaron
Hathaway, Benoni
Henderson, Thomas
Hendrickson, Daniel
Hillman, Josiah
Holme, Benjamin
Holme, John
Holmes, Asher
Houghton, Jacob
Hunt, Nathaniel
Hunt, Stephen
Hyer, Jacob
Jacques, Moses
Johnston, Philip
Lawrence, Elisha
Lindsley, Eleaser
Livingston, Henry Brockholst
Lott, Richard
Lowrey, Thomas
Ludlow, Cornelius
Luse, Nathan
Mackey, John
Martin, Ephraim
Mehelm, John
Middagh, Derrick
Munson, John
Ogden, Abraham
Otto, Bodo
Phillips, Joseph
Potter, David
Preston, Isaac
Quick, Abraham
Read, Charles
Reed, Bowles
Reynolds, Thomas
Ross, John
Salter, Joseph
Scudder, Nathaniel
Scudder, William
Seabrook, Thomas
Seeley, Enos
Seeley, Sylvanus
Shipmann, Matthias
Shreve, Israel
Shreve, William
Shute, William
Smith, Isaac
Smock, John
Somers, Richard
Spencer, Oliver
Starke, John
Stewart, Charles
Stillwell, Enoch
Stillwell, Nicholas
Stockton, Richard
Taylor, George
Taylor, John
Taylor, Robert
Ten Broeck, John
Thompson, Mark
Tonkin, Samuel
Van Dyke, Henry
Vroom, Peter Dumont
Ward, Matthias
West, Jacob
Wetherill, John
White, Anthony Walton
Wikoff, Auke

New York

Antil, Edward
Barker, William
Beekman, Thomas
Bell, Paterson
Bellinger, Peter
Benson, Robert
Birdsall, Benjamin
Blackwell, Jacob
Blair, John
Bratt, Daniel
Brinkerhoff, Abraham
Brinkerhoff, Direk
Bruyn, Jacobus S.
Budd, Gilbert, Jr.
Campbell, Samuel
Cantine, John
Church, Timothy
Clyde, Samuel
Cooper, Gilbert
Crane, Thaddeus
Cuyler, Abraham
De Witt, Charles
Dickinson, Daniel
Drake, Joseph
Drake, Samuel
Du Bois, Lewis
Field, John
Fisher, Frederick
Fisher, John
Fleming, Edward
Freer, John
Gansevoort, Peter
Gordon, James
Graham, John
Graham, Morris
Griffin, Jacob
Hamilton, Alexander
Hamman, James
Hardenbergh, Johannes
Harper, John
Hasbrouck, Abraham
Hasbrouck, Jonathan
Hatfield, Moses
Hathorn, John
Hay, A. Hawkes
Hoffman, Robert
Hogeboom, Stephen
Holmes, James
Hopkins, Roswell
Humphrey, Cornelius
Jansen, Johannes
Jay, John
Jones, Joel
Kirkland, Peter
Klock, Jacob
Knockerbocker, John
Lamb, John
Lansing, Jacob, Jr.
Lasher, John
Lent, Abraham
Lewis, Morgan
Livingston, Henry
Livingston, Henry Beekman
Livingston, James

Livingston, Peter R.
Livingston, Richard
Livingston, William Smith
Lott, Abraham P.
Magaw, Robert
Malcolm, William
McClaughrey, James
McCloskey, Alexander
McCracken, Joseph
McCrea, John
McLarey, James
McPherson, Robert
Moorehouse, Andrew
Morris, Lewis, Jr.
Nicholson, John
Nicoll, Isaac
Nixon, Thomas
North, George
Norton, Berich
Palmer, Thomas
Pawling, Albert
Pawling, Levi
Platt, Zaphania
Quackenboss, Henry
Randall, Benjamin
Remsen, Henry
Rensselaer, Henry Kiliaen van
Rensselaer, John van
Ritzema, Rudolphus
Rodgers, Zabdial
Schemerhorh, Jacob
Schoonhoven, Jacobus
Schuyler, Stephen J.
Seeber, William
Smith, Josiah
Smith, William Stephens
Snyder, Johannes
Stoughtenburg, Isaac
Stoughtenburgh, Tobias
Sutherland, David
Ten Broeck, Abraham
Ten Broeck, Dirck
Thomas, John
Thomas, Thomas
Thompson, Thomas
Thurston, Benjamin
Troup, Robert
Tusten, Benjamin
Van Alstyne, Philip
Van Brunt, Richard
Van Cortlandt, Pierre
Vanderburgh, Garret
Vanderburgh, James
Van Ness, John
Van Ness, Peter
Van Vechten, Cornelius
Van Veghten, Volkert

Van Woert, Lewis
Visscher, Frederick
Visscher, John
Vrooman, Peter
Walker, Benjamin
Waterman, Asa
Webster, Alexander
Weisenfels, Frederick
Wempel, Abraham
Wendell, Harmanus
Whiting, Bradford
Whiting, William Bradford
Willett, Marinus
Williams, John
Wisner, Henry
Witbeck, Andries
Wood, John
Woodbridge, Benjamin Ruggles
Wynkoop, Cornelius D.
Yates, Christopher P.
Yates, Peter
Zedwitz, Herman
Ziele, Peter W.

North Carolina
Armstrong, James
Armstrong, John
Ashe, John Baptista
Avery, Waitstill
Bradford, William, Jr.
Brevard, Alexander
Brewer, Samuel
Brewster, Lott
Brown, James S.
Campbell, Arthur
Clark, Thomas
Cleveland, Benjamin
Collier, John
Davidson, William Lee
Davie, William Richardson
Dawson, Henry
Dawson, Levi
Dixon, Henry
Dudley, Guilford
Eaton, Pinketham
Forbes, Arthur
Graham, William
Hall, James
Hambright, Frederick
Hampton, Andrew
Harney, Selby
Harper, Jonathan
Hawkins, Philemon
Hogg, Thomas
Ingram, James
Isaacs, Elisha

Jarvis, Samuel
Johnston, Jonas
Jones, Allen
Jones, John
Lamb, Gideon
Lillington, John Alexander
Locke, Francis
Lockhart, Samuel
Long, Nicholas
Lowe, Philip
Luttrell, John
Martin, Alexander
McDowell, Charles
Mebane, Robert
Moore, Stephen
Murphy, Archibald
Osburn, Alexander
Patten, John
Perkins, Adam
Phifer, Caleb
Polk, William
Ramsey, Ambrose
Rutherford, Robert
Seawell, Benjamin
Sevier, John
Sheppard, Abraham
Taylor, William
Thackston, James
Tinning, _____
Walker, Felix
Walker, John
Williams, John P.
Williams, Joseph

Pennsylvania
Allen, William
Anderson, John
Antes, Philip Frederick
Atlee, Samuel John
Balliet, Stephen
Baxter, _____
Bayard, John
Bayard, Stephen
Beatty, John
Bell, Patterson
Bicker, Henry
Biddle, Clement
Bord, Mark
Boyd, Matthew
Bradford, William
Bradford, William, Jr.
Brice, John
Bull, Thomas
Bunner, Rudolph
Burd, Benjamin
Burd, James

Appendix Five

Butler, William
Cadwalader, Lambert
Cessna, Charles
Chevalier, John
Clark, Robert
Clymer, Daniel
Coates, William
Connor, Morgan
Cooke, William
Craig, Thomas
Culbertson, Robert
Culbertson, Samuel
Cunningham, James
Davis, John
Dill, Matthew
Dinwiddie, Hugh
Dunlop, James
Elder, Robert
Erwin, Arthur
Evans, Evan
Eyre, Benjamin
Eyre, John
Fairland Nicholas
Farmer, Lewis
Flower, Benjamin
Forrest, Thomas
Geiger, George
Gibbons, William
Gray, Neigal
Greenawalt, Philip L.
Grier, David
Grier, James
Grubb, Curtis
Gurney, Francis
Haller, Henry
Hannum, John
Harmar, Josiah
Hart, Joseph
Hartley, Thomas
Haussegger, Nicholas
Hay, Samuel
Hay, Udny
Hay, William
Hiester, John
Hiester, Joseph
Hosterman, Peter
Hubley, Adam
Hughes, Isaac
Humpton, Richard
Hunter, David
Jeffries, Francis Jacob
Jeffries, Joseph
Johnston, Francis
Johnston, James
Jones, Jonathan
Kachlein, Andrew
Klein, William

Klotz, Jacob
Klotz, Nicholas
Knox, Robert
Lewis, Robert
Lochrey, Archibald
Lowrey, Alexander
Lutz, Nicholas
Lyon, Samuel
Mackay, Eneas
McAllister, Richard
Maclay, Samuel
McClelland, John
McKean, Thomas
Mentges, Francis
Miller, Henry
Montgomery, John
Montgomery, William
Moodie, Robert
Moore, James
Moore, James (different)
Moore, John
Morgan, Jacob, Jr.
Morris, Anthony James
Moylan, Stephen
Murray, John
Nagel, George
Nixon, John
North, Caleb
Parke, John
Parker, William
Patton, John
Penrose, Joseph
Piper, James
Piper, John
Pomeroy, John
Porter, Andrew
Porter, Thomas
Potter, James
Proctor, Thomas
Reigart, Adam
Renner, Francis Jacob
Rice, John
Robinson, Robert
Ross, George
Ross, James
Shee, John
Slough, Mathias
Smith, James
Smith, James (different)
Smith, Jonathan Bayard
Smith, Matthew
Smith, Robert
Stewart, Walter
Stroud, Jacob
Stuart, Christopher
Sutherland, Thomas
Swope, Michael

Taylor, Thomas
Thomas, Richard
Thompson, Archibald
Thompson, Robert
Thornburgh, Joseph
Turbett, Thomas
Udree, Daniel
Vernon, Frederick
Warner, Isaac
Watson, James
Watts, Frederick
Weiser, Benjamin
White, Hugh
Williams, William
Wilson, George
Wood, Joseph

Poland

Kowatz, Michael de

Rhode Island

Angell, Israel
Babcock, Henry
Babcock, James
Barton, William
Belcher, Joseph
Brown, Chad
Brown, Jabez
Brown, Robert
Carpenter, Thomas
Champlin, George
Church, Thomas
Comstock, Adam
Cooke, John
Dyer, Charles
Frye, Richard
Gerdner, Caleb
Gorton, Thomas
Gray, Pardon
Gray, Thomas
Greene, Christopher
Hall, Levi
Hawkins, Nathaniel
Hilyard, David
Hitchcock, David
Hoxie, Gideon
Irish, George
Johnston, Isaac
Kasson, Archibald
Kimball, Stephen
Lowe, John
Malbone, John
Martin, Nathaniel
Maxon, James

Maxon, Jonathan
Miller, William Turner
Noyes, Joseph
Olney, Christopher
Olney, Jeremiah
Peck, George
Peck, William
Peirce, George
Potter, Stephen
Potter, Thomas
Richmond, William
Sears, George
Sherburne, Henry
Stevens, Ebenezer
Talbot, Silas
Tallman, Benjamin
Tillinghast, Thomas
Topham, John
Ward, Samuel, Jr.
Waterman, John
Waterman, Thomas
Williams, James

South Carolina

Beard, Jonas
Beekman, Barnard
Benton, Lemuel
Bond, George P.,
Bratton, William
Brown, Joseph
Butler, William
Cattell, William
Drayton, Stephen
Elliott, Samuel
Erwin, John
Evaleigh, Nicholas
Gadsden, Christopher
Gaillard, Tacitus
Glover, Joseph
Goodwin, Robert
Grimke, John Faucherand
Hammond, Le Roy
Hampton, Henry
Hampton, Wade
Harleston, John
Hawthorne, James
Hayes, Joseph
Hayne, Isaac
Henderson, John
Herriot, Robert
Hicks, George
Hill, William
Horry, Daniel
Horry, Hugh
Horry, Peter

Huger, Francis
Hyrne, Edmund
Kershaw, Joseph
Kimball, Frederick
Kobb, Abal
Kolb, Abel
Ladson, James
Laurens, John
Lisle, John
Maham, Hezekiah
Massey, William
Maybank, Joseph
Mayson, James
McCall, James
McClure, Neil
McCreery, Robert
McIntosh, Alexander
Middelton, Hugh
Motte, Abraham
Motte, Isaac
Nixon, John
Polk, Ezekial
Potsell, James
Powell, George Gabriel
Purcell, Henry
Roberts, Owen
Roebuck, James
Rothmaler, Job
Rowe, Christopher
Savage, John
Scott, William
Simons, James
Stark, Robert
Steward, Charles Augustus
Tarling, _____
Taylor, Thomas
Thomas, John
Thomas, John, Jr.
Thomas, Tristam
Williams, James
Winn, Richard
Yates, William

Vermont

Fletcher, Samuel
Herrick, Samuel
Hunt, Jonathan
Johnson, Thomas
Marsh, Joel
Marsh, Joseph
Mead, James
Olcott, Peter
Robinson, Moses
Webster, David

Williams, William
Wood, Ebenezer

Virginia

Alexander, Morgan
Allison, John
Anderson, Richard Clough
Atwell, Thomas
Ballard, Robert
Barksdale, John
Bass, Joseph
Baylor, George
Blackburn, Thomas
Bland, Theodorick
Bledsoe, A
Blow, Michael
Blunt, Joseph
Bowman, Abraham
Brent, William
Brooke, George
Brooke, Humphrey
Buckner, Mordecai
Bullit, Thomas
Burton, John
Burwell, Lewis
Burwell, Thacker
Byrd, Francis Otway
Cabell, Samuel Jordan
Calloway, James
Calmes, Marquis
Campbell, Richard
Carey, Richard
Carr, Thomas
Carrington, George
Champe, William
Chilton, Thomas
Christian, William
Clark, Jonathan
Cocke, John
Cocke, Nathaniel
Crawford, William
Crockett, Joseph
Cropper, John
Dabney, Charles
Dangerfield, William
Darke, William
Davies, William
Davis, William
Edmunds, Elias
Elliott, Thomas
Eppes, Francis
Evans, John
Falkner, Ralph
Finnie, William
Fitzgerald, John

Fitzhugh, Perigrine
Fleming, Charles
Fleming, Thomas
Gibson, George
Gibson, John
Gist, Nathaniel
Glenn, John
Grayson, William
Green, John
Griffin, Samuel
Harrison, Charles
Harrison, Robert Hanson
Harvie, John
Hawes, Samuel
Hendricks, James
Henry, Patrick
Heth, William
Holcombe, John
Hopkins, Samuel
Innis, James
Jameson, John
Johnston, George
Joynes, Levin
Langbourne, William
Lee, Henry
Lewis, Charles
Lewis, Nicholas
Lynch, Charles
Lyne, George
Magill, Charles
Mallory, Francis
Markham, John
Marshall, Thomas
Mason, David
Mason, James
McDowell, Samuel

Meade, Richard Kidder
Mercer, John Francis
Montague, James
Montgomery, John
Morgan, Haynes
Morrow, John
Morton, John
Nash, John
Neville, John
Neville, Presley
New, Anthony
Parker, Josiah
Peachy, William
Pendleton, Philip
Perkins, Peter
Perkins, William Harding
Pickett, Martin
Porterfield, Charles
Posey, Thomas
Powell, John
Powell, Levin
Preston, William
Randolph, Beverly
Randolph, Thomas Mann
Read, Isaac
Read, James
Richardson, Holt
Rucker, Ephraim
Rumney, William
Russell, William
Sayres, John
Scott, Charles
Shelby, Isaac
Simms, Charles
Smith, Gregory
Smith, John

Spotswood, Alexander
Stubblefield, George
Symmes, John Cleves
Taliaferro, William
Taylor, Henry
Taylor, James
Taylor, Richard
Terry, William
Thornton, John
Thornton, Presley Peter
Thruston, Charles Wynn
Travis, Champion
Tucker, St. George
Vanmetre, Garrett
Walker, Thomas Reynolds
Warneck, Frederick
Washington, John Augustine
Washington, Samuel
Washington, William
Webb, John
Willis, Lewis
Wilson, George
Wood, James
Woodrow, Andrew

Unknown

Barclay, Hugh
De Boze, Baron
Horton, Azariah
Kermovan, John de
Sands, Ray
Stafford, _____
Vrecourt, Count de

Notes

Alexander, William
1. J.T. Headley, *Washington and His Generals*, vol. 1 (New York: Hurst, 1847), 183–185.

Armand, Tuffin Charles
1. Marcel Villaneuva, *The French Contribution to the Founding of the United States* (New York: Vantage Press, 1975); Francis B. Heitman, *Historical Register of Officers of the Continental Army During the War of the Revolution*, reprint (Baltimore: Genealogical Publishing, 1973), 73.

Armstrong, John
1. Charles William Heathcote, "General John Armstrong," *The Picket Post*, November 1959; Heitman, 60.

Arnold, Benedict
1. George Athan Billias, *George Washington's Generals and Opponents: Their Exploits and Leadership* (New York: De Capo Press, 1994); Heitman, 75–76.

Ashe, John
1. Heitman, 77.

Babcock, Joshua
1. Anna Chesebrough Widley, *Genealogy of the Descendants of William Chesebrough, Founder of Stonington, Connecticut* (New York: Press of T.A. Wright, 1903), 43, 100, 101; Heitman, 79.

Bailey, Jacob
1. Frederic P. Wells, *History of Newbury, Vermont, 1704–1902* (St. Johnsbury, VT: Caledonian, 1902); and Hollis R. Bailey, *Bailey Genealogy, James, John, & Thomas and Their Descendants* (Somerville, MA: Citizen, 1899); Ullery, part 2, 12.

Barnwell, John
1. Heitman, 88.

Beall, Reazin
1. *The Yorktown Herald*, February 3, 1949; Heitman, 94.

Bedel, Timothy
1. Robert K. Wright, Jr., *The Continental Army* (Washington, DC: Government Printing Office, 1983), 197; Heitman, 95.

Brickett, James Soldier
1. *Massachusetts Soldiers and Sailors in the Revolutionary War*, vol. 2 (Boston: Wright & Potter, 1896–1908), 483; J.H. Temple, *History of North Brookfield, Massachusetts*, published by the town of North Brookfield, 1887, 236; Heitman, 120.

Brodhead, Daniel, III
1. Robert Walker Smith, *History of Armstrong County, Pennsylvania* (Chicago: Waterman, Watkins, 1883), 585; Heitman, 122.
2. Smith, 585–587.
3. Heitman, 122.
4. Smith, 586–587.

Buchanan, Andrew
1. Heitman, 129.

Bull, Stephen
1. *Charleston* (South Carolina) *Gazette*, May 24, 1772; Heitman, 131.

Butler, John
1. Heitman, 137.

Butler, Richard
1. Heitman, 137.

Cadwalader, John
1. L. Carroll Judson, *The Sages and Heroes of the American Revolution In Two Parts Including the Signers of the Declaration of Independence, Two Hundred and Forty Three of the Sages and Heroes Are Presented in Due Form* (Boston: Lee and Shepard, 1851), 423.
2. Heitman, 139.

Campbell, William
1. Heitman, 142.

Caswell, Richard
1. Judson, 423
2. Letter from Richard Caswell to his son, May 11, 1775, Caswell Papers, North Carolina Archives, Raleigh, N.C.

Chamberlain, James
1. Heitman, 149.

Clark, George Rogers
1. Temple Bodley, *George Rogers Clark: His Life and Public Services* (Boston: Houghton Mifflin, 1926), 1–13; Judson, 424; John Bakeless, *Background to Glory: The Life of George Rogers Clark* (Philadelphia: J.B. Lippincott, 1957), 87–125.

Clarke, Elijah
1. Mark M. Boatner, *Encyclopedia of the American Revolution* (Harrisburg, PA: Stackpole Books, 1994); Heitman, 158.

Clinton, George
1. William L. Stoner, "George Clinton," *Potter's American Monthly* 7, no. 57 (September 1876): 189–191.
2. Heitman, 161.
3. Stoner: 189–191.

Clinton, James
1. Headley, 117.
2. Heitman, 60.
3. Headley, 117.
4. Heitman, 161.
5. Headley, 122.

Cobb, David
1. Heitman, 162.

Conway, Thomas
1. Headley, 221.
2. Villaneuva; Heitman, 168.

Cornell, Ezekiel
1. Heitman, 171.

Crane, John
1. Heitman, 176.

Cushing, Joseph
1. James Cushing, *The Genealogy of the Cushing Family (An Account of the Ancestors and Descendants of Matthew Cushing, Who Came to America in 1638)* (Montreal: Perrault Printing, 1877), 49; *Massachusetts Soldiers and Sailors in the Revolutionary War*, vol. 4, 294; Heitman, 182.

Danielson, Timothy
1. Heitman, 185.

Davidson, William Lee
1. Chalmers Gaston Davidson, *Piedmont Partisan: The Life and Times of Brigadier-General William Lee Davidson* (Davidson, NC: Davidson College, 1968), 3–9.
2. Heitman, 186–187.
3. Davidson, 133.

Dayton, Elias
1. Larry R. Gerlach, *New Jersey in the American Revolution, 1763–1783: A Documentary History* (Trenton: New Jersey Historical Commission, 1975), 11–17; Heitman, 190.

De Fermoy, Matthias Alexis Roche
1. Heitman, 191.

De Haas, John P.
1. John Blair Linn, *History of Centre and Clinton Counties, Pennsylvania* (Philadelphia: Louis B. Everts, 1883); Frank E. Grizzard, Jr., *The Papers of George Washington: Revolutionary War Series*, vol. 10, June-August 1777 (Charlottesville: University Press of Virginia, 2000), 75–76.
2. Heitman, 192.
3. *Pennsylvania Magazine of History* 2: 347.

De Kalb, Johann
1. Headley, 219–220; Judson, 205–208.

De Laumoy, Jean Baptiste Joseph
1. Villanueva.

Dent, John
1. Heitman, 194.

De Woedtke, Frederick William
1. Heitman, 196.

Dickinson, John
1. James V. Marshall, *The United States Manual of Biography and History* (Philadelphia: James B. Smith, 1856), 143–144; Heitman, 197.

Dickinson, Philemon
1. *Magazine of American History*, December 1881: 420–427; Heitman, 197.

Douglas, John
1. Heitman, 202.

Du Buysson, Charles Francois
1. Villanueva, 89; Heitman, 205.

Du Coudray, Philippe Charles Jean Baptiste Tronson
1. Villanueva, 91; Heitman, 172.

Duportail, Louis Le Beque De Presle
1. Charles William Heathcote, "General Chevalier Louis Lebeque dePresle Duportail," *The Picket Post*, February 1959; Heitman, 208.

Dyer, Eliphalet
1. William F. Willingham, *Connecticut Revolutionary: Eliphalet Dyer* (Hartford: American Revolution Bicentennial Commission of Connecticut, 1977); Heitman, 209.

Elbert, Samuel
1. Charles C. Jones, *The Life and Services of the Honorable Maj. Gen. Samuel Elbert of Georgia* (New York: W. Abbatt, 1911), 3–12; Adiel Sherwood, *A Gazetteer of the State of Georgia* (Washington City, GA: P. Force, 1837), 274–275; Heitman, 213.
2. Lawton Evans, *First Lessons in Georgia History* (New York: American Book, 1913), 151–152.
3. Heitman, 213.
4. George White, *Historical Collections of Georgia* (New York: Pudney & Russell, 1854), 438–450.

Enos, Roger
1. Orrin Peer Allen, *The Allen Memorial* (Massachusetts: Press of C.B. Fiske & Company, 1907); Ullery; Heitman, 472.

Ewing, James
1. Heitman, 220.

Febiger, Christian
1. Heitman, 223.

Floyd, William
1. Charles A. Goodrich, *Lives of the Signers of the Declaration of Independence* (New York: William Reed, 1856), 261–282; Heitman, 231.
2. Goodrich, 270–282.

Folsom, Nathaniel
1. *NH: Years of Revolution* (Providence, NH: Profiles Publications and the NH Bicentennial Commission, 1976); Heitman, 231.

Frazer, Persifor
1. John W. Jordan, *Colonial and Revolutionary Families of Pennsylvania*, vols. 1–3 (New York: Lewis, 1911); Heitman, 236.

Freeman, Nathaniel
1. Nathaniel Freeman Papers, Schoff Revolutionary War Collection, William L. Clements Library, The University of Michigan, Ann Arbor, MI; Heitman, 237.

Frye, Joseph
1. Silvio Bendini, "Joseph Frye of Fryeburg, Maine," *Professional Surveyor Magazine*, pt. one, November-December 1989, and pt. two, January-February 1990; William Barrows, *Fryeburg: An Historical Sketch* (Fryeburg, ME: Pequawket Press, 1938).
2. Bendini; Heitman, 239.
3. Bendini; Barrows.

Gadsden, Christopher
1. Heitman, 240.

Gansevort, Peter
1. Judson, 431.
2. Heitman, 242.
3. Judson, 431.

Gates, Horatio
1. Judson, 110–114; Headley, 169–178.
2. Heitman, 244.
3. Judson, 110–114; Headley, 178–190.

Gibson, John
1. Charles William Hanko, *The Life of John Gibson: Soldier, Patriot, Statesman* (Daytona Beach, FL: College Publishing, 1955), 36–37, 42, 82; Judson, 422.

Gist, Mordecai
1. Joe Getty, and Jay Graybeal, "Countians Feared Being Buried Alive," *Carroll County Times*, November 21, 1993; Heitman, 249.

Glover, John
1. Robert K. Wright, Jr., *The Continental Army*, 218; Heitman, 250.

Godfrey, George
1. *Massachusetts Soldiers and Sailors of the Revolutionary War*, vol. 6, 526; Heitman, 250.

Greaton, John
1. Patricia Law Hatcher, *Abstract of Revolutionary Patriots*, vol. 2 (Dallas: Pioneer Heritage Press, 1987), 90; *Vital Records of Roxbury, Massachusetts to the end of the year 1849* (Salem, MA: Essex Institute, 1925), 154; Heitman, 259.

Greene, Nathaniel
1. Judson, 121–122.
2. Heitman, 260–261.
3. Headley, 3–49; Charles Morris and Oliver H.G. Leigh, *The Great Republic By the Master Historians*, vol. 2 (New York: R.S. Belcher, 1902), 260–278.

Gregory, Isaac
1. Heitman, 262.

Gunby, John
1. Woodrow T. Wilson, *Thirty-Four Families of Old Somerset County, Maryland* (Baltimore: Gateway Press, 1974); Wright, 277; Heitman, 265.

Hancock, John
1. Harlow G. Unger, *John Hancock: Merchant King and American Patriot* (New York: John Wiley & Sons, 2000); Goodrich, 71–81; Heitman, 242.

Hand, Edward
1. Mary Virginia Shelly, *The Story of General Edward Hand* (Lititz, PA: Sutter House, 1978); Heitman, 272.

Harrington, Henry William
1. Walter Edgar and N. Louise Bailey, *Biographical Directory of the South Carolina House of Representatives, 1692–1775*, vol. 5 (Columbia: University of South Carolina Press, 1974), 121; William S. Powell, *Dictionary of North Carolina Biography*, vol. 3 (Chapel Hill: University of North Carolina Press, 1979–1996), 43–45; Alexander Gregg, *History of Old Cheraws* (Boyd, 1867), 255, 268, 269; Heitman, 275.

Hazen, Moses
1. James Grant Wilson, John Fiske, and Stanley I. Klos, *Appleton's Cyclopedia of American Biography*, six volumes (New York: D. Appleton, 1887–1889); Heitman, 282.

Heard, Nathaniel
1. William S. Stryker, *Official Register of the Officers and Men of New Jersey in the Revolutionary War* (Trenton, NJ: William T. Nicholson, 1872); Heitman, 283.

Heart, Selah
1. Heitman, 283.

Heath, William
1. Headley, 230–231.
2. Headley, 230–231; Heitman, 284.
3. Headley, 231.

Henderson, William
1. Wright, 309; Heitman, 285.

Herkimer, Nicholas
1. Eugene W. Lyttle, "Nicholas Herkimer," in *Proceedings of the New York State Historical Association* (Albany, NY: n.p., 1904); Heitman, 286.

Hiester, Daniel
1. Valeria E. Clymer Hill, *A Genealogy of The Hiester Family* (Reading, PA: Reading Eagle Press, 1941); Heitman, 289.

Hogun, James
1. Wright, 302.

Holden, Thomas
1. Eben Putnam, *The Holden Genealogy* (Boston: Quintin, 1923, 408–411); Heitman, 295.

Hooper, Henry
1. Donald G. Shomette, *Pirates on the Chesapeake: A True History of Pirates, Picaroons and Raiders on the Chesapeake Bay 1610–1807* (Centreville, MD: Tidewater, 1985); Heitman, 299.

Howe, Robert
1. Headley, 234; Heitman, 304.
2. Henry Steele Commager and Richard B. Morris, *The Spirit of 'Seventy-Six: The Story of the American Revolution as Told By Participants* (New York: Harper and Row, 1967), 1073–1075.
3. Headley, 234; Heitman, 304.

Huger, Isaac
1. Robert W. Gibbes, *Documentary History of the American Revolution*, vol. 3 (New York: D. Appleton, 1855–57), 18; Heitman, 306.

Huntington, Jabez
1. F.M. Caulkins, *History of Norwich, From its Possession by Indians to 1866* (Norwich, CT: self-published, 1866); Heitman, 310–311.

Huntington, Jedediah
1. *The Huntington Family in America: A Genealogical Memoir of the Known Descendants of Simon Huntington from 1633 to 1915, Including Those Who Have Retained the Family Name, and Many Bearing Other Surnames* (Hartford, CT: Huntington Family Association, 1915); Judson, 439–440.
2. Heitman, 311.
3. Charles William Heathcote, "General Jedediah Huntington," *The Picket Post*, May 1956; Judson, 440.

Irvine, James
1. Heitman, 314.

Irvine, William
1. Theodore Diller, *Pioneer Medicine in Western Pennsylvania* (New York: Paul B. Hoeber, 1937), 31–32.
2. Heitman, 314.
3. Diller, 32.

Jackson, Henry
1. *Massachusetts Soldiers and Sailors in the War of the Revolution*, vol. 8, 668; Wright, 210–211; Heitman, 315.

Jackson, Michael
1. Wright, 209–210; Heitman, 316.

Johnson, Thomas, Jr.
1. Edward Delepaine, *The Life of Thomas Johnson* (New York: F.H. Hitchcock, 1927); Heitman, 321.

Jones, Allen
1. Heitman, 323.

Jones, William
1. Heitman, 326.

Knox, Henry
1. Judson, 446.
2. Headley, 65–66; Heitman, 336.
3. Heitman, 336.
4. Thomas Morgan Griffiths, *Major General Henry Knox and the Last Heirs to Montpelier* (Lewistown, ME: Twin City Printery, 1965), 3.

Kosciuszko, Thaddeus
1. Miecislaus Haiman, *Kosciuszko in the American Revolution* (New York: Polish Institute of Arts and Sciences in America, 1943), 3–7.
2. Heitman, 336.

Lacey, John
1. Garland Howard Lacey, *Ancestors and Descendants of Hiram G. Lacey and Sophia Sell* (Hiram, IL: M&D Printing, 1995), 37–40; Heitman, 337.

Lafayette, Marie-Joseph Paul Yves Roch Gilbert du Motier, Marquis de
1. Henry Dwight Sedgwick, *LaFayette* (Chautauqua, NY: The Chautauqua Press, 1928), 9–34; Headley, vol. 2, 180–219; Trevor N. Dupuy, Curt Johnson, and David L. Bongard, *The Harper Encyclopedia of Military Biography* (New York: HarperCollins, 1992), 420–421.
2. Louis Gottschalk, *LaFayette Between the American and French Revolution* (Chicago: University of Chicago Press, 1950), 145–147.

Lawson, Robert
1. J.T. McAllister, *Virginia Militia in the Revolutionary War* (Hot Springs, VA: McAllister, 1913), 40, 68, 81; Wright, 286; Heitman, 343.

Learned, Ebenezer
1. Charles William Heathcote, "General Ebenezer Learned: Courageous Patriot and Friend of Washington," *The Picket Post*, February 1958; Heitman, 343.

Lee, Charles
1. John Richard Alden, *General Charles Lee: Traitor or Patriot?* (Baton Rouge: Louisiana State University Press, 1951), 6–21; Headley, 85–93; Heitman, 344.
2. Headley, 94–95; Heitman, 344.
3. Headley, 96–107.

Lewis, Andrew
1. Wills De Hass, *History of the Indian Wars of Western Virginia*; Heitman, 348.

Lewis, Fielding
1. Paula Felder, *Fielding Lewis and the Washington Family: A Chronicle of 18th Century Fredericksburg* (Fredericksburg, VA: The American History Company, 1999); Heitman, 348.

Lincoln, Benjamin
1. David B. Mattern, *Benjamin Lincoln and the American Revolution* (Columbia: University of South Carolina Press, 1995), 7–9, 13.

2. Ibid., 14–21.
   3. Headley, 69.
   4. Heitman, 351; Headley, 70.
   5. Headley, 71–80.

Lippitt, Christopher
   1. Noah J. Arnold, *The Narragansett Historical Register*, vol. 8, no. 2 (Hamilton, RI: Narragansett Historical Publishing, 1890), 111–112.
   2. Heitman, 352.
   3. Arnold, 112–114.
   4. Richard M. Bayles, *History of Providence County* (New York: W.W. Preston, 1891), 731–733.

Livingston, William
   1. Kathryn Allamong Jacob and Bruce A. Ragsdale, *Biographical Dictionary of the United States Congress, 1774–1989* (Washington, DC: Government Printing Office, 1989); Heitman, 354.

Marion, Francis
   1. Headley, 154–156.
   2. Judson, 248–249.
   3. Heitman, 379.
   4. Headley, 164–180.

Mathews, George
   1. Paul Kruse, "Secret Agent in East Florida: General George Mathews and the Patriot War," Journal of Southern History, May 1952: 193–217; G. Melvin Herndon, "George Mathews: Frontier Patriot," *Virginia Magazine of History and Biography*, July 1969: 307–328.
   2. Kruse, 193–217; Herndon, 307–328; Heitman, 384.
   3. Kruse, 200–217; Herndon, 305–328.

Maxwell, William
   1. Harry M. Ward, *General William Maxwell and the New Jersey Continentals* (Westport, CT: Greenwood Press, 1997), 1–12.
   2. Heitman, 385.
   3. Ward, 181.
   4. Heitman, 385.
   5. Ward, 180.

McClellan, Samuel
   1. Wright, 212–213; Heitman, 365.

McDougall, Alexander
   1. William L. McDougall, *American Revolutionary: A Biography of General Alexander McDougall* (Westport, CT: Greenwood Press, 1977), 1–10.
   2. Heitman, 368.
   3. McDougall, 155–156.

McDowell, Joseph
   1. Thomas Marshall Green, *Historical Families of Kentucky* (Cincinnati: Clearfield, 1889); Heitman, 369.

McIntosh, Lachlan
   1. Harvey H. Jackson, *Lachlan McIntosh and the Politics of Revolutionary Georgia* (Athens: University of Georgia Press, 1979), 3–9.
   2. Charles William Heathcote, "General Lachlan McIntosh: Loyal American and Friend of Washington," *The Picket Post*, February 1957; Heitman, 371.
   3. Heathcote, "General Lachlan McIntosh."

Mead, John
   1. Spencer P. Mead, *Abstract of Probate Records for the District of Stamford, County of Fairfield, 1729–1848* (Salem, MA: Higginson, 1997), 28, 138, 145; Heitman, 386.

Mercer, Hugh
   1. John T. Goolrick, *The Life of General Hugh Mercer* (New York: Neale, 1906); Heitman, 389.

Meredith, Samuel
   1. Heitman, 389.

Mifflin, Thomas
   1. Robert K. Wright, Jr. and Morris J. MacGregor, Jr., *Soldier Statesmen of the Constitution* (Washington, DC: Government Printing Office, 1987), 109–111.
   2. Heitman, 391.
   3. Judson, 457.
   4. Wright and MacGregor, 109–111.

Miles, Samuel
   1. *American Historical Record*, vol. 2, 1873, 49.
   2. Ibid.; Heitman, 391.
   3. *American Historical Record*, 49.

Miller, Nathan
   1. *Biographical Dictionary of the American Congress, 1774–1949* (Washington, DC: Government Printing Office, 1950); Heitman, 386.

Montgomery, Richard
   1. Michael P. Gabriel, *Major General Richard Montgomery: The Making of an American Hero* (Madison, NJ: Farleigh Dickinson University Press, 2002), 18–21.
   2. Judson, 458; Headley, 82.
   3. Heitman, 397.
   4. Judson, 458.

Moore, Andrew
   1. Heitman, 398.

Moore, James
   1. Heitman, 399.

Morgan, Daniel
   1. Headley, 252–255.
   2. Heitman, 401.
   3. *U.S. Legacies Magazine*, July 2004.

Morris, Lewis
   1. Goodrich, 193–196.
   2. Heitman, 403.
   3. Goodrich, 195–197.

Moultrie, William
   1. Headley, 51–53; Heitman, 406.
   2. Headley, 53–54.

Muhlenberg, John Peter Gabriel
   1. E.W. Hocker, *The Fighting Parson of the American Revolution* (Philadelphia: self-published, 1936), 1–27.
   2. Wright, 288; Heitman, 406.
   3. Hocker, 150–200.

Nash, Francis
1. Heitman, 409.

Neilson, John
1. Heitman, 410.

Nelson, Thomas, Jr.
1. Goodrich, 410–415.

Neuville, Chevalier de la
1. Heitman, 411.

Neville, John
1. Wright, 290–291; Heitman, 412.

Newcomb, Silas
1. Wright, 255; Heitman, 412.

Nicola, Lewis
1. Howard R. Marraro, "Unpublished Letters of Colonel Nicola, Revolutionary Soldier," *Pennsylvania History Magazine* 13 (October 1946): 274.
2. Carl Bridenbaugh and Jessica Bridenbaugh, *Rebels and Gentlemen: Philadelphia in the Age of Franklin* (New York: Greenwood Press, 1978), 91; *Pennsylvania Magazine of History and Biography* 42: 126, 213–214.
3. Fred A. Berg, *Encyclopedia of Continental Army Units* (Mechanicsburg, PA: Stackpole Books, 1972), 55.
4. Letter from Lewis Nicola to George Washington, May 22, 1782, George Washington Papers, manuscript collection, Library of Congress, Washington, DC.

Nightingale, Joseph
1. John Russell Bartlett, *Records of the Colony of Rhode Island and Providence Plantations in New England*, vol. 8 (Providence, RI: Knowles, Anthony, 1862), December 10, 1776.

Nixon, John
1. Alfred Sereno Hudson, *The History of Sudbury, Massachusetts, 1638–1889* (Sudbury, MA: n.p., 1889); Heitman, 414.
2. Laura Scott, *Sudbury: A Pictorial History* (Norfolk, VA: Donning, 1989); Heitman, 414.

Ogden, Mathias
1. William Ogden Wheeler, *Ogden Family in America (Elizabethtown Branch) & Their English Ancestor John Ogden, the Pilgrim & His Descendants* (Philadelphia: Quintin, 1907), 132–135.
2. Wheeler, 133–135; Heitman, 415.
3. Wheeler, 134–135.

O'Hara, James
1. Jordan; Heitman, 418.

Orne, Azor
1. Thomas Amory Lee, *The Ornes of Marblehead*, Essex Institute, Historical Collections, vol. 60, Salem, MA, 1924; *Marblehead Messenger*, July 29, 1876, and September 8, 1882.

Palmer, Joseph
1. Allen John and Malone Dumas, *Dictionary of American Biography* (New York: Charles Scribner's Sons, 1930); Heitman, 424.

Parsons, Samuel Holden
1. Charles S. Hall, *Life and Letters of General Samuel Holden Parsons* (Binghamton, NY: Otsiningo, 1905); Heitman, 425.

Patterson, John
1. *Massachusetts Soldiers and Sailors in the Revolutionary War*, vol. 11, 1025; Wright, 212–213; Heitman, 429.

Patterson, Samuel
1. Wright, 273; Heitman, 429.

Pickens, Andrew
1. Heitman, 440.

Pinckney, Charles Cotesworth
1. Wright and MacGregor, 118–119.
2. Heitman, 442.
3. Wright and MacGregor, 119–120.

Polk, Thomas
1. Wright, 301; Heitman, 444.

Pomeroy, Seth
1. Louis DeForest, *The Journals and Papers of Seth Pomeroy* (New Haven, CT: Society of Colonial Wars in the State of New York, 1926), pub. no. 38; Heitman, 445.

Poor, Enoch
1. Charles William Heathcote, "General Enoch Poor," *The Picket Post*, May 1957; Wright, 16, 51; Heitman, 446.

Potter, James
1. Heitman, 449.

Prescott, Oliver
1. *Massachusetts Soldiers and Sailors in the Revolutionary War*, vol. 12, 752; Heitman, 451–452.

Preudhomme de Borre, Philippe Hubert
1. Heitman, 191.

Pulaski, Casimir
1. Dorothy Adams, *Cavalry Hero: Casimir Pulaski* (New York: P.J. Kennedy & Sons, 1957), 9; R.D. Jamro, *Pulaski: A Portrait of Freedom* (Savannah, GA: Printcraft Press, 1979), 11.
2. Jamro, 12–15.
3. Adams, 80–86.
4. Jamro, 10; Heitman, 454.
5. Adams, 117–122.
6. Ibid, 135–138, 148–151.
7. Ibid, 177–183.

Putnam, Israel
1. Headley, 64–72.
2. Headley, 73–74; Heitman, 455.
3. Headley, 75–80.

Putnam, Rufus
1. Wilson, Fiske, Klos; Heitman, 455.

Reed, James
1. *Massachusetts Soldiers and Sailors in the Revolutionary War*, vol. 13, 69–70
2. Wright, 199; Heitman, 461.

Reed, Joseph
1. Marshall, 141–142; Heitman, 461.

Richardson, Richard
1. Heitman, 466.

Roberdeau, Daniel
1. Roberdeau Buchanon, *Genealogy of the Roberdeau Family, Including a Biography of Daniel Roberdeau* (Washington, DC: Joseph L. Pearson, 1876), 43–58.
2. Ibid, 80–99.

Rodney, Caesar
1. Goodrich, 313–315; Heitman, 472.

Rutherford, Griffith
1. *The Salisbury Post*, December 3, 2002.
2. Minnie R.H. Long, *General Griffith Rutherford and Allied Families* (Milwaukee: Wisconsin Cueno Press, 1942); *Knoxville Gazette*, September 6, 1794; Heitman, 478.

Safford, Joseph
1. *Vermont Historical Magazine*, vol. II, 389; Heitman, 479.

Safford, Samuel
1. Ullery; Hiland Hall, *History of Vermont* (Albany, NY: Joel Munsell, 1868), 468; Wright, 320; Heitman, 479–480.

St. Clair, Arthur
1. Headley, 137–152.

Saltonstall, Gurdon
1. Albert C. Bates, *Rolls of Connecticut Men in the French and Indian War, 1755–1762*, vol. 1 (Hartford: Connecticut Historical Society, 1903); Heitman, 480.

Schuyler, Philip John
1. Martin H. Bush, *Revolutionary Enigma: A Re-appraisal of General Philip Schuyler of New York* (Port Washington, NY: Ira J. Friedman, 1969), 5–16.
2. Heitman, 485
3. Judson, 471.
4. Bush, 154
5. Heitman, 485.

Scott, John Morin
1. Dorothy Rita Dillon, *The New York Triumverate: A Study of the Legal and Political Careers of William Livingston, John Morin Scott, William Smith, Jr.* (New York: AMS Press, 1949); Heitman, 456.

Shelby, Evan, Jr.
1. Heitman, 492.

Sheldon, Elisha
1. Heitman, 493.

Silliman, Gold Selleck
1. Heitman, 497.
2. Elizabeth Schenck, *History of Fairfield County, Connecticut* (New York: self-published, 1889), 378, 406, 458; Charles J. Hoadly, *Public Records of the Colony of Connecticut*, vol. 14 (Hartford, CT: Lockwood & Brainard, 1890), 221, 331; Charles J. Hoadly, *Public Records of the State of Connecticut* (Hartford, CT: Connecticut State Library, 1895), vol. 1, 134; vol. 2, 466, 503.

Smallwood, William
1. Heitman, 500–501.
2. Wright, 112.

Spencer, Joseph
1. *Biographical Dictionary of the American Congress*, 1847.

Stanton, Joseph, III
1. William A. Stanton, *A Record, Genealogical, Biographical, Statistical, of Thomas Stanton of Connecticut, and his Descendants 1635–1891* (Albany, NY: Joel Munsell's Sons, 1891); Heitman, 514.

Stark, John
1. Headley, 125–130.
2. Ibid., 130–139; Heitman, 515.

Stephen, Adam
1. Harry M. Ward, *Major General Adam Stephen and the Cause of American Liberty* (Charlottesville: University Press of Virginia, 1989), 1–5.
2. Heitman, 517.
3. Ward, *Major General Adam Stephen*, 142–143.

Stevens, Edward
1. Wright, 289; Yorktown Briefs; Heitman, 519.

Sullivan, John
1. Thomas C. Amory, *The Military Services and Public Life of Major-General John Sullivan of the American Revolutionary Army* (Washington, NY: Kennikat Press, 1968), 8; Arch Merrill, *Pioneer Profiles* (New York: American Book-Stratford Press, 1957), 6.
2. Amory, 9–11
3. Merrill, 9; Heitman, 527.
4. Merrill, 9–10; Heitman, 527
5. Merrill, 11–16.

Sumner, Jethro
1. Wright, 300; Heitman, 527.

Sumter, Thomas
1. Cecil B. Hartley, *Life of General Thomas Sumter of South Carolina* (New York: Derby & Jackson, 1859), 313–314; Heitman, 528.

Swartwout, Jacobus
1. Heitman, 529.

Swift, Heman
1. H. Hull, *Ancestral Record of Mary Eldridge Swift* (New York: American Historical Co., 1945); Heitman, 530.

Ten Broeck, Abraham
1. Howard Kendall Sanderson, *Lynn in the Revolution* (Boston: W.B. Clarke, 1909); Heitman, 536.

Ten Broeck, Petrus
1. Heitman, 536.

Thomas, John
1. *Massachusetts Soldiers and Sailors in the Revolutionary War*, vol. 15, 598; Heitman, 538–539.

Thompson, William
1. Charles William Heathcote, "General William Thompson," *The Picket Post*, February 1961.

Tupper, Benjamin
1. Heitman, 551.

Twiggs, John
1. Heitman, 553.

Tyler, John
1. William Tyler Bringham, *The Descendants of Job Tyler, of Andover, Massachusetts, 1619 to 1700* (Plainfield, NJ: Cornelius B. Tyler; Connecticut: Rollin C. Tyler; n.d.), 95; Heitman, 553.

Van Cortlandt, Philip
1. Pierre C. Van Wyck, "Autobiography of Philip Van Cortlandt," *The Magazine of American History With Notes and Queries*, vol. II, pt. 1 (New York: A.S. Barnes, 1878), 278–283; Heitman, 555.
2. Van Wyck, 284–298.

Van Rensselaer, Robert
1. Cuyler Reynolds, *Hudson-Mohawk Valley Genealogical and Family Memoirs* (New York: Lewis Historical Publishing Company, 1911); Heitman, 557.

Van Schaick, Gosen "Goose"
1. T.W. Egly, *Goose Van Schaick of Albany 1736–1789: The Continental Army's Senior Colonel* (Albany, NY: self-published, 1992); Heitman, 557.

Varnum, James
1. Heitman, 559; Wright, 227.

Von Steuben, Friedrich Wilhelm Augustus
1. Judson, 472; Headley, 191–205; Heitman, 518.

Vose, Joseph
1. *Massachusetts Soldiers and Sailors in the Revolutionary War*, vol. 16, 359; Wright, 203–204; Heitman, 561.

Wadsworth, James
1. Heitman, 562.

Wadsworth, Peleg
1. Richard Henry Dana, Address on General Peleg Wadsworth, February 27, 1908 (Cambridge, MA: n.p., 1908); Heitman, 563.

Ward, Andrew
1. Wright, 240; Heitman, 567.

Ward, Artemas
1. Charles Martyn, *The Life of Artemas Ward; The First Commander-in-Chief of the American Revolution* (Port Washington, NY: Kennikat Press, 1970); Heitman, 567.

Warren, Joseph
1. Leonard Everett Fisher, *Picture Book of Revolutionary War Heroes* (Harrisburg, PA: Stackpole Books, 1970), 24; Heitman, 570.

Warner, Jonathan
1. Heitman, 569.

Washington, George
1. Headley, 1–54 and Dupuy, Johnson, and Bongard, 785–786; Heitman, 571–573.

Waterbury, David
1. Elijah B. Huntington, *History of Stamford, Connecticut From Its Settlement in 1641, to the Present Time, Including Darien, Which Was One of the Parishes Until 1820* (Stamford, CT: self-published), 1868; Heitman, 574.

Wayne, Anthony
1. Headley, 206–207, Thomas Boyd, *Mad Anthony Wayne* (New York: Charles Scribner's Sons, 1929), 5; Heitman, 577.
2. Heitman, 577.
3. Headley, 206.
4. Ibid., 209–216.
5. Judson, 384; Heitman, 577.
6. Judson, 385–386
7. Boyd, 338; Judson, 386.

Webb, Samuel Blachley
1. Rossiter Johnson, *The Twentieth Century Biographical Dictionary of Notable Americans*, vol. 10 (Detroit: Gale Research, 1968), 211; Heitman, 578.
2. R. Johnson, 211.

Weedon, George
1. Heitman, 579.

West, William
1. C.C. Beaman, *An Historical Sketch of the Town of Scituate, Rhode Island* (n.p.: Steam Book and Job Printers, 1877), 3; Heitman, 582.

Whipple, William
1. Goodrich, 139–143.

Whitcomb, John
1. Heitman, 585.

Wilkinson, James
1. Daniel Clark, *Proofs of the Corruption of Gen. James Wilkinson and of His Connexion With Aaron Burr* (Philadelphia: Wm. Hall, Jun. & Geo. Piere, Printers, 1809), 3–20; Alton James, *The Life of George Rogers Clark* (Chicago: University of Illinois Press, 1928), 374; Temple Bodely, *George Rogers Clark: His Life and Public Services* (Boston: Houghton Mifflin, 1926), 259; Heitman, 592.

Williams, Otho Holland
1. Osmond C. Tiffany, "Sketch of the Life and Services of General Otho Holland Williams," *Maryland Historical Society Pre-Fund Publication*, vol. 1, no. 12 (Baltimore: Maryland Historical Society, 1851); Heitman, 596.
2. Wright, 280.

Williamson, Andrew
1. Heitman, 597.

Williamson, Matthias, Sr.
1. Heitman, 597.

Wilson, James

1. Charles Page Smith, *James Wilson: Founding Father, 1742–1798* (Chapel Hill: University of North Carolina Press, 1956); Heitman, 598.

Winds, William

1. Heitman, 600.

Wolcott, Erastus

1. Henry R. Stiles, *The History of Ancient Windsor, Connecticut, Including East Windsor, South Windsor, Bloomfield, Windsor Locks, and Ellington, 1635–1891* vol. 2 (Sommersworth: New Hampshire Publishing Co., 1892), 811–812; George Mackenzie, *Colonial Families of the United States of America, In Which is Given the History, Genealogy, and Armorial Bearings of the Colonial Families*, vol. 6 (Baltimore: Seaforth Press, 1912), 500; Heitman, 602.

Wolcott, Oliver

1. Goodrich, 179–182; Heitman, 602.

Woodford, William

1. Heitman, 604.

Woodhull, Nathaniel

1. George DeWan, "A Hero's Last Words," *New York Newsday*, January 9, 1998, 19.

Wooster, David

1. James Herring, and James B. Longacre, *National Portrait Gallery of Distinguished Americans*, vol. 2 (New York: Monson Bancroft, 1835); Judson, 476; Headley, 223; Heitman, 606.
2. Headley, 223–224.

Bibliography

Books and Booklets

Adams, Dorothy. *Cavalry Hero: Casimir Pulaski.* New York: P.J. Kennedy & Sons, 1957.

Alden, John Richard. *General Charles Lee: Traitor or Patriot?* Baton Rouge: Louisiana State University Press, 1951.

Amory, Thomas C. *The Military Services and Public Life of Major-General John Sullivan of the American Revolutionary Army.* Port Washington, NY: Kennikat Press, 1968.

Arnold, Noah J. *The Narragansett Historical Register*, vol. V8, no. 2. Hamilton, RI: Narragansett Historical Publishing Co., 1890.

Babcock Papers, Babcock House, Westerly, Rhode Island.

Bailey, Hollis R. *Bailey Genealogy, James, John & Thomas & Their Descendants.* Somerville, MA: Citizen, 1899.

Bakeless, John. *Backroad to Glory: The Life of George Rogers Clark.* Philadelphia: J.B. Lippincott, 1957.

Baker, Henry M. *General Nathaniel Folsom: An Address Delivered April 8, 1903 Before the New Hampshire Historical Society.* Concord, NH: n.p., 1904.

Barrows, William. *Fryeburg: An Historical Sketch.* Fryeburg, ME: Pequawket Press, 1938.

Bartlett, John Russell. *Records of the Colony of Rhode Island and Providence Plantations in New England*, vol. 8. Providence, RI: Knowles, Anthony, 1862.

Bates, Albert C. *Rolls of Connecticut Men in the French and Indian War, 1755–1762.* Hartford: Connecticut Historical Society, 1903.

Bayles, Richard M. *History of Providence County.* New York: W.W. Preston, 1891.

Beach, Joseph P. *History of Cheshire, Connecticut from 1694 to 1840, Including Prospect, Which, as Columbia Parish, was a part of Cheshire until 1829.* Cheshire, CT: Lady Fenwick Chapter, D.A.R., 1877.

Beaman, C.C. *An Historical Sketch of the Town of Scituate, Rhode Island.* N.p.: Steam Book and Job Printers, 1877.

Berg, Fred A. *Encyclopedia of Continental Army Units.* Harrisburg, PA: Stackpole Books, 1972.

Billias, George Athan. *General John Glover and His Marblehead Mariners.* New York: Holt, Rinehard & Winston, 1960.

———. *George Washington's Generals and Opponents: Their Exploits and Leadership.* New York: Da Capo Press, 1994.

Biographical Catalogue of the Matriculates of the College 1749–1893 (University of Pennsylvania). Philadelphia: Avil, 1894.

Biographical Dictionary of the American Congress, 1774–1949. Washington, DC: Government Printing Office, 1950.

Blanco, R., *The American Revolution 1775–1783: An Encyclopedia.* New York: Garland, 1993.

Boatner, Mark M. *Encyclopedia of the American Revolution.* Harrisburg, PA: Stackpole Books, 1994.

Bodley, Temple. *George Rogers Clark: His Life and Public Services.* Boston: Houghton Mifflin, 1926.

Boyd, Thomas. *Mad Anthony Wayne.* New York: Charles Scribner's Sons, 1929.

Brady, Cyrus Townsend. *Revolutionary Fights and Fighters.* New York: Doubleday, Page, 1923.

Bridenbaugh, Carl, and Jessica Bridenbaugh. *Rebels and Gentlemen: Philadelphia in the Age of Franklin.* New York: Greenwood Press, 1978.

Brigham, William Tyler. *The Descendants of Job Tyler, of Andover, Massachusetts, 1619–1700.* Plainfield, NJ: Cornelius B. Tyler / Connecticut: Rollin Tyler.

Buchanan, Roberdeau. *Genealogy of the Roberdeau Family, Including a Biography of General Daniel Roberdeau of the Revolutionary Army, and the Continental Congress, and Signer of the Articles of Confederation.* Sinking Valley, PA: Fort Roberdeau Association, 1986.

Bush, Martin H. *Revolutionary Enigma: A Reappraisal of General Philip Schuyler of New York.* Port Washington, NY: Ira J. Friedman, 1969.

Caulkins, F.M. *History of Norwich, From its Possession by Indians to 1866.* Norwich, CT: self-published, 1866.

Champagne, R. *Alexander McDougall and the American Revolution in New York.* Schenectady, NY:

New York State American Revolution Bicentennial Commission, 1975.
Clark, Daniel. *Proofs of the Corruption of Gen. James Wilkinson and of His Connexion with Aaron Burr with a Full Refutation of His Slanderous Allegations in Relation to the Character of the Principal Witness Against Him.* Philadelphia: Wm. Hall, Jun. & Geo. W. Piere, Printers, 1809.
Commager, Henry Steele, and Morris, Richard B. *The Spirit of 'Seventy-Six: The Story of the American Revolution as Told by Participants.* New York: Harper & Row, 1967.
Cowell, Benjamin. *Spirit of '76 in Rhode Island.* Baltimore: Genealogical Publishing Company, 1973.
Cunliffe, Marcus. *George Washington: Man & Monument.* Boston: Little, Brown, 1958.
Cushing, James. *The Genealogy of the Cushing Family (An Account of the Ancestors and Descendants of Matthew Cushing Who Came to America in 1638).* Montreal: Perrault, 1905.
Dana, Richard Henry. *Address on General Peleg Wadsworth, February 27, 1908.* Cambridge, MA: n.p., 1908.
DeForest, Louis. *The Journals and Papers of Seth Pomeroy.* New Haven, CT: Society of Colonial Wars in the State of New York, 1926.
De Hass, Willis. *History of the Early Settlement and Indian Wars of Western Virginia; Embracing an Account of the Various Expeditions in the West, Previous to 1795.* Wheeling and Philadelphia: H. Hoblitzell, 1851.
Delaplaine, Edward. *The Life of Thomas Johnson.* New York: F.H. Hitchcock, 1927.
Dexter, Franklin Bowditch. *Biographical Sketches of the Graduates of Yale College*, vol. 1. New York: Henry Holt, 1885.
The Dictionary of American Biography. New York: Charles Scribner's Sons, 1964
Diller, Theodore. *Pioneer Medicine in Western Pennsylvania.* New York: Paul B. Hoeber, 1937.
Dillon, Dorothy Rita. *The New York Triumverate: A Study of the Legal and Political Careers of William Livingston, John Morin Scott, William Smith, Jr.* New York: AMS Press, 1949.
Dupuy, Trevor N., Curt Johnson, and David L. Bongard. *The Harper Encyclopedia of Military Biography.* New York: HarperCollins, 1992.
Edgar, Walter, and N. Louise Bailey. *Biographical Dictionary of the South Carolina House of Representatives, 1692–1775*, vol. 5. Columbia: University of South Carolina Press, 1974.
Egly, T.W. *Goose Van Schaick of Albany, 1736–1789: The Continental Army's Senior Colonel.* Albany, NY: self-published, 1992.
Emerson, Robert L. *Fort Roberdeau: The Garrison and Military Life, 1778–1780.* Sinking Valley, PA: Fort Roberdeau Association, 2003.
Evans, Lawton. *First Lessons in Georgia History.* New York: American Book, 1913.
Felder, Paula. *Fielding Lewis and the Washington Family: A Chronicle of 18th Century Fredericksburg.* Fredericksburg, VA: American History Company, 1999.
Fisher, Leonard Everett. *Picture Book of Revolutionary War Heroes.* Harrisburg, PA: Stackpole Books, 1970.
Flexner, James T. *George Washington: A Biography*, 4 vols. Boston: Little, Brown, 1965–1972.
Freeman, Douglas Southall. *George Washington: A Biography*, 7 vols. New York: Charles Scribner's Sons, 1948–57.
Gabriel, Michael P. *Major General Richard Montgomery: The Making of an American Hero.* Madison, WI: Farleigh Dickinson University Press, 2002.
Garraty, John A., and Mark C. Carnes. *American National Biography.* New York: Oxford University Press, 1999.
Genealogical and Family History of the State of New Hampshire. Chicago: Ezra S. Lewis, 1908.
Gerlach, Larry R. *New Jersey in the American Revolution, 1763–1783: A Documentary History.* Trenton: New Jersey Historical Commission, 1975.
Goodrich, Charles A. *Lives of the Signers of the Declaration of Independence.* New York: William Reed, 1856.
Goolrick, John T. *The Life of General Hugh Mercer.* New York: Neale, 1906.
Gottschalk, Louis. *Lafayette Between the American and French Revolution.* Chicago: University of Chicago Press, 1950.
Green, Samuel A. *Epitaphs from the Old Burial Ground, Groton, Middlesex, Massachusetts.* Boston: Little, Brown, 1878.
Green, Thomas Marshall. *Historical Families of Kentucky.* Cincinnati: Clearfield, 1889.
Gregg, Alexander. *History of Old Cheraws.* N.p.: Boyd, 1867.
Griffiths, Thomas Morgan. *Major General Henry Knox and the Last Heirs to Montpelier.* Monmouth, ME: Monmouth Press, 1965.
Grizzard, Frank E. *The Papers of George Washington: Revolutionary War Series*, vol. 10, June–August 1777. Charlottesville: University Press of Virginia, 2000.
Guthrie, Alice Baker. *History of Shiloh Presbyterian Church 1793–1847.* Gallatin, TN: n.p., 1938.
Hadley, George Plummer. *History of the Town of Goffstown 1733–1920*, vol. 1. Concord, NH: Rumford Press, 1922.
Hall, Charles S. *Hall Ancestry.* New York: G.P. Putnam's Sons, 1896.
_____. *Life and Letters of General Samuel Holden Parsons.* Binghamton, NY: Otsiningo, 1905.
Hall, Hiland. *History of Vermont.* Albany, NY: Joel Munsell, 1868.
Hall-Quest, Olga. *From Colony to Nation: With Washington and His Army in the War for Independence.* New York: E.P. Dutton, 1967.

Hanko, Charles William. *The Life of John Gibson: Soldier, Patriot, Statesman.* Daytona Beach, FL: College, 1955.

Hartley, Cecil B. *Life of General Thomas Sumter of South Carolina.* New York: Derby & Jackson, 1859.

Hatcher, Patricia Law. *Abstract of Revolutionary Patriots*, vol. 2. Dallas: Pioneer Heritage Press, 1987.

Hawes, Lilla Mills. *Lachlan McIntosh Papers in the University of Georgia Libraries.* Athens: University of Georgia Press, 1968.

Headley, J.T. *Washington and His Generals*, 2 vols. New York: Hurst, 1847.

Heitman, Francis B. *Historical Register of Officers of the Continental Army During the War of the Revolution.* Reprint. Baltimore: Genealogical Publishing Company, 1973.

Herring, James, and James B. Longacre. *National Portrait Gallery of Distinguished Americans*, vol. 2. New York: Monson Bancroft, 1835.

Higginbotham, Don. *Daniel Morgan.* Chapel Hill: University of North Carolina Press, 1961.

Hill, Valeria E. Clymer. *A Genealogy of The Hiester Family.* Reading, PA: Reading Eagle Press, 1941.

History of Walden, Vermont. Written by the History Committee, Walden, VT, Public Library. Randolph Center, VT: Greenhills Books: 1986.

Hoadly, Charles J. *Public Records of the Colony of Connecticut.* Hartford, CT: Lockwood & Brainard, 1890.

_____. *Public Records of the State of Connecticut.* Hartford: Connecticut State Library, 1895.

Hocker, E.W. *The Fighting Parson of the American Revolution.* Philadelphia: self-published, 1936.

Hoenstine, Floyd G. *Military Services and Genealogical Records of Soldiers of Blair County, Pennsylvania.* Hollidaysburg, PA: Blair County Historical Society, 1940.

Hudson, Alfred Sereno. *The History of Sudbury, Massachusetts, 1638–1889.* Sudbury, MA: n.p., 1889.

Hull, H. *Ancestral Record of Mary Eldridge Swift.* New York: American Historical, 1945.

Huntington, Elijah B. *History of Stamford, Connecticut, From Its Settlement in 1641, to the Present Time, Including Darien, Which Was One of the Parishes Until 1820.* Stamford, CT: self-published, 1868.

The Huntington Family in America: A Genealogical Memoir of the Known Descendants of Simon Huntington from 1633 to 1915, Including Those Who Have Retained the Family Name, and Many Bearing Other Surnames. Hartford, CT: Huntington Family Association, 1915.

Jackson, Harvey H. *Lachlan McIntosh and the Politics of Revolutionary Georgia.* Athens: University of Georgia Press, 1979.

Jacob, Kathryn Allamong, and Bruce A. Ragsdale. *Biographical Dictionary of the United States Congress, 1774–1989.* Washington, DC: Government Printing Office, 1989.

James, Alton James. *The Life of George Rogers Clark.* Chicago: University of Illinois Press, 1928.

Jamro, R.D. *Pulaski: A Portrait of Freedom.* Savannah, GA: Printcraft Press, 1979.

Johnson, Allen, and Dumas Malone. *Dictionary of American Biography.* New York: Charles Scribner's Sons, 1930.

Johnson, Rossiter. *The Twentieth Century Biographical Dictionary of Notable Americans*, vol. 10. Detroit: Gale Research, 1968.

Jones, Charles C. *The Life and Services of the Honorable Maj. Gen. Samuel Elbert of Georgia.* New York: W. Abbatt, 1911.

Jordan, John W. *Colonial and Revolutionary Families of Pennsylvania*, 3 vols. New York: Lewis. 1911.

Judson, L. Carroll. *The Sages and Heroes of the American Revolution In Two Parts Including the Signers of the Declaration of Independence, Two Hundred and Forty Three of the Sages and Heroes Are Presented in Due Form.* Boston: Lee and Shepard, 1851.

Kochan, James L. *Joseph Frye's Journal and Map of the Siege of Fort William Henry, 1757.* The Bulletin of the Fort Ticonderoga Museum, n.d.

Lacey, Garland Howard. *Ancestors and Descendants of Hiram G. Lacey and Sophia Sell.* Henry, IL: M&D Printing, 1995.

Lancaster, Bruce. *The American Revolution.* New York: American Heritage Books, 1971.

Langguth, A.J. *Patriots: The Men Who Started the American Revolution.* New York: Simon and Schuster, 1988.

Leamon, James S. *Revolution Downeast.* Amherst: University of Massachusetts Press, 1993.

Lee, Thomas Amory. *The Ornes of Marblehead.* Essex Institute, Historical Collections, vol. 60. Salem, MA, 1924.

Linn, John Blair. *History of Centre and Clinton Counties, Pennsylvania.* Philadelphia: Louis B. Everts, 1883.

Long, Minnie R.H. *General Griffith Rutherford and Allied Families.* Milwaukee: Wisconsin Cueno Press, 1942.

Lossing, Benson J. *Our Country: A Household History For All Readers From the Discovery of America to the Present Time*, vol. 2. New York: Henry J. Johnson, 1877.

_____. *Seventeen Hundred and Seventy-Six or the War of Independence: A History of the Anglo Americans.* New York: Edward Walker, 1852.

Lyttle, Eugene W. "Nicholas Herkimer" in Proceedings of the New York State Historical Association. Albany, NY: n.p., 1904.

Mackenzie, George. *Colonial Families of the United States of America, In Which is Given the History, Genealogy, and Armorial Bearings of the Colonial Families.* Baltimore: Seaforth Press, 1912.

Marshall, James V. *The United States Manual of Biography and History.* Philadelphia: James B. Smith, 1856.

Martyn, Charles. *The Life of Artemas Ward: The First Commander-in-Chief of the American Revolution*. Port Washington, NY: Kennikat Press, 1970.

Massachusetts Soldiers and Sailors in the Revolutionary War, 17 vols. Boston: Wright & Potter, 1896–1908.

Mattern, David B. *Benjamin Lincoln and the American Revolution*. Columbia: University of South Carolina Press, 1995.

McAllister, J.T. *Virginia Militia in the Revolutionary War*. Hot Springs, VA: McAllister, 1913.

McDougall, William L. *American Revolutionary: A Biography of General Alexander McDougall*. Westport, CT: Greenwood Press, 1977.

McDowell, Bart. *The Revolutionary War*. Washington, DC: National Geographic Society, 1967.

Mead, Spencer P. *Abstract of Probate Records for the District of Stamford, County of Fairfield, 1729–1848*. Salem, MA: Higginson, 1997.

Merrill, Arch. *Pioneer Profiles*. New York: Stratford Press, 1957.

Moody, Sid. *'76: The World Turned Upside Down*. New York: The Associated Press, 1975.

Morris, Charles, and Leigh, Oliver H.G. *The Great Republic by the Master Historians*, vol. 2. New York: R.S. Belcher, 1902.

New York in the Revolution as Colony and State: A Compilation of Documents and Records From the Office of the State Comptroller, 2 vols. Albany, NY: J.B. Lyon, 1904.

NH: Years of Revolution. Providence: Profiles Publications and the NH Bicentennial Commission, 1976.

Packard, Aibigne Lermond. *A Town That Went to Sea*. Portland, ME: Falmouth, 1950.

Phillips, Leon. *The Fantastic Breed: Americans in King George's War*. New York: Doubleday, 1964.

Posey, John Thornton. *General Thomas Posey: Son of the American Revolution*. East Lansing: Michigan State University Press, 1992.

Powell, William S. *Dictionary of North Carolina Biography*. Chapel Hill: University of North Carolina Press, 1988.

Putnam, Eben. *The Holden Genealogy*. Boston: Quintin, 1923.

Reynolds, Cuyler. *Hudson-Mohawk Genealogical and Family Memoirs*. New York: Lewis Historical Publishing, 1911.

Roads, Samuel, Jr. *The History and Traditions of Marblehead*. Marblehead, MA: N. Allen Lindsey, 1897.

Sanderson, Howard Kendall. *Lynn in the Revolution*. Boston: W.B. Clarke, 1909.

Schenck, Elizabeth. *History of Fairfield County, Connecticut*. New York: self-published, 1889.

Scott, Laura. *Sudbury: A Pictorial History*. Norfolk, VA: Donning, 1989.

Sedgwick, Henry Dwight. *LaFayette*. Chautauqua, NY: Chautauqua Press, 1928.

Shelley, Mary Virginia. *The Story of General Edward Hand*. Lititz, PA: Sutter House, 1978.

Sherwood, Adiel. *A Gazetteer of the State of Georgia*. Washington City, GA: P. Force, 1837.

Shipton, Clifford K. *Harvard Graduates: Biographical Sketches of Those Who Attended Harvard College*. Cambridge, MA: Harvard University Press, 1968.

Shomette, Donald G. *Pirates on the Chesapeake: A True History of Pirates, Picaroons and Raiders on the Chesapeake Bay 1610–1807*. Centreville, ME: Tidewater, 1985.

Smith, Charles Page. *James Wilson: Founding Father, 1742–1798*. Chapel Hill: University of North Carolina Press, 1956.

Smith, Joseph Jenckes. *Civil and Military List of Rhode Island, 1647–1800*. Providence, RI: Preston & Rounds, 1900.

Smith, Robert Walker. *History of Armstrong County, Pennsylvania*. Chicago: Waterman, Watkins, 1883.

Stanton, William A. *A Record, Genealogical, Biographical, Statistical, of Thomas Stanton of Connecticut, and his Descendents 1635–1891*. Albany, NY: Joel Munsell's Sons, 1891.

Steele, Ian. *Betrayals: Fort William Henry and the Massacre*. New York: Oxford University Press, 1990.

Stiles, Henry R. *The History of Ancient Windsor, Connecticut, Including East Windsor, South Windsor, Bloomfield, Windsor Locks, and Ellington, 1635–1891*. Sommersworth: New Hampshire Publishing, 1892.

Stryker, William S. *Official Register of the Officers and Men of New Jersey in the Revolutionary War*. Trenton, NJ: William T. Nicholson, 1872.

Temple, J.H. *History of North Brookfield, Massachusetts*. Published by the town of North Brookfield, 1887.

Tiffany, Osmond C. *Sketch of the Life and Services of General Otho Holland Williams, Maryland Historical Society Pre-Fund Publication*, vol. 1, no. 12 Baltimore: Maryland Historical Society, 1851.

Trussell, John B. *The Pennsylvania Line: Regimental Organization and Operations, 1775–1783*. Harrisburg: Pennsylvania Historical Museum Commission, 1993.

Tuchman, Barbara W. *The First Salute: A View of the American Revolution*. New York: Alfred A. Knopf, 1988.

Ullery, Jacob G., *Men of Vermont: An Illustrated Biographical History of Vermonters and Sons of Vermont*. Brattleboro, VT: Transcript, 1894.

Unger, Harlow G. *John Hancock: Merchant King and American Patriot*. New York: John Wiley & Sons, 2000.

Van Doren, Carl. *Secret History of the American Revolution*, New York: Garden City Press, 1941.

Villaneuva, Marcel. *The French Contribution to the Founding of the United States*. New York: Vantage Press, 1975.

Vital Records of Roxbury, Massachusetts to the end of the year 1849. Salem, MA: Essex Institute, 1925.

Walker, Anthony. *So Few the Brave*. Newport, RI: Seafield Press, 1981.

Ward, Harry M. *General William Maxwell and the New Jersey Continentals*. Westport, CT: Greenwood Press, 1997.

Wells, Frederic P. *History of Newbury, Vermont 1794–1902*. Johnsbury, VT: Caledonian, 1902.

Wheeler, William Ogden. *Ogden Family in America (Elizabethtown Branch) & Their English Ancestor John Ogden, the Pilgrim, & His Descendants*. Philadelphia: Quintin, 1907.

White, George. *Historical Collections of Georgia*. New York: Pudney & Russell, 1854.

Who Was Who in America, A Component Volume of Who's Who in American History, Historical Volume, 1607–1896. Chicago: Marquis Who's Who, 1967.

Who Was Who in the American Revolution. New York: Facts on File, 1993.

Wildey, Anna Chesebrough. *Genealogy of the Descendants of William Chesebrough, Founder of Stonington, Connecticut*. New York: Press of T.A. Wright, 1903.

Willingham, William F. *Connecticut Revolutionary: Elephalet Dyer*. Hartford, CT: American Revolution Bicentennial Commission of Connecticut, 1977.

William, William. *The History of Portland*. Somersworth: New Hampshire Publishing, 1972.

Wilson, James Grant, John Fiske, and Stanley I. Klos. *Appleton's Cyclopedia of American Biography*, 6 vols. New York: D. Appleton, 1887–1889.

Wilson, Woodrow T. *Crisfield, Maryland 1676–1976*. Baltimore: Gateway Press, 1977.

———. *Thirty-Four Families of Old Somerset County, Maryland*. Baltimore: Gateway Press, 1974.

Wright, Esmond. *Washington and the American Revolution*, London: English University Press, 1957.

Wright, Robert K., Jr. *The Continental Army*. Washington, DC: Government Printing Office, 1983.

———, and MacGregor, Morris J., Jr. *Soldier Statesmen of the Constitution*. Washington, DC: Government Printing Office, 1987.

Manuscript Collections:

Caswell Papers, North Carolina Archives, Raleigh, NC.

Freeman Papers, Schoff Revolution War Collection, William L. Clements Library, The University of Michigan, Ann Arbor, MI.

George Washington Papers, manuscript collection, Library of Congress, Washington, DC.

Newspapers, Magazines, and Periodicals:

American Historical Record, vol. 2, 1873.
Carroll County Times, November 21, 1993.
Charleston (SC) *Gazette*, May 24, 1772.
The Essex Antiquarian, 1901, vol. 5, no. 6.
Heathcoate, Dr. Charles William. "General Lachlan McIntosh: Loyal American and Friend of Washington," *The Picket Post*, February 1957.
Journal of Southern History, May 1952.
Knoxville Gazette, September 6, 1794.
Magazine of American History, December 1881.
The Magazine of American History, with Notes and Queries, vol. II, pt. I. New York: A.S. Barnes, 1878.
Marblehead Messenger, July 29, 1876, and September 8, 1882.
New York Newsday, January 9, 1998.
Pennsylvania History Magazine 13, October 1946.
Pennsylvania Magazine of History and Biography 2, no. 42.
Potter's American Monthly 7, no. 57, September 1876.
The Picket Post, January 1948, May 1956, February 1957, February 1959, November 1959, February 1961. Published by the Valley Forge Historical Society.
Professional Surveyor Magazine, November-December 1989 and January-February 1990.
The Salisbury Post, December 3, 2002.
U.S. Legacies Magazine, July, 2004.
Vermont Historical Magazine 2.
The Yorktown Herald 25, no. 36, February 3, 1949.

Index

Abbe, Rachel 82
Abercrombie, James 81, 152
Abercromby, Robert 67, 71
Aberdeenshire, Scotland 85
Abingdon, Va. 18
Adams, John 41, 64
Adams, Samuel 104, 105, 148, 149
Alamance, Battle of 18, 92
Albany, N.Y. 6, 8, 9, 30, 42, 43, 52, 71, 78, 124, 125, 137, 138, 142, 143
Albemarle County, Va. 19
Alexander, James 78
Alexander, William 5, 28
Alligator Creek, Battle of 21
Altamaha River 58, 84
Amherst, Jeffrey 81, 90, 110, 115, 138
Andover, Mass. 40, 110
Andre, John 61, 68, 105, 128, 131
Annapolis, Md. 63
Arbor Hill, N.Y. 138
Armand, Tuffin Charles 6
Armstrong, Anne 16
Armstrong, John 6, 7, 61, 85, 138
Armstrong, Rebecca 6
Arnold, Benedict 7, 8, 9, 10, 12, 29, 36, 57, 68, 92, 102, 106, 131, 141, 152, 153, 157, 164
Ashe, John 10, 11
Attleborough, Mass. 23
Augusta Academy 91
Augusta County, Va. 18, 74, 80, 91, 106
Augusta, Ga. 11, 21, 81, 107
Auld, Rosanna 52

Babcock, Joshua 11, 77, 101
Babcock, Thankful 130
Bailey, Jacob 11, 12
Baldwin, Lydia 111
Baltimore, Md. 15, 45, 73, 114
Barnwell, Anne 16
Barnwell, John 12
Barnwell, John "Tuscarora" 12
Barton, Rebecca 89
Battle Hill, Battle of 105
Beall, Alexander 127
Beall, Reazin 12
Beaufort, Battle of 16
Beaufort, S.C. 16
Bedel, Timothy 12, 13

Bedford, Va. 74
Belmont, Pa. 87
Beltsville, Md. 12
Bemis Heights, Battle of 110, 137
Bennington, Vt. 122, 132
Berry, Thankful 102
Biddle, Ann Owen 158
Black Mingo, Battle of 79
Black River 79
Blackman, Mehitable 85
Boston, Mass. 12, 13, 27, 39, 46, 47, 48, 55, 62, 65, 70, 76, 78, 101, 104, 109, 115, 129, 134, 138, 139, 146, 148, 150, 158, 161
Bostwick, Hannah 83
Brandywine, Battle of 5, 6, 17, 24, 34, 28, 40, 48, 65, 68, 70, 82, 87, 97, 108, 111, 119, 128, 133, 134, 151, 153, 163
Briar Creek, Battle of 11, 36
Brickett, James 13
Brighton, Vt. 102
Bristol, Tenn. 127
Broadhead, Daniel 14, 15, 45
Brodhead, Hester Wyngart 14
Brooklyn, Battle of 12, 27, 87, 126
Brooklyn, Conn. 117
Buchanan, Andrew 15
Bull, William 15
Bunker Hill, Battle of 13, 37, 41, 48, 63, 65, 70, 95, 102, 106, 109, 116, 118, 131, 148, 149, 155
Bushnell, David 105
Butler, John 16, 135
Butler, Richard 16
Butterfield, Isaac 12

Cadwalader, John 17, 18, 25
Cadwalader, Margaret 87
Cadwalader, Mary 33
Cadwalader, Rebecca 33
Cahokia, Ill. 20
Calhoun, Rebecca 106
Callender, Anne 62
Cambridge, Mass. 8, 13, 41, 55, 57, 60, 70, 134, 139
Cambridge University 98
Camden, Battle of 6, 30, 33, 44, 45, 49, 50, 93, 133, 140
Campbell, Lachlan 79

Campbell, William 18
Cape Briton Island 90
Cape Cod, Mass. 40
Carleton, Guy 24
Carlisle, Pa. 7, 32, 103, 109, 138, 139, 160
Carnan, Cecil 45
Caroline County, Va. 19
Carskerdo, Scotland 160
Carson, Mary 103
Casswell, Richard 18, 19
Castleton, Vt. 124
Catawba River 28
Cathcart, Elizabeth 111
Catherine the Great 112
Cedars, Battle of 12
Centre County, Pa. 29
Chadd's Ford, Battle of 153
Chalmers, Elizabeth 59
Chamberlain, James 19
Chambers, Mary Patterson 111
Chambersburg, Pa. 81
Chandler, Jimima 82
Charles County, Md. 32
Charleston, Battle of 12, 30, 55, 67, 99, 114, 163
Charleston, R.I. 130
Charleston, S.C. 7, 16, 35, 46, 49, 57, 77, 79, 84, 94, 96, 97, 107, 108, 109, 119, 136
Charllier, Amelia 50
Charlotte, N.C. 109
Charlottesville, Va. 19
Chavaniac, France 68
Chesterham, Pa. 89
Chestnut Hill, Battle of 61, 113
Chief Little Turtle 17, 123
Christiana, Del. 106
Clapp, Mary 164
Clark, Elijah 1
Clark, George Rogers 19, 20, 21
Clark, John 19
Clarke, Elijah 21, 22
Clarksburg, Ind. 21
Claverack, N.Y. 142, 155
Clinton, George 22, 23
Clinton, Henry 22, 58
Clinton, James 22, 23, 143
Clyduff, Ireland 51
Clymer, George 87

Index

Cobb, David 23, 24
Cockroft 125
Colchester, Vt. 36
Coldenham Academy 141
Cole, Mary 54
Cole, Ruth 54
Coleman, Gilly 133
Coleman, Mary 103
College of Philadelphia 87
Colson's Mill, Batle of 28
Colt, Mary 140
Colton, Tryphosa 40
Combahee Ferry, Battle of 45
Concord, Battle of 3, 8, 13, 19, 26, 63, 70, 82, 105, 115, 126, 146, 148
Conway, Thomas 17, 24, 25, 44, 151, 158
Cork, Ireland 90, 100
Corlaer's Hook, Battle of 27
Cornell, Ezekial 25, 26
Cornwall, Conn. 137
Cortiss, Elizabeth Waitstill 101
Cosswick's Bridge, Battle of 28
Courtney, Mary 119
Cowan's Ford, Battle of 28
Cowpens, Battle of 49, 80, 93, 107
Cox, Letita 127
Craftsbury, Vt. 149
Crailo, N.Y. 142
Crane, John 26, 27
Cranston, R.I. 77, 78
Cresap's Company Maryland Riflemen 158
Croton, N.Y. 142
Crown Point, N.Y. 11, 31, 39, 90, 109, 115, 131, 138
Cumberland, Md. 132
Cummings, John 13, 111
Cunningham, Robert 159
Curry, Abagail 92
Cushing, Joseph 27
Cushing, Mary 75
Custis, Martha 151

Danbury, Conn. 60, 128
Danielson, Timothy 27
Danville, Pa. 14
Darien, Ga. 80
Davenport, Martha 128
Davidson College 28
Davis, Letita 55
Dayton, Bathsheba 100
Dayton, Elias 5, 28, 29, 160
Deane, Silas 30, 34, 68, 155
De Berdt, Esther 118
DeFermoy, Matthias 29
De Hass, John 29, 30
De Kalb, Johann 30, 31, 33
De Laumoy, Jean 30
Delaware River 34, 37, 46, 84, 101
Demaris, Elizabeth 94
Dennis, Mass. 40
Dent, John 32
Detroit, Mich. 14
DeWitt, Mary 23
De Woedtke, Frederick 31, 32
Dickinson, John 17, 32, 33, 37
Dickinson, Philemon 33
Dickinson College 37, 61

Dingwell, Anne 17
Dorchester, Mass. 104
Douglass, John 33
Dover, Del. 33, 120, 121
Doyle, Christiana 100
Dracut, Mass. 143
Druid Hill, Md. 15
Drum Point, Md. 12
Dublin, Ireland 100
Du Buysson, des Haynes, Charles 33, 34
Du Coudray, Philip 34, 65, 134
Du Portail, Louis 34, 35
Dupui, Elizabeth 14
Durham, Conn. 146
Durham, N.H. 135
Duxbury, Mass. 146
Dyer, Elephalet 35
Dygert, Lana 56
Dygert, Maria 56

East Haddam, Conn. 129
East India Company 43
East Windsor, Conn. 162
Eaton, Pinketam 1
Eaton College 64
Edenton, N.C. 161
Edgartown, Mass. 100
Edgecombe County, S.C. 21
8th Connecticut Infantry 60
8th Massachusetts Infantry 63
8th Pennsylvania Infantry 14, 17
8th Virginia Infantry 96
Elbert, Samuel 36
11th Massachusetts Infantry 139
Elizabeth, N.J. 28
Elizabethtown, N.C. 28
Elizabethtown, N.J. 78, 102, 103, 160
Ellicott, Isabella 127
Ellis, Joseph 2
Emanuel, Ruth 140
England Cross Roads, N.J. 100
Ennalls, Anne 57
Enos, Roger 36, 37
Eutaw Springs, Battle of 49, 55, 109, 135, 159
Eutaw Springs, S.C. 137
Ewing, Catherine 51
Ewing, James 37
Exeter, N.H. 38, 110

Fairfield, Conn. 128
Falmouth, Maine 40, 41
Farmington, Conn. 105
Fassett, John 124
Febiger, Christian 37, 38
Fenwick, Elizabeth 12
Ferguson, Patrick 21
Fermanaugh, Ireland 62
Ferrago Forge, N.J. 67
15th Continental Infantry 106
5th Connecticut Infantry 152
5th Massachusetts Infantry 24, 40
5th North Carolina Militia 28
5th Pennsylvania Infantry 40
5th South Carolina Infantry 59
Fiinen, Denmark 37
Fincastle County, Va. 18

1st Georgia Infantry 36
1st Maryland Infantry 45
1st Massachusetts Infantry 102
1st New Hampshire Infantry 12
1st New Jersey Infantry 5, 100, 103, 161
1st New York Infantry 79
1st North Carolina Infantry 97
1st Pennsylvania Infantry 15
1st Pennsylvania Infantry Battalion 29
1st South Carolina Infantry 12, 55, 59, 108
Fish, Mary 128
Fish Dam Ford, Battle of 136
Fisher, Mary Sprague 38
Fishing Creek, Battle of 136
Fishkill, N.Y. 137
Floyd, Ruth 163
Floyd, William 38, 163
Flucker, Lucy 65
Flying Camp 12, 86, 89, 106, 120
Folsom, Nathaniel 38, 39
Forbes, John 90, 92, 151
Fort Armstrong, Pa. 14
Fort Arnold, N.Y. 46
Fort Augusta, Pa. 85
Fort Barrington, Fla. 58
Fort Canhawa, W.Va. 103
Fort Chambly, Quebec 138
Fort Clinton, N.Y. 22, 23, 41
Fort Cumberland, Md. 135
Fort Cumberland, Nova Scotia 41
Fort Duquesne, Pa. 7, 37, 45, 85, 89, 92
Fort Frontenac, Canada 22, 23
Fort George, Maine 147
Fort Hamilton, Ohio 17
Fort Independence, N.Y. 29
Fort Johnson, N.C. 10
Fort Laurens, Ohio 14, 45, 84
Fort Ligonier, Pa. 133
Fort McIntosh, Pa. 14, 17, 84
Fort Montgomery, N.Y. 22, 23, 61
Fort Motte, S.C. 79
Fort Moultrie, S.C. 7, 79, 96
Fort Necessity, Pa. 73, 99, 132
Fort Niagara, N.Y. 71, 143
Fort Pitt, Pa. 14, 16, 37, 45, 52, 62, 85, 99, 123, 127
Fort Stanwix, N.Y. 17, 42, 56, 70, 81, 141
Fort Stirling, N.Y. 6
Fort Ticonderoga, N.Y. 8, 11, 13, 29, 40, 41, 56, 65, 71, 84, 90, 91, 105, 109, 110, 115, 131, 143, 151, 156
Fort Tuscarora, Ohio 14
Fort Venango, Pa. 85
Fort Washington, N.Y. 158
Fort Wheeling, W.Va. 14
Fort William Henry 115, 131
Fortress Magdeburg, Germany 144
Fosdick, Frances 47
14th Continental Infantry 46
4th Connecticut Infantry 128
4th Continental Infantry 102
4th Massachusetts Infantry 62
4th New York Infantry 141
4th North Carolina Infantry 109

Index

4th Pennsylvania Infantry 14
4th Pennsylvania Infantry Battalion 40
4th Virginia Infantry 69
Framingham, Mass. 102
Franklin, Benjamin 34, 54, 113, 139, 149
Franklin, William 139
Frazer, Persifor 39, 40
Frederick, Md. 12, 64
Fredericksburg, Va. 75, 85, 132, 155, 156, 162
Freeman, Nathaniel 40
Freeman's Farm, Battle of 110
French, Susannah 78
Frye, Joseph 40, 41
Fryeburg, Maine 41
Frye's Massachusetts Regiment 13

Gadsden, Christopher 41, 42, 58
Gale, Hannah 46
Gansevort, Peter 42, 43
Gates, Horatio 3, 27, 30, 40, 43, 44, 45, 47, 82, 93, 99, 102, 126, 129, 132, 133, 151, 157, 158, 159, 162
Gemstone, Carey 136
Germantown, Battle of 5, 7, 17, 24, 27, 28, 38, 45, 48, 61, 67, 70, 80, 83, 87, 97, 108, 111, 119, 128, 133, 151, 153, 155, 163
Gerrard, Alse 50
Gibson, John 44, 45
Gist, Mordecai 45, 46
Gloucester, N.J. 31
Glover, John 47, 48
Godfrey, George 47
Godfrey, Jane 42
Gordon, Catherine 155
Gordon, Isabella 155
Govens, Elizabeth 73
Graham, Elizabeth 121
Graham, Mary 6
Grant, James 95, 159
Gray, Hannah 160
Gray's Ferry, Pa. 97
Great Bridge, Battle of 133
Great Satilla River 16
Greaton, John 47, 48
Green Mountain Boys 8
Green Springs, Battle of 6, 68
Greene, Nathaniel 1, 2, 34, 38, 40, 44, 45, 46, 48, 49, 50, 82, 107, 133, 151, 157, 159, 166
Greensburg, Pa. 123
Greenwich, Conn. 85
Gregorian Calendar 2
Gregory, Isaac 50
Grenadier, Catherine 17
Gridley's Massachusetts Artillery 27
Grindal Shoals, S.C. 55
Groton, Mass. 11
Grovely, N.C. 10
Grymes, Philip 58
Guernsey, Katherine 146
Guilford Courthouse, Battle of 18, 49, 59, 70, 79, 93, 133, 159
Guilford, Conn. 147
Gulph's Mills, Battle of 67
Gunby, John 50

Gwinnett, Button 84
Gwynn's Island, Battle of 18

Hackensack, N.J. 110
Haddondfield, Battle of 114
Hadrell's Point, S.C. 57, 95, 108
Hageboom, Catherine 155
Hager, Frederick 28
Hager, Rosanna 56
Hagerstown, Md. 56, 57
Halifax, N.C. 57, 64
Hamilton, Alexander 35
Hancock, John 50, 51, 52, 62, 104, 148
Hand, Edward 51
Hands, Abagail 118
Handy, Elizabeth 40
Hanging Rock, Battle of 136
Hanover, Mass. 27
Hanover County, Va. 135
Hardin, John 2
Hardwick, Mass. 148
Harlem Heights, Battle of 12, 48, 72, 151
Harrington, Henry 52, 53
Harris, Waite 77
Harvard College 24, 27, 41, 51, 60, 104, 111, 146, 147, 149
Hassell, Mary 42
Haverhill, Mass. 53
Haverhill, N.H. 13
Hayden, Jerusha 36
Hazen, Moses 53
Heard, Nathaniel 53, 54
Heart, Coyprian 54
Heart, Selah 54
Heath, William 54, 55, 129
Heath's Massachusetts Regiment 146
Heitman, Francis 1
Henderson, William 55
Henry, Elizabeth 18
Henry, Patrick 18, 20, 127
Herkimer, Nicholas 55, 56
Herkimer, N.Y. 55
Hiester, Daniel 56, 57
Hillsborough, N.C. 64, 93, 97
Hingham, Mass. 75, 76
Hiram, Maine 147
Hobkirk's Hill, Battle of 49, 59, 159
Hodges, Lydia 47
Hogun, James 57
Holden, Thomas 57
Holly, Mary 152
Hooper, Henry 57, 58
Hooten, Elizabeth 149
Hopewell, Ga. 106
Howe, Robert 58, 59
Howe, Sarah 146
Howe, William 133
Hubbard, Diana 147
Hudson River 54, 66
Huger, Daniel 108
Huger, Isaac 59, 60
Humphrey, Sarah 47
Huntington, Jabez 60
Huntington, Jedediah 60, 61
Hurst, Mary 138
Huston, Anne 12
Huttendorf, Germany 30

Irvine, James 61
Irvine, William 62
Islay, Scotland 79
Ivie, Anne 92

Jack, Samuel 140
Jackson, Henry 62
Jackson, Michael 63
Jamestown, Battle of 18
Jamestown, Va. 119
Jefferson, Thomas 67, 98
Jersey Blues 28
Johnson, Elanor 137
Johnson, John 56
Johnson, Thomas, Jr. 63, 64
Johnson, William 39, 114, 152
Jones, Allen 64
Jones, Hannah 38
Jones, John Paul 64
Jones, William 64
Joppa, Md. 18
Junction, N.J. 92

Kaskascio, Ill. 30
Kensington, Conn. 54
Kettle Creek, Battle of 21, 106
King Augustine III 112
King George III 136, 140
King George's War 40, 41
King's College 132
Kings Mountain, Battle of 18, 21, 28, 80
Kingston, N.Y. 138
Kinston, N.C. 18, 19
Kittery, Maine 156
Klock's Field, Battle of 142
Knox, Henry 27, 34, 35, 65, 66, 72, 134
Kosciuszko, Thaddeus 66, 67

Lacey, John 67
Lafayette, Marquis de 64, 68, 69, 110, 145, 154
Lake George, N.Y. 8, 31
Lake Ontario 23
Lancaster, Pa. 27, 37, 44, 51, 88, 120
Laurens, Henry 59
Laurens, John 73, 160
Lawrence, Mary 124
Lawson, Robert 69, 70
Lawson, Susanna 15
Learned, Ebenezer 70
Lebanon, Pa. 29
Lee, Charles 5, 44, 62, 71, 72, 73, 95
Lee, Elizabeth 105
Lee, Ezra 105
Lee, Harry 18
Lee, Henry 21
Lee, Jeremiah 46
Lee, John 73
Lenox, Mass. 105
Lewis, Andrew 73, 74
Lewis, Fielding 74, 75
Lewis, George 87
Lewis, John 74
Lexington, Battle of 3, 8, 13, 19, 26, 63, 70, 82, 104, 105, 113, 115, 126, 146, 148
Lexington, Va. 92

Index

Lincoln, Benjamin 11, 23, 59, 75, 76, 77, 81, 84, 108, 114, 118, 122
Lippitt, Christopher 77, 78
Lisle, N.Y. 106
Litchfield, Conn. 162
Little Britain, N.Y. 23
Littlefield, Catherine 48
Livermore, Isaac 133
Livingston, Robert 90
Livingston, Sarah 5
Livingston, William 78
Lloyd, Elizabeth 17
Lloyd, Thomas 89
Lockwood, Sarah 54
Locust Grove, Ky. 21
London, England 52
Long Island, Battle of 5, 14, 45, 48, 52, 83, 85, 87, 89, 116, 118, 126, 128, 143, 147, 151, 155
Long Island, N.Y. 38, 48, 71, 72
Longfellow, Henry Wadsworth 147
Lothrup, Deborah 114
Louisville, Ky. 21
Lyman, Phenias 36
Lyme, Conn. 104

Mackilwean, Mary 18
Madison, James 84
Malden, England 43
Malone, N.Y. 124
Maltby, Mary 152
Manchester, N.H. 131
Mandell, Hannah 148
Mansfield, Margaret 8
Marblehead, Mass. 46, 47, 103
Marbleton, N.Y. 14
Marietta, Ohio 118, 143
Marion, Francis 49, 59, 78, 79, 80, 94, 95
Marischal College 85
Marshall, Sarah 32
Marshall's Massachusetts Regiment 24
Marshfield, Mass. 138
Martin, Josiah 19
Martinsburg, W.Va. 133
Mason, George 133
Mastic, N.Y. 163
Mather, Mehitablel 124
Matthews, George 80, 81
Maumee River 20
Maxwell, William 81, 82
McClellan, Samuel 82
McDougall, Alexander 82, 83
McDougall, Nancy 82
McDowell, Joseph 83, 84
McIntosh, Lachlin 84, 85
Mead, John 85
Mercer, Hugh 7, 85, 86, 87, 155
Mercersburg, Pa. 85
Meredith, Samuel 87
Merrill, Edna 13
Merriweather, Sarah 69
Meyer, Anna Barbara 96
Middlebury, Vt. 102
Middleton, Sarah 108
Mifflin, Samuel 15
Mifflin, Thomas 24, 87, 88
Miles, Samuel 88, 89

Miles' Pennsylvania Rifle Regiment 14
Milford, Pa. 15, 26
Miller, Nathan 89
Milligan, Jane 120
Milton, Mass. 146
Moffitt, Katherine 156
Monk's Corner, Battle of 59
Monkton, Robert 43
Monmouth, Battle of 5, 6, 17, 27, 38, 49, 62, 63, 68, 82, 99, 103, 106, 109, 117, 119, 133, 135, 137, 139, 141, 145, 146, 154, 163
Montford, Joseph 64
Montford, Mary 64
Montgomery, Janet Livingston 44
Montgomery, Richard 23, 42, 53, 89, 90, 91, 138, 152
Montgomery County, Pa. 88
Montreal, Canada 8, 12, 53, 84, 91, 122, 152, 161
Montressor's Island, Battle of 63
Moore, Andrew 91, 92
Moore, Ann 60
Moore, Edmund 53
Moore, Mary 10
Moore, Sarah 97
Moore, Susannah 18
Moore's Creek, Battle of 92
Morgan, Daniel 49, 92, 93, 99, 107
Morgan, Nancy 99
Morris, Gouverneur 94
Morris, Lewis 93, 94
Morris, Sarah 87
Morrisanna, N.Y. 93, 94
Morristown, N.J. 30, 110, 112, 142
Moultrie, William 59, 81, 94, 95
Mount Vernon, Va. 150, 152
Muhlenberg, John 96, 97

Nash, Francis 97
Nashville, Tenn. 97
Neilson, John 97, 98
Nelson, Thomas, Jr. 98
Neuville, Chevallier de la 98, 99
Neville, John 99, 100
New Bern, N.C. 19
New Brunswick, N.J. 97, 98
New Haven, Conn. 8
New London, Conn. 61, 124, 140
New York, N.Y. 5, 22, 24, 25, 37, 44, 46, 72, 79, 80, 94, 125, 126, 127, 137, 141, 145, 152, 155, 159, 163
Newburgh, Va. 44
Newbury, Mass. 11
Newbury, Vt. 12
Newcomb, Silas 100
Newport, R.I. 68
Newton, Mass. 63
Newton Square, Pa. 39
Newtonstewart, Ireland 84
Nicola, Lewis 100, 101
Nightengale, Joseph 101, 102
Ninety-Six, Battle of 106
Ninety-Six, S.C. 21, 49, 159
9th Continental Infantry 143
9th Massachusetts Infantry 24, 62
9th Pennsylvania Infantry 61

9th Virginia Infantry 83, 91
Nixon, John 102
Norfleet, Ruth 57
Norris, Mary 32
North Carolina Regulators 16, 18, 92
North Kingston, R.I. 156
Northampton, Mass. 109
Norton, Mass. 47
Norwich, Conn. 7, 60, 61, 124
Noyes, Prudence 4
Nutfield, N.H. 130

Oconee River 21
Ogden, Matthias 102
Ogden, Robert 102
Ogelthorpe, James 80
O'Hara, James 103
Old North Church 47
Oldham, Winifred 99
Oldsborough, Maine 24
Orange County, N.Y. 23
Oriskany, Battle of 56
Orleans, France 34
Orne, Azor 103, 104
Orne, Joshua 103
Osgood, Martha 110
Otis, James 40
Oxford, Mass. 70

Palmer, Joseph 104
Paoli, Battle of 87
Parker, Peter 7
Parker, Ruth 63
Parsons, Samuel 104, 105, 155
Paterson, N.J. 91
Patterson, John 105, 106
Patterson, Samuel 106
Patterson, William 33
Paxton, Pa. 106
Pee Dee River 82
Peekskill, N.Y. 25, 110, 117
Pell's Point, Battle of 46
Pemberton, N.J. 67
Pennsylvania Associators 67
Pepperill, William 109, 164
Philadelphia, Pa. 6, 7, 22, 27, 30, 31, 32, 35, 37, 42, 57, 60, 61, 62, 63, 64, 66, 73, 78, 80, 81, 82, 85, 87, 93, 96, 97, 101, 103, 119, 120, 121, 135, 137, 139, 146, 152, 161
Philadelphia Academy 153
Philadelphia College 160
Phillips, Elizabeth 43
Pickens, Andrew 49, 59, 106, 107
Pinckney, Charles 107, 108, 109, 137
Pittsburgh, Pa. 16, 94, 99, 103
Plainfield, Conn. 33
Point Pleasant, Battle of 74, 80, 127
Polk, James 109
Polk, Thomas 109
Pomeroy, Seth 109, 110
Poniatowski, Stanislaus 112
Pontiac Conspiracy 28
Poor, Enoch 110
Poor, Mehitable 40
Potter, James 111
Prairie du Rocker, Ill. 20
Preble, Jedediah 2
Prescott, Oliver 111

Index

Prescott, William 111
Presque Isle, Pa. 154
Preston, Conn. 141
Preudhomme, De Borre, Philippe 111, 112
Prevost, August 11
Primrose, Benjamin 153
Primrose, Polly 153
Prince Edward County, Va. 97
Prince George County, Md. 158
Prince George County, Va. 69, 129
Prince of Wales Regiment 136
Prince William County, Va. 99
Princeton, Battle of 9, 12, 17, 48, 63, 65, 70, 99, 106, 111, 117, 118, 139, 143, 146
Princeton University 102, 118
Providence, R.I. 46, 101, 102, 156
Prudence Island, R.I. 77
Pulaski, Casimir 6, 112, 113, 114
Pulaski, Ga. 114
Pulaski, Josef 112, 113
Pulaski Legion 6
Putnam, Israel 36, 60, 114, 115, 116, 117, 140, 149

Quaker Hill, Battle of 140
Quaker Meadows, N.C. 83
Quebec, Canada 8, 9, 23, 29, 36, 37, 41, 53, 91, 92, 102, 138
Quinby's Bridge, Battle of 79
Quincy, Dorothy 51
Quincy, Mass. 104
Quitterfield, Lydia 97

Rae, Elizabeth 36
Raleigh, N.C. 64
Ramseur's Mills, Battle of 83, 122
Rappahannock River 74
Read, George 32
Red Bank, Battle of 143
Reed, James 118
Reed, Joseph 118, 119
Reid, Sarah 91
Reynolds, Anastasia 67
Rhode Island College 143
Rice, Persis 117
Richardson, Richard 119
Richmond, Ga. 140
Richmond, Va. 70, 74, 91
Roberdeau, Daniel 37, 119, 120
Robinson, Mary 124
Rockway, N.J. 161
Rocky Mills, Va. 18
Rocky Mount, Battle of 136
Rocky Point Plan, N, C, 92
Rodney, Caesar 35, 120, 121
Roger's Rangers 53
Rolfe, Hannah 28
Ross, Catherine 139
Rowan, N.C. 121
Rowan County, N.C. 27
Roxbury, Mass. 47, 48, 54, 70, 147, 149
Rush, Benjamin 24
Rutherford, Griffith 122
Rutledge, John 64
Rutsen, Catharina 138
Rutsen, Cornelia 142

Saco River 41
Safford, Joseph 122
St. Augustine, Fla. 26, 42, 81, 136
St. Clair, Arthur 17, 29, 123, 124
St. Leger, Barry 56, 126
St. Leonard's, Md. 63
St. Mary's, Battle of 16
Salem, Mass. 46, 114
Salem, N.H. 12
Salem, Va. 73
Salisbury, Conn. 127
Salisbury, S.C. 119
Saltonstall, Dudley 147
Saltonstall, Gurdon 124
Sample, Ann 19
Sandwich, Mass. 40, 137
Santee River 59
Saratoga, Battle of 9, 11, 13, 17, 44, 47, 66, 70, 76, 91, 93, 102, 106, 110, 124, 132, 137, 139, 146, 151, 158, 162
Saussaye, Charlotte 53
Savannah, Ga. 36, 49, 50, 58, 76, 79, 84, 85, 96, 140
Savannah River 84
Schuyler, Philip 91, 123, 124, 125, 126, 143
Schuylkill River 34
Scituate, R.I. 25, 26, 152
Scott, John 126, 127
2nd Canada Regiment 53
2nd Connecticut Infantry 137
2nd Continental Infantry 157
2nd Maryland Infantry 50
2nd New Hampshire Infantry 116
2nd New Jersey Infantry 28
2nd Pennsylvania Infantry 30
2nd Pennsylvania Infantry Battalion 17
2nd Plymouth County Militia Regiment 27
2nd Rhode Island Infantry 77
2nd South Carolina Infantry 95
2nd South Carolina Rifle Regiment 136
2nd Suffolk Militia 76
2nd Virginia Infantry 38
Serrett, Mary 45
17th Regiment of Foot 90
7th Connecticut Infantry 137
7th North Carolina Infantry 57
7th Pennsylvania Infantry 62
Sevier, John 127
Shay's Rebellion 24
Shelby, Evan, Jr. 127
Sheldon, Elisha 127, 128
Shickellamy, Ann 45
Shippen, Margaret 10
Shirley, Richard 138
Shrewsbury, Mass. 147, 148
Silliman, Gold 128
Sinkler, Dorothy 119
16th Continental Infantry 63
6th Massachusetts Infantry 139
6th Pennsylvania Infantry 62
6th South Carolina Infantry 55
Skiff, Mary 137
Smallwood, William 128, 129
Smallwood's Rifle Regiment 5

Smith, Dorothy 38
Smith, Mary 159
Society of the Cincinnati 15, 44, 46, 59, 61, 106, 155
Somersworth, N.H. 133
Sons of Liberty 26, 60, 83, 126
Southold, N.Y. 161
Spencer, Joseph 129, 130
Spottsylvania County, Va. 74
Spratt, Susanna 109
Stamford, Conn. 152
Stanton, Joseph 130
Stark, John 39, 44, 51, 130, 131
Startwout, Jacobus 137
Startwout, N.Y. 137
Stateburg, S.C. 137
Staten Island, Battle of 6
Stephen, Adam 132, 133
Stevens, Edward 133
Stevenson, John 50
Stirling, Earl of 5
Stockbridge, Ruth 27
Stockton, Md. 50
Stone, Mary 53
Stone Arabia, Battle of 142
Stono Ferry, Battle of 31, 50, 59, 76, 135
Stony Point, Battle of 38, 154
Stoughton, Mass. 139
Stratford, Conn. 163
Strong, Joanna 38
Sudbury, Mass. 102
Sudbury West Side Minuteman Company 102
Sugaw Creek Academy 27
Sullivan, John 39, 43, 44, 46, 48, 51, 112, 133, 134, 135, 157
Sullivan's Island, Battle of 136
Sumner, Jethro 135
Sumter, Thomas 49, 55, 135, 136, 137
Susquehanna Land Company 35
Sutton, Mass. 117
Swett, Hannah 62
Swift, Heman 137
Swords, Ireland 89
Symmes, John 105

Tappen, Cornelia 22
Tarleton, Banastre 21
Taunton, Mass. 24
Taylor, Mary Worrall 39
Ten Broeck, Abraham 137, 138
Ten Broeck, Maria 143
Ten Broeck, Petrus 138
10th Continental Infantry 140
10th Massachusetts Infantry 139
10th Virginia Infantry 133
3rd Continental Artillery 27
3rd Maryland Infantry 45
3rd Massachusetts Infantry 148
3rd New Hampshire Infantry 118
3rd Rhode Island Infantry 25
3rd South Carolina Infantry 55
3rd Suffolk Militia 75
3rd Virginia Infantry 83, 86
Thomas, Anthony 27
Thomas, John 138
Thomastown, Maine 65

Index

Thompson, William 138, 139
Thompson's Pennsylvania Rifle Battalion 51, 157
Threadcraft, Sarah 80
Three Rivers, Battle of 62, 84, 131, 139, 153
Towamencin, Pa. 97
Transoconee Republic 21
Trappe, Md. 32, 33
Trappe, Pa. 96
Tregaron, Wales 127
Trenton, Battle of 5, 9, 12, 17, 48, 56, 63, 65, 70, 86, 99, 106, 117, 118, 123, 128, 133, 134, 139, 143, 155
Trenton, N.J. 33, 37, 118
Trinity College 62, 90
Trowbridge, Sarah 147
Troy, N.Y. 53
Trumball, Faith 60
Tupper, Benjamin 139, 140
12th Massachusetts Infantry 78
21st Continental Infantry 139
24th Continental Infantry 47, 146
Twiggs, John 140
Tyler, Eliza 159
Tyler, John 124, 140, 141
Tyron, William 27

Ulster County, N.Y. 22
Union College 138
Union Farm, N.J. 82
University of Aberdeen 132
University of Georgia 140
University of Halle 96
University of Pennsylvania 119, 157

Valcour Bay, Battle of 152
Valley Forge, Pa. 6, 7, 35, 57, 60, 68, 70, 84, 88, 110, 111, 134, 141, 143
Van Cortlandt, Cornelia 125
Van Cortlandt, Philip 143, 144
Van Rensselaer, Catharine 125
Van Rensselaer, Elizabeth 137
Van Rensselaer, Robert 142
Van Schaick, Catrina 43
Van Schaick, Gosen 142, 143
Varnum, James 105, 143, 144

Vermont University 37
Vincennes, Battle of 20
Von Steuben, Friedrich 144, 145, 146
Voorhees, Catharine 97
Vose, Joseph 146

Wabash River 20
Wadsworth, James 146
Wadsworth, Peleg 146, 147
Walcott's Connecticut State Regiment 54
Wallace, George 45
Walton, Mary 93
Ward, Andrew 147
Ward, Artemus 70, 109, 147, 148, 149
Warner, Ezra 1
Warner, Jonathan 148, 149
Warren, Joseph 149, 150
Warren, N.C. 135
Warren, R.I. 89
Warwick, R.I. 48, 57
Washington, Augustine 150
Washington, Catherine 74
Washington, D.C. 23, 57, 84
Washington, George 1, 6, 7, 8, 11, 14, 17, 24, 25, 41, 44, 48, 52, 60, 63, 65, 66, 68, 72, 73, 76, 79, 85, 87, 88, 91, 92, 96, 97, 99, 109, 111, 113, 114, 116, 118, 128, 132, 134, 135, 144, 148, 150, 151, 152, 155, 158
Washington, Lawrence 150
Waterbury, David 152
Wayne, Anthony 40, 67, 72, 118, 133, 153, 154
Waynesboro, Pa. 154
Webb, Samuel 154, 155
Weedon, George 155, 156
West, William 156
West Point, N.Y. 10, 35, 46, 47, 49, 58, 66, 79, 101, 105, 117, 118
Westerly, R.I. 11, 130
Westernville, N.Y. 38
Westminster Prepatory School 107
Westmoreland County, Pa. 17
Wethersfield, Conn. 154
Wheeler, Mehitable 25

Whipple, William 156, 157
White, Huldah 139
White Clay Creek Hundred, Del. 106
White Plains, Battle of 12, 52, 76, 77, 83, 85, 105, 126, 127, 128, 129, 141, 143, 155, 163
Whiting, Nathan 147
Wilkes County, Ga. 21
Wilkinson, James 157, 158
Williams, Hannah 60
Williams, Otho Holland 158, 159
Williamsburg, Va. 17
Williamson, Andrew 106, 159, 160
Williamson, Matthias 160
Williamsport, Md. 159
Williamsport, Pa. 159
Wilmington, Del. 33, 129
Wilmington, N.C. 11, 19, 49, 92, 122
Wilson, James 160, 161
Windham, Conn. 35
Winds, William 161
Windsor, Conn. 36, 161
Winiary, Poland 112
Winthrop, Rebecca 124
Winyah, S.C. 81
Witcomb, John 149
Woburn, Mass. 118
Wolcott, Erastus 161, 162
Wolcott, Jerusha 161
Wood, Rachewl 25
Woodbridge, N.J. 53
Woodford, William 162, 163
Woodhull, Nathaniel 163
Woodward, Elizabeth 16
Wooster, David 8, 9, 137, 163, 164
Worcester, Mass. 80, 92, 93, 97, 120
Worster, Lydia 134
Wragg, Ann 42
Wrightstown, Pa. 67
Wyoming, Pa. 35

Yale College 27, 35, 60, 93, 105, 124, 161, 162, 163
Yorktown, Battle of 23, 28, 35, 65, 68, 77, 98, 133, 142, 155

www.ingramcontent.com/pod-product-compliance
Ingram Content Group UK Ltd.
Pitfield, Milton Keynes, MK11 3LW, UK
UKHW050526150426
5217IPUK00026B/1821